UPGRADING THE IBM PC FAMILY 8088 TO 486

Michael Hordeski

PTR Prentice Hall
Englewood Cliffs, NJ 07632

Library of Congress Cataloging-in-Publication Data

Hordeski, Michael F.
Upgrading the IBM PC family 8088 to 486 / Michael F. Hordeski.
p. cm.
Includes index.
ISBN 0-13-948225-3
1. Microcomputers—Upgrading. 2. IBM microcomputers. I. Title.
TK7887.5.H67 1993
621.39′16—dc20 93-9122
CIP

Editorial/production supervision
and interior design: *BooksCraft, Inc.*
Prepress buyer: *Mary Elizabeth McCartney*
Acquisition editor: *Bernard M. Goodwin*
Editorial assistant: *Diane Spina*

The publisher offers discounts on this book when ordered in bulk quantities. For more information contact:

Corporate Sales Department
PTR Prentice Hall
113 Sylvan Avenue
Englewood Cliffs, New Jersey 07632

Phone: 201-592-2863
Fax: 201-592-2249

Printed in the United States of America
10 9 8 7 6 5 4 3 2 1

ISBN 0-13-948225-3

Prentice-Hall International (UK) Limited, *London*
Prentice-Hall of Australia Pty. Limited, *Sydney*
Prentice-Hall Canada Inc., *Toronto*
Prentice-Hall Hispanoamerica, S.A., *Mexico*
Prentice-Hall of India Private Limited, *New Delhi*
Prentice-Hall of Japan, Inc., *Tokyo*
Simon & Schuster Asia Pte, Ltd., *Singapore*
Editora Prentice-Hall do Brasil, Ltda., *Rio de Janeiro*

CONTENTS

	PREFACE	ix
	Acknowledgments	xiii
1.	**THE IBM PC FAMILY**	1
	Computer Architectures	1
	The PC Architecture	1
	PCs, Minis, and Mainframes	5
	PC Family Characteristics	8
	XT/AT Compatibles	9
	Share of Market	16
	IBM PC Construction	17
	The IBM PS/2 Family	20
	PS/2 Models	25
	The 386-486 Family	27
	The IBM XP 486 Family	37
	Other Typical 486 Machines	39
2.	**UPGRADING THE SYSTEM UNIT**	46
	Should I Upgrade or Trade In?	46
	The Upgrade Path	46
	The System Unit	47

System Upgrades 58
Upgrading Decisions 65

3. **MEMORY UPGRADES** **68**
Introduction—Basic Concepts 68
Know Your System Unit 69
Static and Dynamic RAM 69
RAM Chips 69
Handling Memory Chips 75
Memory Problems 75
RAM Limits 76
Expanded and Extended Memory 77
Adding Memory 83

4. **VIDEO SYSTEMS** **91**
The Video Output 91
Monitor Operation 91
Adapters 95
Monitors 101
The Use of Multiple Display Adapters 111
Details of Display Operation 111
Problems During Upgrading 112
Monitor and Video Board Specifications 113
Large-Screen Monitor Characteristics 113
Factors Affecting Display Quality 114
Monitors for Desktop Publishing and CAD 116
Add-On Products 119
Summary of Monitor Types 120

5. **UPGRADING DISK DRIVES** **123**
Floppy Drives 123
Hard Drives 135

6. **UPGRADING YOUR COMPUTER'S INPUT** **160**
Keyboards 160
Other Input Devices (Pointing Devices) 166

	Optical Data Input	179
	Video Input Upgrade Options	183
	Scanner Types	188
	Verbal Input	200
	CD-ROMs	207
7.	**UPGRADING YOUR PRINTER**	**214**
	Evolution of the Printer	214
	Types of Printer Mechanisms	216
	Important Factors in Choosing a Printer	225
	Dot-Matrix Printers	227
	Inkjet Printers	233
	Laser Printers	235
	LCS and LED Printers	245
8.	**UPGRADING WITH POWER, OPTICAL, AND TAPE BACKUP SYSTEMS**	**249**
	Why You Need Power Backup	249
	Power Problems	250
	Protecting Your Power Supply	253
	Tape Backup Systems	260
	Optical Backup Systems	273
9.	**UPGRADING WITH FAX AND MODEM UNITS**	**278**
	Fax	278
	Modems	287
	Modem Communications	296
10.	**UPGRADING YOUR SYSTEM WITH SOFTWARE**	**310**
	MS-DOS 5.0 Upgrade	310
	DR-DOS	314
	Windows	316
	OS/2	320
	Using Windows Applications	324
	SOURCE LIST	**337**
	INDEX	**371**

PREFACE

If you understand how your IBM or compatible PC is designed and how it works, you will find it easier to upgrade for more productivity. If you use your PC to be more productive, this book will help you to be even more productive by showing you how to develop the full capabilities of your PC.

If your work is becoming more computer-intensive, while at the same time your existing system is being taxed by more powerful operating systems and software programs, you can solve this double whammy by improving your system. With all the products available today, it is easier than ever to enhance your existing system.

You can add more hard disk space for storage, more random access memory (RAM) for modern programs, modems for communications and exchange of data, and video graphics array (VGA) boards and monitors for improved visual output. This book details all of these upgrades in easy-to-understand language.

We will show you how to perform your own upgrading services so that you won't have to rely on technicians to upgrade and modify your system.

For example, we will show you how to:

- Add memory to your system easily.
- Use plug-in modules to add megabytes to speed throughput and for memory-hungry software.
- Save money by adding more memory yourself.

- Use small, rugged single inline memory module (SIMM) boards that add 1 megabyte (MB) or more and plug into connectors on the system board.
- Select the memory products that meet your computer's exact specifications.
- Optimize resources by liberating lower memory and creating expanded and extended memory.
- Move terminate-and-stay-resident programs (TSRs), utilities, and device drivers above the 640 kilobyte (K) barrier, making room for a RAM disk or print spooler.
- Reconfigure the 640–1,024K range to improve speed and performance.
- Upgrade now and be ready for Windows, OS/2, XENIX, and UNIX.

This book will help you to be more proficient technically, providing a good working knowledge of how PCs are built and how they function. You will gain in-depth information about how performance-critical hardware and software elements of your system function and practical tips for dealing with problems that impede performance.

You will learn how to select and employ the newer easier-to-use programs to achieve the best gains in productivity. While you can replace your existing memory chips with faster devices, there are much easier ways to get more performance with your existing memory using commercial software. You can also speed up the operation of your hard disks and make better use of disk space before crowding problems occur using the state-of-the-art programs available today.

We will show you how to upgrade processors, memory, hard disks, and even power supplies using a few simple tools. By learning more about your system and how to maintain it, you can reduce downtime and the costs associated with it.

You can learn how to diagnose computer performance problems, and then decide if you can cure it yourself (in many cases, all that is required are your fingers—no tools) or if you need to go to another system. Since you can solve most performance problems by replacing a system component, simple upgrades can be lifesavers.

If you are nontechnical or a novice, you can perform upgrades with no prior knowledge and lose your fear of PCs. If you are a more experienced user, you can improve on your knowledge and perform upgrades for others.

With the understanding gained from this book, you will be able to identify and solve most performance problems quickly and easily. You will also be able to make more informed decisions regarding your PC's performance and functionality. You will learn about the most cost-effective approaches to improving performance at the data input, output, and processing levels.

We will explain the architecture of the IBM PC and compatible families, define common PC buzzwords and acronyms, and detail upgrade solutions.

There are many ways to improve a PC, and you will need to know how to select the best options among the available products and how to install the appropriate components. It is important to understand the operation of the more critical parts of the PC, such as the inner workings of hard disk drives. Bottlenecks in the PC's data storage are often critical since so many programs require frequent access of data.

Not all upgrades require hardware changes. You can make many performance improvements with software. This book will help you determine which system failures require hardware upgrade and which can be handled with software.

This book will be helpful to anyone who works with an IBM PC/XT/AT 286, 386, or 486 system. If you are an end user, you can save hours of time by taking care of simple upgrades on your own. If you are a data-center staff member who supports end users, you can learn valuable tips that will help you with your job. If you are responsible for equipment purchases, you will be able to make intelligent decisions.

Suppose you are concerned with the analysis and management of replacement and upgrade options. You must deal with analyzing applications versus upgrade benefits; decide when upgrades are necessary and cost-effective; and analyze component upgrades versus system upgrades and replacement versus upgrade. This book, developed specifically to be a valuable on-the-job reference, will give you many alternatives for handling these situations. You should find it helpful when making upgrade choices as well as maintaining systems.

Chapter 1 describes the IBM PC families and clarifies the different generations, components, and their interrelation. It also includes an analysis of the IBM PC- and AT-type systems, major compatible computers, and compatibility levels, along with upgrade features and built-in security features.

Chapter 2 discusses the components of the system unit—this includes the upgrade path for the system unit, clocks and crystals, expansion boards, and expansion slots. You can make system upgrades with accelerator boards, math coprocessors (MCP), and memory caches. Upgrade decisions also include replacing the power supply.

Chapter 3 shows how to change motherboard memory and memory boards and includes valuable tips on solving memory upgrade problems. You will learn about static and dynamic RAM chips, parity checking, RAM limits, expanded and extended memory management, expansion boards, modules, and solid-state RAM drives. You will also find out how to handle memory chips.

Video systems are explained in chapter 4, which includes topics like monitor resolution and color, adapter boards, monitor and adapter compatibility, application software compatibility, manufacturer specifications, and important considerations. It offers tips on video system upgrades and common problems and their solutions. We explain interlacing as well as multifrequency and double-scan monitors, graphics coprocessor boards, and special monitors. Problems during upgrading include monitor and video board compatibility. Important monitor characteristics include flicker, brightness, phosphors, and glare.

Chapter 5 is concerned with upgrading disk drives, including the operation and types of floppy disks, drive controllers, drive types, options, installation, reconfiguration, manufacturer specifications, and related considerations. It offers tips on disk drive selection, preventive maintenance techniques, and speed adjustments. Chapter 5 also covers the operation of the different types of hard disks and controllers and their installation. It explains the use of cylinders and tracks, along with the different data formats. Data compression along with the application of buffers and caches can improve the drive's usefulness. Intelligent drives using the small computer system interface (SCSI) bus can reduce many problems when expanding your system.

Chapter 6 covers various input components such as lightpens, trackballs, joysticks, and mouse units. Accessory keyboards and keyboard enhancers can result in improved productivity in many specialized applications. Other input devices such as some of the newer trackball and joystick variations present opportunities for increasing efficiency. Optical data input is available with low-cost scanners. Digital cameras allow image and data collection at remote locations. Speech-recognition products allow verbal input, and CD-ROMs provide access to large amounts of specialized information.

Printers are the subject of chapter 7, including the different types of printers, adapters, and cables. We offer printer construction and selection tips as well as maintenance techniques and common problems and their solutions. Manufacturer specifications and considerations are presented for laser, light-emitting diode (LED) and liquid crystal types.

Chapter 8 is concerned with power and optical and tape backup systems. Power problems include sags, surges, noise, and oscillations. Among the solutions are the use of surge suppressors and standby, uninterruptible, and intelligent power systems. We also discuss various types of tape backup and present examples of these. Optical backup includes rewritable optical disks, and there are a number of different types of optical drives available.

Chapter 9 considers faxes and modems, starting with the different fax standards and features and illustrating the available PC options. We talk about different types of modem units, along with their associated specifications and performance factors. Modem application software packages are easier to use with graphic interfaces such as Windows. We cite examples of these products.

Chapter 10 covers the wider range of software available to enhance computer operations. These include MS-DOS 5.0, DR-DOS, OS/2, Presentation Manager, Windows, NewWave, Adobe Illustrator and Streamline, Aldus PageMaker and Persuasion, Ami Pro, CorelDraw, Correct Grammar, Lotus 1-2-3, Microsoft Mail, and PowerPoint. Chapter 10 also discusses the different operating systems available, including DOS and OS/2 versions. We also cover compatibility problems between DOS and OS/2, and offer tips on installing, configuring, and customizing application software.

We include a list of sources for most of the products mentioned herein in the appendix. Use this list to contact manufacturers for additional product information and/or current availability and cost.

ACKNOWLEDGMENTS

Many thanks to Dee, who did many of the illustrations, word processing, proofreading, and correcting; and to Joe and Sharron Carro of Comco for their help in obtaining many of the photographs.

1

THE IBM PC FAMILY

COMPUTER ARCHITECTURES

In general, all computers have three main facilities: a central processing unit (CPU), internal read/write or random-access memory (RAM), and some type of external storage such as floppy disks or hard or tape drives.

The CPU operates at the heart of the computer system, executing the instructions of the software programs. The CPU is usually a single chip (the microprocessor) in most personal computers (PCs). This chip is designed with a specific instruction set. In larger computers, several chips often make up the CPU. There may be a special processor for input/output (I/O) and the control of peripherals such as printers, disk drives, and modems.

THE PC ARCHITECTURE

The CPU

The original IBM PC (Fig 1-1) is equipped with a CPU designed and manufactured by the Intel Corporation. The CPU is the Intel 8088 (Fig 1-2), and the primary operating system is a disk operating system from Microsoft—MS-DOS. The Intel 8088 is a 16-bit processor, which means that it can process 16 bits (0s or 1s) of data at one time. In addition, for the more mathematical, number-crunching tasks, an Intel 8087 numeric coprocessor is available, which installs in an empty socket next to the 8088

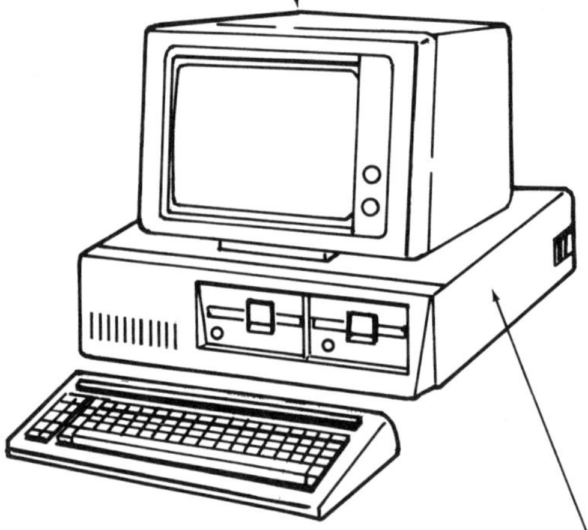

Figure 1-1 IBM PC with two 5.25-inch full-height floppy drives

CPU. The 8087 can process 80 bits of data at one time and will execute numerical calculations much faster than the 8088. Many scientific and engineering programs for the IBM PC or compatible computers require the installation of a numeric coprocessor. Numeric coprocessors are also commonly referred to as floating-point processors.

The CPU executes instructions using a machine cycle. This is the period that is controlled by an oscillating crystal that produces the clock frequency for timing computer events. The Intel 8088 in the original IBM PC operates at a clock rate of 4.77 million cycles per second (4.77 megahertz [MHz]).

The bit size, also called the "word size," and the clock rate of the microprocessor are among the primary parameters that determine the processing power and speed of the computer. The memory-addressing capacity, I/O speed, and the data transfer capacity (data bus width) are other important factors.

Internal Memory

The internal memory capacity of a computer is measured in bytes. One byte consists of 8 bits and can represent a single text character. In a

Figure 1-2 The 8088 CPU, 16-bit processor for 8-bit data bus

16-bit computer, integers can be stored in 2 bytes, single-precision numbers (7 or fewer digits) in 4 bytes, and double-precision numbers (8 to 16 digits) in 8 bytes. In many programs, double-precision numbers are used to reduce numerical round-off problems.

The internal memory that is used for storing data from the keyboard or data generated by the program is generally volatile unless the read/write or RAM has an internal battery (Fig 1-3) for power. If the electronic memory is powered from the system power supply, the information in RAM is lost when the computer is turned off. Data to be saved is normally written to an external storage device such as a disk or tape drive before shutting down the computer. Read-only memory (ROM) contains information that is more permanent and is generally encoded before the chips are installed.

The internal memory capacity or maximum size of the computer's internal memory depends on the amount of memory that can be addressed by the computer's CPU as well as the memory-handling capacity of the computer operating system. The Intel 8088 can address 1 million bytes (generally referred to as 1MB) of memory, but MS-DOS versions to 3.3 can address only 640,000 bytes (generally referred to as 640K) of internal memory. Additional memory can be used as external storage in the form of a RAM disk or virtual memory.

External Storage

Data can be stored externally on either disk or tape drives. The larger disk or tape units can store more than 500MB of data. Many existing PCs have hard disks that can store 10–40MB of data. These can be upgraded

Figure 1-3 Batteries in the computer are used to power RAM with critical system parameters

with larger units. Floppy disks have a capacity ranging from 360K to 1.2MB.

Capacities are increasing as storage technology improves. Compact laser (CD-ROM) disks have capacities of 500MB or more. These are read-only—data can be written once to the disk and then can only be read. This type of storage is ideal for storing large amounts of reference material.

The speed with which you can access the data is important to the performance of an external storage device. Disk and tape drives that are faster are also more expensive. Floppy drives are slower than hard drives and less expensive. Even if you use the fastest external storage devices, you can access data much more quickly from internal memory since it is electronic and has no moving parts such as drive spindle motors and read/write heads.

Upgrading

Upgrading to increase the use of excess, or expanded, internal memory as an external storage facility is an effective way to improve performance. Before shutting the computer down, you save the information in RAM on disk or tape. Internal memory that you use as an external storage device is known as a RAM disk or virtual memory.

You must have the proper utility software for handling internal memory as a RAM disk. When you need RAM disk space, you designate the internal memory space as an external storage device, such as drive D, and format it like another disk or tape drive.

You can use RAM disks only if you have the excess memory. For example, suppose your program uses 512K of memory. In a machine with 640K of memory, with DOS 3.3 using 66K of RAM, this leaves less than 70K for a RAM disk. For many programs, 70K of RAM is not enough for storing data files during calculations. The solution is to use an expanded-memory option such as the Intel Above Board, which can support as much as 8M bytes of additional memory. The software must be designed to access the expanded memory.

PCs, MINIS, AND MAINFRAMES

There are three general categories of computers: mainframe, mini, and micro or PC. The engineering workstation is somewhere between the mini and the PC. These categories have been changing quickly due to the advances in microprocessor technology and the increasing overlap in processing power in each of these categories. However, these machines still differ significantly.

Mainframe Computers

Until about 1980, virtually all complex analysis was performed on mainframe computers. Mainframe computers are large multiuser, multitasking machines that provide a central processing facility for large engineering and manufacturing companies, research and financial institutions, and other corporations requiring high-capacity computing power. Fully configured mainframe computers can cost well over $1 million and require separate air-conditioned rooms and a high level of maintenance and vendor support.

A typical mainframe used in the engineering industry is the Cyber 180, by Control Data Corporation. This machine has a 64-bit, single-processor CPU and supports up to 130MB of main memory. For number-crunching tasks, the Cyber 180 can support 40 users. It uses a number of peripheral processors for handling I/O. This frees up the CPU for arithmetic operations since most of the other tasks are distributed among multiple processors.

The primary characteristic that distinguishes the mainframe from mini- and microcomputers is the processor size, which is typically 60 to 64 bits (as opposed to 8 to 32 bits). The large processor provides the processing power required for extremely complex analysis in addition to the capability of supporting a large number of users. Mainframes can also support a large number of external storage units with capacities of over 500MB each. A typical mainframe configuration might include 10 of these large 500MB disk drives. As with minicomputers, mainframe operating systems are designed to use virtual memory.

While mainframe programs are generally run in batch mode, interactive usage has become popular with the increase of graphics in many programs. However, large analysis problems are still more suited to run in the batch mode.

Resource contention can also be a problem on mainframe computers. When a lot of users are performing large number-crunching analysis simultaneously, mainframe performance can deteriorate, causing waiting times for results.

Minicomputers

Minicomputers are 32-bit machines with multiuser, multitasking, and support for up to 40 users. Supporting this many users and handling multiple computation-intensive tasks requires higher memory capacities. Minimum memory capacities for minicomputers range from 4MB to 16MB. Minicomputers usually take advantage of virtual memory.

Some minicomputers require special air-conditioned rooms. However, there are many models available that are designed to operate in a normal office environment.

Minicomputers normally use disk and tape drives with storage capacities of 400–500MB. Many minicomputer systems are configured with gigabyte (GB) storage capacities.

Most of these systems can network, allowing machines in different locations to share programs and files with other computers on the network. Fully configured minicomputers such as the Digital Equipment Corporation's VAX can exceed $100,000, depending on the amount of memory and peripherals such as disks, tapes, and printers.

Minicomputers can run programs interactively or in batch mode. In batch mode the user prepares a file of instructions and submits this with the data set to be executed by the computer. The file to be executed is placed in a queue and the computer executes it according to its priority. The system might complete a high-priority job within half an hour, while a low-priority job might run overnight. Interactive usage is more common with minicomputers than batch mode. Each user runs the program directly from his or her own terminal.

Minicomputers offer the flexibility and power to support multiple tasks and users, but users often find themselves contending for resources on the system. If accounting, word processing, and engineering all run on one minicomputer, this limits performance for all users, and long waits can occur.

One solution to this resource-contention problem is to move engineering applications to dedicated engineering workstations. These engineering workstations are 32-bit machines designed for single-user operation and number-crunching calculations. The engineering workstations can network with other workstations so that data can be shared among the users.

A typical engineering workstation might use a 32-bit processor operating at a clock rate of 15 MHz or more. Virtual memory built into the system will support at least 16MB of main memory.

In general, engineering workstations use the UNIX operating system, which supports multitasking and virtual-memory operation. Workstations range in price from $8,000 to $35,000, depending on memory, storage, and networking options. The Sun Microsystems Sun-3 series machines are typical engineering workstations.

The Microcomputer

We usually define the microcomputer or PC as a single-user, single-processor desktop system with a CPU size ranging from 8 to 16 bits. The main memory capacity of the microcomputer is usually 1M byte or less; and multiuser or networking capability, although available, has not been practical for number-crunching tasks such as engineering analysis.

In general, the microcomputer is a single-tasking machine, meaning that applications or programs are operated one at a time. Multitasking software is available but not practical for applications involving complex analysis. A more common application for a microcomputer involves word processing or spreadsheet analysis. Generally, microcomputer programs are interactive, meaning that the computer executes user instructions immediately rather than in batch mode.

Microcomputers generally have one or two 5.25- or 3.5-inch floppy drives and one or two hard drives with hard disk capacities ranging from 10MB to 40MB. Virtual-memory usage is generally not a built-in feature of microcomputers, but you can add it with the appropriate software and hardware additions. Memory-expansion boards are available that support up to 8MB of virtual memory.

For simple business applications, microcomputers must have at least 512K of main memory, some graphics capabilities, and at least 10MB of hard disk storage. You can use a numeric coprocessor if you are doing many calculations.

Graphics boards and monitors can range from a few hundred to several thousand dollars depending on the resolution and color capabilities required. For most purposes, inexpensive graphics equipment is adequate. You must ensure that the software is compatible with the selected graphics hardware. You can generally use inexpensive dot-matrix printers with graphics capability for printing, although ink jet and laser printers will give you better-quality output.

The dominant microcomputers are the IBM AT and XT and compatible machines from other vendors. You can purchase a microcomputer system suitable for simple applications for less than $1,000.

PC FAMILY CHARACTERISTICS

The IBM PC family includes the PC, XT, and AT (see Table 1-1). The original IBM PC uses the Intel 8088 microprocessor which runs at 4.77 MHz. Internal memory ranges from 128K to 640K of RAM and 40K of ROM. Storage is minimal, with one or two 5.25-inch floppy drives. The IBM PC uses 5 expansion slots, and an optional expansion unit is available for holding 8 additional boards. You can increase storage by adding two 10MB hard disks.

TABLE 1-1 IBM PC Family

Company	Processor	MHz	Memory	Storage
IBM PC	8088	4.77	256K to 640K RAM; 40K ROM	One or two 5.25-in floppies
IBM XT	8088	4.77	256K to 640K RAM; 40K ROM	One 5.25-in floppy; one 10MB hard
IBM AT	80286	6	256K to 3MB	1.25MB floppy; one 20MB hard

IBM XT

The IBM XT uses the same Intel 8088 CPU running at 4.77 MHz. The memory is also 128K to 640K of RAM with 40K of ROM. Storage is either one or two 5.25-inch 360K floppy disks, or one 5.25-inch 360K floppy disk and one 10MB hard disk.

The XT has an additional 3 expansion slots, bringing the total to 8, with one floppy and one hard drive. An expansion unit can add 8 additional slots. The main difference is the increased storage capacity, with a 10MB hard disk and one 180K or 360K floppy.

IBM AT

The IBM AT offers more raw processing power by using the more powerful Intel 80286 CPU running at a faster rate of 6 MHz. Internal memory was expanded to range from 256K to 3MB RAM. A 1.2MB floppy disk and a 20MB hard disk increase capacity.

There are 7 I/O expansion slots for adding peripherals. You can increase the standard AT memory to 3MB RAM and improve the storage capacity with an available 40MB hard disk.

In the mid-1980s, many computer makers marketed PC and XT versions following IBM's lead in the personal computer market. While these manufacturers were still following IBM by developing PC- and XT-compatible systems, IBM developed and released the AT, leading the way into a second generation of microcomputers. The use of Intel's 80286 microprocessor chip allows the AT to process data faster than its predecessors that use the 8088 processor.

A number of manufacturers then released AT clones in an attempt to gain a part of this new market. Typical of these AT-compatibles are Compaq's Deskpro 286, Corona Data Systems' Corona ATP, Texas Instruments' Business Pro, TeleVideo System's TeleVideo AT, and Kaypro Corporation's Kaypro 286i.

IBM first released the AT higher-end system in August 1984. By March 1985, the AT was about 10% of IBM's microcomputer market. By July 1985, there were about 110,000 ATs in use.

The manufacturers of compatible systems include upgrades from the AT with improved clock speeds and higher disk storage (Fig 1-4). With its more powerful features, the AT and its clones are more useful in business applications. Enhanced versions allow users to expand hard disk storage capacity to 60MB or more.

XT/AT COMPATIBLES

Other manufacturers' XT- and AT-compatible systems are listed in Tables 1-2 and 1-3 and are discussed in this section. Table 1-4 shows the microprocessors used in the PC family machines. While IBM machines use some version of PC-DOS, compatibles generally use the latest release of MS-DOS. The BIOS manufacturer and release date refer to the brand name and revision date of the BIOS (basic I/O system) firmware chip. Early chips may not be completely software-compatible. The type of main processor used in the PC determines the relative performance of the machine.

AT&T

The AT&T PC 6300 uses the more powerful Intel 8086 CPU running at 8 MHz. The internal memory ranges from 128K to 640K of RAM for the

Figure 1-4 Typical AT-compatible with keylock, 1.2MB floppy disk, and four drive bays; two additional drive bays are just below the two slots shown

TABLE 1-2 Typical XT-Compatible Computers*

Company	Processor	MHz	Memory	Storage
Athena Canon	8086	4.77	256K to 512K RAM; 16K ROM	Two 360K 5.25-in floppies
AT&T Personal Computer	8086	8	128K to 640K	One 360K 5.25-in floppy and one 10MB hard; two 360K floppies and one 10MB hard
Bios	8088	10	640K	360K floppy; 40MB hard
Commodore PC	8088	4.77	640K	Two 360K 5.25-in floppies
DTK Data	8088	4.77/10	640K	360K, 20MB hard

Epson Equity I Plus	8088	8	640K	360K 5.25-in floppy
Ericsson PC Model S02	8088	4.77	256K to 640K RAM; 8K ROM	Two 360K 5.25-in floppies
Headstart II	8088	10	640K	5.25- & 3.5-in floppies; 360K & 720K
ITT Xtra	8088	4.8	128K to 640K RAM; 320K ROM	One 360K 5.25-in floppy
Leading Edge Personal Color Computer	8088-2	7.16/ 4.77	256 K to 640K RAM; 20K ROM	Two 360K 5.25-in floppies or one floppy and one 10MB hard
NCR PC4	8088	4.77	128K to 640K RAM; 8K ROM	Two 360K 5.25-in floppies or one 360K floppy and one 10MB hard
Tandy 1000	8088	4.77	128K to 640K	One 360K 5.25-in floppy
Z-150 Zenith Data	8088	4.77	320K to 720K RAM; 32K ROM	Two 5.25-in 320K/360K floppies or one floppy and a 10MB hard

*Although some of these computers were marketed as XTs, the hard disk was not included.

TABLE 1-3 Typical AT-Compatible Computers*

	Processor	MHz	Memory	Storage
AGI/Everex 1700C	80286	12	1MB RAM	1.2MB, 40MB
AST Premium	80286	6/12	512K RAM	1.2MB floppy; 1.2MB, 40MB
Compaq E Model 1	80286	12	1MB RAM	1.2MB
DTK Tech 1260	80286	8/12	640K RAM	1.2MB, 20MB

Epson Equity II Plus	80286	12	640K RAM	1.2MB, 40MB
Leading Edge D2	80286	8/12	640K RAM	1.2MB, 50MB
Packard Bell PB-286	80286	8/12	640K RAM	1.2MB, 40MB

*Although some of these computers were marketed as ATs, the hard disk was not included.

TABLE 1-4 PC Family Characteristics

Processor Type	Description and Use
Intel 8088 Intel 8086	Used in the IBM PC, XT, and most turbo compatibles; usually found in higher-performance XT-type machines such as the AT&T PC 6300.
NEC V20/V30	Clones of the Intel 8088 and 8086 chips; operate faster than the Intel versions; found in some compatibles or installed to improve performance.
Intel 80188/ 80186	Later versions of the 8088 and 8086 chips; similar functionally to the earlier processors, but can process instructions faster and run at a faster clock rate; often found on early accelerator boards.
Intel 80286	Generally used in AT-class PCs; used in the IBM AT and most PC-compatibles of the 286 class.
Intel 80386SX	Found in machines using a 16-bit bus like the AT but which are faster and operate at higher speeds.
Intel 80386DX	Found in machines using a 32-bit bus for faster information processing and which operate at higher speeds than the AT computer.
Intel 80486	A more powerful version of the 386 that can run at higher speeds; has a built-in math coprocessor.
Bus Type	
XT Bus	Refers to an 8-bit bus like that found in an IBM PC or XT; XT bus used in machines with an 8088, 8086, V20, or V30 processor.
AT Bus	Refers to the 16-bit bus used in the IBM AT or compatibles.
Micro Channel	Refers to the IBM Micro Channel bus used in the PS/2 Model 50 and other more powerful models.

floppy version, 256K to 640K of RAM for the 10MB hard version, and 512K to 640K RAM for the 20MB hard version.

Storage is two 5.25-inch 360K floppy disks, or one 5.25-inch 360K floppy and one 10MB or 20MB hard disk. There is a socket provided for an optional 8087 math coprocessor (MCP). The floppy disk system has 7 available expansion slots, and there are 6 available slots on the hard disk system. There is a 16/8-bit, data-bus converter provided for communications interfacing.

Compaq

The Compaq Deskpro (Model 4) also uses the 8086 CPU which runs at either 4.77 or 8 MHz. The internal memory is 128K to 640K of RAM with 8K of ROM. Standard storage is one 5.25-inch 360K floppy disk and one 10MB hard disk.

The Model 4 includes a 10MB tape backup system, and storage capacity can expand to accommodate a 30MB hard disk. The system has a socket for an 8087 MCP and includes 1 parallel and 1 serial port with 4 available expansion slots. A switchable clock speed allows software compatibility with older programs.

The Compaq Deskpro 286 (Model 2) uses an 80286 CPU running at 6 or 8 MHz. The memory is 512K to 8.2MB of RAM with 8K of ROM. Standard storage is one 3.5-inch 1.2MB floppy disk and one 30MB hard disk. Storage capacity can be expanded with a 70MB hard disk, and a 10MB tape backup system is also available.

The system performance will improve with an optional 80287 math processor, and there are 4 available expansion slots. The Model 2 has 1 parallel and 1 serial port and a switchable clock speed for improved software compatibility.

Corona

The Corona ATP-6-QD from Corona Data Systems uses an 80286 CPU running at 6 MHz. The internal memory range is 512K to 16MB RAM. Standard storage is one 5.25-inch 360K and one 3.5-inch 1.2 MB floppy disk.

You can upgrade this system with an Intel 80287 math processor, and the unit has 5 expansion slots. One serial and 1 parallel port are also included in the system. The Corona ATP-6-Q20 is standard with a 1.2MB floppy and a 20MB hard drive controller.

Ericsson

The Ericsson PC Model S02 from Ericsson Information Systems uses an 8088 CPU running at 4.77 MHz. Internal memory is 256K to 640K of RAM with 8K of ROM. Standard storage is two 5.25-inch 360K floppy disks.

The Ericsson PC has a socket to allow upgrading with an optional

Intel 8087 MCP. There are 5 IBM bus-compatible expansion slots and 1 serial and 1 parallel port.

Hewlett-Packard

The Touchscreen II from Hewlett-Packard uses an 8088 CPU, which runs at 8 MHz. Internal memory is 256K to 640K RAM. Standard storage is two 3.5-inch 710K floppy disk drives or one 3.5-inch 710K floppy and one 10MB, 20MB, or 40MB hard disk.

This is an upgraded version of the HP-150, with touchscreen features. The standard system has 4 available expansion slots and 4 serial ports. A 10MB, 20MB, or 40MB hard disk gives additional storage capacity.

ITT

The ITT Xtra XP from ITT Information Systems uses an 80286 CPU running at 4.77 or 6 MHz. Internal memory is 512K to 1.6MB of RAM and 64K of ROM. Standard storage is one 5.25-inch 360K floppy disk and a 10MB or 20MB hard disk.

You can upgrade the ITT Xtra XP with an optional Intel 80287 math coprocessor and expand the memory to 1.6MB. The XP has 4 available expansion slots after the monitor board is added. There are 3 on the hard disk version after the controller board is installed and 1 parallel and 1 serial port. A switchable clock speed improves applications software compatibility.

ITT also introduced 80286-based PCs that are called Xtra XL PCs and run under both DOS and XENIX operating systems. They use Intel's 80286 microprocessor running at 8 MHz. These systems have 640K of RAM (expandable to 1.6MB) and a 1.2MB disk. Model 1 used a 40MB disk, and Model 2 used a 72MB disk with ITT's version of DOS 3.1. ITT designed Model 3 with a 40MB disk and Model 4 with a 72MB disk to function as multiuser computers when running under ITT's version of XENIX System V.

These units also feature zero-wait-state memory, which allows tasks to proceed without interruption, and I/O caching, which keeps data in memory for quick access. Unlike other versions of DOS, ITT's version bypassed the 32MB disk-partition requirement.

Kaypro

The Kaypro 286i (Model A) uses an 80286 microprocessor running at 6 MHz. The internal memory is 512K to 15MB of RAM and 32K of ROM.

Standard storage is one 5.25-inch 1.2MB floppy disk. This is a typical clone of IBM's AT. The Kaypro 286i has a socket for adding an 80287 math coprocessor. The system has 7 expansion slots, and system memory can be expanded up to 15MB RAM with additional boards.

The Model B has one floppy and one 10MB hard disk, 5 expansion slots, 1 serial and 2 parallel ports, and a red-green-blue interface (RGBI) for an AT-compatible monitor.

Leading Edge

The Leading Edge PC Model D uses an 8088 CPU which runs at 4.77 MHz. Internal memory ranges from 256K to 640K of RAM. Storage is two 5.25-inch 360K floppy disks, or one floppy and one 10MB hard disk.

The system has 4 IBM-compatible expansion slots and a socket for upgrading by adding an optional 8087 MCP. Also included are 1 parallel and 1 serial port.

NCR

The NCR PC6 uses an 8088-2 CPU which runs at 4.77 or 8 MHz. The standard internal memory is 256K or 512K to 640K of RAM and 40K of ROM. Storage is two 5.25-inch 360K floppy disks; or one 360K floppy and one 20MB hard disk; or one 360K floppy, one 20MB hard disk, and one 10MB streaming tape backup. The unit has 6 expansion slots available for additional cards. There are 5 slots available on the hard disk versions. One RS232 and 1 parallel port are standard equipment.

The NCR PC8 uses an 80286 microprocessor running at 6 MHz. Internal memory is 256K to 4MB of RAM and 40K of ROM. Standard storage is one 5.25-inch 1.2MB floppy disk drive. The unit has 6 expansion slots available, and the system's storage capacity can include a 40MB hard disk drive.

The PC8 enhanced version has 512K RAM, 5 expansion slots, a 1.2MB floppy and 20MB hard disk, and 1 serial and 1 parallel port.

Tandy

The Tandy 1200 HD uses an 8088 CPU running at 4.77 MHz. Internal memory is 256K to 640K of RAM. Storage is one internal 5.25-inch 360K floppy disk and a 10MB hard disk. The motherboard on the Tandy 1200 HD allows the addition of an Intel 8087 MCP. Five IBM-compatible expansion slots are available. There are 4 available after the monitor board is installed. An external hard disk of 35MB is available, and 1 parallel port is standard.

Televideo

The TeleVideo AT (Model I) from Televideo Systems uses the 80286 CPU running at 6 or 8 MHz. The internal memory is 256K to 15MB of RAM and 32K of ROM. Standard storage is one 5.25-inch 1.2MB floppy disk. The TeleVideo AT has 8 expansion slots available for adding peripheral cards, along with a socket for an 80287 MCP. Additional memory boards upgrade the memory to 15MB. The storage capacity can expand to 40MB. One serial and 1 parallel port are standard equipment.

The Televideo TeleCat 286 is a desktop PC with a 20MB hard disk. A version with a 30MB disk is also available. These disk drives operate more slowly than those on IBM's AT, and the power supply is smaller. The 80286 microprocessor runs at either 6 MHz or 8 MHz.

The TeleCat has 512K of RAM and a monochrome monitor. Also included is a display adapter that offers the capabilities of IBM's monochrome and color graphics adapters.

Wang

The Wang PC-PK6 from Wang Laboratories uses the 8086 microprocessor running at 8 MHz. Internal memory can range from 128K to 640K of RAM. Standard storage is one 5.25-inch 360K floppy disk and one 10MB hard disk. There are 4 available expansion slots, and an RS-232C port and a parallel port are standard.

Zenith

The Z-200 Advanced PC from Zenith Data Systems uses the 80286 CPU running at 6 MHz. Internal memory is 512K to 16MB. Storage is one 5.25-inch 1.2MB floppy disk, and you can purchase the Z-200 with or without a 20MB hard disk. The computer has 7 available expansion slots and a socket for adding an 80287 math coprocessor.

SHARE OF MARKET

Early in 1985, the combined sales of the AT and compatibles were between 15,000 and 20,000 units per month. For the first part of the year, IBM sold about 80% of these units, but the competition slowly began to improve its share. By the end of 1985, a total of 700,000 units had been sold, 70% of which were IBM.

Table 1-5 shows the approximate U.S. market shares for all PCs built in the mid-1980s.

TABLE 1-5 PC Market—Mid-1980s

1984 Total: $8 billion		1985 Total: $11 billion		1986 Total: $14 billion	
IBM	32%	IBM	29%	IBM	28%
Apple	18%	Apple	11%	Apple	9%
Tandy	7%	AT&T	4%	AT&T	6%
Hewlett Packard	5%	Compaq	4%	Tandy	6%
Compaq	4%	Hewlett Packard	4%	Compaq	4%
Epson	4%	Tandy	4%	Hewlett Packard	4%
Wang	3%	Epson	3%	Epson	3%
Zenith	3%	Zenith	3%	Zenith	3%
All Others	24%	All Others	38%	All Others	37%

Most of the compatibles are clones of the IBM desktop machines, but some manufacturers, such as Corona Data Systems and Compaq, offer portable XT- and AT-compatible machines. Most of the portables use the same circuitry, but the size of most circuit boards is reduced in order to provide units that can be transported easily. These portable PCs generally are not hardware-compatible, although some may use standard expansion boards.

IBM PC CONSTRUCTION

The IBM PCs use a modular design, which makes them easy to install, comfortable to operate, and easily accessible to added functions. The original PC has an 8088 microprocessor, which is a 16-bit processor internally with an 8-bit data bus. This means that the processor can operate directly on 16-bit words, but data transfers in or out of the processor chip must be in 8-bit chunks.

The block diagram in Figure 1-5 shows the basic functions for the 8088-based machine. The 8088 processor controls the functions required from the computer system, such the disk drive's reading and writing of data and the control of the monitor, keyboard, communications connectors, and other options added to the system.

The original PC uses only 16–64K of main memory, a byte represent-

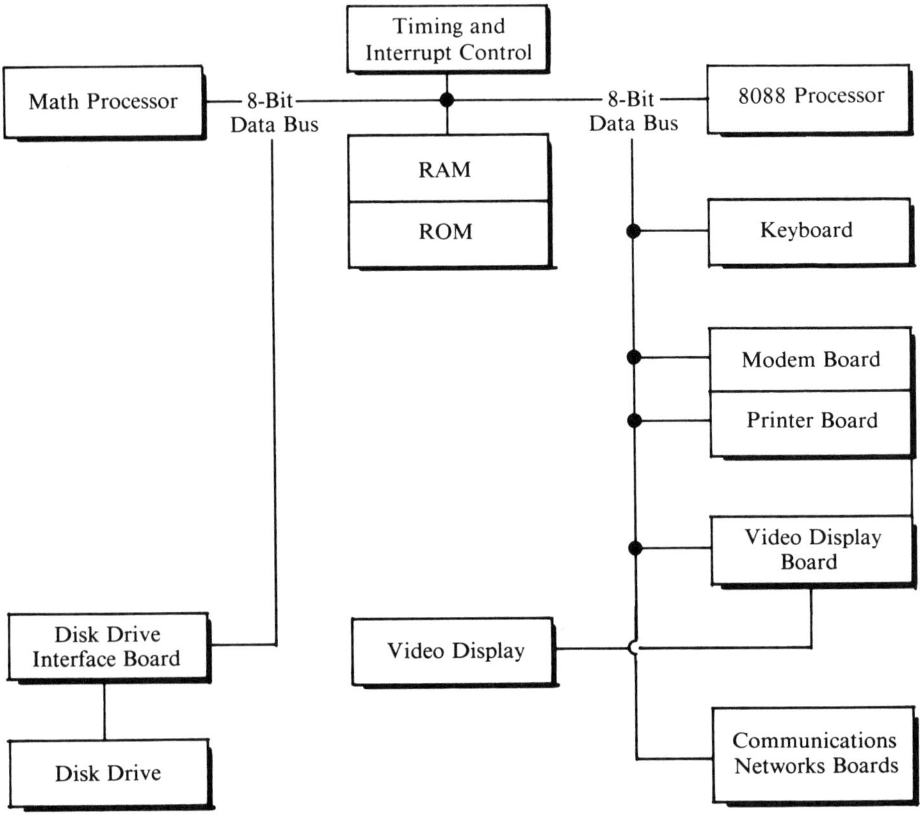

Figure 1-5 IBM PC, block diagram

ing one character position. The user can expand this memory to 256K with the addition of a memory extension option. The computer's disk holds 180 or 360K of auxiliary memory on single- or double-sided 5.25-inch disks. A second disk drive brings the total auxiliary memory to 720K.

The PC's modular design makes it flexible and adaptable to many needs. Its 3-component structure allows the components to be placed in different arrangements. A floor stand can be used to hold the system unit upright and free up desk space. The components are relatively light, compact, and portable. The keyboard comes with a 6-foot cord that lets you place it anywhere that is comfortable, even on your lap.

The Monitor

The PC's monitor contains a video screen with a diagonal dimension of 12–14 inches that supplies visual information in the form of characters or graphics on the screen. A wide variety of monitors is available for different applications.

The video control system resides on the system board or on a separate video adapter expansion board inside the system unit. Controls on the monitor's back or side let you adjust the screen's brightness and contrast levels as you would on a television set.

The Keyboard

The original PC uses a low-profile keyboard that has eighty-four keys, (Fig 1-6). The standard keys at the center and left provide the uppercase and lowercase alphabet, numbers, and punctuation. To the right of the standard keys are the basic editor keys—Insert, Delete, End, Home, Print Screen, Page Down, Page Up, Number Lock—and the cursor arrow keys. On the same side is the numeric keypad. The extended keyboard used in the AT series has separate calculator and cursor arrow keys. You do not have to use the shift key when inserting numbers on a matrix such as those found in spreadsheets.

The special function keys on the left side of the original PC's standard keyboard perform operations in different types of applications such as word processing, electronic mail, accounting, and spreadsheets. The functions keys on the AT's extended keyboard are in a single line across the top.

Some keyboards use a mechanical click that sounds when a key is pressed, while others use a quiet switch with an internally generated keyclick. You can usually turn the keyclick feature on or off or adjust its volume through a set-up feature.

The keyboard is typematic, so there is an automatic repeating of all keys on the main keypad array, the numeric keypad, and the function keys (including Space, Del Char, and Tab).

The keys are arranged in an electrical switching matrix, which is scanned for keys that are pressed. A single-chip, 8-bit processor detects when a key is pressed and transmits this information to the system unit.

Many keyboards have lights that the system can turn on and off. These lights have specific functions assigned to them during normal system operation (an example would be the caps key lock).

The Floppy Disk Drive

The PC family uses a compact disk (CD) subsystem consisting of a drive controller board and a floppy drive that controls the floppy disks on a single spindle. These disks provide mass storage, data exchange, and file backup capabilities. The early disks stored 180–360K bytes of information. Later, this was expanded to 1.2M or 1.4M bytes.

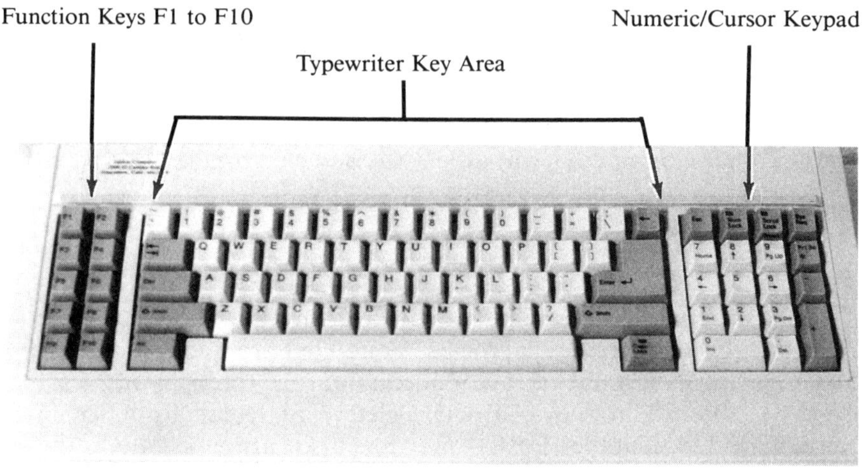

Figure 1-6 The 84-key keyboard

There are two sizes of floppy disks. The first PCs used 5.25-inch floppy disks (180K bytes). These now have a capacity range of 360K to 1.2M bytes. Most of the more recent machines have additional facilities for 3.5-inch disks, which have a capacity range of 720K bytes to 1.4M bytes.

We usually express disk storage capacity in terms of kilobytes (1,000 bytes rounded off from 1,024) and megabytes (1,000,000 bytes rounded off from 1,048,576). We might, for example, refer to a 40MB hard disk or a 360K floppy disk.

The CPU does not directly access items stored on disk—a drive controller interfaces the disk to the CPU. The controller can be a separate expansion board or it can be a part of the main system board.

The disk drive has a single spindle (Fig 1-7) that is turned by the drive motor. The drive accesses the disks with a single-head carriage assembly if it is single-sided or with a dual-head assembly if it is double-sided. In either case, a stepper motor/lead screw mechanism moves the assembly.

The disk drive has two sensors that detect the installation of a disk. These sensors also look for the notch on the side of the disk's protective cover to see if the disk is write-protected. If this notch is covered, the disk drive cannot write on the disk.

THE IBM PS/2 FAMILY

Since the introduction of the IBM PC in 1981, the use of the personal computer has grown, and the size of applications has also increased. Disk storage requirements have grown significantly, as has the need for greater access to information and greater system resources.

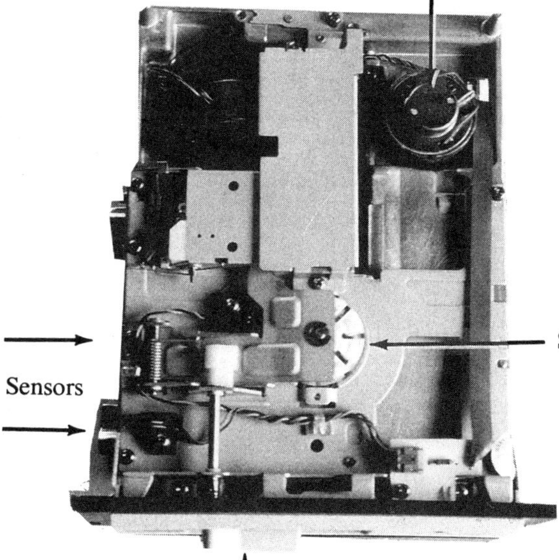

Figure 1-7 Floppy drive, top view, showing spindle in center and drive motor in upper-right corner

The software available for personal computers has more function and ease-of-use characteristics. This has increased program size, so program memory requirements have grown as well. Many applications can also coexist with other programs, which further increases the memory requirements. The computer needs other performance enhancements to accommodate the quickly growing application load.

The reliance on personal computers has also led to the need to process multiple applications concurrently (multitasking), a capability that has been limited in the earlier PCs. In addition, the system designs have become more important. The size of the components has decreased, and the proliferation of personal computers in all areas has been significant. There have been substantial advancements resulting in higher-capacity, faster, smaller, and less expensive systems.

The IBM Personal System/2 (PS/2) family leans on technology from IBM's large systems and customized IBM circuit integration. In developing the PS/2 family, IBM wanted to enhance reliability, improve overall quality, and increase component mean-time-between-failures. The result is a repackaged physical component design. IBM also added security facilities to protect user assets. The overall design goal was to reduce size, weight, heat, and noise.

One of the major changes is a new bus/channel architecture. System throughput and overall capacity has increased, and new graphics capabilities have been introduced. The design provides for some growth within the PS/2 family and application compatibility.

The PS/2 family is made up of desktop models as well as floor-standing models along with the IBM PC Convertible (see Tables 1-6 and 1-7). All models use front controls and indicator lights. The power-on switch is in the front of the system. Low-profile 3.5-inch floppy disk drives are used with a single push-button disk release. The noise levels on the PS/2 models are up to 75% less than the IBM PC, due mainly to the fan and airflow.

TABLE 1-6 PS/2 Model Characteristics

Model	25	30	50	60	80
Microprocessor Type	8086	8086	80286	80286	80386
Speed (MHz)	8	8	10	10	16 or 20
Permanent memory (ROM) (K)	64	64	128	128	128
User memory (RAM)					
Base	512K/640K	640K	1MB	1MB	1MB/2MB
Maximum	640K	640K	7MB	15MB	16MB
Hard Disk Storage					
Standard (MB)		20	20	44/70	44/70
Maximum (MB)		20	20	185	628
Floppy Disk 3.5-in capacity	720K	720K	144MB	144MB	144MB
Number Standard	1-1 2-2	2 1	1	1	1
Integrated functions:					
Parallel/serial/pointing device port	X	X	X	X	X
MCGA graphics	X	X			
VGA graphics port			X	X	X
Floppy drive controller	X	X	X	X	X
Hard disk adapter		X	X	X	X
Clock/calendar		X	X	X	X
Optical disk drive					
Internal				X	X
External	X	X	X	X	X
Max. storage (GB)	4	4	12	16	16
6157 Tape drive	X	X	X	X	

Expansion slots	2–3	3	3	7	7
Operating systems					
PC DOS 3.3	X	X	X	X	X
OS/2					
Standard			X	X	X
Extended			X	X	X

TABLE 1-7 Comparative Performance

PS/2 Computer	IBM PCs	Performance Ratio
Model 80	AT (339)	3.5
Model 60	AT (339)	2.0
Model 50	AT (339)	2.0
Model 30	XT (089)	2.5
Model 30	PC	2.4
Model 25	PC	2.4

Models 30, 50, 60, and 80 use the enhanced keyboard with replaceable keytops and a detachable keyboard cord. Model 25 uses the IBM Space Saving Keyboard or the Enhanced PC Keyboard.

Models 25 and 30 are based on the traditional IBM PC architecture. Models 50, 60, and 80 use the Micro Channel architecture.

Micro Channel Architecture

The initial IBM PC architecture was designed in 1981 for entry-level personal computing requirements. These stand-alone systems handled one application at a time using a small or moderate amount of memory. IBM designed the PS/2 line for more advanced applications. It expands the limits of connectivity.

The Micro Channel architecture (MCA) was first used in PS/2 Models 50, 60, and 80 and includes features for multitasking support, 32-bit data paths, and an analog channel for voice and analog signals. It also has a redesigned interrupt-servicing scheme, automatic attachment detection, and automatic configuration optimizing.

System-Board Integration

The PS/2 system-board design integrates the functions that occupy four or five adapter cards on an IBM PC AT system using very large-scale integration (VLSI) and surface mount technology (SMT). The system board includes memory expansion; display; and parallel, serial, and mouse ports. There is also a video subsystem on the system board as well as the floppy drive controller.

IBM custom-designed gate arrays are used to replace lower-level components. The internal data paths have been designed to reduce cables with direct connections between components.

Memory

IBM uses single inline packaging (SIP) technology in the PS/2 Models 25, 30, 50, and 60. The memory modules snap onto a custom-designed connector on the system board. They use SMT that requires less space and power and produces less heat. Model 80 uses high-speed (80-nanosecond [ns]) 1-megabit (Mb) technology. This is the same memory used in the 3090, 9370, and other IBM systems. By using higher densities and reducing the number of components, it is possible to provide larger amounts of standard memory on the system board.

Storage Media

Models 30 and 50 use a 20MB 3.5-inch hard disk. Model 30 has an integrated controller. Models 60 and 80 have 5.25-inch hard disks with capacities of 40MB, 70MB, 115MB and 314MB.

IBM also introduced an optical disk drive with removable cartridge disks. Each removable disk holds up to 200MB of data and can be used for archiving data. The optical disk uses light-beam access with write-once-read-many (WORM) technology.

A 6157 streaming tape drive is also available for the PS/2. The 6157 stores up to 55MB of data using a small cassette.

Hard Disk Interleaves

The hard disks on PS/2 Models 50, 60, and 80 use a one-to-one sector interleave. This is much more efficient than the three-to-one interleave used on the Model 30, IBM PC, XT, and AT. The system stores programs and data on a disk in 512-byte sectors. Because of the processing required for each sector and the limitations of the original IBM PC bus, you cannot transfer data to contiguous sectors. The system writes the data into every third sector, resulting in a three-to-one interleave. A one-to-one sector interleave allows you to write data onto contiguous sectors, thereby improving system performance.

Graphics

The PS/2 Models 25 and 30 integrate the graphics function on the system board by using a gate-array chip called the multicolor graphics array (MCGA). The MCGA uses an improved 8 x 16 character box and is fully compatible with the IBM color graphics adapter. The MCGA also determines which type of display is attached and appropriately converts the image to 64 shades of gray for a monochrome display. This process is called color summing. The MCGA can display 256 colors from a palette of more than 256,000 colors. In the entry-addressability color graphics mode (320 x 200), the MCGA can display 256 colors simultaneously for a television-type image. In the high-addressability mode (640 x 480), high-quality graphics can be displayed in greater clarity with 2 colors simultaneously.

Models 50, 60, and 80 use a higher-addressability character box (9 x 16) in the video graphics array (VGA). VGA gives better performance and color variety than enhanced graphics adapters (EGA). The IBM 8514/A provides functions beyond VGA, including 1024 x 768 screen modes and increased color capability for PS/2 Models 50, 60, and 80.

PS/2 MODELS

Model 25

Model 25 uses the Intel 8086, which runs at 8 MHz, and can accept the addition of an 8087 MCP. Internal memory is 512K on the system board for the standard unit and 640K on the system board for the collegiate unit. The standard unit has one 720K 3.5-inch floppy disk, while the collegiate unit has two 720K 3.5-inch floppy disks. Options include a second 720K 3.5-inch floppy disk, a 4869 5.25-inch external floppy disk, or an external 3363 optical disk drive.

A 12-inch analog monochrome or color display is available. The MCGA has an 8 x 16 character box with either 640 x 480 or 320 x 200 resolution. There is a 64K video RAM along with an analog display interface.

Integrated functions include serial I/O up to 9.6 kilobytes per second (Kbps), parallel I/O, an audio earphone connector, and floppy drive controller. Expansion includes one full-size expansion slot and one 8-inch expansion slot. The unit is 15.38 inches high, 12.63 inches wide, and 14.88 inches deep. A monochrome unit weighs 31 pounds, and a color unit weighs 36 pounds. A special space-saving keyboard is available that is 15.86 inches wide and 7.5 inches deep. The monochrome unit uses a 90-watt power supply, and the color unit uses a 115-watt supply.

Model 30

This unit uses an Intel 8086 running at 8 MHz and has the capacity for an added 8087 MCP. The system board has 640K of RAM. Storage is either two 720K 3.5-inch floppy disks or one 720K 3.5-inch floppy disk and a 20MB hard disk. Options include an external 3363 optical disk drive, a 6157 streaming tape drive or a 4869 5.25-inch external floppy disk.

Video and integrated functions are the same as the Model 25 except that a hard drive controller is also available. There are 3 expansion slots available to accept IBM PC cards. The unit is 4.0 inches high, 16.0 inches wide, and 15.6 inches deep. It weighs 17.5 pounds and has a 70-watt switching power supply.

Model 50

This unit uses an Intel 80286 running at 10 MHz and accepts the addition of the 80287 MCP. The system board has 1MB RAM, which is expandable to 7MB on adapter cards. There is one 1.44MB 3.5-inch floppy disk and one 20MB hard disk. Options include an external 3363 optical disk drive, a 6157 streaming tape drive, and a 4869 5.25-inch external floppy drive. The VGA uses a 9 x 16 character box with a 720 x 400 text mode. Graphics modes are 640 x 480 with 16 colors from a 256K palette and 320 x 200 with 256 colors from a 256K palette. The system uses a 256K video RAM with an analog display interface.

The Model 50 includes serial and parallel interfaces along with a floppy drive controller and a hard drive controller adapter. There are 3 available expansion slots housed in a box 5.5 inches high, 14.2 inches wide, and 16.5 inches deep. The unit weighs 21 pounds, and the power supply is a 94-watt switching unit.

Model 60

The Model 60 uses an 80286 processor running at 10 MHz and the capacity for an added 80287 MCP. There is 1MB RAM on the system board, which is expandable to 15MB with adapter cards. Storage is one 1.44MB 3.5-inch floppy disk with a 44MB or 70MB hard disk. You can add a second 1.44MB 3.5-inch floppy disk along with a second hard disk of 44MB. A 115MB hard disk is available along with an internal or external 3363 optical disk drive, a 6157 streaming tape drive, and a 4869 5.25-inch external floppy drive.

The VGA uses a 9 x 16 character box with a 720 x 400 text mode. Graphics modes are 640 x 480 with 16 colors from a 256K palette and 320 x 200 with 256 colors. There is a 256K video RAM and an analog display interface.

Enhanced small device interfaces (ESDI) and serial and parallel interfaces are included along with the floppy drive controller and hard drive controller adapter. Smaller hard drives use an ST-506 interface, and large hard drives use an ESDI.

There are 7 expansion slots. The tower case is 23.5 inches high, 6.5 inches wide, and 19.0 inches deep. The weight is 47 pounds. The system uses a 207-watt or 225-watt switching power supply.

Model 80

The Model 80 uses an 80386 running at 16 or 20 MHz. An 80387 MCP is an option. The 16-MHz system board has 1MB of RAM on the system board, which is expandable to 2MB. The internal memory is expandable to 16MB with adapter cards. The 20-MHz system board has 2MB of RAM on the system board, which is expandable to 4MB. The system is expandable to 16MB of RAM using adapter cards. Storage ranges from one 1.44MB 3.5-inch floppy disk drive and one 44MB hard disk to one 1.44MB 3.5-inch floppy disk and one 314MB hard disk. Options include a second 1.44MB 3.5-inch floppy disk and a second hard disk of 44MB to 314MB. There is also an internal or external 3363 optical disk drive, a 6157 streaming tape drive, and a 4869 5.25-inch external floppy disk drive.

The VGA uses a 9 x 16 character box with a 720 x 400 text mode. Graphics modes are 640 x 480 with 16 colors from a 256K palette or 320 x 200 with 256 colors from a 256K palette. The system uses a 256K video RAM along with an analog display interface.

Serial and parallel interfaces are included with a floppy drive controller and hard drive controller adapter. The smaller hard drives include an ST-506 interface, and the larger hard drives include an ESDI.

There are 4 16-bit expansion slots and 3 16/32-bit expansion slots available. The tower case is 23.5 inches high, 6.5 inches wide, and 19.0 inches deep. It weighs 52 pounds and uses a 207-watt or 225-watt switching power supply.

THE 386-486 FAMILY

The 386 Architecture

Introduced in 1986, the 386 microprocessor was designed for power users. This chip allows desktop computers to use more powerful applications and moves them into areas like parallel computers, file servers, and workstations. The 386 computer is based on a 32-bit family of chips.

Benefits of the 386 architecture include: multitasking of DOS programs, the ability to run larger programs, and the more efficient use of memory. Multitasking allows the user to run multiple applications at the same time. The 386 CPU has the ability to run multiple DOS applications simultaneously using the virtual 8086 mode. This feature is used with the windowing environment provided by programs such as Windows 386 from Microsoft and DesqView from Quarterdeck. Other programs, including products from Interactive Systems and Locus Computing, allow DOS-under-UNIX operation.

Memory accessibility is another improvement with the 386 family. The 386 DX microprocessor has 32 address lines and can directly access 4 gigabytes (4GB) of main memory and 64 terabytes (64 trillion bytes) of virtual memory. This large addressing capability becomes important in large databases. The virtual-memory addressing capabilities allow systems to operate with less physical memory, and this reduces the system cost.

Table 1-8 lists some typical 386 computers.

TABLE 1-8 Typical 386 Computers

Company	Processor	MHz	Memory	Storage
AST Model 45	80386DX	16	1MB RAM	1.2MB or 1.4MB, 40MB
Compaq Model 40	80386DX	20	1MB RAM	1.2MB, 40MB
DTK	80386DX	20	0K RAM	Optional
Epson Equity	80386DX	20	1MB RAM	1.2MB, 40/90MB
Hewlett-Packard HP Vectra QS/20	80386DX	20	1MB RAM	108MB
Leading Edge D-3	80386DX	16	1MB RAM	1.2MB, 65MB
Televideo Teloas III, Model NH	80386DX	16	1MB RAM	1.2MB, 40MB
Zenith Z-386	80386DX	16	1MB RAM	1.2MB,80MB

The 386 Workstation

Many of the techniques used in the 386 microprocessor come from mainframe computers. The result is an inexpensive microcomputer with the performance previously associated with larger and more expensive machines. The 386 computer offers a platform for many computing needs and blurs the prior distinctions between PCs, workstations, and minicomputers. Since 1986, the 386 DX CPU performance has increased at least 25% per year with the introduction of new speeds, including 33-MHz chips (the 386 DX CPU, 387 MCP, and 82385 cache controller).

The 486 Microprocessor

The introduction of the 486 microprocessor in 1989 extended the 386 architecture to even greater performance. The 486 CPU integrates a 386 DX CPU that is enhanced using reduced instruction set computer (RISC) technology, a 387 MCP, and a cache memory. The result provides at least double the performance of the 386 DX CPU at the same clock speed. At a clock speed of 25 MHz, the 486 CPU performance is equivalent to most 32-bit RISC processors.

386-486 Compatibility

The 486 processor shares the same 32-bit software architecture as the 386 family and improves the 386 architecture's performance within the bounds of compatibility with earlier processors. Like the 386 processor, the 486 CPU runs all 8086 and 80286 software. Software that runs on the 386 will run with no changes on the 486 CPU, and software written for the 486 processor will also run on any 386 processor.

386 Software

Because of the high power offered in systems based on the 386 architecture, many applications traditionally reserved for minicomputers and mainframes are now available for 386 family-based computers. For example, IBM Interleaf Publisher, a popular mainframe publishing package, is now available for the desktop environment. Other applications in areas such as risk analysis, resource management, computer-aided design (CAD), and manufacturing have been migrating to the 386 platform. Multiuser software solutions are available using products like Banyan's Vines 386 or Novell's NetWare 386 for the same type of connectivity achieved with minicomputers.

386 SX

The 386/486 family has a wide range of price and performance, from the 386SX at 3 MIPS (millions of instructions per second) to the 486 processor at 20 MIPS. Systems based on this architecture can meet needs from the office automation market to high-performance minicomputers.

The 386 SX processor delivers 386 functions at a 16-bit price. The 386 architecture, including the 486 processor, runs software written for DOS, Operating System 2 (OS/2), 32-bit OS/2, and UNIX and XENIX 386. The 286 systems run only a subset of 386 family software.

The 16-MHz 386SX is an inexpensive business machine capable of running today's software. For a 33% faster performance at a slightly higher cost, there is the 20-MHz SX chip, which gives the system more power to run CPU-intensive applications like Windows 3.0, WordPerfect 5.1, and Paradox. These machines generally have a higher capacity for drives, expansion boards, and fast (CPU-speed) RAM (Fig 1-8). The faster machines also hold their value longer and keep pace with new applications and their increasing demands for more RAM and mass storage.

The faster, more powerful 25-MHz 386DX systems cost about $1,000 more than the 386SX. Price differences among most machines are small, except for Compaq. The capacity for fast RAM is significant especially if you run Windows, since the program will slow down if memory is short. Windows 3.0 needs a minimum of 4M RAM. It also needs a 100MB or slightly larger hard disk, one floppy disk drive, an EGA or VGA video controller, an EGA or VGA monitor, a keyboard, a mouse, and DOS 3.3 or 4.01. The system should include floppy and hard drive controllers and at least 1 parallel and 1 serial port and should support 16MB of fast RAM.

Typical SX computers are covered in this section.

Typical SX Machines

ALR PowerFlex. ALR's PowerFlex 20CSX has good performance for a 20-MHz machine, but it has a 5MB limit on CPU-speed RAM. The CPU board plugs into a special slot, which makes it easy to upgrade to a 486 by changing boards. However, since a 32-bit 486 has to access motherboard memory through the 16-bit memory bus, you do not get the full benefits of the 486. In addition to the SX CPU, the motherboard has a 286 that is normally used. Therefore, if the CPU or processor board fails, you can use the PowerFlex as a 286. VGA is not built into the motherboard, so you have to use a separate board. ALR's VGA video board also contains the system's mouse port. This VGA board runs in 800 x 600 super-VGA mode.

While it has room for four drives, the chassis is not designed for moving drives around. If you need to change a drive in one of the center drive bays, you have to remove the CPU board, any full-length expansion boards, and the drives in the right-hand bays. Installing expansion boards and the right-hand drives is easier.

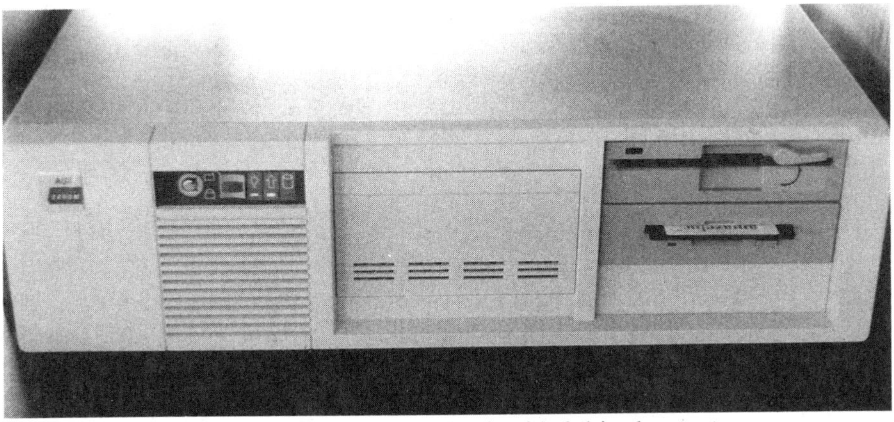

Figure 1-8 A typical 386 system chassis with 6 drive bays

The fan and hard drive may seem a little noisier than other machines, and the keyboard does not have a lot of tactical feedback. The right-hand floppy drive mounts vertically, which makes it easy to use if you want to stand your computer end-up on the floor to save desk space.

AST Premium II. This is a small-footprint PC with the CPU, system memory, and math coprocessor on a removable CPU board, so it is easy to upgrade it to a 25-MHz or 33-MHz 386DX or a 25-MHz 486. The system has good expansion capacity with 5 drive bays and 5 available expansion slots. Thumbscrews make it easy to open and close the case, and the internal design lets you change drives without having to remove expansion boards or other drives.

The power switch and monitor controls are on the front panel, and the system has a reset switch along with a second serial port and a mouse port. The fan is not as quiet as other systems, and the keyboard is without an audible click. Performance on disk-intensive tasks is lacking for programs like Paradox or dBASE, but the upgrade path is made easier by the design.

Compaq Deskpro. Compaq's 20-MHz 386SX system is the Deskpro 386s/20. The system includes a 4K RAM cache and uses a wait state only about 7% of the time. The 60MB and 120MB hard disks have average access times under 19 milliseconds (ms).

A computer will not become obsolete as fast if it has the potential for memory expansion. The Deskpro 386s/20 comes with 2MB of RAM and can be upgraded to 16MB on the motherboard. It comes with a 3.5-inch floppy disk drive and either a 60MB or 120MB hard disk. You can add a second hard drive internally. You can also upgrade the 386s/20 with a 20-MHz 80387SX math coprocessor.

This system is well designed. Loosening a few thumbscrews will remove the case. Adding RAM or a MCP is easy, and changing a drive requires removing a few screws. The memory uses standard single inline memory modules (SIMMs) instead of the special memory modules used in some Compaq units.

The fan is quiet, and all power and monitor controls are on the front panel. The keyboard may not have the feel you like, and a key-press click sounds from the speaker instead of from the keyboard.

The Deskpro 386s is one of the first 386SX computers. This machine processes data with less than one wait state using a page-mode memory architecture. It has an integrated-VGA adapter and 2MB of RAM that you can upgrade to 13MB using a special high-speed RAM expansion slot. There are four 8/16-bit expansion slots, one of which is used for ordinary operation.

This system has a 1.44MB floppy disk, with a 40MB or 80MB hard disk installed in its internal drive bay. The hard disks use a one-to-one interleave for access times under 29 ms.

Deskpro 386N and 286N. Compaq designed the Deskpro 386N and 286N as LAN workstations, but they can also run as stand-alone machines.

The 386N is a 16-MHz 386SX computer that is 15.0 inches wide, 3.9 inches high and 14.9 inches deep. It weighs only 13.25 pounds empty or 16.75 pounds with hard and floppy drives. It has built-in serial, parallel, and mouse ports along with built-in floppy and hard drive controllers and a high-performance 16-bit VGA controller.

The 386N has 3 expansion slots. Two of them are industry standard architecture (ISA) standard 8/16-bit slots (full-length), and the third is a high-speed memory slot. With 1MB of RAM as standard, you can upgrade the 386N with 7MB of additional memory on the motherboard and 8MB more in the memory slot.

A power-on password controls initial access to the 386N, and a quicklock feature lets you temporarily disable the keyboard without exiting an application. A system administrator can disable the floppy drive or set it up so that users can read files but cannot copy information from the network. A hacker may be able to use the parallel or serial ports on even a diskless workstation to extract programs and data from a LAN. The 386N allows an administrator to disable these ports when the system is not being used in a secure environment.

The 386N uses a dual-speed fan that seems quieter than those of many other desktop PCs. The Deskpro 286N has all of the features of the 386N, but it uses a 12-MHz 286 instead of a 386.

Dell. This was one of the first 386 20-MHz units. It is also a large-footprint system, which provides more room for boards and drives, but which needs more room on a crowded desk. This machine tends to be slow compared to others since it does not use a memory cache.

It is easy to work on the Dell due to the larger AT-style case. The design is open and not crowded. Drives slide in and out easily, and all slots can hold full-length boards. The keyboard has tactile feedback which can improve accuracy during fast keying. The fan is noisy compared to other systems and the power switch is on the right side of the unit.

NCR. This system has a built-in super VGA (SVGA), and the motherboard includes the drive. There is also a socket for upgrading the system's video memory for super VGA capability to 1024 x 768. The system has four available expansion slots, but room for only three drives. There is a built-in port for an external floppy disk drive.

The fan is quiet, and there is a volume control for the PC's audio output. The case is only a little over 5 inches high and can fit in small spaces, but the keyboard can block the lower floppy drive. The keyboard has no audible or tactile feedback. This system has good performance for Lotus 1-2-3 and Paradox.

NEC PowerMate. Expandability on the PowerMate is not good since the system uses custom boards and each must fit into its own dedicated slot on the motherboard. The CPU and math coprocessor are on one of these boards, but there is no upgrade option. Other proprietary boards provide an 800 x 600 SVGA adapter and RAM expansion. If you use the built-in Integrated Drive Electronics (IDE) controller, there are 4 available expansion slots. You are also limited to 3 drive bays.

The keyboard and mouse ports, on/off switch, and monitor controls are on the front. However, the lower drive bay is too low to clear the back of the keyboard, and the fan and hard drive are noisier than most other machines. The keyboard has good tactile feedback, but the Ctrl and Alt keys may be too close together for many users.

The lack of memory caching limits performance, and the system has a 12MB limit for fast RAM.

Upgrading from SX to DX

Expandability is important to long-term functionality, especially if the system is used as a server. The number of drive bays and expansion slots ensure that you can upgrade your PC with new life-extending technology over the years. Many systems offer the Extended Industry Standard Architecture (EISA) bus, which allows higher throughput as well as backward compatibility with standard AT-style boards.

The standard 80386 chip is faster and has more RAM capacity than the less expensive SX. The maximum for the SX chip is 16MB of CPU-speed RAM. For a workstation, 16MB (which is OS/2's and Windows' current capacity) may be sufficient. However, in a server, larger buffers and larger caches mean faster performance. For example, Novell's NetWare 386 can take advantage of up to 4GB.

Memory beyond 16MB is useful if the server is used in a large busy NetWare 386 local area network (LAN). As the demand on the network grows, you can add more RAM to improve performance, but you will need a place to put it. A 386 with 33 Mhz is a good choice as a small server or a high-end workstation, and the expandability of a machine like the AST Premium 386/33TE allows it to handle and network almost any power-computing application in the near future. Typical 386 DX machines are covered in this section.

Typical DX Machines

ALR. This is a small-footprint desktop machine, and the unit is cramped internally. It will accept two third-height and two half-height drives, but it will not take a full-height drive. This places a limit for off-line storage since the bigger drives need a full-height bay.

The CPU-board design allows you to upgrade to a 25- or 33-MHz 486. There are 6 available expansion slots, and 3 of these are EISA. However, the CPU board is in the way, so that one of the 16-bit slots can take only a half-length board. If you install more than 17MB of RAM, you will obstruct another 16-bit slot. Performance is good for NetWare and Paradox, but the unit is too cramped to act as a server for large networks.

Arche Legacy. This system uses an AT box with 5 half-height drive slots, and it can accommodate a full-height drive. There are 5 available expansion slots, but, if you use more than 8MB of RAM, you will need to use 1 of the 2 RAM slots, which can also take standard 8/16-bit cards. To bring the memory up to its full 32MB capacity, you will need to use 2 of these slots.

There is no front-panel on/off switch, and installing a coprocessor requires removing the motherboard. There is a front-panel reset button and an LED display to indicate the processor speed. The motherboard uses several proprietary chips that reduce the component count and increase the machine's reliability. Performance is good for dBASE IV and NetWare.

AST Premium. This is a tower case with good expandability and 80MB of RAM capacity. The tower case provides 8 available EISA slots and 6 drive bays. The CPU is upgradable and the fan is quiet.

AT&T. The AT&T machine uses a floor-standing case and has 8 drive bays. The front panel has a reset button, but the on/off switch is down near the floor. Configuring RAM, printer, and serial-port settings can be time-consuming since a number of jumper pins must be changed on the system board. Otherwise, the system is very expandable.

Compaq. A 386 processor cannot deliver good performance without the proper subsystems. These include a memory cache, EISA expansion bus, and high-performance disk drives. The Deskpro 386/33L has good expandability with a modular processor board, 7 available EISA slots, optional drive-array technology, and a 100MB capacity for RAM.

Compaq worked with Western Digital to develop IDE hard drives, which run from a controller located on the motherboard. The drive-array technology is designed for serving a large, growing LAN. Its multiple hard drives act as one, improving both access speed and data integrity. Two 110MB drives can perform as a fast 220MB drive or as a single 110MB drive that backs itself up as it is used. The drive-array technology must be used with Compaq drives.

The basic unit comes with a 120MB, 19-ms hard disk that uses the built-in controller. A 320MB or 650MB system uses the ESDI controller that provides data transfer and access times below 18 ms.

The Deskpro 386/33L's 7 bays for mass storage devices can store up to 1.3GB internally. You can add more storage with an external hard disk expansion unit and then back up your data with the Digital Audio Tape (DAT) drive, which fits into the front panel and holds up to 4GB.

The Deskpro's 33-MHz 386 processor uses a dedicated processor card that also holds sockets for both Intel 80387 and Weitek 3167 MCPs. An Intel 82385 cache controller and 64K of static RAM reduce wait states to less than 2% of the processing time. The processor card uses one of two dedicated 32-bit slots. The other 32-bit slot can accept a memory card for expansion to 100MB of RAM. The base unit comes with 4MB of RAM.

The Deskpro 386/33L requires the use of proprietary memory modules, which cost several times as much as standard SIMMs. You can upgrade to a 33-MHz 486 CPU by changing processor cards. The system case uses thumbscrews. Performance is fair.

Compaq's small-footprint case appeared in 1988 with the Deskpro 386s. The case measures 15.8 by 14.8 by 5.9 inches, which is a little wider than most monitors. Compaq uses a longitudinal 140-watt power supply that runs along the full depth of the machine.

The Deskpro 386/33L comes with 7 expansion slots. Each slot can accept an 8-bit card (as used in the original IBM PC), an AT-style 16-bit card, or a 32-bit EISA card. There are 3 front-panel bays for storage, which can include 3.5- and 5.25-inch floppy disk drives with a tape backup drive. They have room for 1 or 2 internal hard disks with 4 full-length 8/16-bit ISA expansion slots.

Built-in controllers and interfaces include integrated-VGA graphics with graphics accelerator, built-in floppy, hard, and tape drive controllers, with motherboard-based serial, parallel, and mouse ports. These functions would normally take several expansion cards.

In addition to saving a slot, the IDE hard drive controller provides faster data transfer than the earlier ST-506 controllers. IDE hard disks also tend to cost less than others. The Compaq flex architecture separates the system-memory bus from the peripheral bus for high-speed access to memory.

The Deskpro 386/25e comes with a 25-MHz 386 processor, 4MB of RAM, 32K of static-RAM cache, and a socket for either an Intel 80387 or Weitek 3167 math coprocessor. It has a 60MB hard drive, with a high-speed memory expansion slot for RAM up to 16MB, and it supports 2 internal hard disks.

A ROM-resident program provides security functions and lets you make changes to the system configuration without using a setup disk. Compaq's Advanced VGA is faster than ordinary VGA adapters and delivers 256 simultaneous colors at a resolution of 640 x 480 pixels.

Another compact unit is the Deskpro 386/20e. It is a full 32-bit machine using the 386DX processor. It is much faster than a 386SX system, especially when running 386 software. The system has a 82385 cache controller with 32K of dedicated RAM.

The Deskpro 386/20e comes with 4MB of RAM, expandable to 16MB using a dedicated RAM expansion slot. You can install 2 hard disks internally, along with an Intel 80387 or Weitek 3167 MCP.

Dell. This DX system lacks the storage and RAM capacities desirable in a large server, but it is useful as a smaller server or a workstation. There are 6 available AT-style slots and 4 half-height drive bays. You can expand the system 16MB of CPU-speed RAM, which makes it useful as a workstation but not as a large server. The system also includes SVGA graphics. The unit has a small-footprint chassis and opens with thumbscrews. It also has front-panel on/off and reset switches.

NEC PowerMate. This machine has room for expansion, but it is limited by 16MB of fast RAM. It provides good performance when using Windows, but in other areas it might be slow.

The PowerMate uses a proprietary application-specific integrated circuit (ASIC) chip for memory management—usually a problem in Windows applications. The memory management improves performance for Windows, but not for NetWare.

The architecture is a mixed bag. All 5 open slots are EISA, but you must flip motherboard switches to set up the system. The system includes a floor stand, so you can stand the unit up like a tower.

Tandy. This machine has 4 drive bays with a 16MB fast-RAM limit. Performance is low with NetWare, but there is a RAM cache. The 80386 is mounted on a modular board, but initially a 486 board was not available for future upgrades. There are 5 available AT-style expansion slots and 4 drive slots, but 2 of these are for third-height drives. The compact chassis has on/off and reset controls on the front panel.

Zenith. This machine uses a caching drive controller, which can operate 4 ESDI, 7 SCSI (small computer system interfaces), and 2 floppy drives at the same time. It is slow in NetWare applications, and initial systems had NetWare compatibility problems. The large 3-layer caching controller should improve performance. It uses 1 EISA slot, but takes up space that could be used for another slot. VGA and I/O take up 2 more slots, leaving 4 available slots. The standard AT-style chassis allows 5 half-height drives.

THE IBM XP 486 FAMILY

The IBM PS/2 XP 486 line consists of 4 machines. There are two Model 90 desktops and two Model 95 towers. They offer 25- and 33-MHz 486 configurations and easily upgradable CPUs. These 486s have a much better capacity for memory and drives than other PS/2s.

The XP line uses next-generation graphics hardware that comes with every system. The extended graphics array (XGA) is built into all Model 90 motherboards and comes standard as an expansion board with all Model 95 towers.

Like IBM's 8514/AZ, XGA offers 1024 x 768 resolution with 256 colors. However, a special mode allows XGA to display up to 65,536 colors at standard-VGA resolution. This can provide realistic screen shows for multimedia and other applications.

XP Performance

Like other 486s, XPs can handle tasks that earlier PCs cannot. This includes generating large CAD drawings, multitasking under OS/2, running multiuser data-base applications, and doing similar jobs. The tower case offers a good complement of drive bays and slots, but, other than that, the tower and desktop configurations are similar internally.

There is a removable CPU board that fits into a Micro Channel slot. This board holds the 486, memory controller, and related circuitry, making it easier to upgrade to more powerful CPUs.

All XP models come with 4MB of CPU-speed memory, which you can expand to 32MB. The standard memory uses 70-ns chips, so the upgrade from 25 to 33 MHz does not require new chips or added wait states. You upgrade with pairs of 1MB, 2MB, or 4MB SIMMs.

The memory architecture gives the 486 interleaved access to 2 32-bit memory banks. You can also add a 256K secondary memory cache designed to speed multiuser and multitasking applications. Many competing boxes either have a hardwired secondary cache or cannot be upgraded.

XPs store part of the BIOS on disk and copy it into RAM, which aids both performance and future upgrades. IBM has increased the throughput for serial ports from 19,200 bits per second to a potential 345,000 bits per second for high-speed modems. Parallel and mouse ports are standard.

Unlike many 486 systems, the XPs have good mass-storage options. All the systems use IBM's 32-bit SCSI bus-master controller, which is built in and handles up to 7 SCSI drives for gigabytes of storage. A high-performance 2.3GB tape backup unit is also available.

Model 90 Desktop

The Model 90 is a little larger than the 386-based Model 70, at $17\frac{1}{4}$ inches wide, $16\frac{7}{8}$ inches deep, and $5\frac{1}{2}$ inches high. With XGA on the system board, the Model 90 offers 3 available 32-bit Micro Channel slots. One of the slots has a special pass-through extension that hooks into XGA for future graphics options like IBM's M-Motion multimedia board.

This unit holds up to 5 storage devices. Two 5.25-inch bays can hold CD-ROM drives, tape backup units, or a half-height 5.25-inch floppy drive. On the motherboard, 2 vertical racks of sockets hold up to 4 SIMMs each. The power supply is 194 watts, and 2 serial ports and 1 parallel port are standard.

Model 95

The Model 95 is the most powerful PS/2, in a tower configuration slightly smaller than the Model 80. This machine holds 8 32-bit slots, with 6 of them free. Two of the slots have XGA pass-through extensions. The SIMMs plug into the system board.

Model 95 uses a 329-watt power supply and has 7 storage bays. There are 2 for floppy disks, CD-ROM drives, or tape backup and 5 for hard disks. This allows up to 1.6GB with IBM drives.

There is also an external storage enclosure for up to 7 SCSI devices—a Model 95 case with a 320MB drive, power supply, and connecting cables.

By adding more SCSI controllers and storage enclosures, you can upgrade the system to 28 hard disks and 8.96GB. To do this, you would need some mixture of DOS, OS/2, AIX, and UNIX, since OS/2 supports 24 hard drives and DOS handles only 7. However, you would probably run into many data-transfer problems if you were to install a few dozen drives. The tower case has an 8-character LED diagnostic display in front.

The IBM Model 95 and the Compaq Systempro are in a high-powered class sometimes referred to as a super network server or a super server. A super server is a machine designed to run a standard LAN operating system with the utmost in both reliability and speed. The 95 is actually targeted for networks of 36 or fewer workstations rather than much larger installations. It does not have Compaq's dual-processor architecture or proprietary intelligent drive array (IDA) disks. The 95 could be a true super server with a few additional features, such as a bus-master coprocessor card and bus-master network adapters.

OTHER TYPICAL 486 MACHINES

Compaq Systempro

Compaq's Systempro was the first super server on the market. It has the power of a minicomputer with the flexibility and compatibility of a PC. You can increase its speed by adding a processor or drive arrays without removing any existing components.

The floor-standing tower system (Fig 1-9) has room for 11 mass-storage devices and 11 full-size expansion slots. Compaq's Flex/MP architecture, which is dedicated for up to 256MB of RAM and for CPU expansion, uses 4 expansion slots. There is a processor card in one of the Flex/MP slots that can employ either a 33-MHz 80386 or 33-MHz 80486. The 80386 processor card has a 64K RAM cache and supports the Weitek 3167-33 and Intel 80387-33 MCPs. The 80486 processor card has an integrated coprocessor, 8K of on-chip cache, and a server cache that uses 512K of 25-ns static RAM in a second-level cache.

You can speed up the Systempro by adding an additional 386 or 486 processor card. The dual processors can be used with LAN Manager, Vines, UNIX, and NetWare.

In most LANs, the server's disk performance is more critical than processor speed. Instead of a single, large hard drive, the Systempro uses

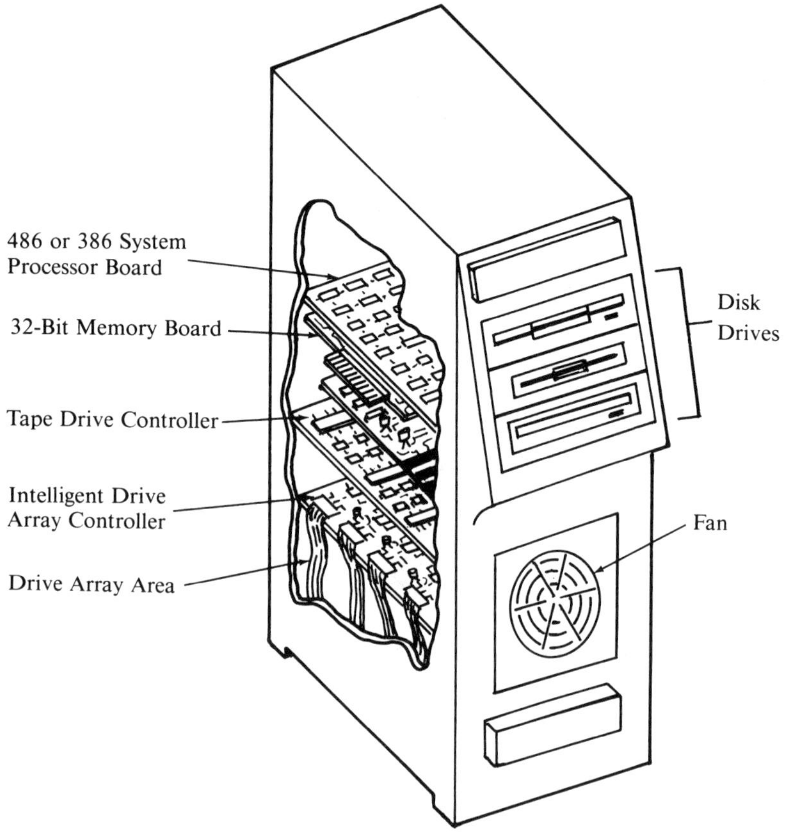

Figure 1-9 Compaq Systempro floor-standing tower system

drive-array technology, which employs teams of smaller drives that act like one drive to the operating system and the user. The system splits up the incoming data and writes it to several drives simultaneously. This makes reading and writing the data go faster, since the head movement is decreased.

There is also a data-guarding feature that stores an image of the data. Each time a byte is written to any drive in the array, the IDA controller reads the byte occupying the same position on all the other drives. It performs a mathematical calculation on the byte values and writes the result on the data guard drive. Then, if a drive fails, the system reconstructs its contents by reading the guard drive and interpreting the stored values. This technique is used with four or eight drives and would fail if two drives in the same array crashed at the same time. For critical data, you can set up the controller so it automatically and continuously performs drive mirroring, using half of the system's storage to duplicate information written to the other half. You can also use controller duplexing with two IDA controllers and two sets of drive arrays. This provides redundancy for the two disk subsystems, and the data is always accessible.

As a super server, the Systempro also provides storage capacity that goes well beyond other microcomputers. If you need more than 2.04GB of storage, you can use the Compaq intelligent array expansion system. This unit has its own 367-watt power supply and space for up to 11 mass storage devices. It comes with two 1.3GB hard disks. You can install 2 expansion controllers per Systempro unit, and each can support an expansion system with up to 9.1GB of storage, bringing the upgraded Systempro to 20.24GB of storage.

A dual-486 Systempro with an intelligent array expansion system has better performance in disk-intensive applications than some minicomputers. It runs 70% faster than a DEC VAX 6310 and 40% faster than an HP 9000. The base configuration has 240MB of storage, 8MB of RAM, and one 386 processor. The intelligent array expansion system has 2.6GB of mass storage.

The PS/2 Model 70 486 does not have enough mass storage and memory capacity for a 486 machine. The XPs have made up for these shortcomings and added super-XGA graphics (a newer industry standard).

Deskpro 486/33L

The Compaq Deskpro 486/33L was the fastest personal computer until Compaq announced an even faster machine, the Deskpro 486/50L. Although this computer is fast, speed should not be the only reason to buy one. Whatever model you buy today, it will not be the fastest PC next year. Compaq's original Deskpro 386 was introduced in 1986, and since then clock speeds have increased steadily.

The Deskpro 486/33L is a good-quality system, with an EISA expansion bus and an integrated-VGA adapter. This machine is useful as a LAN server or workstation. It comes in a wide-body chassis with seven 8/16/32-bit EISA expansion slots.

Controllers and interfaces that are built in include: floppy drive controller, hard drive controller, parallel port, tape drive controller, mouse port, 2 serial ports, and an integrated video graphics system with a graphics accelerator.

In addition to the 7 EISA slots, there are 2 additional 32-bit slots. One holds the processor card with the 33-MHz 80486 CPU and a socket for a Weitek 4167 numeric coprocessor. This 486 includes an integrated

80387-compatible MCP for CAD and other math-intensive applications. The second slot can hold up to 100MB of RAM.

The processor has 8K of on-chip cache memory, and Compaq has added 128K of cache to increase the system performance. The 486 runs programs about twice as fast as a 386 system operating at the same clock speed. A faster 386 would not be as quick at 32-bit operations that will be needed to run 32-bit applications such as Windows and OS/2.

The Deskpro 486/33L Model 120 comes with a 120MB IDE hard disk that provides 19-ms access times. The 320MB or 650MB systems provide access times of 18 ms and an even faster data transfer, due to the improved performance of the ESDI controller used with these drives. Seven bays for mass storage devices allow the Deskpro to store up to 1.3GB internally. If you need even more storage, you can use a fixed disk expansion unit, which is an external box that comes with either a 650MB or 300MB hard disk. The Deskpro 486/33L can also use the same IDA controller used on the Systempro. The base model uses a 120MB hard disk, and the top end of the line is a 650MB unit.

AcerPower 486SX

The AcerPower 486SX was one of the first 486SX systems. It is a compact ISA workstation designed for the desktop for business users who use a graphical-windowing environment such as Windows or computer-intensive applications such as CAD.

The 16-bit ISA I/O bus provides a lower-cost product for users who do not need the additional data-processing power provided by the 32-bit EISA bus. The lower cost of manufacturing the 486SX systems translates to a lower cost for the user who does not require the 32-bit I/O bus.

Standard features include an Intel 20-MHz 486SX processor, 2MB of system memory, an integrated ultra-VGA graphics chipset, a 101-key enhanced PS/2 keyboard, a PS/2 mouse, 4 expansion slots for 16- or 8-bit ISA board, 2 serial ports (9-pin and 25-pin), and a parallel port.

The system also comes standard with a 3.5-inch 1.44MB floppy disk. It has 4 3.5-inch half-height storage bays. You can convert 2 of the 3.5-inch bays to a 5.25-inch half-height bay. In the server environment, most server software comes in the 5.25-inch format, but in the desktop workstation environment the trend is toward the 3.5-inch disk drive.

Hard drives for this system include 120MB, 200MB, and 500MB IDE disks. It comes with Microsoft Windows, MS-DOS 3.3, Microsoft GW-BASIC, and Version 4.0 of the LIM-EMS memory manager. Also included is a disk buffer that increases I/O performance up to 50%, depending on how much memory is configured in the cache.

Upgrade Features. One of the AcerPower 486SX's features is its ChipUp technology. This allows a user to insert a 25- or 33-MHz chip into the socket intended for the 487SX upgrade. There is a speed improvement since the 487SX, like the 486SX, is a 20-MHz chip. The system automatically detects the type of CPU installed, so the user does not have to worry about setting switches or configuring software when the 486DX chip is installed. A second socket is designed for the Weitek 4167 coprocessor for users who need more floating-point capability.

Internal Memory. The 486SX accesses memory through a separate 128-bit memory bus. The system memory uses page-mode interleave, which speeds up the processing task. The internal memory is made up of dynamic RAM (DRAM), which has to refresh itself constantly to keep from losing data. The time DRAM spends refreshing itself is time lost from processing tasks, slowing the system down.

Page-mode interleaving splits the DRAM into two banks. The system accesses even-numbered addresses from one bank and odd-numbered addresses from the other bank. This reduces the time the CPU spends waiting (wait states) for DRAM to refresh itself and bring up the data.

Along with page-mode interleaving, the unit uses an 8K internal RAM cache to improve system performance. The RAM cache uses static RAM to hold frequently used instructions and data. Static RAM is faster than DRAM since it does not have to continually refresh itself.

There is also a cacheable BIOS feature, which lets you put BIOS code into the 8K RAM cache. This can increase performance by 25%. Cacheable BIOS is sometimes confused with shadow RAM, in which a section of conventional RAM is designated for the BIOS. Therefore, when you boot up the machine, the contents of system and video BIOS are copied into shadow RAM, which is faster than the EPROM (erasable programmable read-only memory) that is normally used to store the BIOS.

Memory Upgrading. The AcerPower 486SX offers a sizable memory-upgrade path. In addition to the base memory configuration for 2MB, the system includes 3 available SIMM sockets. When you use 16MB DRAM chips, the AcerPower 486SX will support up to 98MB of memory on the system board.

The memory-upgrade path is also extremely flexible, with 63 different combinations of SIMM chips possible. The AcerPower 486SX sup-

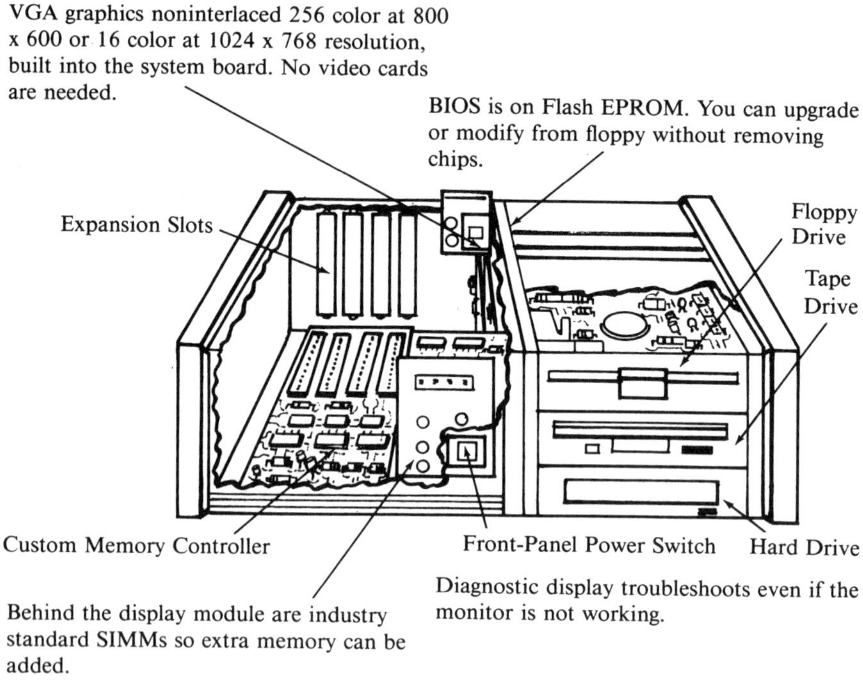

Figure 1-10 Typical 486 desktop system chassis

ports 6 types of commercial SIMMs: 1MB, 2MB, 4MB, 8MB, 16MB, and 32MB. The benefit of using SIMM chips is that it lets the end user upgrade memory incrementally instead of having to purchase a proprietary memory expansion board. It is also more efficient, as a memory board must typically be replaced by a new board each time the user wants to upgrade memory.

Security. A number of software, hardware, and mechanical techniques are built in to safeguard against unauthorized system access or data transfer. There are two levels of booting password control: either standalone or network mode. You can also use passwords to disable the keyboard. You can control access to the floppy drive, hard drive, and ports using software configurations, with comparable hardware controls available using switch settings.

The user must insert a mechanical key in the machine and turn it toward the unlocked position in order to open the hardware case. This feature allows you to maintain control of distributed, unsupervised work-

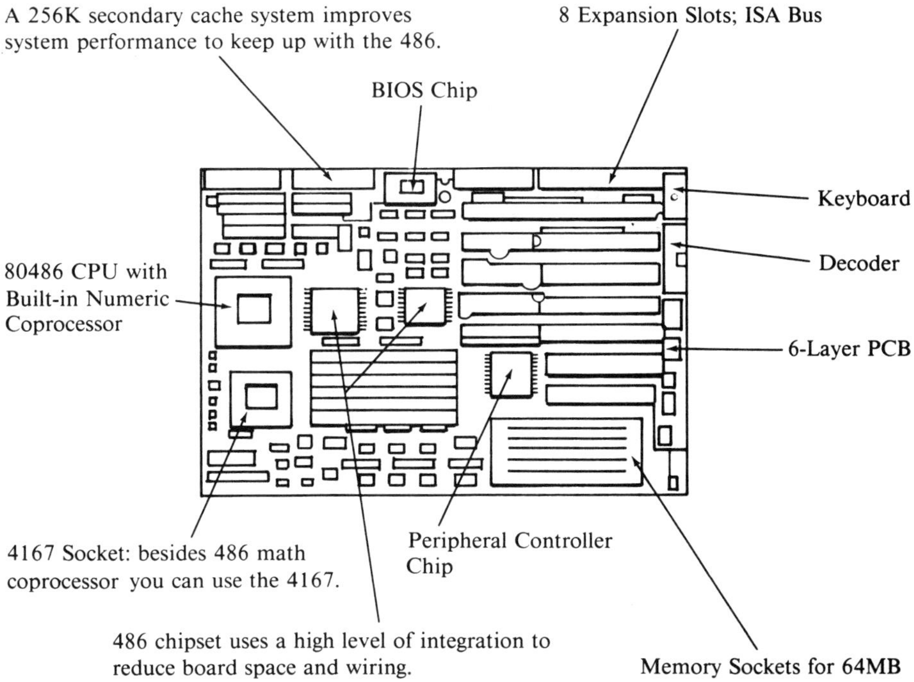

Figure 1-11 Typical 486 system board

stations by keeping the keys for each workstation. This level of security is due to the demand for added security in the PC environment to satisfy the applications in large office or corporate environments.

Summary

Features on 486 computers will continue to grow. A typical 486 desktop system is detailed in Figure 1-10, and a typical 486 system board is illustrated in Figure 1-11. These features, as well as others introduced in this chapter, are discussed in the remaining chapters.

2

UPGRADING THE SYSTEM UNIT

SHOULD I UPGRADE OR TRADE IN?

Sometimes your PC may seem like it is too slow. It could be that you have seen a 486 run, or maybe you are just impatient. You can always rationalize the need for a faster machine: You will be able to increase your productivity by reducing the time spent waiting during a data search or calculations; the quality of your output will improve because you will be free to experiment with different data output formats.

If you have an older PC, it may not be wise to upgrade. An upgrade would have to include a bigger power supply in order to overcome the original PC's weak points. However, no matter which PC you own, there are upgrade options available that let you move to a different level of performance.

Deciding whether or not to upgrade is easier than deciding *how* to upgrade.

THE UPGRADE PATH

With all the different options available today for the IBM PC family, the process of upgrading has become complicated. Some of the basic approaches to upgrading include system upgrades, memory expansion, and accelerators.

In order to give you a better idea of the options, we will review the

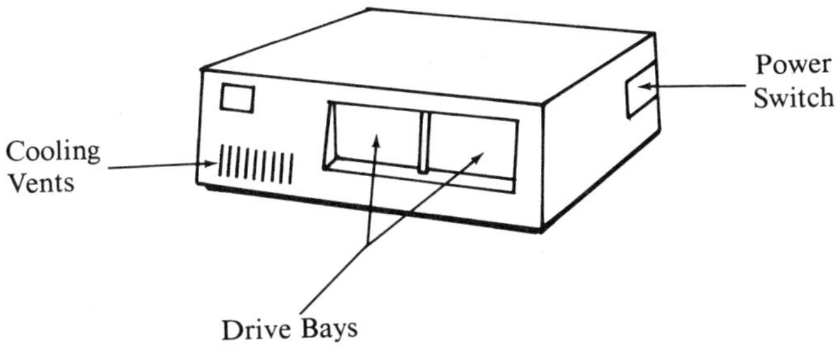

Figure 2-1 System unit or system box showing drive bays

construction and operation of the system unit and discuss the different types of upgrades available, such as accelerators for PCs, for the components of the system unit. Memory upgrades are a special form of a system upgrade and are considered in Chapter 3.

THE SYSTEM UNIT

The system unit, shown in Figure 2-1, contains the power supply, the system board, disk drives, a fan, and the system power switch. The standard desktop unit can be placed horizontally on a desk or vertically in a floor stand. The tower type of case (Fig 2-2) sits on the floor. Placing the system unit on the floor reduces the amount of desk space needed by the personal computer. For desktop units, floor stands are available to hold the unit upright and permit adequate airflow.

The design of the components of the PC's system unit make the installation of upgrade options and the removal of old components easy. The

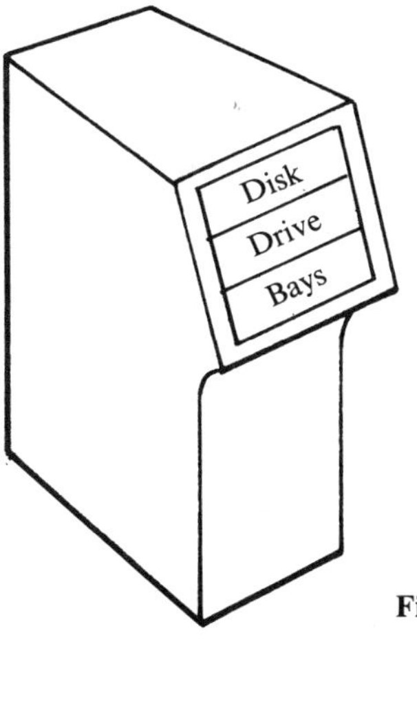

Figure 2-2 Tower type of PC case

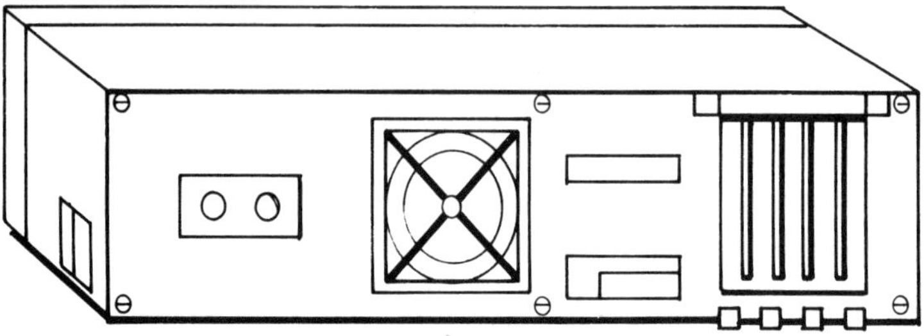

Figure 2-3 The rear of the system unit (Remove the screws or thumbscrews at the rear of the system unit in order to remove the cover. Some units also have screws on the sides.)

system unit's cover is secured by screws or thumbscrews at the rear and, on some units, on the side of the system box (Fig 2-3). You can remove the disk drives and power supply by disconnecting their cables and removing their mounting screws.

Power Supply

The power supply is a shielded cube (Fig 2-4) usually found in the right-rear section of the chassis. In 286-compatibles, it is likely to be a 190- to 200-watt power supply. The unit's power-on switch is usually part

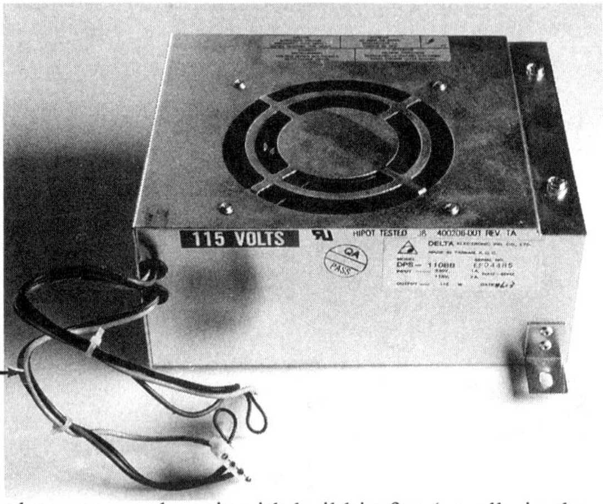

Figure 2-4 Typical power-supply unit with build-in fan (usually in the right-rear section of the system chassis)

of the power supply, as are the internal cables that connect to the drives. A switch on many units lets you select 220-volt (V) operation when you use the unit outside the United States. If you need more power cables for additional drives, you can get an inexpensive Y power cable that connects to one of the cables and splits its output in two. You should not use more than one Y cable per system since it is possible to overload the power supply.

The System Chassis

The system chassis is the metal cage inside the metal cover of the system unit. It slides out the back of this cover, as shown in Figure 2-5. The chassis has expansion connectors for mounting the drive controller, memory extension options, and other options. The connectors for the peripheral devices are at the back of the system unit, as shown in Figure 2-6. The chassis holds the system board with its electrical components and circuits. The board holds major components of the computer such as the microprocessor and related parts as well as memory chips. The power supply is usually attached to the metal cage and/or the system board. The system may also have the drive controller for controlling the reading and writing on the disk drives located on this board, or there may be separate controller boards which plug into the expansion slots.

The system chassis has connectors for mounting memory extension options and other expansion-board options. You can expand the system's memory by adding a memory extension board. The system chassis also has a ROM section, which contains diagnostic tests and a bootstrap program for power-up.

The microprocessor controls the monitor, keyboard, and printer if

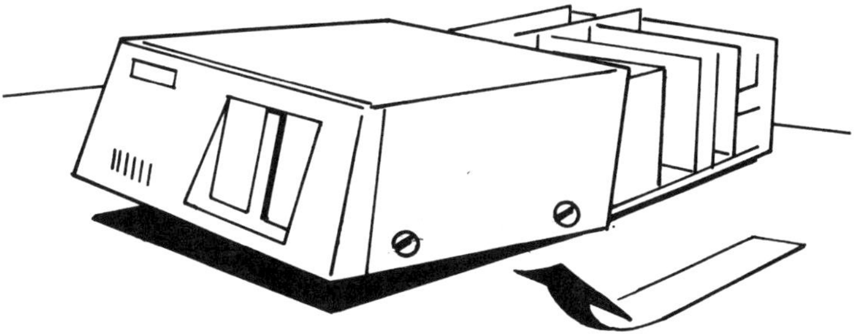

Figure 2-5 Removing the desktop unit's cover (Most desktop unit covers are removed by sliding the cover forward and then up after removing the rear screws. Some units, like the Leading Edge Computer, also have screws on the sides.)

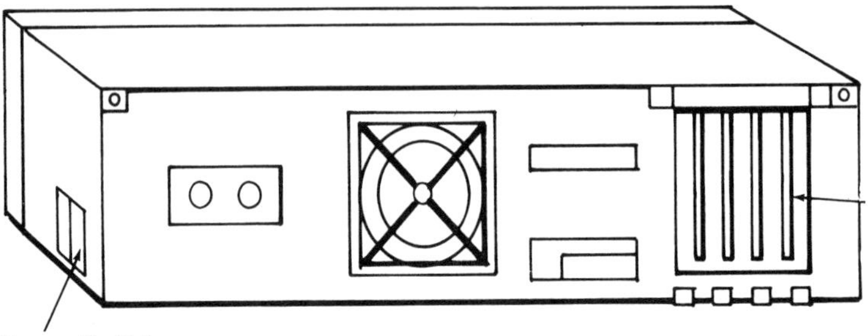

Figure 2-6 Rear of system unit, showing peripheral connector slots

connected. It also controls any additional options that may be added to the system unit.

Clocks and Crystals

The computer's clock sets the basic timing for all of the computer's operations—a faster clock speed implies a faster, more powerful computer. A crystal provides the clock timing for all of the computer functions. Computers generally run at half their crystal speed—if a 16-MHz crystal is used, the computer will run at 8 MHz. If the rest of the circuitry will run at higher speeds, you may be able to change to a faster crystal like a 24-MHz unit, which would speed the system up to 12 MHz.

A typical crystal looks like a little tin pellet with two wires (Fig 2-7). One side is often attached to the system board by an adhesive pad. To change crystals, you pull the old crystal loose from the adhesive pad and slide it off the holder. Then install the new crystal on the holder, with the printing side faceup, and stick it down on the adhesive pad.

Expansion Boards

The IBM AT and compatibles can address a maximum of 16MB of memory. You can upgrade the internal memory by adding a memory board or card. This board will occupy an expansion slot of the system unit.

You can use other expansion slots for a printer, modem, or other external device. Depending on the device, you may need a serial or parallel port, and these will also take up expansion slots.

Multifunction cards combine additional memory with serial and/or parallel ports—and offer additional features—on a single card. As with all

Figure 2-7 Clock crystal package

add-in cards, it is important that the card be designed to run on the system clock speed.

The AT system uses a 16-bit bus, but, in many units, some of the expansion slots are designed for an 8-bit card.

Expansion Slots

There is an area of the system chassis with long connecters. These connecters are designed to expand the computer bus, and they hold the additional circuit boards or cards required by the user. In most AT desktop systems, the expansion slots are in the left-rear section of the system box as shown in Figure 2-8.

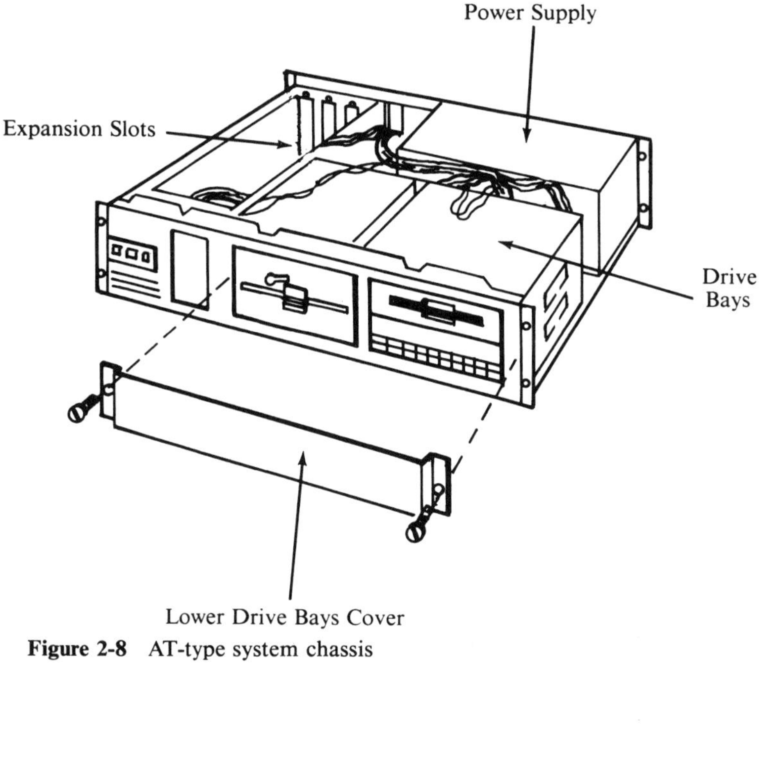

Figure 2-8 AT-type system chassis

Each connector slot provides space for either a short or long circuit board (Fig 2-9). There is a rectangular hole in the back of the chassis for each of the circuit board's output connectors. Metal plates called slot covers go over this hole when the slot is empty. The end plate of the expansion card covers the hole when the slot is occupied. The metal plate provides a continuous electrical shield for the system chassis.

When you add a card to the system, you remove the slot cover and insert the board into the data bus connector which runs along the bottom of the slot. A slot cover screw secures the end plate of the card to the back of the chassis.

Short cards (Fig 2-10) are less than half the length of standard boards. Short cards were designed for the IBM XT and compatibles, which have one or more short expansion slots behind the left-hand disk drive, where only about half the usual space is available. These short slots work in the same way as long slots, but require a card that fits physically into a small space.

Most 286 computers have no short slots, but you can still use short cards in these machines. The short cards are all 8-bit cards and must have the same criteria (speed, configurability, and physical compatibility with 16-bit slots) required to use any 8-bit card. Some, but not all, 8-bit cards will run in a 16-bit slot.

You can install an 8-bit card in a 16-bit slot if the card is physically compatible with the 16-bit connector pins. The difference lies in the bottom edge of the card next to the 8-bit connector pins. If there is a wide cutout on the card next to the 8-bit tab connector, or if the edge goes straight out from the tab, it is physically compatible. If the edge of the card dips down again next to the 8-bit tab connector, it is physically incompatible—you cannot install this card in a 16-bit slot because this part of the card will interfere with the second connector on the system board.

The end plate of the expansion card will hold cable connectors so that a monitor or a printer can be plugged into the card. The end-plate bracket also anchors the card to the system chassis and completes the metallic shield protecting the circuitry from electromagnetic interference.

Expansion Card Installation. The actual replacement of cards in expansion slots is simple. Find an empty slot, and remove the screw holding the slot cover to the back of the chassis. Slide the card into place, with its tab(s) meeting the grooves in the expansion slot. The end plate of the card should now be in the same place just occupied by the slot cover. When the tab meets the groove, press carefully on the top edge of the card. The tab will snap into place.

A primary source of "how to" information for replacing peripheral cards is the installation manual or instructions that come with the product.

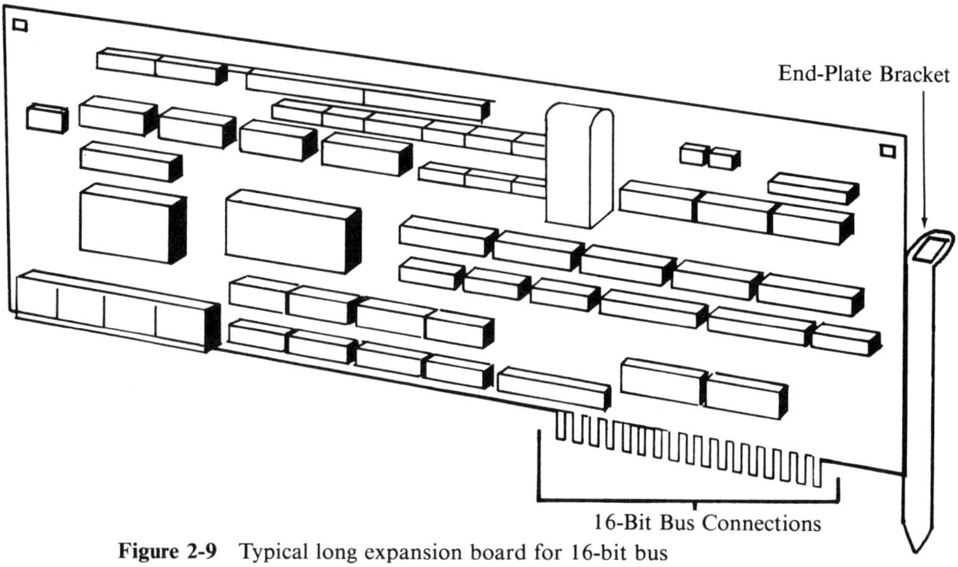

Figure 2-9 Typical long expansion board for 16-bit bus

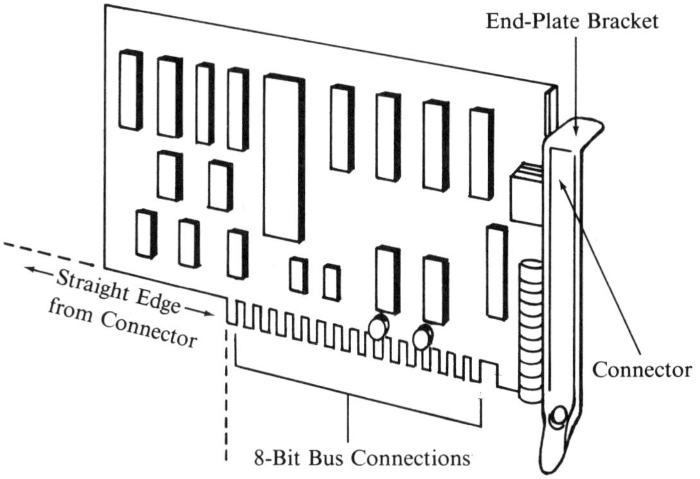

Figure 2-10 Typical short card for 8-bit bus with connector on end-plate bracket

These vary widely in their usefulness. The following general rules should apply in most installations:

1. Circuit boards are sensitive to static electricity, and one discharge can permanently damage sensitive electronic chips. You should rid your

hands of static electricity by touching the system chassis every time before touching a circuit board.

2. It is generally a good idea to install cards that attach to ribbon cables (such as drive-controller cards) to the right of cards without cables. That way the cables are not in the way of other expansion slots.
3. Tighten the holding screw of the end-plate brackets of your cards, and keep slot covers in place over every unused slot. This reduces the possibility of radio-frequency interference (RFI) entering.
4. Do not let metal parts such as screws drop into the computer. If you drop a screw on the system board, you must take the time to find it and remove it before you apply power to the computer. Otherwise, it could cause a short circuit and do serious damage.

The PC Expansion Bus

The original IBM PC uses a clock of 4.77 MHz with the Intel 8088 microprocessor. The IBM PC is a single-board computer—all of the main CPU parts are on a single printed circuit board, usually called the motherboard or system board (Fig 2-11). The microprocessor, along with supporting components, and some of the I/O circuits and memory are found on this board, along with the edge connectors used for adding expansion boards.

The expansion-board connections are essentially the same as found on the microprocessor pins. There is an 8-bit bidirectional data bus, 20 address lines, 6 interrupt lines, direct-memory-access (DMA) control lines, and several other data control and status lines.

A total of 62 pins is used in the IBM PC bus. They are split into two rows (A1–A31 and B1–B31) in the edge connectors that make up the expansion slots. The edge connectors provide the following functions: Data transfers take place on pins A2–A9; addresses use pins A12–A31.

The PC uses an Intel 8288 bus controller. The 8288 control signals are brought out to the bus, including ALE (Address Latch Enable) and AEN (Address Enable) which use pins B28 and A11. Other 8288 signals that are also on the bus include I/O Read (IOR)—pin B14; I/O Write (IOW)—pin B13; MEMory Read (MEMR)—pin B12; and MEMory Write (MENW)—pin B11.

In the original IBM PC, bus cycles take four clock cycles, or 0.84 microseconds. DMA cycles take five clock cycles, or 1.05 microseconds. An 8288 bus controller running at 4.77 MHz controls the cycles.

You can use a bus handshake line—I/O CH RDY, pin A10—to increase the current bus cycle. Strobing this line refreshes the dynamic mem-

Expansion-Board Connectors

Slots for Holding Expansion Boards

Figure 2-11 XT-type system board

ory. The refresh is handled by one channel of the system DMA controller, which uses the bus.

There are six interrupt pins: B21–B25 and B4. These are connected to an interrupt controller on the main board for interrupt servicing. There is no interrupt-acknowledge signal on the PC bus.

Three pairs of DMA handshake lines include DRQ1-3 on pins B-18, B-6, and B-16. The system uses these for DMA requests. $\overline{\text{DACK}}$1-3—pins B-15, B-17, and B-26—are the acknowledge lines. $\overline{\text{DACK}}$0—pin B-19—refreshes DRAM boards that may be plugged into the bus. T/C—pin B-27—indicates when the correct number of DMA bus cycles have occurred during a DMA transfer. OSC—pin B-30—runs a 14.31818-MHz clock; and CLK—pin B-20—is the 4.77-MHz clock for the 8088 microprocessor. RESET DRV—pin B2—is a reset signal for all cards plugged into the bus.

Power inputs for the expansion cards include: +5 volts (V)—pin B-3; −5V—pin B-5; +12V—pin B-9; and −12V—pin B-7. Three ground pins are used: B-1, B-10, and B-31.

Following its introduction, the IBM PC bus became one of the most popular microprocessor backplane buses. Hundreds of companies have designed thousands of boards to plug into the PC bus.

The AT Bus

The AT is a full 16-bit computer based on the Intel 80286 microprocessor. The 80286 uses a 16-bit data bus, and the AT expansion slots use this wider data path with more interrupt lines and more DMA signals.

Like the PC bus, the AT bus signals resemble the microprocessor signals on which the computer is based. In order to maintain compatibility with expansion boards designed for the PC, the original 62-pin connector and pin definitions remain the same. There is an added second connector with 36 pins to carry the additional signals.

The second connector is in front of the 62-pin connector. Some older boards that were originally designed for the IBM PC can physically interfere with the AT expansion connector. Since there is no standard board size or shape for the PC expansion boards, some manufacturers make use of the available space by dropping the bottom edge of the board just in front of the PC's edge connector.

Most of the signals on the AT's 62-pin connector use the same names they had on the PC's bus. However, some signals have new names, but similar functions. For example, $\overline{\text{DACK0}}$ on the PC is renamed $\overline{\text{REFRESH}}$ for the AT bus. Pin B-8 on the PC bus is not used, but on the AT bus it is 0WS (Zero Wait State) and allows an expansion board to indicate that it does not require the main board to insert wait states in the bus cycle. The $\overline{\text{MEM CS16}}$ (pin D-1) and $\overline{\text{I/O CS16}}$ (pin D-2) enable an expansion board to indicate that it can accept a 16-bit, 1-wait-state transfer. These added signals are on the 36-pin connector.

Since the introduction of the original AT, the clock speeds of 286-compatible computers have increased to over 20 MHz as Intel and other microprocessor vendors have improved their manufacturing processes.

The Institute of Electrical and Electronics Engineers (IEEE) created the P996 Bus committee to study the feasibility of standardizing the AT bus. However, before the committee could produce a standard, IBM introduced its PS/2 line of personal computers that use a completely different and incompatible bus.

The PS/2 Micro Channel Bus

In 1987, IBM introduced the PS/2 computers along with the new Micro Channel bus. IBM patented several areas of the PS/2's bus, and competitors must pay IBM for a license to use the Micro Channel. A few companies have announced that they are making computers with PS/2 busses, but many others have chosen not to market machines using this bus.

While the Micro Channel has some similarities to both the new- and the old-style PC busses, it also has its differences. The PS/2 bus supports three types of cards: 16-bit, 16-bit with a video extension, and 32-bit.

The Micro Channel contains a set of signals that allow expansion cards to become bus masters. Up to fifteen masters are allowed to share the bus with the system board.

The power and ground scheme is also different. Compared to the number of ground and power pins on the earlier PC and AT busses, there are more power pins on the PS/2 bus. The extra ground and power pins provide a low-impedance path to the computer's power supply, thereby allowing expansion cards to draw more power from the computer. The low-impedance paths also help to drain RFI from the expansion cards. This results in improved data integrity by reducing noise on the bus.

The Micro Channel bus also provides a set of pins labeled AUDIO and AUDIO GND. This allows expansion cards to make use of the PS/2's audio amplifier and speaker. These two pins allow users to inject sound signals into a mixing amplifier.

Most of the signals in the Micro Channel bus are similar to those of the PC/XT/AT busses. The data bus uses signals D0–D15 on the 16-bit Micro Channel slot and D0–D31 on the 32-channel version. A0–A23 make up the address bus for the 16-bit bus, and the 32-bit bus adds A24–A31.

The Micro Channel differs from the AT bus in that the memory and I/O read and write control lines are not used. Instead, three lines, M/—I0, —S0, and —S1 are used for reading and writing as shown in Table 2-1.

TABLE 2-1 Micro Channel Bus I/O and Memory Control

M/—I0	—S0	—S1	
0	0	1	I/O read
0	1	0	I/O write
1	0	1	memory read
1	1	0	memory write

*The (—) used as a prefix means the signal is low-true.

The MADE 24 and TR32 signals are used with the address lines. MADE 24 indicates that the address bus has a 24-bit address. TR32 (Translate 32 bits) indicates a 32-bit wide memory-data transfer.

When a bus cycle starts, the computer sends an ADL (Address Decode Latch) signal. The expansion card that recognizes the address on the bus then sends either a —CD DS 16 or —CD DS 32 bus signal to indicate the presence of a 16- or 32-bit card, and a —CD SFDBK to acknowledge the cycle. The PS/2 system board generates a —DS 16 RTN or —DS 32 RTN signal to acknowledge the width of the transfer.

Bus Setup. The Micro Channel design does not use addressing and option-configuration switches on the expansion cards. The scheme that is used is called the Programmable Option Select (POS), a technique originally developed by Computer Automation. During power-up, the PS/2 motherboard individually addresses each expansion card using a −CD SETUP line. This line is not bussed across the PS/2 backplane; each slot has its own −CD SETUP signal. When a card observes a signal on its −CD SETUP line, it provides access to I/O addresses 100–107. This allows the motherboard processor to read a 16-bit identification (ID) code from the expansion card. The processor on the motherboard matches the ID with the configuration data stored in the computer's nonvolatile memory and downloads that data into the expansion card.

Different cards from different manufacturers have unique POS ID codes. IBM issues these codes to vendors who make PS/2-compatible products.

Bus Timing. Normally, a bus transfer on the Micro Channel requires 250 ns, representing four clock cycles for a 16-MHz microprocessor. Matched memory cycles occur in three clock cycles and therefore take 187.5 ns for 16-MHz microprocessor speed. The faster processor speeds found in the newer models of the PS/2 family provide correspondingly faster bus transfer times.

Physical Specifications. The board dimensions for Micro Channel expansion cards must meet specific tolerances. This differs from the previous IBM policy used in the PC and AT busses which use larger connectors. A Micro Channel card is 11.5 inches long and 3.475 inches high, including the edge connector.

The PC and AT busses use edge connectors with fingers placed on a 0.100-inch pitch. The Micro Channel places fingers on a 0.050-inch pitch—a more precise fit is needed to prevent shorted fingers. There are plastic positioning keys on each side of the printed circuit board that mate with notches in the expansion-card edge connectors.

A full-size Micro Channel expansion card is about 40% smaller than a full-size AT card. The reduced card size forces the use of denser ICs and surface-mounted components, which require less room on a printed circuit board than other IC packages. Thus, the cost of PS/2 expansion boards can be higher than that for AT boards.

SYSTEM UPGRADES

A system upgrade gives a PC new capabilities. The upgrade may be a new drive, a port, color support, power supply, or a memory board. Depending on the features offered, system upgrades can range widely in cost and complexity. The most important thing to do before buying a system upgrade is to make sure that your PC can support the features the upgrade offers.

A memory upgrade is a good way to enhance performance, especially if you are getting messages saying OUT OF MEMORY. The upgrade options available depend on the PC you own. The upgrade you buy now will also affect your upgrade options in the future.

Accelerator Boards

For improved productivity with a faster computer, consider upgrading with an accelerator board. Basically, this type of board boosts performance by replacing the processor already installed in the PC with a faster one. If you own an older PC such as an XT, you might consider selling it and purchasing either a new or used faster PC.

Math Coprocessors (MCPs). Accelerators vary in their performance for math calculations. The PC's processor is not efficient with floating-point calculations (calculations involving decimal points), which are often used in CAD and spreadsheet applications. Most accelerators let you add a math coprocessor or floating-point unit (FPU), and you should use this option if you perform tasks with floating-point calculations. Generally, the clock speed of the FPU should match the clock speed of the microprocessor. For example, if you add a 20-MHz 386 accelerator, you should also use a 20-MHz 387.

A math coprocessor is an inexpensive way to speed up operations when you are using complex spreadsheets or graphics. A PC will perform most calculations faster if you install an FPU, which is optimized for handling floating-point calculations. These specialized chips take over the math that slows down any CPU, with the exception of the 80486 which has its own math coprocessor. For the 486 SX, there is also a special math coprocessor that is the 16-bit version of this chip. Table 2-2 shows the available Intel math coprocessors.

When you are running spreadsheet, database, engineering, scientific, and graphics packages, the math coprocessor off-loads complex math functions from your computer's main processor and, in one instruction, handles what the standard processor would have required many steps to do. Depending on your application, your software can run up to five times faster. Programs like Lotus 1-2-3, Microsoft Excel, Borland's Quattro Pro and Paradox, Ashton-Tate's dBASE IV, Lotus Freelance Plus, and Generic CADD run faster and without a compatibility problem. Nor do you have to worry about hardware incompatibilities since virtually every IBM-compatible PC contains a socket (Fig 2-12) specifically for an Intel math coprocessor, so you can upgrade your computer's performance for just a fraction of the cost of a new system. The Intel 387 DX-33 math coprocessor works in 16-, 20-, 25-, and 33-MHz DX systems. There is also a 387 SX-20 coprocessor for 20-MHz SX systems and a 387 SX-16 coprocessor for 16-MHz SX systems.

TABLE 2-2 Intel Math Coprocessors

Model Number	Application
8087	IBM-compatible PCs with an 8088 or 8086 running at 5-MHz or less, including the IBM PC, XT, and Compaq Portable Plus
8087-2	IBM-compatible PCs with an 8088 or 8086 running at 8-MHz or less, including the IBM PS/2 Model 30 and Compaq Deskpro
8087-1	Any 8088- or 8086-based computers or accelerator boards running at 10-MHz or less
80287	Compaq 286 systems (8 MHz), IBM XT 286, IBM AT, and compatibles or accelerator boards requiring a 6-MHz 80287
80287-8	Compaq 286 systems (12 MHz), Compaq Portable III, Tandy 4000, and other 80286-based systems or accelerator boards requiring an 8-MHz 80287
80287-10	IBM PS/2 Models 50 and 60, WYSEpc 286, and other 80286-based systems or accelerator boards requiring a 10-MHz 80287
80C287A	Compaq SLT/28, Toshiba 1600, Zenith Supersport/286 laptop, Compaq 286e, and other 80286 computers that use the 80C287A CMOS* processor
387SX	386SX-based systems, including the Compaq 386s and the IBM PS/2 Model 55SX
387 SX-20	20-MHz 386 SX-based systems
387 DX-16	386 DX-based and Intel Inboard 386-line systems or accelerator boards running at 16 MHz including Compaq Deskpro 386, and IBM PS/2 Models 70 and 80
387 DX-20	386 DX-based systems running at 20 MHz including 20-MHz IBM PS/2 Models 70 and 80 and Compaq Deskpro 386/20e
387 DX-25	386 DX-based systems running at 25 MHz, including 25-MHz IBM PS/2 Model 70 and Compaq Deskpro 386/25
387 DX-33	386 DX-based systems running at 33 MHz including the Zenith Z-386/33 and Compaq Deskpro 386/33

*Complementary metal oxide semiconductor.

Coprocessor
Socket

Figure 2-12 Coprocessor socket on AT-compatible system board

For additional 486 number-crunching capabilities, such as that needed in some financial-modeling applications and engineering, there is the Intel 487 SX math coprocessor. It adds over seventy operations to the 486 SX CPU instruction set. This product is designed for the performance-upgrade socket of Intel 486 SX microprocessor-based systems. It extends the instruction set to include trigonometric, logarithmic, exponential, and arithmetic instructions for all data types. The 487 SX MCP can provide up to 70% higher performance than a 33-MHz Intel 387 DX math coprocessor.

Installing the Accelerator. Some accelerators may be difficult to install because of the tight fit inside the case. You must have a slot that is designed for add-in products. Some of the earlier accelerators attach with clip-on connectors that can cause reliability problems.

The interior of most PCs is easily accessible, but you have to be careful not to damage other components. To install many accelerators you remove the existing processor chips. Intel provides a special tool (a chip puller) to make this job easier. In general, the accelerators from most vendors include clear instructions and are relatively easy to install. Exercise care when inserting a new adapter board into the sockets that once contained the original processor; otherwise, you may damage the new processor's pins, and the accelerator will be useless.

Some PC models present problems that prevent using accelerators in them. Processors that have been soldered in are difficult to remove. The processors in the majority of PCs are not soldered in.

Accelerators can also have compatibility problems. Most vendors have solved previous problems with timing-dependent operations. In the event that a problem appears, most units let you turn the accelerator features on and off to circumvent most potential difficulties. Be sure that the accelerator you purchase works with the monitor you have—some combinations are incompatible.

Processor Power

When an accelerator is present to do much of the overhead other than disk access, processor-intensive operations—such as redrawing a graphics file, grouping objects in a graphics file, performing a find and replace, and sorting databases—will improve.

However, raw computing power depends on the type and speed of the processor. The PC and XT use the comparatively slow 8088 processor, so you can improve the performance of these machines—often dramatically—by adding an accelerator with a faster 80286 processor. Similarly, you can noticeably improve the 80286-based AT speed by adding a 80386.

As we have shown previously, math-intensive tasks, such as recalculating a spreadsheet and running a calculation in several places, can improve with the use of a math coprocessor or FPU on the accelerator.

Processors and Speed. An accelerator containing the same processor as the 386SX-20 may not make an AT's overall performance equal to that of the 386SX. For overall performance, the AT must have a balanced hardware design. The amount of memory, the speed of the hard drive, and the bus configuration all play important roles in system performance. (Also, the system may use a comparatively slow SCSI port. Reading data from and writing data to a hard drive remains relatively slow on this unit.)

For example, a 40-MHz system can require four wait states to work with 80-ns RAM. This is because the processor is faster than the RAM and must wait for the RAM. There is a performance degradation in products that compensate for slower-speed RAM by adding wait states. For instance, a 25-MHz version may require 70-ns RAM to run at one wait state, but one with 80-ns RAM may require two wait states to synchronize the processor with memory. This means that a board with 70-ns RAM can be faster than the same board equipped with 80-ns RAM if it has less wait states.

Intel Enhancement Boards. The Intel Inboard 386/PC is a 386-based performance-enhancement board for IBM PC, XT, and XT-compatibles with 8088 CPUs. It provides performance that is up to ten times faster with 1MB of fast, 32-bit memory that replaces the existing memory in the computer and is expandable to 5MB total memory with a piggyback option. The Inboard 386/PC supports an optional Intel 387 DX-16 math coprocessor. There is also a special Windows/386 for the Inboard 386/PC board.

The Inboard 386 is a 386-based performance-enhancement board for IBM PC AT computers and AT-compatibles. It allows performance that is two to three times faster and provides conventional, expanded (EMS 4.0), and extended memory. The Inboard 386 is expandable to 1MB on the board with 256K chips and to 3MB total memory with a piggyback option. The board supports an optional Intel 387 DX-16 math coprocessor and requires a special installation kit, which you use to connect the Inboard 386 to an IBM AT or to 3270 AT computers. The AT kit includes cables, software, chip pullers, crystal, jumper, storage containers for 80286 and 80287, and a plug for the empty 80287 socket.

Another kit is available to connect the Inboard 386 to Compaq Deskpro 286 (8 MHz), Tandy 3000, and other compatibles with a removable 80286. The kit includes cables, software, chip pullers, socket covers, storage containers for 80286 and 80287, and a plug for the empty 80287 socket.

PS/2 Accelerators. For more power and improved performance, you can upgrade your 286 PC to a faster, more powerful 386SX. The Intel SnapIn 386 module for PS/2 models offers a 200% boost in power. For less cost than a new machine, it opens up a range of 386 software that you could not run before, such as Windows 3.0 in 386-enhanced mode.

Installation is easy—you take out the existing 286 microprocessor and replace it with the SnapIn 386 module. Then you run the software included with the module to configure your system. The Intel SnapIn 386 is available for PS/2 Models 50, 60, and compatibles.

SX/Now

This is a processor upgrade that can bring 386SX power and performance to your 286-based system. For OS/2 and most contemporary software, including Windows, you need 386SX processing power. With SX/Now, you can replace the processor on your 286-based computer instead of replacing the entire system—you just remove the 286 processor and replace it with the SX/Now module. By combining a 20-MHz 386SX processor with 16K of cache memory and an on-board clock, you can increase system performance by over 250 percent without taking up an expansion slot. You may need expansion slots for other functions such as modems, communications, and tape-backup cards. The SX/Now module replaces the 286 processor by plugging directly into the processor socket on the system board. A cache improves your operating system's performance, whether you are using DOS or OS/2. You can also add a 387SX math coprocessor for math-intensive applications.

The SX/Now module is available for the following upgrades:

1. 20-MHz 386SX upgrade for IBM PS/2 Models 50, 60.
2. 20-MHz 386SX upgrade for IBM PS/2 Model 50Z.
3. 20-MHz 386SX upgrade for IBM PS/2 Model 30/286.

Memory Caches

Upgrading a PC with a faster processor will not address the whole speed problem, however. That is because the PC still needs to transfer data from the main memory on the main board to the processor over a data path or bus. With a faster processor, the bus becomes a bottleneck in attaining more speed. One solution to this problem is to add a small amount of 20-ns static RAM (SCRAM) to the accelerator. This SCRAM acts as a cache between the accelerator and the main system memory. SCRAM stores data from the main system memory, where the processor can use it with only a small delay.

Another solution is to place RAM directly on the accelerator board so that data transfers directly between the processor and the memory, bypassing the data bus completely.

You need to match the faster processor with faster memory. For instance, 150-ns RAM is adequate for the 8-MHz 80286 processor installed in AT machines. If you upgrade one of these ATs with an accelerator that uses a 16-MHz or faster processor, however, the 150-ns RAM becomes inadequate. You need at least 120-ns RAM with a 16-MHz processor. Accelerators that add a 33-MHz 80386 or faster processor without using cache may require high-speed 50-ns RAM. These faster chips are more expensive. You may be able to delay the processor so that slower memory can synchronize with it, causing a wait state. The number of wait states an accelerator has varies depending on how much time is required to synchronize the processor with the RAM.

UPGRADING DECISIONS

Often, the decision of whether to buy a new system or upgrade an existing one is not easy, and a bad purchase can be expensive. Here are a few common problems and some suggestions of how to solve them. These examples may not address your exact system configuration or computing needs, but they should give you a good idea of the available options. Later, we will consider these add-on products in more detail.

Slow CPU

Suppose you are using a 12-MHz or slower CPU with large, demanding applications, such as relational database managers, spreadsheets, or Windows applications. You may have already added more RAM and have enough hard disk storage to handle the increasing databases, spreadsheets, and graphics files. As your files have grown, you may have noticed that your system's performance seems slower.

Upgrade Options. To correct slow performance, you can:

1. Add a math coprocessor. This will upgrade an older computer like a 10- or 12-MHz AT to more power for number-crunching operations and improve performance in large spreadsheets. Your motherboard has a socket for this purpose. An Intel 12-MHz 80287 should cost a few hundred dollars.
2. Add a high-speed processor card, such as Intel's Inboard 386 for 8088-based machines or Microway's Fastcache SX for 286-based systems. You can also combine this with additional memory, such as the Intel Above Board with 2MB of RAM. The total cost should be about a thousand dollars, and you may have added a few more years to the useful life of your computer.
3. Replace the motherboard with a 33-MHz 80386 version that includes a 64K memory cache and sockets for additional RAM. This costs about a thousand dollars, plus the cost of the additional RAM.
4. Buy a new computer system. An equivalent 386/33 system will cost two to three times the cost of a motherboard replacement. The systems should be roughly equivalent, depending on the drives of your existing system. A 25-MHz system will cost a little less. This option may be a better choice for those who do not like to work with hardware and who want a full factory warranty on the system.

Memory Inadequate for Graphic Applications

Suppose you want to produce professional-looking newsletters or catalogs with a desktop-publishing program, such as Aldus' PageMaker or Ventura Publisher. These programs require at least 640K of RAM and high-resolution graphics.

Upgrade Options. You can:

1. Upgrade your computer using items 2 or 3 above, and add a graphics card and monitor, which should cost several hundred dollars for gray scale or double this for color.
2. Buy a new computer system.

Power Supply Inadequate for Upgrade's Needs

The power supply inside the system unit provides power for the system board, adapters, floppy drive(s), hard drive(s), monitor, and keyboard. The power supply is designed to operate the maximum number of drives that can be added inside the system unit. IBM AT-compatible computers have a total output of 175–200 watts. Earlier PCs have much smaller power supplies, and you will often need a power-supply upgrade to support additional drives and memory. Since the original IBM PC was not designed for operating any hard drives, adding a hard drive requires upgrading at least to an XT power supply.

The AT-type power supply is typically rated at 100/130 volts, alternating current (VAC), 5.0 amps (A), or 220/260VAC, 2.5A. The power supply provides +5, −5, +12, and −12 volts, direct current (VDC). Table 2-3 shows typical load current and regulation tolerance for a 200-watt supply.

TABLE 2-3 Typical AT Power-Supply Output Characteristics

Output	Load	Tolerance	Ripple
+5VDC	20.0A	±2%	50MV*
+12VDC	7.3A	±5%	100MV
−5VDC	0.3A	±10%	100MV
−12VDC	0.3A	±10%	100MV

*Millivolts.

Figure 2-13 Power-supply components

If any output becomes overloaded, the power supply will switch off within about 20 ms. This will normally prevent an overcurrent condition from damaging the power supply.

Power Supply Upgrades. The power supply is a switching oscillator type with the functional components shown in Figure 2-13.

It is simple and usually economical to replace the power supply—you can purchase one from most computer-supply outlets for less than $100. Just make sure that the replacement has the proper wattage for expansion of your system.

3

MEMORY UPGRADES

INTRODUCTION—BASIC CONCEPTS

A memory upgrade is one of the most common upgrades you can do. There are two basic types of internal memory: read-only memory and random-access memory. ROM and RAM components provide the basic electronic memory for the unit. ROM and RAM are both fabricated on computer chips, and both are measured in terms of kilobytes or megabytes.

A ROM chip is a read-only device—you can read its contents but not change them. The information is permanently burned into the chip during manufacturing or at some later time using special equipment. The ROM chips hold fixed instructions that are not expected to change. These instructions allow the PC to boot following the application of power. These chips hold other instructions or information relating to the specific hardware or configuration parameters for that machine.

A RAM chip is reusable since it provides the temporary storage that the computer needs to process program instructions and data. The RAM chips hold data and instructions only when the power is on. When you turn the power off, the RAM chips lose their contents.

A RAM-disk utility has been included in DOS versions since 3.1. It allows you to create a RAM disk in your PC's memory. The RAM disk acts like another hard or floppy disk attached to the system, but, since electronic memory is used with no disk mechanically attached, the access time is much faster.

KNOW YOUR SYSTEM UNIT

The system unit contains the main printed circuit board—the system board or motherboard—along with the power supply and the disk drives. The system board contains RAM, support chips to produce the clocking signals, a set of chips for the ROM programs, and I/O chips to connect the computer to the peripherals. The original IBM PC (5150) system board contains about 100 chips as well as the connectors for the expansion boards. Each short connector or slot will accept 62 connection pins.

The connector slots are wired in parallel so they will form the output bus for the 62-pin expansion boards that plug into the connectors. The layout for the IBM 5150 system board is shown in Figure 3-1.

The internal program selects the correct expansion board, or card even though they are all wired in parallel. These cards add the peripherals to the computer. For example, the drive-controller card connects the disk drives to the system board. You need a video adapter and a printer card to connect the monitor and printer to the system board.

Other cards are available for the expansion of the computer. You could add a modem along with additional disk drives, additional memory, printers, and other peripherals.

STATIC AND DYNAMIC RAM

Dynamic RAM or DRAM, takes up less circuit-board area, uses less power, and costs less than static RAM. It is used whenever there is a need for RAM of about 4K or more. Static RAMs use binary switching—flip-flop circuits that can hold a high or low voltage level (1 or 0 bit) as long as power is applied to the chip. Dynamic RAMs use the capacitance on the gates of field-effect transistors (FET) to hold the high or low voltage levels. These are held as a charge or a noncharge in the capacitance between the FET gates and ground.

Once a logic state is established in a static RAM, it stays the same as long as the device is powered. In a dynamic RAM, however, the charge on the capacitors will leak off in a short time unless the levels are recharged. Every few milliseconds, refresh circuits recharge, or "refresh" the capacitors to keep up the proper bit levels. Refreshing usually starts at the bottom row of memory and continues to the top row.

RAM CHIPS

The early PCs use the 16K-bit 4116 RAM chip. The actual memory array used for storage has 128 rows and 128 columns (Fig 3-2). The 16 address bits are used in the following manner:

Signal/Voltage Source	Signal Designations	Pin	Pin	Signal Designations	Signal/Voltage Source
	Undefined	36	18	(+) 5 Volts	Printer
—	Undefined	35	17	Chassis Ground	Common
—	Undefined	34	16	Logic Ground	Common
—	Undefined	33	15	Oscillator Transmit	Printer
Printer	Fault (Active Low)	32	14	Supply Ground	Common
Computer	Input Prime (Active Low)	31	13	Select (Active High)	Printer
Common	Input Prime —RETURN	30	12	Paper End (Active High)	Printer
Common	Busy—RETURN	29	11	Busy (Active HIGH)	Printer
Common	Acknowledge —RETURN	28	10	Acknowledge (Active Low)	Printer
Common	Data Bit 8— RETURN	27	9	Data Bit 8 (MSB)	Computer
Common	Data Bit 7—	26	8	Data Bit 7	Computer
Common	Data Bit 6— RETURN	25	7	Data Bit 6	Computer
Common	Data Bit 5— RETURN	24	6	Data Bit 5	Computer
Common	Data Bit 4— RETURN	23	5	Data Bit 4	Computer
Common	Data Bit 3— RETURN	22	4	Data Bit 3	Computer
Common	Data Bit 2— RETURN	21	3	Data Bit 2	Computer
Common	Data Bit 1— RETURN	20	2	Data Bit 1 (LSB)	Computer
Common	Data Strobe— RETURN	19	1	Data Strobe— (Active Low)	Computer

Figure 3-1 IBM PC 5150 system-board layout

- The system uses two highest bits for chip selection.
- The next seven most significant bits address the 128 rows.
- The seven least significant bits address the 128 columns.

The system addresses each bit cell by first addressing a row and then addressing a column.

The 4116 chip connects in parallel groups of eight (Fig 3-3). By wiring the chips in parallel, each byte of 8 bits spreads over the 8 chips, with 1 bit in a corresponding location in all 8 chips. The group of 8 chips provides a total of 16,384 total bytes, or 16K bytes. The 8 chips are usually numbered 0–7.

The top view of the 4116 chip is shown in Figure 3-4. This chip uses both transistor-transistor-logic (TTL) circuits and metal-oxide-semiconductor (MOS) circuits. The system uses the TTL circuits for I/O functions, and the MOS circuits make up the memory array used to store the logic states.

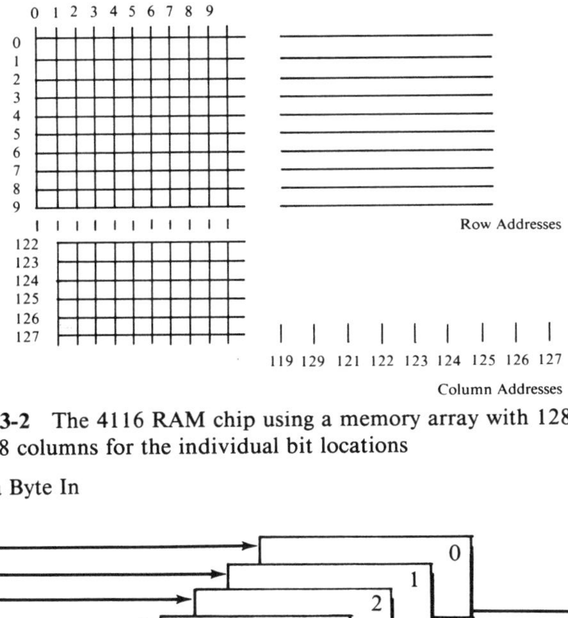

Figure 3-2 The 4116 RAM chip using a memory array with 128 rows and 128 columns for the individual bit locations

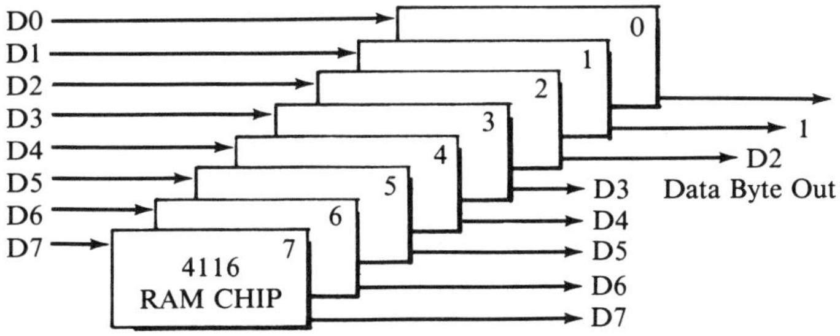

Figure 3-3 Eight chips connected to make up a byte

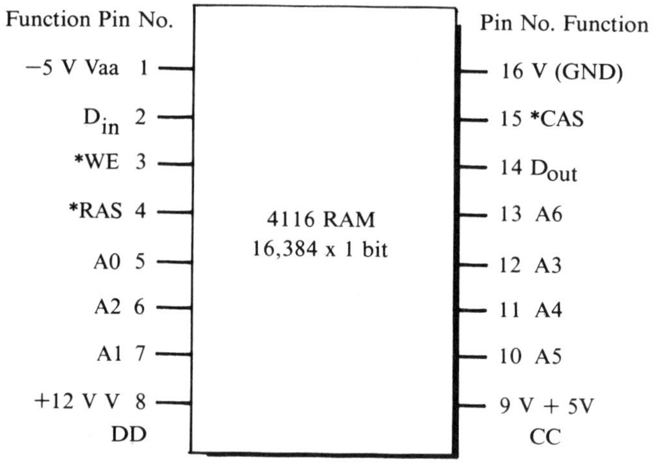

Figure 3-4 A 4116 RAM chip with 16,384 individual bits, using a 16-pin dual inline package (DIP)

There are 7 address lines (A6–A0) (Fig 3-5, 3-6). These lines connect in parallel with all of the address lines for the rest of the chips in the 16K-array.

You need a total of 14 address bits to address the memory matrix—7 bits for the 128 rows and 7 bits for the 128 columns—so the system uses a multiplexing technique. This splits the use of the available address lines, so that you can address a total of 14 bits. The multiplexing technique uses two signals: the row address strobe and the column address strobe.

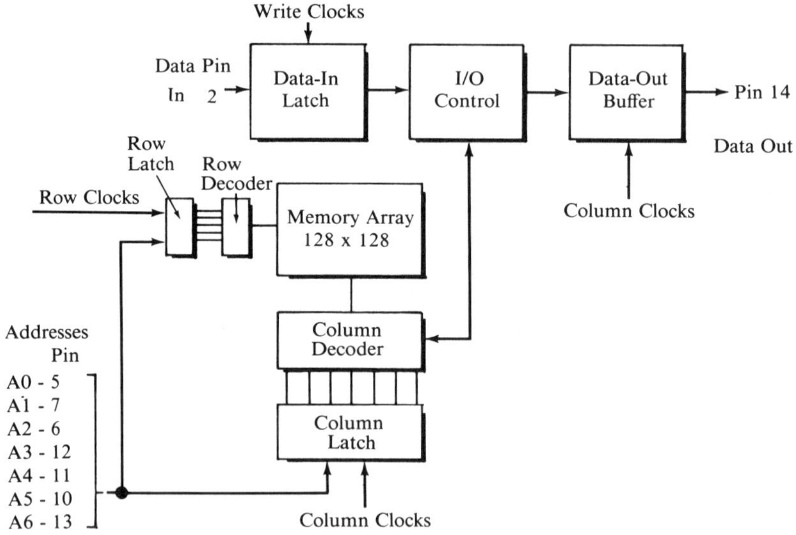

Figure 3-5 Block diagram of 4116 RAM chip

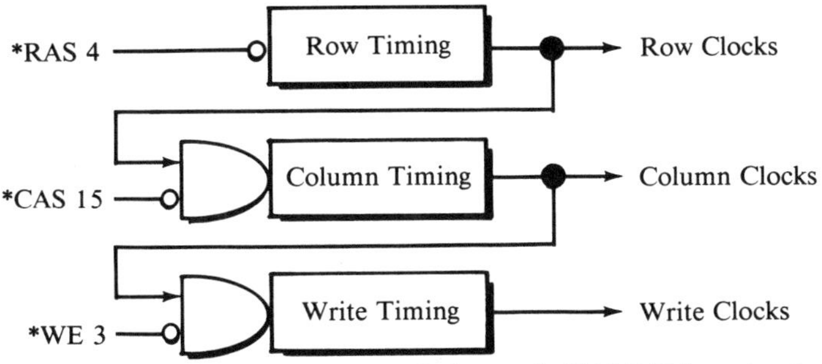

Figure 3-6 The timing signals (Applied to each 4116 RAM at pins 4, 15, and 3. These are gated logically as shown to produce the different clock signals.)

Special multiplex chips receive the 14 address bits and separate them into two sets of bits (Fig 3-7). Then they send the two sets alternately to the array. Multiplexing saves 7 pins on the chip. There are only 2 data pins—Data In and Data Out.

RAM Chip Upgrades

You can upgrade the 16K 4116 RAM chip with other denser chips. One of these is the 64K 4164 which uses the same 16-pin package as the 4116 (Fig 3-8). The 4164 chip uses a 256 x 256 bit cell matrix (Fig 3-9) and has only 2 power pins instead of the 4 power inputs used in the 4116. This frees up an additional address pin for the 64K bits.

The 41256 chip, also shown in Figure 3-8, has 262,144 bit cells. This chip gives you a density increase of four by doubling the numbers of rows and columns with a matrix of 512 rows and 512 columns.

The 41256 is similar to the 4164 and the 4116 in the way it operates.

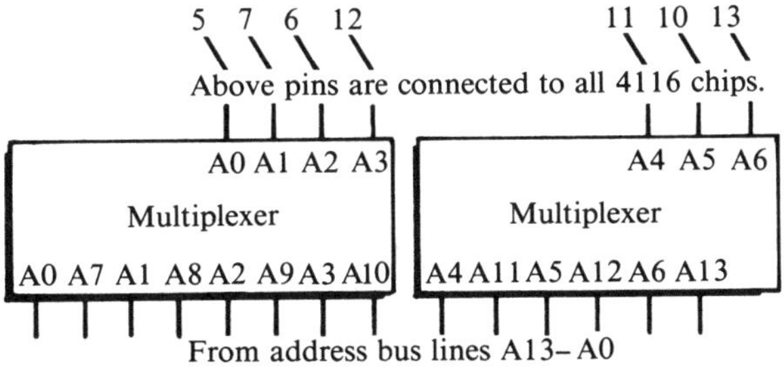

Figure 3-7 The multiplexer chips receive 14 bits from the address bus (During the 4116 *RAS time, they send 7 bits [A6–A0] to the 4116s. During the 4116 *CAS time, they send the other 7 bits [A13–A7] to the RAM chips.)

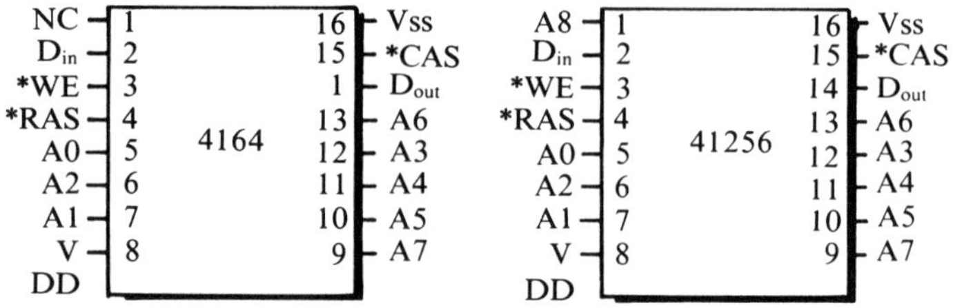

Figure 3-8 4164 and 41256 RAM chip pins (The only difference between these is the extra address bit on the 41256 [A8].)

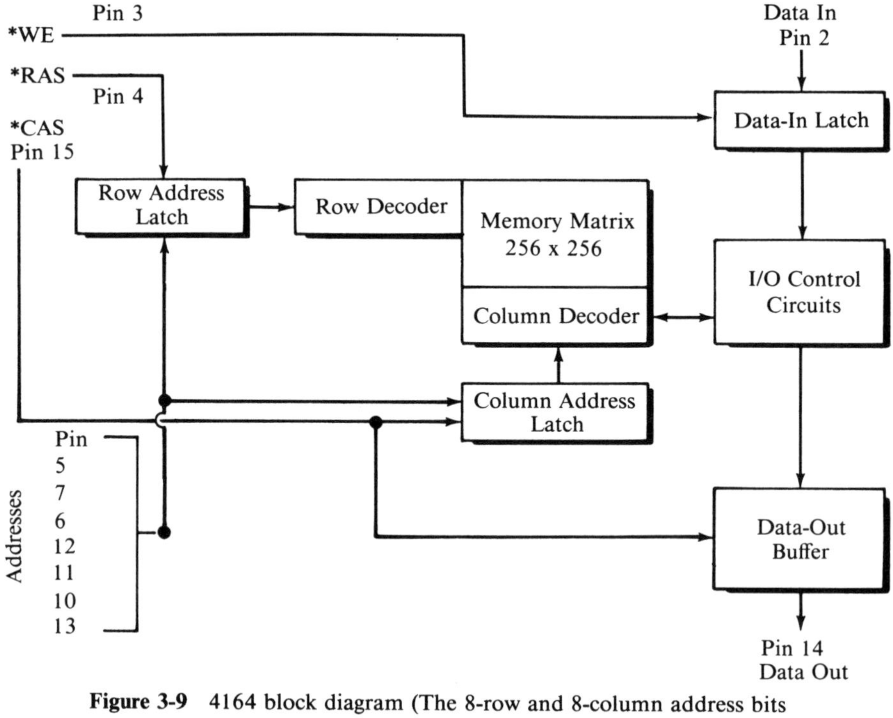

Figure 3-9 4164 block diagram (The 8-row and 8-column address bits take turns entering through the 8 address pins. *RAS switches the row address into its latch, and *CAS switches the column address into its latch.)

The major difference is the number of address lines. The 4116 uses 7 data inputs to provide 14 multiplexed address bits—7 at a time. The 4164 uses 8 data inputs to provide 16 multiplexed address bits—8 at a time. The 41256 needs 9 data lines to input 18 multiplexed address bits—9 at a time. These three RAMs all use the same package, but the 1MB RAMs use a different package.

1M Bit RAMs. The one megabit RAM has a bit cell matrix of 1024 x 1024 (Table 3-1). A group of eight can provide a million bytes of dynamic memory. In order to address this much memory, you need 20 address bits. The 1MB chips use 10 data input pins for multiplexing the 20 address bits.

TABLE 3-1 Memory Chips

Chip Number	4116	4164	41256	411024
Total bits	16K	64K	256K	1024K
Bit array	128 x 128	256 x 256	512 x 512	1024 x 1024

One type of package is a 26-pin surface mount device (SMD) where 3 pins on each side of the pin arrangement are removed in the center. This provides space for additional components or circuit paths.

In the larger chips, the bit matrixes divide into several sections (Fig 3-10). The sense amplifiers aid in the refreshing operation which must be performed every few milliseconds.

HANDLING MEMORY CHIPS

Memory chips should always be handled carefully. They use very small MOS circuits for the memory cells, and these are sensitive to static electricity. Static charges can damage these chips and destroy the small circuits paths found inside them. You can use a wrist strap connected to ground and other precautions to avoid damage due to static electricity.

Parity Checking

Eight chips usually connect in parallel to provide a byte, but sometimes a ninth chip is used as a controller of the set or as a parity checking bit. Parity checking involves counting the bit states and determining if the total is odd or even. You then compare this total with a previously stored total to determine if a bit was lost during an operation.

MEMORY PROBLEMS

If RAM or ROM fails to function, there is usually a short or open somewhere in one of the internal circuits. This causes a problem in storing data when a program is running. In some cases, a short might produce some smoke from the chip when it occurs, and the chip package may become charred and visually damaged. Most of the time, however, the bad chip looks the same as the other chips.

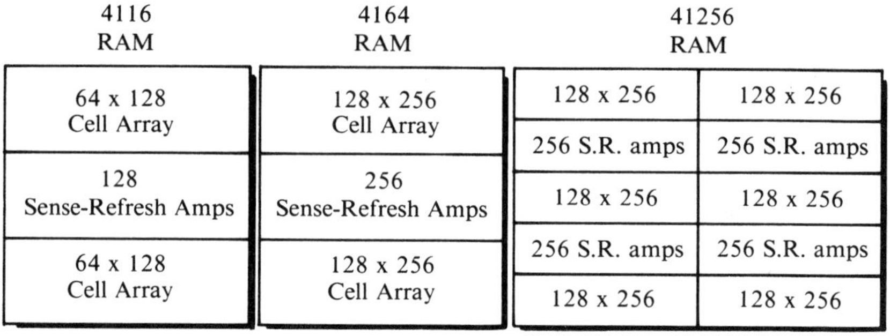

Figure 3-10 The 41256 chip (The cell arrays in the DRAM chips use amplifiers for memory-cell refreshing. The 41256 is actually like four 4164 chips.)

Usually only one chip at a time is defective, although multiple chip failures can happen if there is a chain reaction from, for example, a power-supply problem. In this case, you need to correct the power supply before you replace the memory chips.

A defective memory chip will usually cause a problem in running part of a program. A shorted cell location could cause faulty data or addressing to occur. The results could be minor, like a slight error in calculations, or the program may not run at all.

RAM LIMITS

The 8088 and 8086 microprocessor chips can only recognize addresses up to 1MB of memory. Of this 1MB, the older DOS versions can access addresses from 0K to 640K for RAM. This 640K of RAM is the conventional or working memory. The area above 640K is used for system functions such as video and ROM instructions. The 1MB limit has its roots in the older PC and XT computers that used the 8088 microprocessor chip capable of accessing only 1MB of addresses.

The AT used the 80286 microprocessor chip, which can access 16MB of memory (actually 16,777,216 storage addresses). The PCs that use 386s can access 4GB, or more than 4 billion addresses. None of this extra storage space exists for the older DOS versions.

Although an AT system can access 16MB, it may contain only 1MB of RAM. Even this is more memory than your DOS may be able to access. The DOS may only be able to access 1MB, and, out of that 1MB, it will use only 640K of RAM to run a program. There are two types of memory that you can add to upgrade these systems. They are expanded memory and extended memory. Both of these use RAM beyond the 640K limit.

EXPANDED AND EXTENDED MEMORY

Add-on Memory

Expanded memory is a type of add-on memory that has no corresponding physical memory addresses. Expanded memory was originally developed to get around the physical memory constraints of the XT. On an XT there are no addresses above 1MB. Lotus, Intel, and Microsoft developed a standard for an add-in memory board called the Expanded Memory Specification (EMS) board.

Extended memory is a type of add-on memory that is standard in many 286 and 386 computers and is linear with its addresses starting at the 1MB limit.

Figure 3-11 shows an XT-compatible system board with the RAM chips arranged in four rows. These rows make up the logical banks. The first row may be designated as bank 0 while the next rows are designated as banks 1–3. A bank must be either completely full or completely empty—you can never have one row or part of a row empty.

Most XTs and ATs can use 64K or 256K RAM chips. You should always use chips with a speed of 150 ns or faster for the AT. A dip switch on the system board often selects the RAM chip configuration.

Table 3-2 shows some typical configurations of the system-board RAM for an XT and demonstrates how the type of chips used in the two banks affect the total memory. In this case, there are 9 chips total per bank. You will need 9 chips if you are upgrading one bank, or 27 chips if you are pulling out the existing 64K chips and populating the board entirely with 256K chips. Bank 3 is left blank.

TABLE 3-2 Typical XT Memory Bank Arrangement

SWITCHES 1	SWITCHES 2	BANK 0	BANK 1	BANK 2	BANK 3	TOTAL
ON	ON	4164	4164	4164	4164	256K
ON	OFF	41256	4164	4164	4164	440K
OFF	ON	41256	41256	4164	4164	640K
OFF	OFF	41256	41256	41256	—	640K

Each chip has a pin 1, which is marked with a notch or a dot. Under each empty chip socket, there is usually an outline of the chip in its proper orientation. Pin 1 is usually toward the front of the chassis. You need to install each chip in the correct orientation, with all the pins completely pressed down in the socket. It is easy to bend the pins that fit into the

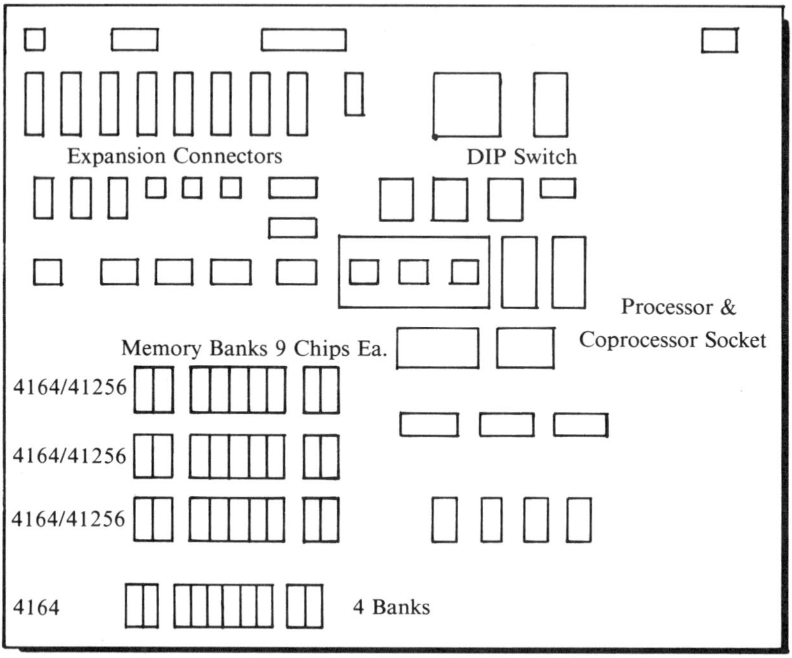

Figure 3-11 XT system board showing location of memory banks

socket out of shape. Since it does not take a great deal of force to install the chips, if you have to exert much force, you are probably bending a pin. If you make an error and need to remove a chip from a socket, insert the tip of a small flat-blade screwdriver under one end of the chip and twist or pry up gently. As the pin begins to loosen, move the screwdriver to the other end and loosen in the same way. Work gently back and forth until the chip is freed; then straighten the bent pin with pliers and start over.

Memory Management

Hardware such as expanded memory boards (Fig 3-12) adds memory to the system. Memory-management software does not add any chips, but it upgrades the system by making more efficient use of the existing RAM. Since DOS was developed for the 8088 and 8086 microprocessors, which cannot work directly with anything over 1MB of RAM, 384K of this is set aside for system use, leaving only 640K for programs.

Both expanded and extended memory are available for upgrading for programs that need more than 640K. Expanded memory is RAM on an expansion board and is accessible only through a window or page frame as shown in Figure 3-13. The window holds different pages of memory that

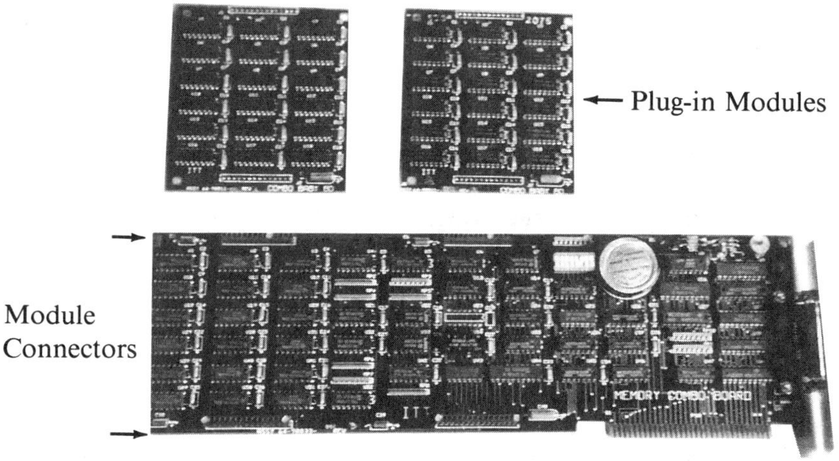

Figure 3-12 Memory-expansion board for XT systems with plug-in modules

are swapped as required into the processor's address space. In order to use expanded memory, you need a memory board and software that meet the EMS standard. EMS version 4.0 will let you run programs and store data using up to 32MB of paged RAM and will work on machines from XTs to 486s.

Extended memory is more of an extension of RAM. You cannot use it on 8088 and 8086 machines. You can add 15MB of extended RAM starting at the end of 1MB in an 80286 or 386SX machine. The 386DX and 486 machines can handle an additional 4,095MB.

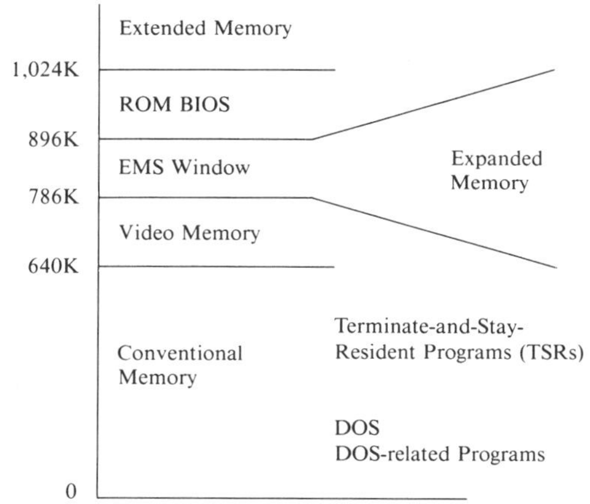

Figure 3-13 Memory map showing the relationship between conventional, expanded, and extended memory

Operating systems like OS/2 and UNIX can use extended memory directly, but DOS cannot. To run in extended memory, a program needs to have a DOS-extender, which switches the CPU between the real mode (used by DOS) and the protected mode, which can access memory beyond 1MB. The three standards that are in use are:

1. Extended Memory Specification (XMS).
2. Virtual Control Program Interface (VCPI).
3. DOS Protected-Mode Interface (DPMI).

Extended memory is easier to use than EMS, but it will not work in XT machines. It is newer than EMS for 286s and 386s. EMS has established itself as a popular standard for all three classes of PCs. Most of the more recent hardware and software products may use either one or a combination of the two memory types.

Expanded memory uses existing addresses that are available within the DOS 1MB address limit. As discussed earlier, expanded memory swaps additional blocks of memory into those unused addresses using a technique known as bank switching. An expanded memory manager (EMM) accesses the memory located outside RAM through a window or page frame. The page frame is inside the 1MB that the older DOS versions recognize and allows DOS to access up to four blocks or pages of memory at once. If the program needs data that is located in expanded memory, the EMM searches for the page or pages the program is looking for and moves it into the 64K page frame so that DOS can use it.

If you want to use expanded memory, you need to install an EMS board or a software emulator. The emulator mimics an EMS board. You can add expanded memory to an XT, AT, or 386 machine—this gives you more memory space for those programs that can take advantage of EMS. The hardware expansion normally takes the form of an EMS 4.0 memory board. Software products emulate the expanded memory by swapping sections of code using the hard drive or extended RAM. This results in a simulation of an EMS-paged RAM.

Above Disk Emulator. A typical software emulator is Above Disk. While it is mainly an EMS emulator, it also has utilities for using 96K of EGA or VGA video memory for nongraphics programs and for relocating Novell Netware terminate-and-stay-resident programs (TSRs). You can use it to simulate the entire 32MB EMS limit in extended memory or on a hard drive.

Above Disk is one of the easiest memory managers to install. First, it asks if this is a first-time installation and which disk and subdirectory to copy files to. Then a configuration screen appears to show the settings for emulating EMS memory in the system. During the installation, Above Disk adds a device driver to the CONFIG.SYS file and a memory-resident module to AUTOEXEC.BAT.

Above Disk will not work with some programs like Windows/386. The protected mode only works on 286s or 386s with CPUs that are dated August 1987 or after and that run DOS 3.3 or later. Above Disk includes a Lotus 1-2-3 EMS emulator for additional memory management that is not available in the main program. It provides space for large 1-2-3 worksheets.

TC Power Emulator. This program also supplies EMS emulation. During the installation procedure, you create a new hard drive subdirectory and then copy the program files. TC Power adds a command line to CONFIG.SYS. It can combine extended, expanded, and hard drive memory in any combination up to the 32MB of EMS 4.0.

TC Power can run on an XT, but since XTs do not support extended RAM, the program will use only the machine's hard drive for EMS emulation. This disk-based emulation can provide the full 32MB of EMS 4.0 memory.

Memory Manager Characteristics. Some software products make room for the application program by moving TSRs and drivers out of the lower 640K and relocating them to expanded or extended memory, the hard drive, or gaps between 640K and 1MB if the system has memory in this range. These gaps are found in some 286- and 386-compatibles with 1MB on the system board.

A few products stretch DOS RAM to 704K or 736K—the value depends on the type of video card used. Monochrome and color graphics adapter (CGA) cards do not use the memory addresses immediately above 640K, so a memory manager can assign the empty space to DOS.

Some memory-management products for 386s convert extended memory to expanded memory. These products use the 386 chip's memory-mapping facility as a substitute for the actual EMS board. They convert extended memory to EMS RAM and then use memory-mapping to relocate TSRs and drivers.

Extended-Memory Application

The first 640K of DOS is sometimes called the user-addressable base memory. In the 286, this memory is linear, which means that it proceeds theoretically but not physically in a straight line from bit 1 through the highest bit in the memory.

DOS can use the base memory for any purpose. Memory from the 640K point up to the 1MB point is used for ROM, which acts like a type of built-in permanent software for the system's basic functions. This includes video processing and the start-up procedures, which is also called booting up or booting. The user does not normally have access to the memory in the reserved area between 640K and 1MB. Above 1MB, the extended-memory region begins.

The earlier DOS versions do not recognize extended memory, but many applications programs use it. Extended memory goes from 1MB to 16MB for a 286 system. If you install 1MB of RAM on the system board, the first 640K goes to base memory, and the remaining 384K jumps above the reserved area for ROM to become the first 384K of extended memory.

One application for extended memory is a RAM disk. DOS versions 3.1 and above usually include a program for creating a RAM disk in extended memory. The RAM disk is electronic memory that acts like a fast disk drive. DOS treats it like an extra floppy or hard drive connected to the system. Since there is no physical disk involved, the access time to and from the RAM disk depends only on the speed of the memory chips. Even though it works as if it were storage, the RAM disk is volatile memory, and the contents of the RAM disk need to be saved to a long-term storage device after a computing session.

Extended and Expanded Memory Differences

Extended memory is different from expanded memory in that only 286s and 386s can use it. Extended memory is also linear, and its addresses start at the end of the DOS limit, going from 1MB on up to 16MB in a 286 and 4,996MB in a 386. Extended memory does not use bank switching like expanded memory—it is all available simultaneously, instead of being used in 64K chunks. You will need extended memory for multitasking (running several applications at once) and for the operating systems that are designed to handle multitasking OS/2 and UNIX.

When 286s and 386s use extended memory, they are working in protected mode. Some software programs are written for 286-and-above machines, so these programs can use the extended memory. ATs and 386s can also run in real mode, the conventional 640K RAM limit, using conventional DOS-compatible software. When running in real mode, ATs and 386s pretend to be XTs.

DOS works within a 1MB limit. Expanded memory is memory that lies completely outside that limit but that is switched into and out of a 64K window so DOS can work with it. Extended memory is a linear extension of that 1MB and can all be accessed directly by the CPU. Extended memory is only available with 286 and 386 computers.

ADDING MEMORY

A 286 machine may only have 512K of RAM on the system board. You can upgrade this to 640K or 1MB or more by installing more RAM chips on the system board. The RAM chips are located in rows on the system board. Some rows will be filled with chips while other rows will have empty sockets.

The rows are divided into logical banks, as discussed earlier. In a 16-bit system like the 286, each of the logical banks contains 16 memory chips plus 2 organizers or parity chips; an 8-bit system will use 8 memory chips plus 1 organizer or parity chip. Each bank can send 16 bits—one from each memory chip—to the data bus at one time.

If you have empty rows of sockets on the system board, you can upgrade the memory. Suppose you have 512K and you want to upgrade to 640K memory. Your board has 9 sockets per row (Fig 3-14)—one chip is used for parity testing and 8 chips are used for actual memory per row. A total of 64K bits times 8 chips equals 64K bytes per row. Two rows of 64K bytes gives you 128K bytes added to the system. This 128K bytes plus the original 512K bytes provides 640K.

If your upgrade goes to 1MB of RAM, you will use eighteen 256K RAM chips. If you want to downgrade the total system memory to 256K, then you pull two rows of existing 256K chips and fill four rows with 64K chips.

There is no difference between a chip used for parity and a chip used for RAM. Any RAM chip can be the organizer if it is installed in the ninth socket of the bank.

RAM chips are available in different speeds, which indicate how long it takes the chip to send a bit of information to the microprocessor. Chip speeds are measured in nanoseconds, or one-billionths of a second. The lower the number of nanoseconds, the faster the chip. In high-performance machines, with the faster 386 or 486 microprocessor units, you need memory chips that can deliver information fast. The microprocessor cannot be kept waiting for a slow RAM chip. The recommended speed for RAM chips in most 286 machines is 150 ns.

There are also programs that swap applications or TSRs in and out of the 640K working area. This lets you switch between programs without exiting one and starting up another. When tasks are switched, the program saves a snapshot of the suspended program while you work with the new task in the foreground. These products differ from true multitasking environments such as provided by DesqView or Windows, which run several programs simultaneously.

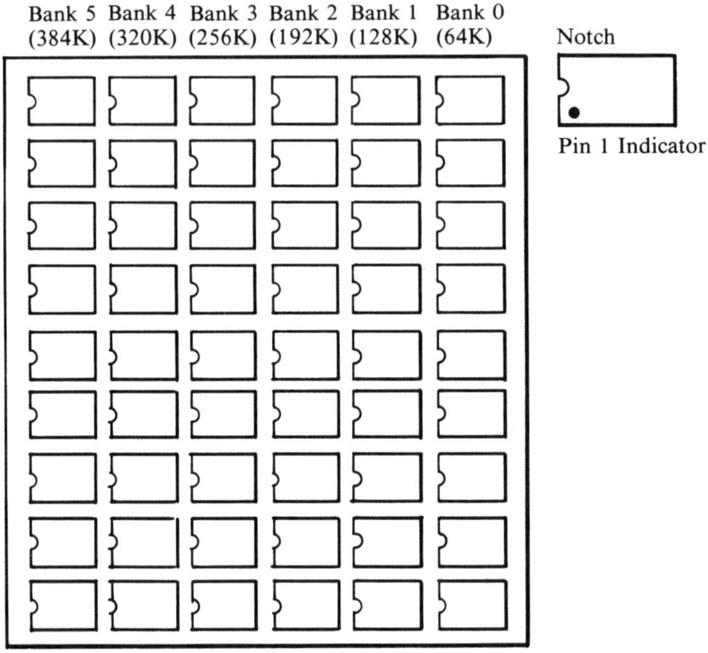

Figure 3-14 Section of memory sockets with 8 chips of memory and 1 chip for parity

Upgrade Problems and Solutions

A PC- or XT-class machine can use an EMS expanded memory board that fits into an 8-bit slot. This allows improved performance for task-switching programs. You can use a hard drive for a slower, but often satisfactory, solution with a task switcher or EMS emulator. In a 286 system, if you use hard drive swapping without adding memory, you may find it too slow. A better solution is to combine these programs with an expanded memory board. In a 386 system, it is best to use all of the extended RAM that you can on the motherboard or in a 32-bit memory slot, instead of a slower expansion-board slot. A 386 memory manager will allow EMS access, and you can use a task switcher to make sure that all of the RAM is fully utilized.

Memory Options

Both software caching and RAM disks require more RAM. One of the quickest ways to get more out of your PC and improve your system is to add more memory. Prices on upgrades should continue to drop.

Memory chips are packaged in different ways: SIMMs, just the chips themselves (usually called DRAMs), single inline pin packages (SIPPs), and DIPs. Your PC can use only one of these forms of RAM. You also need to buy memory of the right capacity and speed. It is sometimes possible to mix, for example, 256-kilobit (Kb) and 1-megabit (1Mb) 80-ns chips and 100-ns chips on the same motherboard, but you should avoid it.

When you add RAM to the motherboard, you generally set it up as extended memory. You can only use extended memory with the 80286 and later CPUs. The 80286 and newer PCs can access many megabytes directly, eliminating the concept of conventional RAM and the 640K barrier, but older CPUs must use special techniques to move information between conventional RAM and added RAM. A second option—expanded memory—swaps a certain section of conventional RAM with expanded RAM. While this technique was popular for the 8088 and 8086 machines, the more advanced CPUs depend on extended memory.

Expanded memory is a quick and simple way to add memory to a system. It is sold on expansion cards (Fig 3-15) that you can buy already populated with RAM. Popular programs like Lotus 1-2-3 and DesqView use expanded memory. If you add RAM to an expansion card (Fig 3-16), it is usually much easier to add chips to one of them than it is to add them to your motherboard. You can set the card down on a table to work on it. One of the most popular expansion cards, Intel's Above Board Plus 8 I/O, is a full-size card that comes with 2MB of RAM and software installation program.

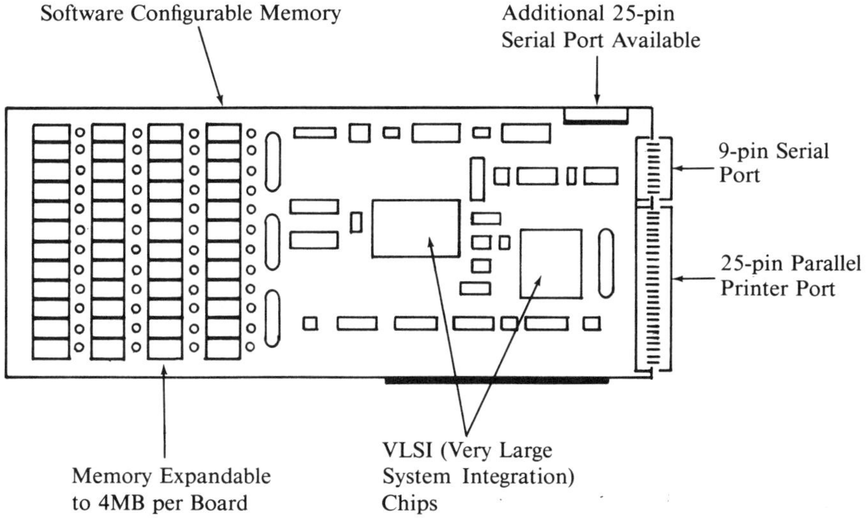

Figure 3-15 AT I/O card for 286- or 386-based systems with expandable memory

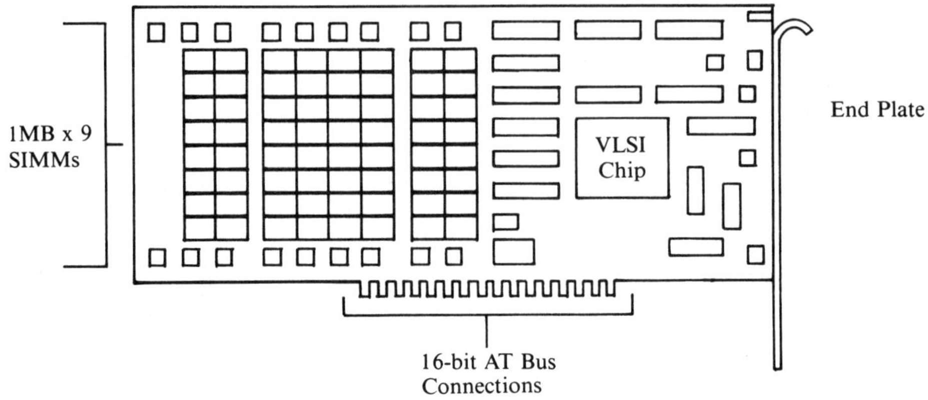

Figure 3-16 AT memory board for memory expansion of up to 8MB for conventional, EMS, or extended memory in 2MB increments

You may be able to get more memory out of the system you already have without using expanded or extended memory. DOS does not take full advantage of the memory in the system. Programs like Quarterdeck's QRAM for 8088 and 80286 machines and QEMM for 386 machines can free almost 100K of memory for direct use by programs. However, these programs and others like them do not always work because not every machine has hidden memory that can be freed. Programs that can free RAM from large programs and TSR programs include Mark and Release. These are a part of a freeware package from TurboPower called TSR Utilities. Mark loads TSRs into memory, and Release takes them out of memory.

SIMM Modules. A single inline memory module is a small circuit board with DRAM chips soldered to it. The type of chips used on a SIMM determines its capacity. There are 256-kilobit chips on a 256K SIMM; and there are 1-megabit chips on a 1M byte SIMM. SIMMs are available in 256K, 1M, 2M, 4M, and 16M bytes.

A SIMM's size is expressed as a particular capacity followed by an "x" and a number. The number indicates how many chips there are on the SIMM. For example, "1MB x 8" means there are eight 1-megabit chips on the SIMM. The PC accesses RAM data 8 bits at a time, or in bytes.

The use of parity SIMMs is common in the IBM PC. Parity SIMMs contain an extra parity chip for error checking and correction. You must have the parity-checking capability to take advantage of such SIMMs.

The speed of the chips determines how fast the CPU can retrieve information from memory. The lower the SIMM-speed number, the faster the SIMM is. Faster CPUs need faster SIMMs. You can usually determine the SIMM speed by looking at the chips on the SIMM. You will see a part number, a dash, and then more numbers. Multiply the numbers after the dash by ten to find the speed. For example, if an "8" follows the dash, then you have an 80-ns SIMM.

As long as your SIMMs are equal to or faster than the recommended speed for your PC, they will work. Installing SIMMs that are faster than the PC needs does not create a problem. Many companies sell 100-ns and 80-ns SIMMs. If you put 80-ns SIMMs in a PC, the PC will continue to access memory at, for example, 150-ns, even if the SIMMs can go faster.

SIMMs come with different profiles, or heights, due to the type of RAM chip soldered to the module. Low-profile SIMMs use surface-mount chips—the leads of the chip are soldered directly to the board. High-profile SIMMs use DIP chips—the leads are soldered into holes on the SIMM board. Because of their height, high-profile SIMMs could interfere with future expansion. They can also block the air circulation, causing heat problems.

Memory-Expansion Boards. The Intel Above Board MC32 is a 32-bit memory board for the PS/2 Model 70 (16 and 20 MHz) and PS/2 Model 80. It provides expanded (EMS 4.0) and extended (OS/2) memory to 8MB using 1MB SIMMs rated at 100 ns or faster. It is expandable to 2MB with 256K SIMMs.

The Above Board 2 is a 16-bit memory board for the PS/2 Model 50, 50Z, 55SX, and 60. It provides expanded (EMS 4.0) and extended (OS/2) memory to 8MB with 1MB SIMMs rated at 120 ns or faster. It is expandable to 2MB with 256K SIMMs.

The Above Board Plus 8 provides conventional (to 640K), expanded (EMS 4.0), and extended (OS/2) memory for the PC, XT, and compatibles with bus speeds up to 8 MHz. You can also use it for the AT and compatibles with bus speeds up to 12.5 MHz and for the PS/2 Model 25 and 30 and the Compaq 386. The board is a hardware implementation of EMS 4.0 and is expandable to 8MB with 120-ns or faster 1MB DRAM. It is expandable to 14MB total, with a 6MB piggyback option, and is available with a parallel and serial port. Other Above Board options include a 2MB piggyback and a second port on the board.

Extended Memory Boards. Typical extended memory boards include those available from Newer Technology. The Attention!2 and Attraction boards allow you to add up to 8MB of high-speed AT extended memory using one slot. You can use these for 286/386 computers running DOS Windows and OS/2. They will enable you to increase the conventional (DOS) memory and extended memory simultaneously for the best memory utilization in 2M byte chunks of one megabit RAM chips or one megabit SIMMs as your memory needs grow.

You can also maximize performance in a 286/386 with up to 16MB of EMS 4.0 on one board. These boards provide full hardware and software support of EMS 4.0 and 3.2. You can increase conventional (DOS) memory, AT-extended, EMS 4.0, and RAM disk memory simultaneously for the best possible memory utilization. Thus, four memory modes are available from one board which can support DesqView and Windows multitasking environments. You can add 256K or 1MB SIMMs as memory needs grow.

There are also boards that allow you to access up to 8MB of memory for the 16-bit MCA computers or 8MB of 32-bit memory using one expansion slot. The 16-bit boards fit PS/2 models 50, 50Z, 55, 60, and 65. The 32-bit board works in PS/2 models 70, P70, and 80. You can start with 2MB to 4MB and expand as your memory needs grow.

PS/2 SIMMs offer a flexible solution for high-speed motherboard or memory-board upgrades. There are 512K, 1MB, 2MB, and 4MB upgrade kits available. You can use these memory products with a variety of system hardware. Fast 80-ns chips are available for these SIMMs.

Memory Modules. More memory can boost software performance, and, with extended memory, you can improve the performance of DOS applications and run applications like Windows and OS/2.

Intel Matched Memory Modules offer 1MB, 2MB, or 4MB of fast 32-bit memory on 72-pin SIMMS. This means you can add memory as you need it. Installation is usually easy since you just plug it into the system board. Modules are available for the following system boards:

1. 1MB for PS/2 Models 55, 65, 70; Compaq 386N, 386s/20; Hewlett-Packard Vectra 486; Zenith 386/20, 25, 30.
2. 2MB for PS/2 Models 50Z, 55, 65, 70; Compaq 386N, 386s/20; Hewlett-Packard Vectra 386/25.
3. 2MB for PS/2 Model 70.
4. 4MB for PS/2 Models 55, 65; Compaq 386N, 386s/20; Hewlett-Packard Vectra 486; Zenith 386/20, 25, 33.

Solid-State RAM Drives. The SCSI Dart from Newer Technology is a solid-state, nonvolatile, RAM drive with up to 128MB of SIMM memory, which can reduce hours of disk-intensive jobs into minutes. Dart handles files with a 0.5-ms access time and 0.5-ms seek time. These access times are much faster than even the best conventional hard drives.

This solid-state RAM drive uses industry-standard SIMMs, resulting in a small physical size. You can configure the drive for present requirements and then expand it in the future. This product uses a drive bay or comes in an external version.

The DartCard is a similar product that runs up to 96MB of nonvolatile RAM drive for internal use in ISA 286/386 and EISA 386/486 computers. It has similar access and seek times. The data access time is fifty times better than a fast hard drive. This RAM drive comes with its own dedicated high-speed controller card that fits in an expansion slot. The DartCard unit mounts in an internal 5.25-inch full- or half-height drive bay like a standard hard drive. The modular design allows upgrading with 8MB cards, so the system can grow with your needs.

Ultima from Newer Technology is a nonvolatile motherboard-based RAM disk drive. It is accessed at full CPU speed, and you can upgrade it in 4MB increments. The unit comes with a small internal uninterruptible power supply (UPS) battery backup to provide up to five days backup for power outages. Depending upon the CPU speed, you can get a 4–15MB/second data transfer rate, which is far better than even the fastest hard drives. It is easy to set up since there are no switches to deal with.

Compaq Upgrades. You can increase your system memory up to the maximum with 16-bit and 32-bit high-speed memory for Compaq Systempro, Deskpro, Laptop, or Portable computers. There are 1MB, 2MB, 4MB, and 8MB modules available for use with Compaq Deskpro and Systempro models; and 1MB, 2MB, and 4MB memory modules are available for the Laptop, Portable, and network-oriented line of computers. All of these modules support parity error checking. Simple plug-in installation makes the upgrade quick and easy to install.

Multiplication and Multiplication/S are memory upgrade boards for Compaq computers. They are available in either 1MB or 4MB configurations for the Deskpro 386/20e and 386/25e, and there is a 4MB configuration for the Deskpro 386s. You can add more 1MB and 4MB boards as your computing needs increase. The multiplication boards allow for a clear upgrade path. They support parity error checking and are compatible with Compaq's 1MB and 4MB System Memory boards. Neither installation nor configuration is difficult.

Compaq Portables. Compaq has some of the highest-performance notebook PCs available. These can be used like a desktop PC if you add the desktop expansion base to your CompaqLTE 386s/20 personal computer. The desktop expansion base has two full-sized 8-/16-bit industry-standard expansion slots to customize your system and tie you into a network. You can choose from a variety of tape and floppy disk drives for backup and media flexibility.

For more comfort, you can attach a full-size 101/102-key enhanced keyboard. Using the attached monitor support cover, you can enhance your system with a full-size VGA color monitor.

You can use all the standard interfaces to connect to the peripherals you need without connecting them directly to your notebook. When you need to travel with your PC, you do not have to disconnect the peripherals and move the monitor.

The expansion base also gets your PC ready for travel. An AC adapter powers the system and charges the battery while you work. When you need to disconnect, press the release button.

4

VIDEO SYSTEMS

THE VIDEO OUTPUT

The IBM family of personal computers uses a separate monitor, and the video outputs to the monitor are often on plug-in expansion cards. The video outputs are designed to be used with specific types of monochrome or color monitors with low to high resolutions. *Resolution* is quantified by (1) the number of pixels displayed on a monitor per horizontal line by (2) the number of horizontal lines displayed on the vertical axis. For example, a resolution of 640 x 350 indicates 640 pixels wide by 350 lines of pixels vertically. A *pixel* is the smallest unit available for display on a raster screen. It represents a single graphics point and is also called a picture element.

A *raster display* is a common type of video display that operates like a television set—images are created by illuminating individual pixels using a line-by-line scan of the screen by an electron beam (Fig 4-1 and Fig 4-2). Depending on the type of monitor used, the output of the video circuits must contain all the elements needed to create the desired image on the display screen.

MONITOR OPERATION

A monochrome monitor uses a display face with a single color phosphor—usually green, amber, or white (Fig 4-3). At the other end of the cathode-ray display tube is an electron gun. This part of the tube sends a controlled beam of electrons that lights up the display screen. As the beam hits the

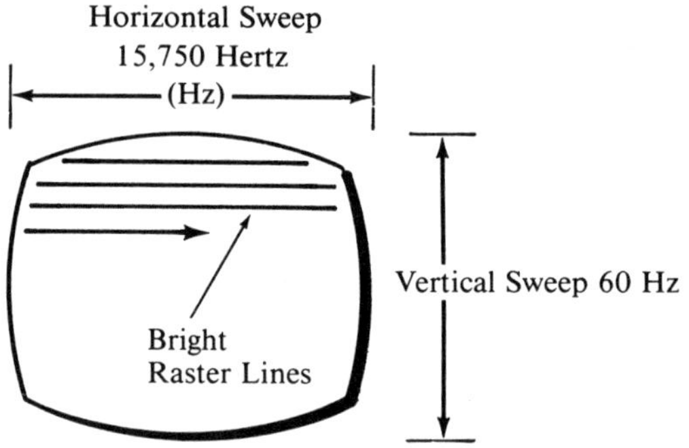

Figure 4-1 Raster display (The raster lines are created by moving the electron beam across the screen and then down the screen on a line-by-line basis.)

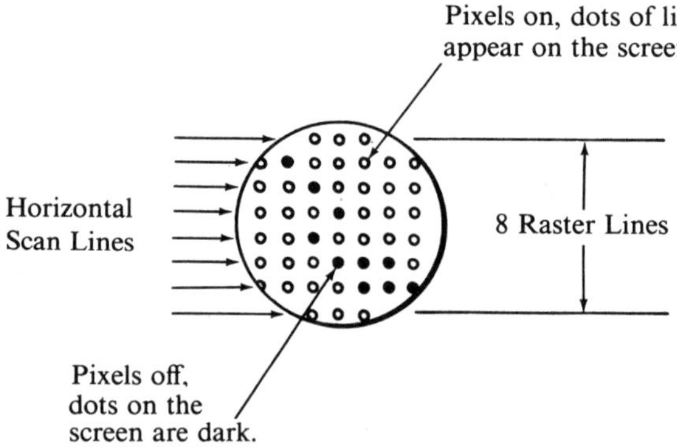

Figure 4-2 Close-up showing raster lines and pixels

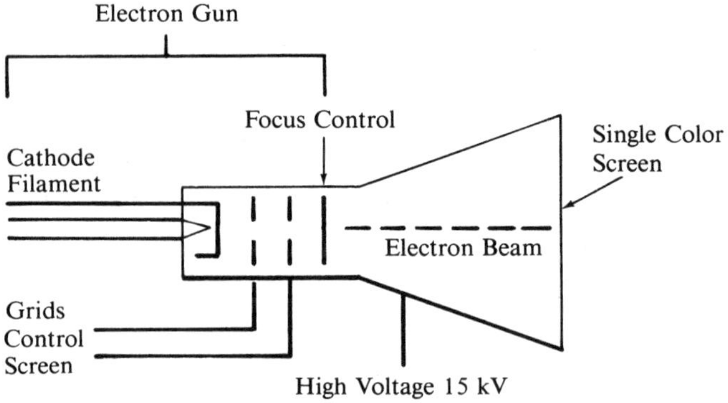

Figure 4-3 Monochrome cathode-ray tube

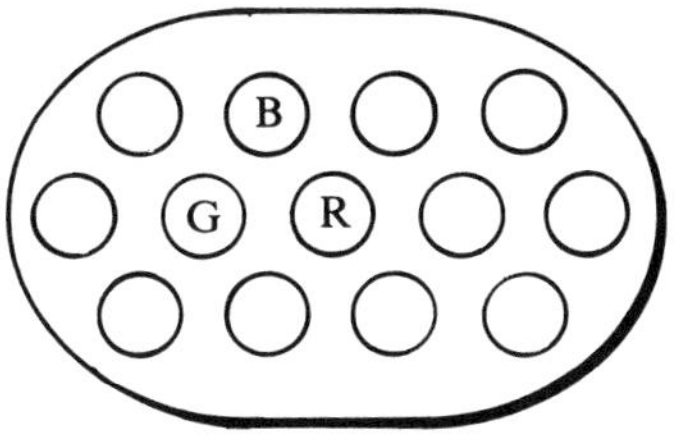

Figure 4-4 Color tube screen with alternating red, blue, and green dots on the face of the screen

phosphor in the screen, it causes a glowing effect. Only a small dot on the screen lights up at any one time.

A color tube uses small patterns of color phosphor dots (red, green, and blue [RGB]) on the face of the screen (Fig 4-4). Three electron beams come from the electron gun (Fig 4-5). One beam controls the red dots, the second controls the green dots, and the third controls the blue dots. The three colors mix on the screen to produce the desired colors for a color image.

High-resolution monitors pack the color dot patterns close together to produce a more natural color display. Pixels (the picture element) are the individual points of light that make up the patterns on the screen. The resolution of the display will depend on the numbers of pixels across and up and down the screen, as shown in Figures 4-6 and 4-7.

The electron-beam scan moves across the face of the tube and down the tube on a line-by-line basis. When the scan occurs, it switches each dot either on or off. Video circuits control the scanning operation and move and focus the beam. Most tubes use electromagnetic focusing. When the beam goes from the electron gun to the screen, it must travel through a series of focusing coils. One coil is used for horizontal focusing and the other for vertical

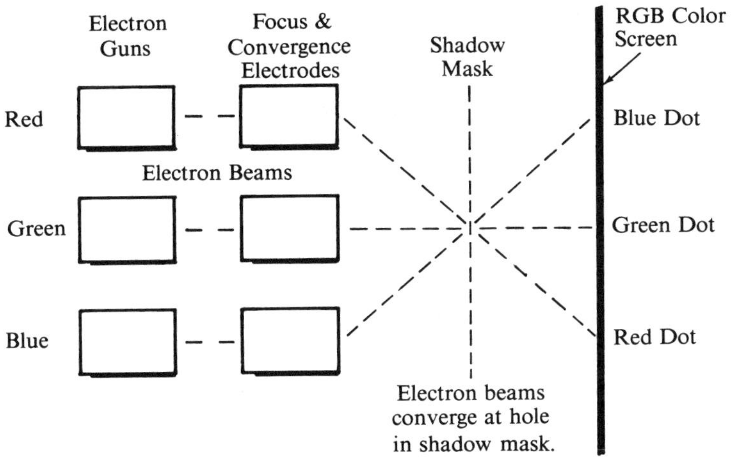

Figure 4-5 Color tube operation

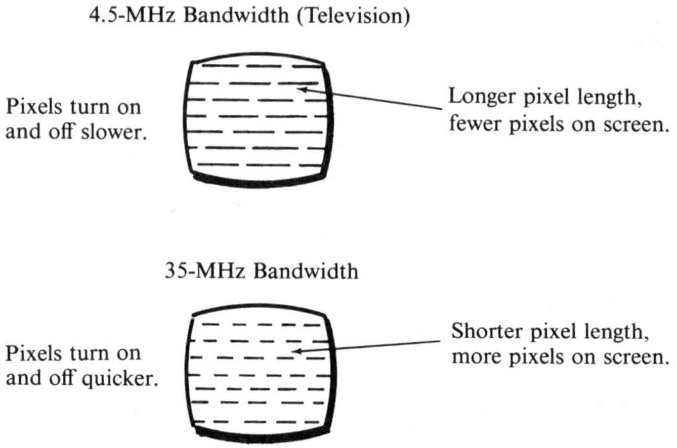

Figure 4-6 Horizontal bandwidth and pixel length (A higher horizontal bandwidth provides a shorter pixel length and higher resolution.)

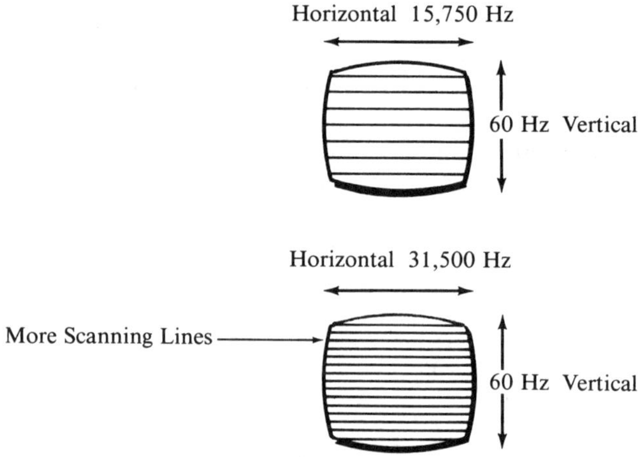

Figure 4-7 Horizontal bandwidth and scanning lines (A higher horizontal bandwidth will produce more scanning lines and a higher resolution.)

focusing. The horizontal coil moves the beam from side to side at a rate of more than 15,000 times every second. The vertical coil moves the beam up and down about 60 times a second. This scanning operation results in writing 264 lines of light on the screen 60 times a second. The scanning is done using the timing of the monitor's sweep circuits.

The scanning operation needs to be in sync with the computer's clock. The computer sends horizontal and vertical synchronization (sync) signals to the sweep circuits, which lock the horizontal and vertical oscillators in step with the computer's operating frequencies.

ADAPTERS

Monochrome Adapters

The original IBM PC family uses a separate adapter card (Fig 4-8) that plugs into one of the I/O slots and provides a connector on the rear of the system unit for the monitor cable. The modular approach makes it easy to upgrade the different components of the video system. The disadvantage of the adapter card is that it takes up one expansion slot, and some later machines have a built-in video adapter on the system board. In many of these machines, it is still possible to add another adapter and use both or inhibit the original on-board adapter.

The adapter uses a video-output chip. Many monochrome systems use the 6845 cathode ray tube (CRT) controller (Fig 4-9). It is the main chip for the conversion of digital bits from the computer to the image on the monitor. The monochrome supporting chips also include 4K of SCRAM and an MK-36000-character ROM in many systems. The RAM holds the system memory map, and it acts as a video RAM. The system memory map is often called a "bit map." It is the computer representation that defines the color and intensity of each pixel needed on a raster screen to create the image.

On a monitor screen of 80 x 25 characters, there are 2,000 characters total. Each character will use 2 bytes of RAM to function. One byte will hold the ASCII code representing the character, while the second holds the bits controlling character features such as blinking and intensity.

The address of the video RAM will go from hexadecimal B0000 to B0F9F, starting at the upper left-hand corner of the screen and ending at

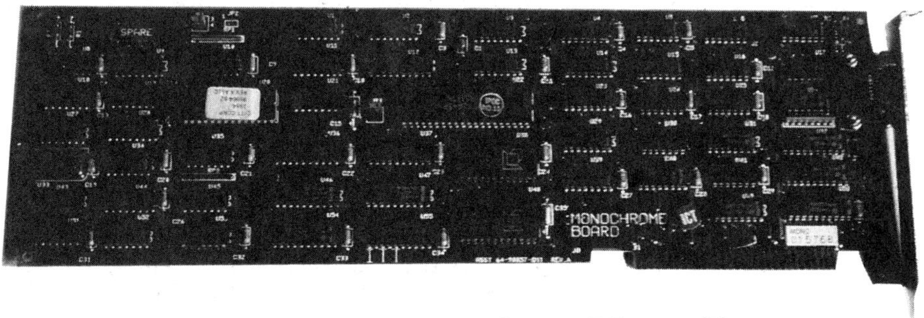

Figure 4-8 Monochrome adapter used in many PC-compatibles

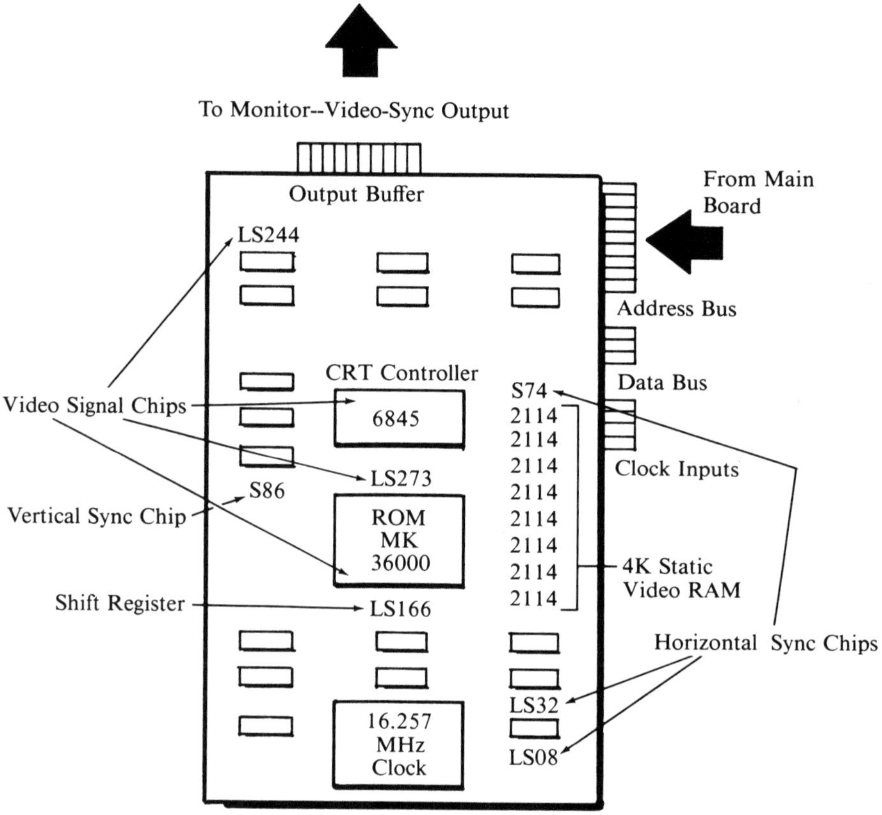

Figure 4-9 Monochrome adapter layout

the lower right-hand corner with the last RAM address. The system constantly scans the video RAM and uses the contents of each byte to turn the dots on and off.

The monochrome adapter uses a 9-pin connector. Pins 1 and 2 are used for grounding, and pins 3 and 4 are not used. The other pins are used for the following functions: pin 6—intensity; pin 7—video; pin 8—horizontal sync; and pin 9—vertical sync.

The CRT controller receives address, data, and clock signals from the computer. It uses the address information to access the video RAM and send the data bits to the video RAM. The controller uses the clock information to generate the horizontal and vertical sync signals. The CRT controller works as the video processor; uses the video RAM to update the dot information on the screen; and reads the video-RAM data and sends this information to the character-generator ROM where the actual character generation is done. When the ASCII-coded byte arrives at the ROM, the

ROM codes it into the correct character byte. The character bytes then travel to a shift register, which converts the parallel byte to serial format. The controller conditions this signal, and it becomes the video output (pin 7). The CRT controller also provides the horizontal and vertical sync information through pins 8 and 9.

Color/Graphics Cards

A color/graphics card will use the same types of circuits as a monochrome card, with the addition of the color and graphics circuits needed. Many manufacturers make these cards for the IBM PCs (see Table 4-1). The cards have different features, but the basic operations remain the same. The IBM color/graphics adapter (CGA) uses the circuits shown in Figure 4-10. A 6845 CRT video processor controls the input from the computer. The video RAM is dynamic rather than static, and it holds 16K bytes. It

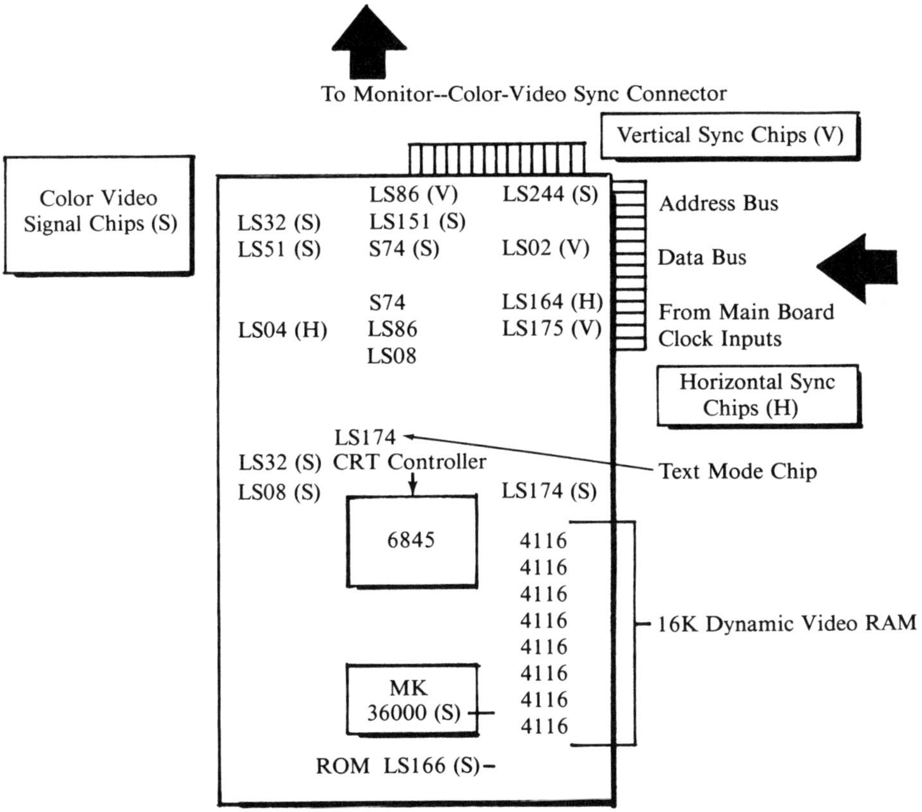

Figure 4-10 IBM CGA layout, showing main chips and connectors

TABLE 4-1 Medium-Resolution Video Boards

Type	Manufacturer/Model	Data Bus	MDA	Hercules	CGA	EGA
Monochrome graphics adapters (MDA/HGCO*)	Amdek Adapter 110	8-bit	X	X		
	Hercules Graphics Card Plus	8-bit	X	X		
Mono/color (MDA/CGA†)—supports monochrome and color monitors	Paradise Basic Video	8-bit	X	X	X	
	ATI Technologies Graphics Solution	8-bit	X	X	X	
MonoCGA displays CGA on mono monitors	STB Chauffeur HT	8-bit	X	X		
MonoEGA displays EGA on mono monitors	Paradise Auto Switch Monochrome	8-bit	X	X	X	X
EGAs	Paradise AutoSwitch	8-bit	X	X	X	X
	STB AutoEGA	8-bit	X	X	X	X
Extended EGA	Personal Computer Graphics Photon MEGA/VGA	8-bit	X	X	X	X
	Video Seven VEGA Deluxe	8-bit	X	X	X	X
VGA Adapters	Amdek VGA Adapter/132	8-bit	X	X	X	X
	Video Seven VEGA VGA	8-bit	X	X	X	X
Extended VGA	AST Research AST-VGA Plus	16-bit	X	X	X	X
	Orchid ProDesigner	8/16 bit	X	X	X	X
Supports MD/HGC graphics on color monitor in monochrome or color	Hercules InColor	8-bit	X	X		

*Monochrome display adapter/Hercules graphics color output.

†CGA = color graphics adapter.

uses 14 address lines, the locations of which are accessed through multiplex chips. The DRAM sends its contents to an MK-36000 character ROM. The ROM outputs are conditioned and sent to the 9-pin DIN adapter connector (Fig 4-11). Pins 1 and 2 are ground, and the colors are on pins 3, 4, and 5 (red, green, and blue). Pin 6 is used for intensity or brightness, and pins 8 and 9 are used for the horizontal and vertical sync signals.

CGAs also use additional output connectors. Some use an RCA-type jack to provide a composite video signal. The three color outputs, the color burst, and clock signals are combined using a multiplexer chip, buffered, and then sent to the RCA jack as shown in Figure 4-12. Another output connection found on some older adapters is a 4-pin Berg-type strip. It provides the same outputs as the RCA jack plus a connection to the +12V power supply. You can use this to connect the PC to a television with a radio frequency (RF) modulator. The RF modulator provides the modulation frequencies for channel 3 or 4. The +12V power the modulator.

Video Display Adapters

The video display adapter is the expansion card that plugs into one of the expansion slots. It acts as the interface between the system board and the monitor and must be compatible with the monitor. For example, you cannot use a color monitor with a display adapter that is designed only for monochrome monitors.

Types of Video Display Adapters. The PC family uses the following types of adapters:

- **Monochrome display adapter (MDA)**: This is the simplest video card since it can display only text characters in one color.
- **Hercules graphics adapter (HGA)**: This is a popular video card and, because of its popularity, it has become a defacto standard. It emulates an MDA card but it also supports high-resolution monochrome graphics.
- **Color graphics adapter (CGA)**: This early video card can display text and graphics in any of 8 colors.
- **Enhanced graphics adapter (EGA)**: This improved video card can display text and graphics in any of 16 colors from a palette of 64. It also supports a higher resolution than CGA video cards.
- **Multi-color graphics adapter (MCGA)**: This video card is a cross between a CGA and a VGA. It supports all CGA modes and can display graphics in up to 256 simultaneous colors.

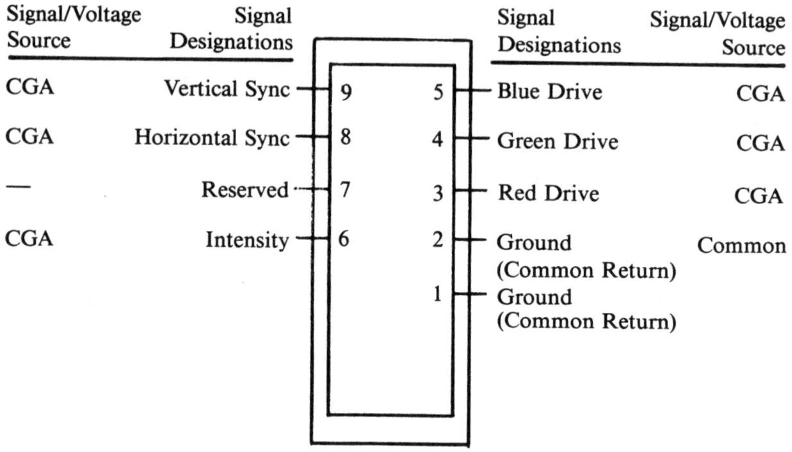

Figure 4-11 IBM PC color monitor interface

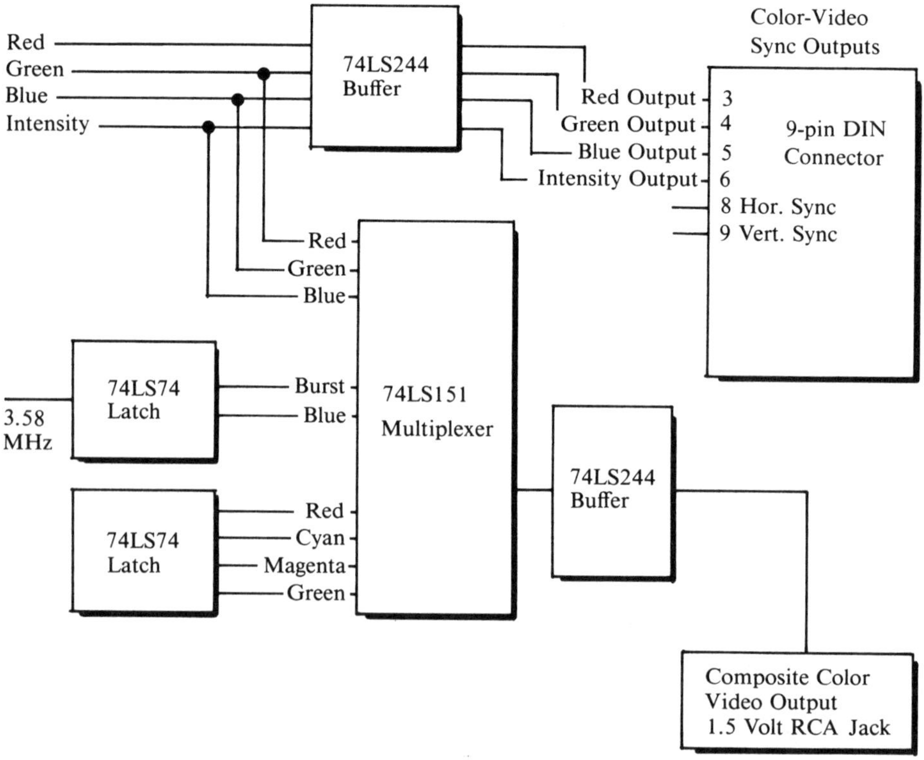

Figure 4-12 Color/graphics card block diagram showing multiplexed color signals

- **Video graphics adapter (VGA)**: This video card can display text and graphics in any of 256 colors from a palette of 262,144. It also supports a higher resolution than CGA, EGA, or MCGA video cards.
- **Super VGA (SVGA)**: This enhanced VGA card provides a higher resolution than standard VGA. The colors may be reduced at the higher resolutions.

Display-Adapter Installation. The display adapter installs in one of the expansion slots. Most are designed for 8-bit slots, but there are some 16-bit display adapter cards that are generally older color adapters. Some display adapters will run two or more monitors. Others offer features such as 132-column extended display, dual displays, and the ability to run color graphics software on a monochrome monitor.

Many older display adapters do not run reliably at the higher MHz speeds used in today's processors. This can be a problem if you intend to upgrade your system unit and keep your older monitor.

Some computers have a slide switch on the system board that you can set to have the system boot up in either color or monochrome mode. You need to set this switch to the correct position. Many display adapters have several different display modes, which are set by jumpers or DIP switches. It is important to use the correct switch settings, since you can damage some monitors by attaching them to a display adapter configured for the wrong mode.

MONITORS

Monochrome Monitors

A monochrome monitor runs at a horizontal frequency of 18.432 kiloHertz (kHz) and a vertical frequency of 50 Hz. These monitors are available in black and white, amber, or green. A monochrome monitor will display a 9-x-16-pixel text character with 25 rows of 80 characters. The monochrome video adapter will typically provide 720-x-348-pixel graphics and may emulate CGA, EGA, or VGA displays. The adapter does this emulation by displaying the colors as varying tones of gray, amber, or green.

Sync Adjustments. Some monitors have external vertical and horizontal sync adjustments, which you may need to adjust the sync frequencies for different video modes. Sometimes temperature changes will cause the monitor to shift its sync characteristics. This can cause the image to roll vertically due to the change in vertical sync frequency. You may need to adjust the vertical sync control to correct this problem.

The early IBM monochrome monitors do not have external sync controls, and you have to remove the case to make minor adjustments of the sync frequency. Newer monochrome monitors use phase lock loop (PLL) circuitry to control drifting of the input sync signal. Many color emulation boards will not work properly unless the monochrome monitor is equipped with PLL. In order to reduce interference from external sources, some monitors filter the input signal to remove electrical noise. Color emulation boards alter the signal characteristics to produce grey shades, and the filter circuit can interpret these changes as noise and convert them to a clean signal, thereby modifying the shading effects. Monitors that use only a shielded cable for filtering do not have these problems.

CGA Monitors

A CGA monitor (also called an RGB monitor) has an input frequency of 15.75 kHz horizontal and 60 Hz vertical. It uses separate red, green, blue, and intensity inputs (RGBI format) to allow a total of 16 colors to be displayed. The characters are 8 pixels high by 8 pixels deep with an 80 x 25 character display. The monitor normally displays graphics at 640 x 200 pixels, and there is an enhanced version that provides a 640-x-350-pixel display. This type of multivideo adapter allows an RGB monitor to also display monochrome and EGA graphics. The adapter uses an interlacing technique to produce the 350 lines required for EGA or monochrome graphics.

Interlacing. Interlacing creates a virtual screen in memory and forms the display area using two alternating 200-line segments. This simulates a screen with 400 lines. Interlacing does not affect the vertical frequency, but it does cut the screen refresh rate to 30 Hz, and a certain amount of flicker can result. Using an RGB monitor with a high-persistence phosphor reduces the flickering effect. You will need external sync controls if you are using EGA or monochrome emulation boards with an RGB monitor. Changes in vertical sync characteristics can distort screen images and make the text characters difficult to read.

Multifrequency Monitors

A multifrequency monitor is a display that can operate at several frequencies. A dual-frequency monitor can operate with either monochrome or color sync frequencies. These monitors usually have a monochrome screen and produce different shades of grey when operating in the color mode. They switch from monochrome sync frequencies (18.432-kHz horizontal, 50-Hz vertical) to color sync frequencies (15.75-kHz horizontal, 60-Hz vertical), depending on the input sync frequency. Some monitors test the pin configuration—usually pins 3, 4, and 5—to determine if a color adapter is connected.

If you use a dual-frequency monitor as a monochrome display, you get a higher resolution and do not need interlacing. A color adapter will have connections for pins 3, 4, and 5; and, in order to use monochrome operation, a special cable is needed between the monitor and the adapter to disconnect these pins.

EGA Monitors

An EGA monitor displays an 8-x-14-pixel character on an 80 x 25 display. It can be driven by either a CGA adapter (15.75 kHz) or an EGA adapter (21.8 kHz) to provide resolutions from 320 x 200 pixels to 640 x 350 pixels. The vertical sync frequency is 60 Hz. A total of 16 colors from a pallet of 64 can be displayed at any one time. Red, green, and blue inputs (RGB format) generate the colors. Most EGA adapters also emulate monochrome text and graphics on the EGA display. Some EGA monitors do not support the 15.75-kHz horizontal scan frequency, which limits them to EGA resolution (640 x 350).

As discussed earlier, some video adapters double-scan CGA graphics to produce better graphics. Most EGA monitors can handle the frequency changes, but some tend to lose vertical sync.

Double-Scan Monitors

There are 25-kHz monitors that provide better CGA graphics by double-scanning each of the 200 lines used on a CGA graphic screen. Some adapters are only CGA-compatible, but others can emulate EGA and provide their own 640-x-400- and 752-x-410-pixel graphics modes on the 25-kHz monitor.

There is no established industry standard for double-scan monitors, and many manufacturers have developed their own specifications for video frequencies and color format. The horizontal frequencies range from 23 kHz to 27 kHz. Some of the 25-kHz monitors even combine the horizontal and vertical sync signals into a composite sync signal.

Sync polarity is an important part of matching a 25-kHz monitor to a video adapter. CGA monitors use a positive sync for the horizontal frequency and a negative sync for the vertical frequency. An EGA monitor uses the opposite sync polarity in high-resolution modes, and it switches to a positive horizontal/negative vertical sync in CGA resolutions. A 25-kHz monitor may use one of these formats, or it may use its own.

VGA Monitors

VGA monitors are another IBM PC graphics standard. They use a horizontal frequency of 31.5 kHz and a vertical frequency of 70 Hz. These monitors provide 640-x-480-pixel resolution.

A VGA monitor uses an analog-RGB type of input in order to provide the 262,144 different colors available in VGA modes. By switching the vertical and horizontal sync polarity, the VGA adapter signals the monitor to change its vertical-sizing characteristics for lower vertical-resolution modes. Figure 4-13 shows a VGA card.

Multisync and Multimode Monitors

Multisync monitors are able to adapt themselves to the sync characteristics of the video board. They can operate with most video boards, including many special-purpose workstation adapters.

Multimode monitors are more limited than multisync monitors, since they can only match input sync characteristics within one of several frequency ranges (they are designed for specific modes). Most multisync and multimode monitors support both digital (monochrome, CGA, and EGA) and analog (VGA and graphics workstations) video.

Some multisync monitors will not sync on frequencies below 21

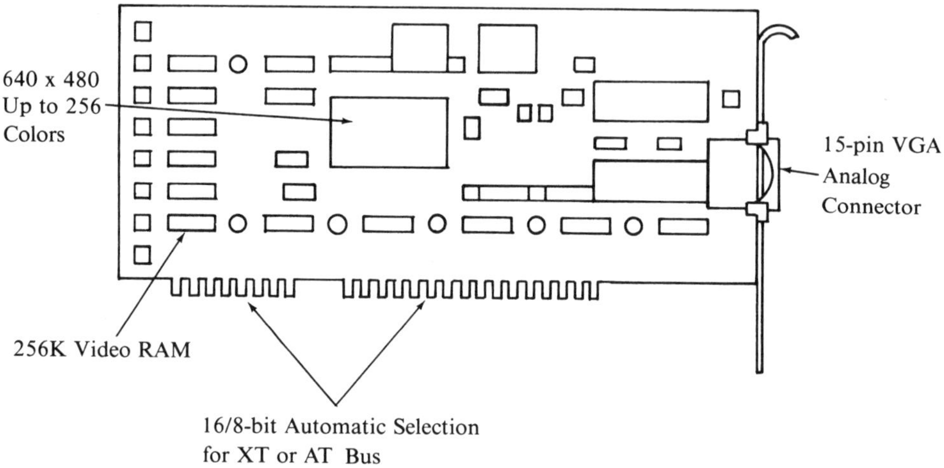

Figure 4-13 VGA card with automatic selection feature for XT or AT bus

kHz, so you cannot use them with CGA adapters. However, you can use them with video boards that double-scan CGA. When you use multimode monitors, some multivideo-board emulation modes may be within an unsupported frequency range. This can occur with EGA and VGA boards.

Not all high-resolution modes will work when using these adapters on multimode monitors. In order to connect a multisync or multimode monitor to a VGA adapter, you will need a special cable to mate the video board's connector with the monitor's analog input connector. The VGA adapter may cause a multisync monitor to experience shifts in the vertical display size when the video mode changes. This will occur if the monitor does not sense the sizing signals that the VGA adapter sends.

SVGA Monitors

SVGA monitors are an upgrade beyond VGA. An SVGA graphics board will give you at least 800-x-600-pixel capability and can go up to 1024 x 768.

You can get an SVGA board that provides 256 colors at the lower resolution, or one that has 1024 x 768 at 16 colors. Multiscan monitors are also compatible with the VGA standard. Most multiscan monitors support only interlaced scanning at 1024 x 768. This means the electron gun inside the monitor tube is making two passes to create an image instead of one, which can cause some screen flicker. Boards with special graphics coprocessors can speed up performance, but they can cost a few hundred to a few thousand dollars.

In most business applications, you spend a lot of time manipulating text. In a graphics environment like Windows, an SVGA board running at 800 x 600 in 16 colors on a 14-inch multiscan will give you about one and a half times the Windows desktop at standard VGA resolution. Text will be slightly smaller, but the characters will be sharper and easier to read.

If your VGA is built into the PC's main system board, you probably have basic VGA. If you decide to buy and install a new board and monitor, you will also have to disable the built-in VGA.

If you install a Windows driver for SVGA resolution, most Windows applications will be able to use it, and you will not have to install a separate driver for each application.

There are many graphics hardware solutions that include SVGA for applications like CAD and desktop publishing (Fig 4-14). The boards and monitors that are available support 800 x 600 to 1024 x 768 resolution.

If you need more room on the screen for multiple applications, you can upgrade to a larger monitor. The typical monitor measures 14 inches

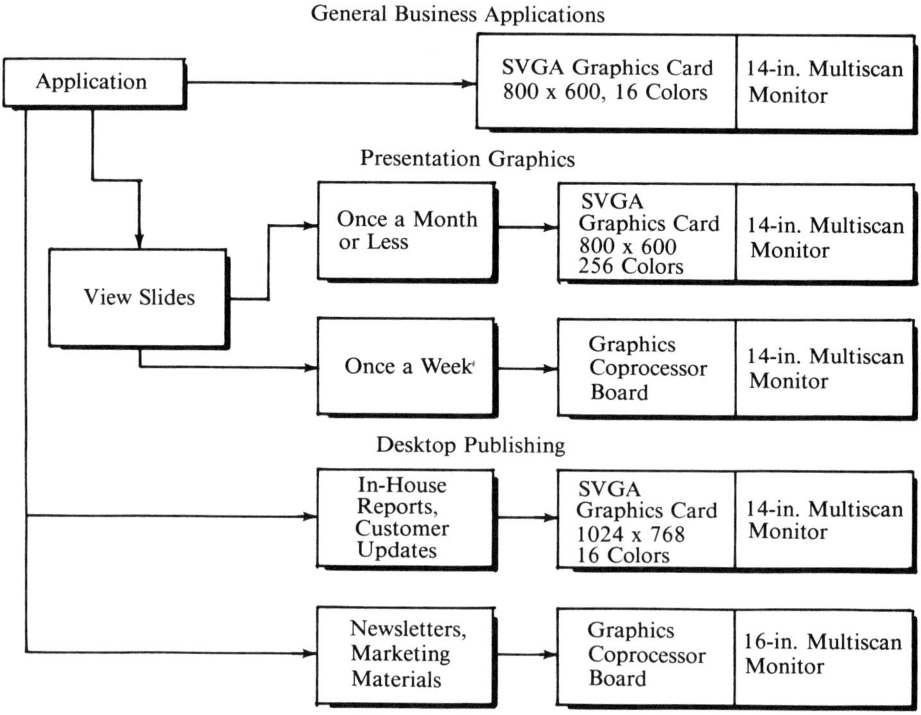

Figure 4-14 SVGA and graphics coprocessor applications

diagonally, and if you upgrade to a 16-inch monitor, you will improve the utility of the screen.

Graphics Coprocessor Boards. The IBM 8514/A was one of the first boards to offer resolution beyond standard VGA boards. The 1024 x 768 boards available today divide into two groups: the clones of IBM's 8514/A board, and the boards that use Texas Instruments' 34010 coprocessor. The 8514/A-compatible boards are less expensive than the 34010-based boards. Resolution, colors, and the ability to emulate VGA all affect the cost.

To run VGA software, you need VGA capability. Most graphics coprocessor boards have optional VGA modules or provide VGA pass-through—a feature that enables you to use the VGA you already have. Coprocessor boards generally provide a greater selection of drivers than SVGA boards do, but most of them are for desktop publishing and CAD applications.

If you plan to use Windows for everything, you do not need VGA capability. All you need is Windows compatibility, which many boards have. Outside of the Windows environment, more business software supports the 8514/A-based boards than the 34010.

Most graphics coprocessor boards drive noninterlaced monitors running at 1024 x 768, but a few will not interlace at this resolution. Some graphics-intensive applications will run up to 20 times faster on a graphics coprocessor board than on a VGA. The increase from 8514/A and 34010 boards depends upon the application. In some applications, the speed advantage of a graphics coprocessor board over a fast SVGA board is too small to justify the higher price. Most boards use video RAM (VRAM), which makes memory upgrades more expensive than they are with SVGA boards. Most boards have enough VRAM for 1024 x 768 at 16 colors (see Table 4-2).

TABLE 4-2 Graphics Coprocessor Boards

		VGA Colors—Interlaced/Noninterlaced		
Manufacturer/Model	VRAM	640 x 480	800 x 600	1024 x 768
Artist Graphics XJi	768K		256	256/256
ATI Tech. 8514/Ultra	1MB			256/256
Compaq Computer Advanced Graphics 1024	1MB	256		256/256
Desktop Computing AGA 1024	1MB	256	256	256/256
Hercules Computer Graphics Station	1MB	32000	256	256/256
Hewlett-Packard IGC10	512K	16	16	0/16
IBM 8514/A	1MB			256/0
Matrox MG-108	1MB	16		256/256
NEC MultiSync Graphics Engine	1MB	256	256	256/256
SOTA Technology 340i	1MB	256	256	256/256
Vectrix EX1280	1.28MB	256	256	256/256
Vermont Microsystems Cobra Plus	768K	256	256	256/256
Western Digital Imaging 8514/A Combo	1MB	16	16	256/256

Special Monitors

There are also monitors with high-resolution graphics for applications such as CAD. These monitors usually accommodate the monitor manufacturer's proprietary video system. If you use another video system, then it becomes important to match the monitor's sync characteristics with those of the video adapter. The following characteristics must match:

1. Vertical/horizontal sync frequency.
2. Analog/digital signal.
3. Sync polarity.
4. Color format.
5. Composite/separate sync.

Dual Display

Some adapters give you the ability to run two monitors at the same time, with different displays on each one. Some software packages, such as Lotus 1-2-3 and Symphony, support this feature. If you use a dual display adapter and run one of these packages, you can have a graph on a color monitor and simultaneous text on a monochrome monitor. You can type changes to the text on the monochrome monitor, and the graph on the color monitor will modify itself to show the changes.

Dual monitor support means the system supports two different types of monitors, while dual displays refers to the dual, simultaneous, independent display on two separate monitors.

IBM Compatibility

Many display adapters are compatible with several types of monitors. The graphics capabilities of a particular adapter include the resolution and the number of colors. These vary depending on what type of monitor you use and which display adapter you need to simulate. The capabilities of a particular monitor can be affected when you install other graphics display adapters in your system. The following shows the available IBM monitors and display adapters (prior to the PS/2) that are compatible. The characteristics of these monitors appear in the following sections.

- **5151 Monochrome Display (MD)**—use with the MDA.
- **5153 Color Display (CD)**—use with the CGA.
- **5154 Enhanced Color Display (ECD)**—use with the EGA.

Tables 4-3 and 4-4 show the compatible graphics and text modes that are possible.

Monochrome Display Monitor (5151). The IBM 5151 MD monitor and the IBM MDA are compatible. This monitor uses a screen refresh rate of 50 Hz (noninterlaced) and has a maximum bandwidth of 16.257 MHz. The MD monitor is TTL-compatible and uses a horizontal scan frequency of 18.432 kHz.

TABLE 4-3 Typical Graphics Modes (CGA/EGA)

Adapter	No. of Colors	Resolution (pixels)	Monitor
EGA	16/64*	640 x 350	ECD
EGA	16	640 x 200	CD/ECD
EGA	16	320 x 200	CD/ECD
EGA	4/64	640 x 350	ECD
EGA	2	640 x 350	MD
CGA	4	320 x 200	CD/ECD
CGA	2	320 x 200	CD/ECD
CGA	2	640 x 200	CD/ECD

*16 displayable colors from a 64-color palette; usually requires 256K of graphics memory on the adapter.

TABLE 4-4 Typical Text Modes (MDA/CGA/EGA)

Adapter	Number of Colors	Character Size (pixels)	Characters on Screen	Monitor
EGA	16/64*	8 x 14	80 x 25	ECD
EGA	16/64*	8 x 8	80 x 43	ECD
CGA/EGA	16	8 x 8	80 x 25	CD/ECD
CGA/EGA	16	8 x 8	40 x 25	CD/ECD
CGA/EGA	2	8 x 8	80 x 25	CD/ECD
CGA/EGA	2	8 x 8	40 x 25	CD/ECD
MDA/EGA	2	9 x 8	80 x 43	MD
MDA/EGA	2	9 x 14	80 x 25	MD

*16 displayable colors from a 64-color palette; usually requires 256K of graphics memory on the adapter.

Color Display Monitor (5153). The IBM 5153 CD monitor and the IBM CGA expansion board are compatible. This monitor can display 16 different colors by combining digital outputs of red, green, blue, and intensity values.

Monitors of this type are also called digital RGB monitors since they combine red, green, and blue hues to create color variations. The CD has a high-contrast black screen. There are many IBM-compatible RGB monitors, but some of the older monitors provide only 8 colors instead of 16. The maximum bandwidth for this type of monitor is 14.318 MHz, and the screen refresh rate is 60 Hz (noninterlaced). The monitor is TTL-compatible and uses a horizontal scan frequency of 15.750 kHz.

Enhanced Color Display Monitor (5154). The IBM 5154 ECD is compatible with the EGA. This type of monitor will usually support software written for either the EGA or the CGA. The ECD monitor has a screen refresh rate of 60 Hz, and the horizontal scan rate can be either 15.75 kHz or 21.850 kHz. This type of monitor can be considered to be an RGBI monitor since each color can be intensified.

If an adapter is compatible with an IBM standard like EGA, it will also be supported by the Virtual Device Interface (VDI) specification described by IBM and Graphics Software Systems (GSS). Software that is written for the VDI interface will run on most adapters with an EGA driver. Some, but not all, CGA software that runs on IBM's EGA will also run on other EGA adapters.

PS/2 Displays

The PS/2 displays have improved graphics support integrated into the system and display adapter. There are also improvements in resolution and color capabilities. There are double-scan 200-line modes available, as well as a palette of more than 256K colors. The following sections describe the monitor types used.

PS/2 Monochrome Display (8503). The PS/2 MD has an analog input signal with a display size of 12 inches (diagonal measurement). The display is white on black or black on white, with a palette of 64 shades of gray. You can get resolution modes of 720 x 400 text and 640 x 480 or 320 x 200 graphics. The monochrome mode uses an 8 x 16 character box, and the VGA mode uses a 9 x 16 character box. All modes use a 31.5-kHz horizontal scan frequency. The monitor is noninterlaced with up to a 70-Hz vertical refresh rate.

PS/2 Color Display (8512). This monitor also has an analog input signal, but the display size is 14 inches (diagonal). The palette contains 256 out of more than 256K colors. The resolution is 720 x 400 text and 640 x 480 or 320 x 200 graphics. The character size is 8 x 16 pixels for MCGA and 9 x 16 for VGA. All modes use a 31.5-kHz horizontal scan frequency. The monitor is noninterlaced with up to a 70-Hz vertical refresh rate. The display screen uses a 0.41-millimeter (mm) stripe format.

PS/2 Color Display (8513). This monitor has an analog input signal with a display size of 12 inches (diagonal). It has a color palette of 256 out of more than 256K colors. The resolution is 720 x 400 text and 640 x 480 or 320 x 200 graphics. MGCA uses an 8 x 16 character box, and VGA uses a 9 x 16 character box. All modes use a 31.5-kHz horizontal scan frequency. Operation is noninterlaced with up to a 70-Hz vertical refresh rate. It is compatible with the PS/2 Display Adapter 8514/A. The screen uses a 0.28-mm dot phosphor pitch.

PS/2 Color Display (8514). This is another analog monitor, but the display size is 16 inches (diagonal). The color palette is 256 out of more than 256K colors. If you use the 8514/A adapter, you can get 1024 x 768 graphics for all modes of the 8512 and 8513 displays. This resolution uses either a 12 x 20 character box to provide 85 columns x 38 rows or a 7 x 15 character box for 146 columns x 51 rows. A 35.5-kHz horizontal scan frequency is interlaced at a 43.5-Hz vertical refresh rate. The display screen uses a 0.31-mm dot phosphor pitch.

THE USE OF MULTIPLE DISPLAY ADAPTERS

Depending on your software applications, you may wish to use a new display adapter along with an existing display adapter. Most color adapters will only work with another display adapter if one adapter is operating in a color mode and the other is in a monochrome mode. For example, if a color adapter coexists with a CGA, then you must configure one color adapter in monochrome mode.

When two display adapters are connected, you must specify which adapter is primary and which is secondary. You do this through switch or software settings. The adapter that you designate as primary will be the adapter in use when you boot up your system. The secondary adapter will be inactive until it is activated through a DOS MODE command. For example, to switch over to a monochrome display adapter designated as secondary, you would enter the following command at the DOS prompt:

```
C> MODE MONO <Enter>
```

DETAILS OF DISPLAY OPERATION

During system power-up, one of the BIOS routines initializes and starts the CRT controller and tests the video read/write storage. In an XT system, the program causes the 8088 CPU to check the setting of the video switch SW1 by reading port A of the 8255 PPI. This port connects to the two configuration switches SW1 and SW2. The CPU logically ANDs the port data with the hex value 30H and thus checks the settings of switches SW1-5 and SW1-6. If they are not off, the program jumps to a subroutine that tests to see which type video card is installed. If SW1-5 and -6 are off, the program goes into an I/O memory parity test and then into setting the video mode. If a parity error occurs, a message appears. If a problem occurs setting the video mode, another error message appears.

The program will also test the video storage memory. If a failure exists, the speaker will beep. By reading the CRT-controller status port and logically ANDing the reading with binary 1000, the system makes a test to see if the video/horizontal line changes state. If it does not go low during this timed test, a timer clocks out and an error message appears and the speaker beeps.

In many newer systems, software stores the settings instead of hardware switches. The basic test procedure outlined above will be similar.

PROBLEMS DURING UPGRADING

If you experience problems during your upgrade, you can localize the problem to the display unit or the system board by connecting a good monitor with a good cable to the PC and rechecking the problem. If the problem disappears, then try the other display unit with the good cable. If this works, replace the cable. If it does not work, the problem is in the display unit.

If there is no video using the test monitor and cable and no cursor appears, check to see if there are any configuration switches on the system board. These switches configure the system for the particular type of monitor adapter that you are using.

You can also clean the pins and reinstall the adapter card. Sometimes not all of the pins make the proper contact, especially if you have moved the unit. On some of the older adapter cards, the bracket on the adapter must be grounded to the chassis for proper operation. Error code 501 will appear when there is a problem in the CGA card.

When problems occur on systems that have a monochrome display/printer adapter installed, you can do the same types of checks. Connect the system to a good monitor with a known good cable to eliminate the display unit and cable as the problem cause. A 401 error code will appear if there is a problem.

If there is no video, there may not be +5V on the adapter board. If there is no cursor on the screen, the problem could be the system board configuration switches. These are SW1 and SW2 in the IBM PC 5150. Both of these switches should be in the OFF position. A loose piece of wire or a piece of solder could cause a short, and one of these switches could appear to be on.

MONITOR AND VIDEO BOARD SPECIFICATIONS

Pitch is a measurement of the density of the pixels displayed on the screen. Color monitors refer to the *dot pitch* of the display, giving the measurement of the space between pixels, or the *stripe pitch*, which is the measurement between horizontal scans. These measurements are usually in millimeters.

The *horizontal scan frequency* is the rate at which the monitor updates the screen image. Higher horizontal scan frequencies correspond to higher screen resolutions. Monitors that have multiple scan frequencies or can multisync and lock in on a range of horizontal scan frequencies are compatible with multiple video standards.

LARGE-SCREEN MONITOR CHARACTERISTICS

When considering an upgrade to a large-screen monitor, it is important to understand a number of video characteristics that determine the quality and suitability of a large-screen monitor.

Screen *resolution* is a function of the pixel density (pixels per inch, discussed earlier) and the scan rate. The scan rate is a measure of the number of horizontal scan lines that the monitor draws each second. This is measured in kHz, with a better monitor having more than 30,000 lines per second or 30 kHz (a standard broadcast-television receiver has a value of 4.5 kHz, or 45,000 lines per second).

High-resolution monitors generally have more than 700,000 pixels displayable on the screen. You can determine the number of pixels by multiplying the horizontal and vertical pixel densities. A monitor with a 1024 x 768 resolution, for example, displays 768,432 pixels.

In general, desktop publishing applications benefit from a monitor that has a vertical resolution of 72 dots per inch (dpi) because there are 72 points to the printer's inch. This matched value provides a truer display of what screen images will look like when printed. A good indication of monitor resolution is the clarity of the characters along the edges of the screen.

The dpi measurement is a gauge of the number of pixels contained in one linear inch, either horizontally or vertically. The higher the dpi value, the greater the appearance of image sharpness, and the smaller the image will appear relative to the screen it was designed for, assuming that it was not originally designed for a high-resolution display. When the computer uses a 72-dpi screen display, then a large-screen monitor that also utilizes

72 dpi will maintain the same proportional relationship and provide a WYSIWYG (what-you-see-is-what-you-get) view. A monitor that has a greater dpi value than the computer system it supports will produce sharper screen images, but each image will be smaller.

FACTORS AFFECTING DISPLAY QUALITY

Flicker and Brightness

The refresh rate can be significant, since a refresh rate of less than 60 Hz will produce a visible flicker or movement. Screen flicker can be a real problem, resulting in eyestrain, headaches, and fatigue. It is best observed by viewing the screen from the corner of the eye, since peripheral vision is more sensitive to it. In general, a high-quality monitor will have a refresh rate of 63 to 66 Hz. Once you eliminate the problem of flicker, there is no need to increase the refresh rate.

Image clarity is a characteristic that has a number of elements. The spot, or pixel shape, should be square so that graphic images and typographic characters are properly rendered. When the pixel shape is not square, the images that are displayed will be distorted relative to the deviation from a true square. The pixel aspect ratio should be 1:1.

The spot size should be as small as possible to make the image sharp and clean. The screen should be free of electronic noise, which can appear as breaks or fuzzy images on the screen—this condition is similar to snow on a regular television set. You can get a good indication of acceptable clarity by drawing a large circle on the screen using a CAD or paint program. If the image clarity is good, the circle will be round and not oval. Also important in a desktop publishing environment is the display of small type, which should appear crisp and sharp.

The range-of-brightness setting on the monitor should be wide enough so that the setting is not on maximum for sufficient contrast and clarity. If you need to set your monitor on maximum brightness, it will generally have a reduced life. The range-of-brightness settings should be able to meet the direct and ambient lighting conditions normally encountered.

Linearity refers to the correct representation of lines, circles, and squares on any part of the entire screen surface. Lines should seem straight, circles round, and squares equilateral. Lines and shapes should maintain their character even when placed along an outer edge or corner of the screen.

The raster lines should be straight, and the screen edges should not be bowed. As images are moved around the screen, they should appear equally well in any area.

Phosphors and Glare

Phosphor is the chemical that determines the color of the screen and controls a number of screen characteristics. The quality of the phosphor determines the smallest-attainable spot size, the screen persistence (a measure of the screen's ability to redraw quickly with no ghosts), and the screen grain. You can check ghosting or smearing, which leaves an undesirable afterimage, by moving the cursor around rapidly. P104 Phosphor provides a high-quality white color that is pleasing to the eye. It is also efficient when comparing the light output against the power input.

Some studies have shown that a screen that uses black characters against a white background is easier to read and not fatiguing to the eye. Some monitors can switch to a reverse video screen that is activated through hardware or software control. The screen phosphor should be bluish-white, and the characters should appear black in reverse video.

Glare is due to the reflection of light onto the surface of the monitor screen from overhead illumination, outside windows, highly reflective surfaces, and other sources. Excessive glare can result in eyestrain and headaches. The better monitor screens have an antiglare coating applied during manufacture that not only reduces glare, but also results in improved screen contrast. An antiglare coating such as the OCLI HEA can reduce glare by a factor of 14. You can usually purchase antiglare screens as a monitor upgrade (Fig 4-15). Without any coating or screen filter the presence of glare will be noticed when the monitor is placed in certain light situations.

Software and Hardware Upgrades

You can enhance the utility of a monitor by adding software that dims or turns off the screen when it is not in use and by using tear-off menus that allow you to place all or part of the menu bar in a more convenient location. There are other utilities that can make your monitor functional. Chapter 10 discusses some of these software packages.

Hardware, such as a graphic input device with a high sampling rate, can reduce the time needed to move a cursor or other object on the screen. These devices are discussed in Chapter 6.

These software and hardware accessories must be compatible with your monitor.

Interlacing

Interlacing is the process of alternating the refresh rate of alternate horizontal lines. Interlaced screens produce flicker, and this can be a real

Figure 4-15 An antiglare screen for use with a monitor to reduce glare

distraction. They use a refresh rate of thirty times per second for every second raster line. Noninterlaced monitors are better, since they display all of the raster lines at a constant rate. A noninterlaced monitor will display a single thin, horizontal line as a steady image with no flicker.

Screen Flatness

Generally, the flatter the screen the better. Curved screens tend to produce more glare and distort the image. The curve of the screen is directly related to the amount of image distortion. Positioning identical images in the corners and the center of the screen will provide you with a good check of curvature distortion.

MONITORS FOR DESKTOP PUBLISHING AND CAD

Some desktop publishing and CAD applications may require the use of multiple monitors, of various types, on a single computer system. The three major types of large-screen monitors are monochrome, gray-scale, and color. Each has certain characteristics for specific types of desktop publishing and CAD work.

A large-screen monochrome monitor is an extended version of a standard computer monitor. Its major benefit is the increased viewing area.

Large-screen monochrome monitors are usually black and white, while standard computer monitors are often green and black or amber and black.

Large-screen monochrome monitors provide the same benefits as all large-screen displays. These include a greater surface area for the simultaneous display of multiple applications, full or multiple-level views, and visible details using close-up views. The display will generally have more utility.

A gray-scale monitor provides multiple gray levels for each pixel. This makes it possible to display more realistic photo-like images with better detail. A gray-scale monitor is useful in desktop publishing applications when you are working with different text fonts, since it displays the characters with better legibility compared to an equivalent-resolution color monitor. Typical applications include:

1. The display and alteration of gray-scale images.
2. The composition and layout of documents with gray-scale images.
3. 3-D solid modeling.

A color monitor can display all or a portion of the colors that the host computer can generate. Applications include:

1. The use of color to organize screen layouts or highlight selections, menu choices, and screen elements.
2. The specification and display of spot color, multiple flat colors, color graphics, and color photographs.
3. The creation, display, and manipulation of color graphics.
4. The display and manipulation of full-color photographic images.
5. The display and capture of real-time color video images.

Amdek

The AM/732+ is a PC-compatible color VGA monitor designed for color graphics applications. It provides crisp color images on a 14-inch maximum-resolution display. It is compatible with IBM's VGA and PS/2 MCGA standards and allows up to 256 simultaneous color variations with any VGA-compatible adapter.

Compaq

The Video Graphics Color Monitor from Compaq gives you the capability to display as many as 256 colors in 320 x 200 graphics resolution and

16 colors in 640 x 480 resolution. The Video Graphics Color Monitor uses a 14-inch (diagonal) antiglare screen and a fine dot pitch for more precise color graphic images.

Compaq also provides a Reduced Emissions VGA Monitor. It reduces extremely low-frequency (ELF) emissions, very low-frequency (VLF) emissions, and electrostatic potential on the face of the screen in compliance with the emissions recommendations of the Swedish MPR 1990 documents. This monitor has a 14-inch (diagonal) antiglare screen, 640 x 480 resolution, adjustable brightness and contrast, a tilt/swivel stand, and non-interlaced scanning. It supports up to 256 colors simultaneously for applications like graphics-based spreadsheets and presentation graphics.

Epson

Epson offers two VGA displays—a 12-inch monochrome model and a 14-inch extended color model. Both monitors have a tilt/swivel base as well as accessible power, contrast, and brightness controls. They use an etched, antiglare faceplate that reduces eyestrain and fatigue. Both monitors are compact units. Epson's monochrome and color monitors are compatible with other display software like MCGA, EGA, or CGA.

The 12-inch monochrome VGA monitor displays up to 64 gray shades with 640 x 480 resolution. It uses a paper-white screen to enhance viewing clarity in text and numerically based documents.

The 14-inch extended color VGA is for use with color-intensive graphics and design work. This multisync monitor provides up to 1024 x 768 resolution for detailed images. With this monitor, you can simultaneously display 256 different colors from a palette of 256,000. The multimode feature provides 5 user-selectable display resolutions. A 0.28-mm dot pitch helps the images look crisp and the colors vibrant.

NEC

MultiSync monitors offer sharp images as well as compatibility. NEC's MultiSync 2A color monitor works with VGA and SVGA (800 x 600). You can use the display images for presentation and business graphics. The 14-inch (diagonal), direct-etch screen provides maximum contrast and minimum glare. The analog input signal provides an unlimited palette of colors. The controls are in front for easy access to the most commonly made adjustments. A dedicated signal cable minimizes installation time. This monitor also has a tilt/swivel base.

The MultiSync 4DS color monitor has all the features of the MultiSync

4D monitor, and it incorporates reduced magnetic field (RMF) technology and an antistatic screen. NEC designed this monitor to address the potential concerns regarding the effects of magnetic fields. The 4DS also complies with MPR II ELF and VLF emission guidelines. The MultiSync 4DS monitor supports 1024 x 768 at 70-Hz refresh noninterlaced resolution.

The MultiSync 4DS monitor uses a dynamic-beam focus for clearer images on the entire screen. It also uses a microprocessor-based memory and digital controls to allow preset and custom graphics modes for automatic screen configuration.

The MultiSync 3DS 14-inch color monitor has 1024 x 768-pixel resolution with a 0.28-mm dot pitch. It uses RMF technology and an antistatic screen. It supports VGA, SVGA, 8514/A, XGA and extended video modes, including 132 column and terminal emulation. The digital controls that contain microprocessor-based memory eliminate the need to readjust controls each time you switch modes.

ADD-ON PRODUCTS

Hercules

Hercules started the PC video add-in industry and now offers a wide variety of graphics cards for your personal computer. The Hercules Graphics Station is a family of graphics adapters for the IBM PC that you can use with many types of analog monitors from inexpensive VGA screens up to high-performance, high-refresh monitors with 1024 x 768 noninterlaced resolution. You can enhance your existing VGA with a Hercules graphics station. This video card is a full-size adapter designed to fit into a 16-bit slot of an AT or compatible ISA bus 386/486 computer.

The Hercules graphics station models use 1MB of VRAM. If you need to run AutoCAD Release 11, AutoDesk 3D Studio, or Hercules art-department software, the graphics station +2 adds an extra 2MB of DRAM for more realistic color.

The Hercules graphics station MC provides 24-bit color and advanced graphics processing for the IBM PS/2 Micro Channel family. The 60-MHz TI 34010 processor can increase the PS/2's graphics speed and resolution beyond the capabilities of the on-board VGA. It gives you 24-bit color, resulting in realistic images in up to 16.7 million colors. Graphics station MC's VGA pass-through allows compatibility with your current VGA applications. The card comes with 1MB VRAM, and you can upgrade to 4MB or 8MB DRAM.

The Graphics Card Plus is a powerful monochrome video card. The

Hercules RamFont mode combines the speed of text display with the versatility of graphics display. Using WordPerfect 5.0 or 5.1, you can display more than 3,000 different characters with attributes, such as underline, overstrike, italics, and different sizes.

The Hercules VGA card is fully compatible with the IBM VGA. This graphics card works with each of the seventeen IBM standard video modes, including CGA and EGA, so all software for the IBM VGA runs identically on the Hercules VGA card. This card is easy to install and use since you do not have to install any software or set switches or jumpers.

Smoothing Graphics Boards

If you work with the small elements found in CAD or publishing files, graphics boards from ATI and Icon can be easier on your eyes. These boards use anti-aliasing methods to smooth the jagged edges out of curved and diagonal lines. ATI uses software fonts to smooth the edges, while Icon uses a special chip. The Icon board has more colors and better legibility, but the ATI 8514/Ultra board is faster.

ATI 8514/Ultra. The ATI 8514/Ultra board can anti-alias text under Windows 3.0, but not for DOS applications. ATI's Crystal Fonts make small text legible. The 8514/Ultra includes 13 PostScript fonts which take up about 30K per font. The board uses a proprietary graphics coprocessor to increase the speed of CAD applications, desktop publishing, and Windows. The 8514/Ultra includes both SVGA and 8514/A 1024 x 768 noninterlaced mode, which refreshes the screen one line at a time to reduce flicker.

Icon Photo Board. The Icon Photo Board is a VGA board that uses an Edsun Labs chip to reduce jagged edges on letters and graphics. It has 1MB of memory and will support a 1024 x 768 noninterlaced monitor with resolutions of 800 x 600 and 680 x 480. There are drivers for Windows 3.0, AutoCAD, Lotus 1-2-3, and Symphony. You can also use a 132-column driver for Lotus 1-2-3 and Symphony. The Icon Photo Board gives more color and greater legibility, but it is slower than the ATI 8514/Ultra.

SUMMARY OF MONITOR TYPES

Table 4-5 lists a sampling of monitors of different resolutions and screen sizes.

TABLE 4-5 Typical Monitors

Type	Manufacturer/ Model	Screen Size	Maximum Resolution	Scan Frequencies Horizontal	Vertical
Amber MDA	Packard Bell PB1272	12-in	720 x 350	18.43 kHz	50 Hz
	AOC International MM-411R	14-in	1000 x 900	18.43 kHz	47–63 Hz
Green MDA	Goldstar 2195G	12-in	720 x 350	18.43 kHz	50 Hz
	AOC International MM-411R	14-in	1000 x 900	18.43 kHz	47–63 Hz
	Samsung MA2571	12-in	720 x 350	18.43 kHz	50 Hz
	AOC International MM-411R	14-in	1000 x 900	18.43 kHz	47–63 Hz
Amber MDA/CGA	Packard Bell PB1472	14-in	720 x 350	15.75–18.43 kHz	50/60 Hz
	AOC International MM-411R	14-in	1000 x 900	15.75/18.43 kHz	47–63 Hz
Green MDA/CGA	Packard Bell PB1472	14-in	720 x 350	15.75–18.43 kHz	50/60 Hz
Paper-White MDA/CGA	AST Research Premium Monochrome	14-in	720 x 348	15.75/18.43 kHz	50/50 Hz
	AOD International MM-411R	14-in	1000 x 900	15.75/18.43 kHz	47–63 Hz
Amber MonoCGA	Magnavox BM7622	12-in	900 x 350	15.75 kHz	50 Hz
Green MonoCGA	Magnavox BM7652	12-in	900 x 350	15.75 kHz	50 Hz
Amber Monochrome Multisync	NEC Multisync GS/A	14-in	720 x 480	15.7/18.4/ 21.8	49.6/59.9/ 60.0
Green Monochrome Multisync	NEC Multisync GS/G	14-in	720 x 480	15.7/18.4/ 21.8	49.5/59.9/ 60.0
Paper-White Monochrome Multisync	NEC Multisync GS/W	14-in	720 x 480	15.7/18.4/ 21.8	49.5/59.9/ 60.0
Amber VGA	Hewlett-Packard Monochrome VGA/A	14-in	640 x 480	31.5 kHz	60–70 Hz
	AOC International MM-413	14-in	1000 x 900	31.5 kHz	50/60/70 Hz
Green VGA	Hewlett-Packard Monochrome VGA/G	14-in	640 x 480	31.5 kHz	60–70 Hz
	AOC International MM-413	14-in	1000 x 900	31.5 kHz	50/60/70 Hz
Paper-White VGA	Tatung MM-1233	12-in	640 x 480	31.5 kHz	50–70 Hz
	AOC International MM-413	14-in	1000 x 900	31.5 kHz	50/60/70 Hz

TABLE 4-5 Typical Monitors (cont'd)

Type	Manufacturer/ Model	Screen Size	Maximum Resolution	Scan Frequencies Horizontal	Vertical
Paper-White High-Resolution	Princeton MAX-15	14-in	1024 x 768	15–36 kHz	45–120 Hz
	Ventek PS2000	20-in	1280 x 1024	64 kHz	60–70 Hz
Paper-White Full-Page Display	Packard Bell PB1518DT	15-in	1006 x 1048	62.75 kHz	59.88 Hz
	Princeton LM-300	15-in	1200 x 1664	74.63 kHz	N/A
Paper-White System with PC/XT/AT-compatible video board	Micro Display System The Genius Plus	15-in	736 x 1008	62.76 kHz	60 Hz
	Moniterm Viking 2400/IBM PC	24-in	1280 x 960	66 kHz	N/A
Paper-White System with AT Video Board	Elite Business App	19-in	1280 x 1024	64 kHz	64 Hz
	NANAO Flexscan 6300	21-in	1664 x 1200	31.5, 48–55, 64–78 kHz	60–80 Hz
Paper-White System with PS/2 Micro Channel Video Board	Micro Display Genius MC	15-in	736 x 1008	62.76 kHz	60 Hz
CGA-Compatible	NANAO 7030H	12-in	640 x 200	15.75 kHz	49–61 Hz
	Princeton HX-12E	12-in	640 x 350	15.75/21.85 kHz	60 Hz
CGA/EGA-Compatible	AMDEK 722	13-in	640 x 350	15.75/21.85 kHz	60 Hz
	Princeton HX-9E	9-in	640 x 350	15.7/21.85 kHz	60 Hz
EGA/VGA-Compatible	AST Research	14-in	720 x 480	21.85/31.47 kHz	60/70 Hz
Multisync Monitors	Princeton UltraSync	12-in	800 x 600	15–35 kHz	45–120 Hz
	IDEK SpectraSync	15-in	800 x 600	15.75–37 kHz	50–90 Hz
VGA-Compatible	Princeton SR-12	12-in	640 x 400	31.5 kHz	60 Hz
	NEC Multisync 2A	14-in	800 x 600	31.5/35.2 kHz	56/60/70 Hz
High-Resolution	NEC MultiSync 30	14-in	1024 x 768	15.5–38 kHz	50–90 Hz
	Toshiba P20CU00	21-in	1280 x 1024	30–70 kHz	50–70 Hz

5

UPGRADING DISK DRIVES

Magnetic disks are the most popular method of storage for PCs. There are two types of disks used: floppy disks and hard disks. Both are similar in function, but different in their actual operational details.

FLOPPY DRIVES

The Floppy Disk

The 5.25-inch floppy disk (shown in Fig 5-1) is the standard drive in the IBM PC family. IBM introduced the 3.5-inch floppy disk with the PS/2 family, and it has some advantages. The smaller drives are more compact and rugged, and they represent the trend for future drives.

The actual disk is made of a flexible mylar material. It has a magnetic oxide coating and rotates in a plastic jacket (5.25-inch) or case (3.5-inch). There is a long opening in the jacket or case to provide access to the read/write head (Fig 5-2). The plastic case used to hold the 3.5-inch disk has a spring-loaded metal cover that also protects the media opening.

Spots, Tracks, and Sectors. If you strip away the protective case, a floppy disk looks like a small phonograph record. However, while a record uses grooves that a needle travels in to produce the vibrations that are converted into audio frequencies, computer disks are more like magnetic tape. The layer of magnetic iron oxide on the mylar disk allows

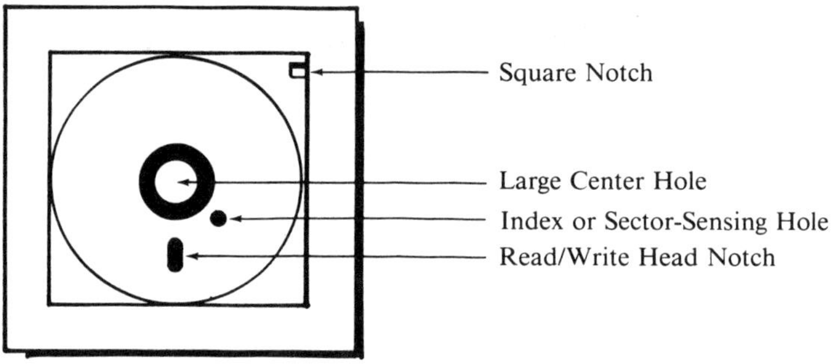

Figure 5-1 Overhead view of a 5.25-inch floppy disk

Figure 5-2 3.5-inch floppy disk with plastic case and spring-loaded metal cover for media read/write opening

microscopic spots to be magnetized in small spots on the coating. Each of the spots acts like a very small magnet. When a spot is magnetized, it can indicate a "true" or "one" state by fixing the magnetic poles in one direction. If the spots are magnetized in another direction, they can indicate a "false" or "zero" state and thus can be used to record digital data.

A line of spots becomes a track. A floppy disk might have 40 of these concentric tracks, the outside of which is usually numbered "0" and the inside of which is numbered "39" (Fig 5-3). The tracks do not form a continuous spiral like a phonograph record. Instead, each track is an isolated closed circle.

The disk is divided up like pieces of a pie into sections called sectors. There could be 10 sectors on each track, and each sector has its own address. With 40 tracks of 10 sectors each, there are the 400 sector addresses which are numbered 0–399.

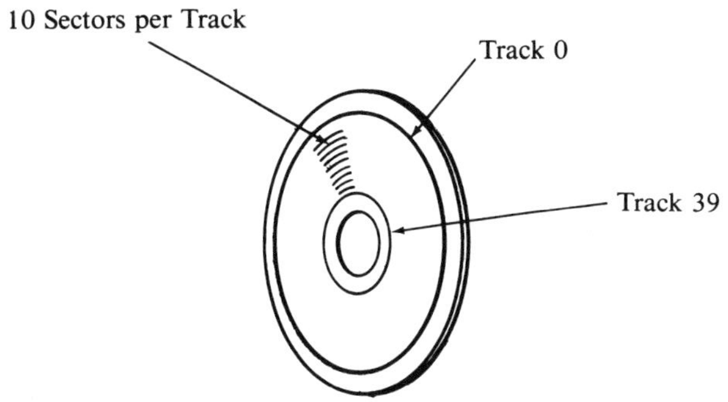

Figure 5-3 Tracks and sectors on a floppy disk

Disk Drives

The disk drive is the mechanical system that spins the disks and moves the magnetic recording head. It houses the mechanical components, along with the motors and the electronics required to control the rotation of the disk and access data (see Fig 5-4).

The drive is similar to a small record player in some ways, but it is much faster. When you place the disk in the drive, the mechanism starts rotating the disk to a specific speed, usually 300 revolutions per minute (rpm). (A hard disk usually rotates at ten times this speed.) Rotating at 300 rpm, the floppy disk moves at a spacing of about 30 microinches from the read/write magnetic head, which is positioned up and down the tracks. The disk head moves on a shaft between the outer and inner tracks of the disk. An indexing system allows the head to be accurately positioned over any of the 40 tracks. With the disk rotating at 300 rpm, the 10 sectors on each track pass under the head 5 times a second. The head positioning takes about a second to locate a sector.

The same head is used for read/write and erase. It is moved to the proper track by a positioning motor—usually a stepping motor. The jacket has an index hole, which is punched in the disk and marks the beginning of the first sector. A light-sensing circuit detects the hole.

Drive Operation. In addition to moving the head to the proper track, the drive must be able to perform either a read, write, or erase operation. It also has to generate or interpret control signals or status information for the computer, including index-hole detection, while turning the spindle motor at a constant speed. A read or write operation requires the drive to access the specified track and sector, and then it must transfer a block of data. Usually, a stepping motor positions the head,

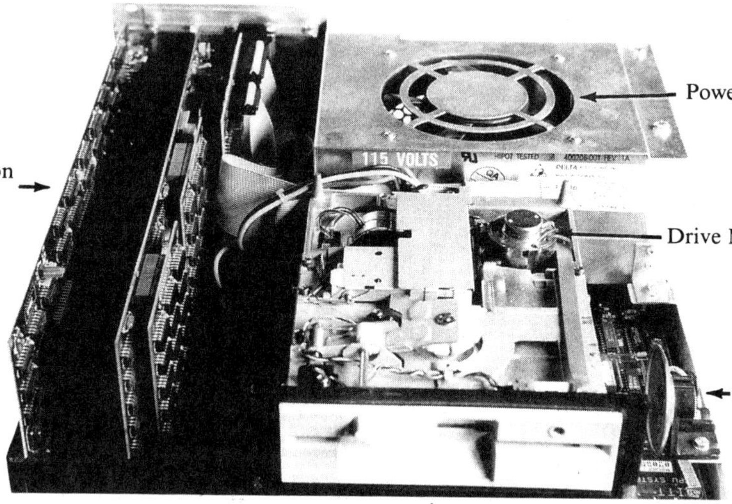

Figure 5-4 Floppy drive shown mounted in XT chassis

which takes 3 to 10 ms per step. A head-settling delay of 8 to 15 ms allows vibrations to die out.

The drive electronics verifies the head position by reading the coded track number on the disk and comparing it to a track-number register. It uses a direction signal to select the direction in which the head will be moved. Pulsing the stepping motor causes the actual motion. This pulse will move the head by one track position toward or away from the center of the disk.

Hard and Soft Sectoring. The drive issues a signal whenever a hole is sensed in the disk. There are two types of holes: an index hole and a sector hole. The index hole marks the beginning of the first sector on the disk.

A hard-sectored disk uses several holes to mark the beginning of every sector. Most personal computers, including the IBM family, use soft sectoring. In a soft-sectored disk, the drive issues one pulse per revolution at the beginning of a track. This is usually done every 200 ms. In a soft-sectored disk, a code identifies the sectors at the beginning of the data. This is called a header. The header uses up some of the data space, so less data can be stored compared to hard sectoring, but reliability and flexibility are better.

An index hole, detected by a photosensitive circuit, provides a pulse marking the beginning of the first sector. There is also a notch or hole on the protective disk cover that can be covered with a small tab or tape. An optical sensor in the drive detects whether the notch is covered. This protects the disk from accidental writing—if the notch is covered with a tab or tape, you will not be able to change the contents of the disk; you will only be able to read data from it.

Disk Formatting

Soft sectoring, then, begins the division of the disk or track into sectors. In hard sectoring, a series of holes in the disk (Fig 5-5) indicates the beginning of each sector. In a soft-sectored disk, each track is marked by a pulse that occurs relative to the detection of the index hole on the disk. This is done during the formatting operation.

A unique identifier marks each data record and gaps separate successive records. These gaps protect the following or the preceding data record. Because of speed variations in the disk-drive motor, when a record has all or some of its contents rewritten, the end of the record may extend beyond the previous record end. The gaps allow these overlaps without the loss of any data.

Magnetic Recording

Information records on the tracks of the disk in binary format. Usually, recording is done using an NRZ (nonreturn to zero) technique, and each bit position is magnetized in one direction (1) or the other (0). This is called NRZ because there is no intermediate state (or true zero). The basic modulation technique is FM (frequency modulation) encoding. Variations of the basic recording methods are used to increase the bit density.

Double-density disks use modified frequency modulation (MFM) or a variation of MFM to increase the recording density. Data on the disk is structured in bytes (groups of 8 bits). The system gives each block of information a marker. When the disk is first used, the system initializes or formats it with these markers. The drive controller (usually) uses serial-to-parallel conversion to assemble the bits into bytes.

Density. There are two methods of increasing the amount of information that can be stored on a floppy disk: dual heads and increased density. Dual heads read and write both sides of the floppy disk. This allows double-sided disks with double the capacity of single-sided disks. Double-density doubles the number of bits per track by using a packed recording technique, such as modified MFM (M2FM). M2FM encoding requires tighter tolerances for reliable operation and is less speed-tolerant

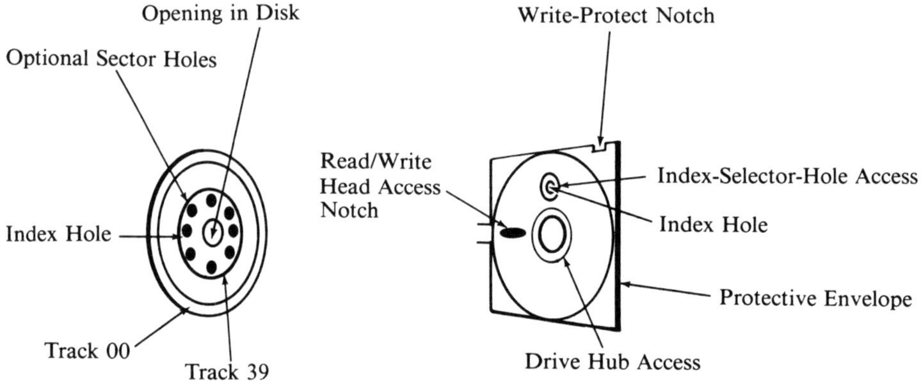

Hard-sectored 5.25-inch floppy disk.

Soft-sectored (single-hole) 5.25-inch floppy disk with protective envelope.

Figure 5-5 Floppy disk configurations

than regular FM encoding. The 360K disks used in the original PC are double-sided, double-density disks.

Double-Density versus High-Density. Many computer users get confused about the difference between double-density and high-density disks. The basic difference is in the size of the magnetic particles. The difference in particle sizes applies to both 5.25- and 3.5-inch disks.

The magnetic particles used in the coating of high-density media are smaller than those found in the double-density media. The smaller the particles, the more data bits will fit on the surface of the disk. The smaller particles allow the high-density disk to have a higher capacity to hold data. Since the particles are smaller, they emit a lower voltage or signal strength. To compensate for this lower voltage, the read/write head used on a high-density drive must be more sensitive so that it can read the signals accurately.

On a double-density disk, the magnetic particles are larger. These larger particles will send out a stronger voltage or signal strength. Therefore, the read/write head used in a double-density disk drive can be less sensitive than that found in a high-density drive.

You cannot use high-density disks in a low-density drive because the read/write heads will not be able to read the signals clearly. This can result in data errors, problems in retrieving the data, and/or the inability to format the disk properly. You can use low-density disks in a high-density drive if you format the disk properly, but you may have a problem reading a low-density disk (360K) in a 360K drive if it was formatted and written to in a high-density drive (1.2MB).

Future High-Density Trends. Increasing the storage capacity of floppy disks is simple in principle. You can either increase the amount of data stored on each track or increase the number of tracks. Double-density 5.25-inch diskettes use 40 tracks of data with nine 512-byte sectors per track, for a total capacity of 360K. A high-capacity disk like the 1.44MB 3.5-inch disk has 80 tracks and eighteen 512-byte sectors.

The larger number of tracks on the 1.44MB disk requires the tracks be placed closer together; and the larger amount of data in a single, smaller-circumference track results in the data bits being placed closer together. When you increase the data density, the magnetic head that reads the data must be positioned more accurately over a track. Positioning motors control accuracy. Also, since more data exists on the track, the "read" electronics need to process the data faster because more data moves by the read head in a given time. Increasing the data density reduces the signal from the magnetic material, and it becomes harder for the read electronics to detect the true and false states.

Most media manufacturers refer to an unformatted storage capacity, while drive manufacturers specify formatted capacity. A 1.44MB floppy disk has an unformatted capacity of 2MB. The newer 4MB disks have a formatted capacity of 2.88MB.

Higher-density disks (beyond 1.44MB floppy disks), manufactured by companies like Toshiba, use a different magnetic material. The floppy disk circle of mylar is coated with a thin layer of magnetic material. Typically, disks have a ferric-oxide coating, in which the magnetic particles are acicular (needle-shaped). These particles tend to lie flat so that the needles are in line with the mylar. To obtain the higher data density needed for 4MB disks, a different magnetic material, barium ferrite, is used. Barium ferrite particles are hexagonal platelets (thin hexagonal disks) that lie flat on the mylar.

When you encode data onto a ferric oxide-coated disk, the rod-like particles become magnetized along their length. One end of the rod becomes a north pole and the other a south pole. This is called longitudinal encoding (Fig 5-6).

When you encode data on a barium-ferrite-coated disk, the magnetization axis is *through* the pill-shaped particles rather than *across* them. An individual particle will have a north or south pole at the top and a south or north pole at the bottom. This is called perpendicular or vertical encoding (Fig 5-7).

The read head, which detects the magnetic information stored on the disk, passes over the surface. This head must be able to detect the transition between the areas where particles are magnetized in one direction and the areas where the particles are magnetized in the other direction. On a ferric-oxide disk, the transition area is not distinct since the particles may

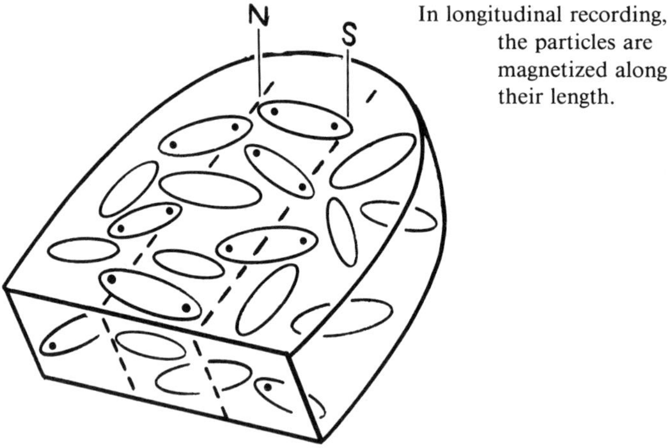

Figure 5-6 Ferric oxide-coated, low-density floppy disk

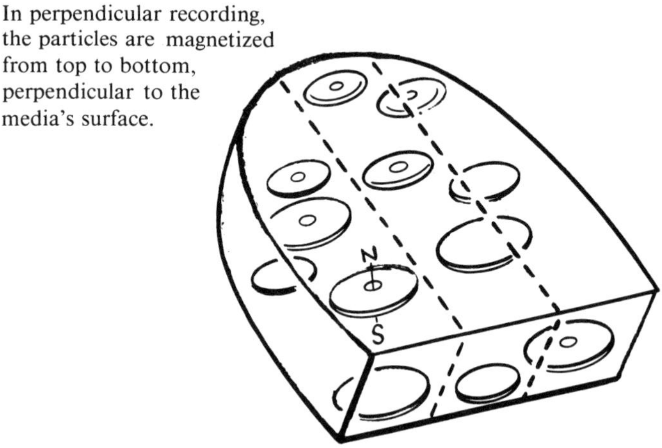

Figure 5-7 Barium ferrite-coated, 4MB floppy disk

lie in different directions. In a barium-ferrite disk, the distinction is much clearer, so the data density can be increased because the edges can still be detected. A 1.44MB floppy disk (ferric oxide) has a density of 17,434 bits per inch, while a barium-ferrite disk has almost double that—34,768 bits per inch.

By packing more data into a single track, the barium-ferrite disks have advanced the floppy disk. Some companies are building 2.88MB disks. Others have extended the technology further with better head-positioning accuracy. Using 4MB unformatted disks with different encoding methods, manufacturers have increased the disk's data capacity to about 20MB. These companies add additional information to the disk that allows the head to be positioned more accurately. They also increase the density by placing more tracks on disk. The manufacturer must precondition the disk prior to its use, which adds to the media cost.

Brier Technology uses a proprietary technology called Twin Tier Tracking to record two levels of information. The data level is on the surface, and a feedback-control layer is deeper into the media's surface.

Insite Technology provides track location information with small grooves that are carved in the disk's surface. An infrared light reflects off the disk, and the signal obtained from the light allows the head to be positioned more accurately, thus permitting a higher data density on the disk.

The disk drives that can read and support the 20MB of data do not allow downward compatibility, so you cannot read low-density disks (1.44MB and 720K) in the same drive.

Error Checking

Drives typically use a checksum technique for detecting errors when data is written on the disk. Cyclic-redundancy-checking (CRC) is one method of error checking. The drive uses special CRC bytes at the end of a group of data bytes and then divides the data bits using a special equation, usually a polynomial. The remainder from this division becomes the CRC bytes. When reading data from the disk, the drive checks the CRC bytes for errors. The floppy drive controller performs the CRC generation and checking.

Drive Controllers

The IBM PC and XT units use a drive-controller card that plugs into one of the expansion slots. The drive-controller card has a ribbon data cable that connects to the disk drive. A typical controller card can support four disk drives. Some XT-compatibles have a built-in controller on the main board. If you wish to upgrade your floppy disk drive from the standard 360K to a 1.2MB, you also will need to add a controller board. Most users prefer to add a high-density drive and keep the original 360K drive in place. This allows you to use both drives for loading your hard disk or storing files. You can also purchase 3.5-inch drive kits, enabling you to use 3.5-inch disks in addition to 5.25-inch disks. Sony, Teac, and Epson have upgrade kits available for both 5.25-inch (1.2MB) and 3.5-inch (1.44MB) disks.

Data Transfers

A DMA controller chip (Fig 5-8) on the main board typically controls the data that moves between the disk and the processor (data transfer operations). This chip controls the movement of data from the disk to computer memory, from the computer memory to the disk, and from one disk drive to another disk drive. When a disk drive needs to send data, it sends a signal to the DMA controller. The chip first sends back an acknowledge and inhibits the other I/O devices. Then the drive sends the starting address and the number of bytes to be transferred to the DMA controller. The data travels from the disk through the drive controller to the data bus and then into RAM. After the transfer is complete, control of the data bus returns to the processor.

The floppy drive controller converts data from serial-to-parallel format and from parallel-to-serial format. This matches the data bus in the computer with the disk drive. The data from the bus converts from parallel to serial and is conditioned for the format needed by the disk drive. When data is moving the other way, from the floppy disk to the computer, the bits must also be conditioned. The system uses sync bits on both ends of the actual data to minimize errors due to variations in the speed of the rotating disk.

Maintenance of Disk Drives

It is normal to have some contamination due to oxide buildup on floppy disks, caused by dust and other particles in the air. The distance between the disk runs and the read/write head is small enough to allow some of these oxides to collect on the head over a period of time. If enough oxide rubs off the disks and collects on the head, the drive will begin to make read or write errors. Eventually this can result in damage to the disks or the head.

You can clean the heads with isopropyl (rubbing) alcohol and a cotton swab. Try to use a lint-free material and apply the alcohol sparingly so that you do not wet any of the components around the head.

To clean the heads, you will have to remove the system unit cover and usually the head cover from the disk drive. Drive manufacturers use a number of methods to cover or protect the head assembly. It helps to make some notes on how the cover is assembled before you remove it. Once you have access to the head, then you can clean the oxides off. When the head appears to be clean, let the area dry completely before you reassemble the head cover and the system unit.

You can also use a head-cleaning disk (Fig 5-9), which is easier. There is a special cleaning solvent on this disk designed to clean the head. You insert the cleaning disk into the disk drive and allow it to turn. The turning

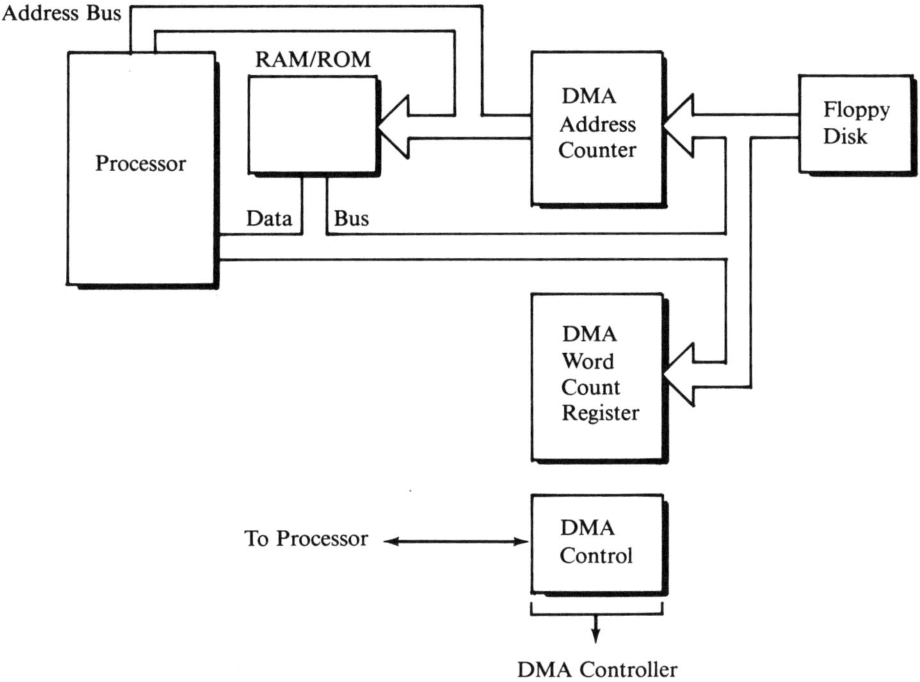

Figure 5-8 A DMA controller (used to transfer data between the hard disk and the processor)

motion of the drive rubs some of the solvent material against the head, and the disk is cleaned.

Floppy Drive Adjustments

Floppy drives are vital to your system. Other than a modem or a network, floppy disks are usually the only way you can exchange data between your computer and the outside world. Like other mechanical components, these drives may need adjustments.

In much the same way that a VCR player can develop tracking problems and display a fuzzy picture on the screen, floppy disks can be out of alignment, making the data difficult to read. The symptoms of a misaligned drive or other mechanical problems are easy to overlook and problems can go unnoticed for long periods of time. This is because a misaligned drive may have no trouble reading data *it* wrote, but it may have trouble installing commercial software or reading disks from another computer. Conversely, other computer drives can have a hard time reading disks written by the misaligned drive.

Figure 5-9 A head-cleaning disk with cleaning solvent (Run it through the floppy drive to clean it.)

DOS tries to read data from a floppy disk several times before giving up. If you notice your drive taking longer to copy files or being more noisy than usual, this can indicate read problems.

Most people back up their hard drives with floppy disks, and they assume that they can restore their data when needed. If you back up with a faulty drive and then try to restore the data, some of your data may be lost. You may only discover this problem after you send the computer in for repairs and attempt a restore on a different drive. If the two drives differ significantly in their alignment, your backup may be unreadable.

It is also a common practice to copy and exchange data files. If the two drives being used are not properly aligned or if the drive speeds are not compatible, the data may be unreadable. You may also have trouble loading someone else's software on your system. These are all signs of an alignment or other mechanical problem. Typically you would see a message like:

```
Data Error Reading Drive A:

Abort, Retry, Fail ? -
```

and

```
Not Ready Reading Drive A:

Abort, Retry, Fail ? -
```

Sometimes these messages appear because of bad media, but other common reasons are head alignment and rotational speed (rpm).

There are programs that you can use to test the mechanical operation of your floppy disk drives. Some use a special minispiral disk to measure the operating characteristics of the drive and then compare them to the drive specifications. The test program will measure how well the drive is aligned and report how far it is out of normal alignment. If one drive is within the tolerance but on the low end, while another drive is within tolerance but on the high end of the specification, you may have trouble exchanging files between these two drives. Therefore, it is best to keep all drives as close to the standard as possible. If your drive is out of alignment, you can have it adjusted. You usually do not need to replace the drive because of an alignment problem.

Floppy disks spin like records to either read or write data on them. Disks that are formatted on a drive that is too fast or too slow may produce a "Drive Not Ready" message on other drives. You can test how fast the drive is spinning. The normal values are: 300 rpm (+/−5 rpm) for 360K, 720K, and 1.44MB disks; and 360 rpm (+/−5 rpm) for 1.2MB disks. You can have a drive that is out of tolerance adjusted (see Fig 5-10).

The location of track 0 is also important since it determines the areas your drive can read. Problems with this include failure to boot from floppy disks or trouble with formatting new disks. These problems can usually be cured by adjusting.

Problems can also occur if the disk is not centered. When you insert a disk and close the door, the center of the disk is grabbed by a mechanism that is supposed to center the disk. If this does not happen, the tracks written on the disk will not be true. Then, when you insert the disk again, the data may be difficult to read unless the disk is inserted in the same way. This usually means a worn clamping mechanism, and the drive must be replaced.

Hysteresis measures the drive's ability to move from one track to another and to be exactly in the center of the track. If this alignment problem exists, it means there is some physical play in the drive's read/write head mechanism.

HARD DRIVES

Hard drives are similar in concept to floppy disk systems. The main difference is the disks (also called platters) themselves, which are made of aluminum instead of plastic. These aluminum disks have a coating of magnetic particles similar to floppy disks, but, since they are more rigid, the drive speed can be much greater (about ten times that of a floppy). The magnetic particles are also much closer which allows more data on a hard disk compared to a floppy.

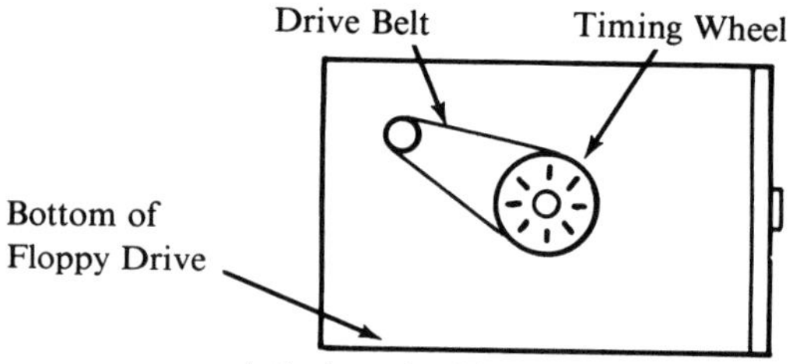

A timing wheel is located on the bottom of some disk drives.

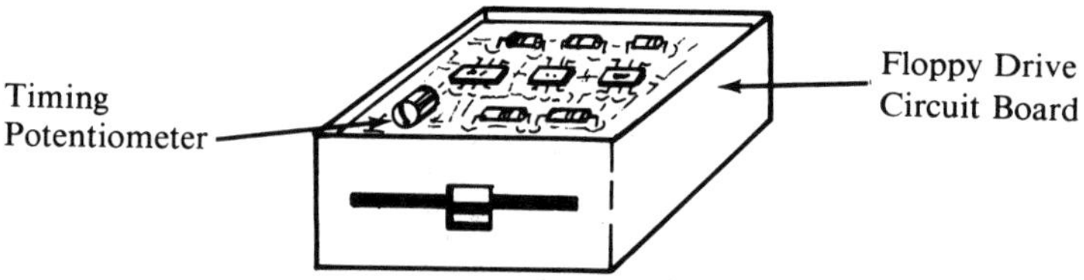

To adjust the timing, you will need a diagnostic disk and a 60-Hz timing light (ordinary fluorescent light) to sync or stop the pattern.

Figure 5-10 Adjusting a floppy drive

We generally use the term *media* to refer to the type of surface that coats the surface of the hard disk platters. Current technologies include oxide media and thin-film media, as well as the newer glass media drives.

Because the speed is much higher with the rigid aluminum disks, the heads must be much closer for read/write operations (Fig 5-11). The drive assembly (Fig 5-12) is sealed to prevent dust from getting between the heads and the disk. Thus, the disk is fixed (hard drives are also called fixed disk drives). The form factor of a drive is its physical size. A 5.25-inch disk is 5.25 inches wide, and a 3.5-inch disk is 3.5 inches wide.

A hard drive includes the actual drive mechanism which turns the disks and supporting parts (Fig 5-13). There are usually several disks,

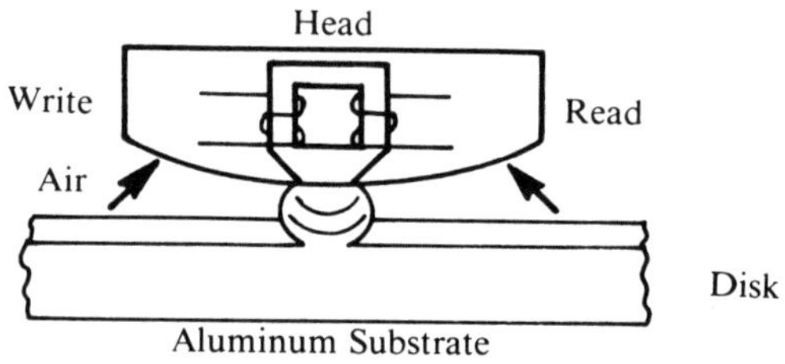

Figure 5-11 Typical flying head used in hard drive (Note the head is above the magnetic surface and separated by a thin air cushion.)

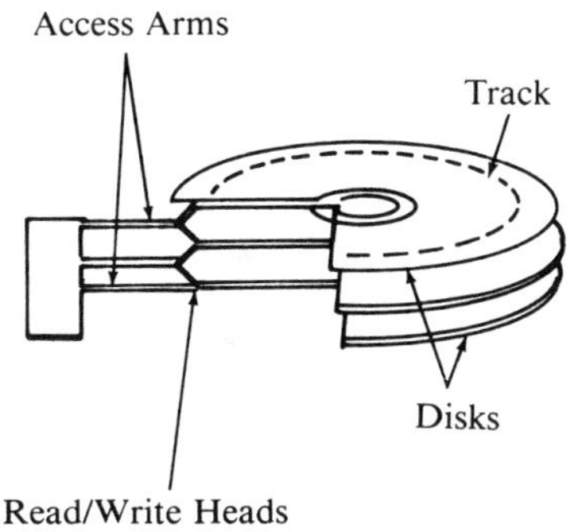

Figure 5-12 Sealed components of hard drive, showing the use of several disks and heads

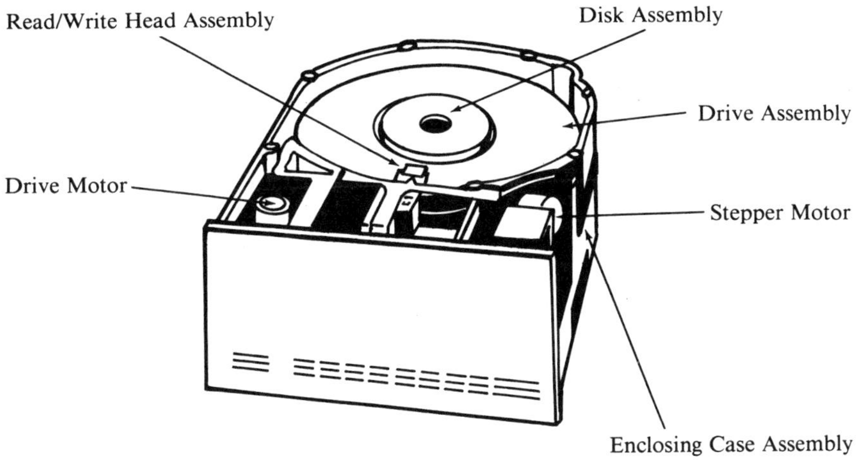

Figure 5-13 Typical hard drive

except for very small drives, and each disk has its own read/write heads. The drive mechanism holds the spinning disks and the read/write heads, which are sealed in a metal enclosure. There is also a circuit board to transfer data between the read/write heads and the drive's connectors (Fig 5-14) and a drive controller or adapter to interface with the PC bus. Figure 5-15 shows the power cable, and Figure 5-16 shows the power connector. The number of heads used depends on the number of platter surfaces that are used to record the actual data.

The actuator mechanism in the hard drive positions the drive head, moving the head to a specific track of data. Some manufacturers use one or two surfaces to record information that the drive uses to position a stepper motor. Voice-coil actuation is generally faster than a stepper-motor actua-

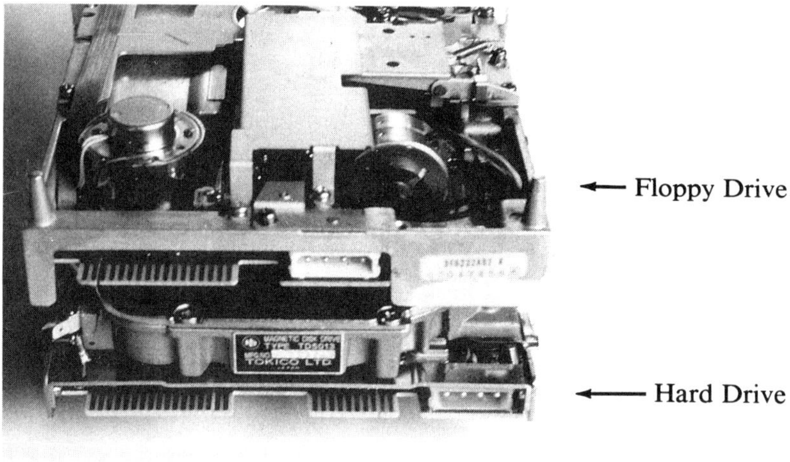

Figure 5-14 Drive connectors (Rear view of floppy and hard drives, showing connector pins and sealed hard-drive construction. Note that the hard drive takes both a data connector and a control connector.)

tor. A voice-coil actuator can quickly move the head to the desired location, while a stepper motor steps from track to track to get to a specific track. The track-to-track speed is the minimum access time in milliseconds that it takes the drive head to move from one track to the next adjacent track of data. The average access time of the drive is the average amount of time in milliseconds that it takes the disk drive to locate a track of data. Average access time is an indicator of the overall performance of the drive and is calculated by averaging the speed of every possible combination of head seeks.

Cylinders and Tracks

The number of cylinders in a drive refers to the number of tracks per data surface. Think of cylinders as the cross section of the tracks on each platter. You can use this information, along with the number of heads, to determine the drive type when formatting a drive for use on a PC. Some AT-compatible computers have a table of compatible drives that are listed in their BIOS chips. To install a drive, you must match up that drive's specifications to a specific number listed in the drive-type table.

Drive Capacity

The first consideration in any hard drive is capacity. A good rule is to buy a drive large enough to meet your needs for the next few years. Hard

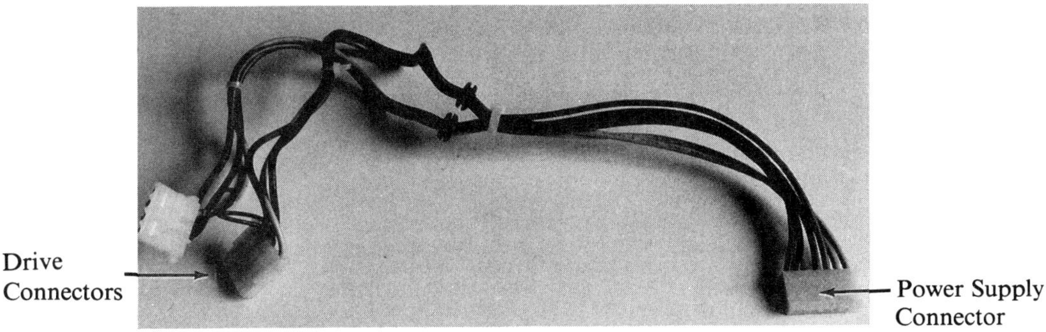

Figure 5-15 Power cable for drives

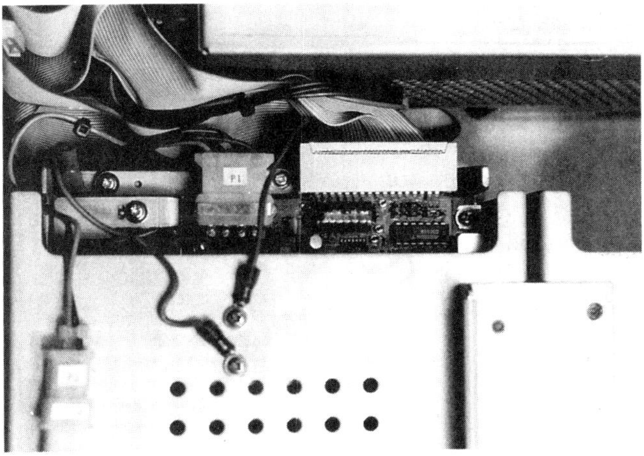

Figure 5-16 Rear view of floppy drive installed in AT system

drives can wear out, and the additional capacity you will need in two years' time should be less expensive than it is now.

If you have outgrown a 30MB or even an 80MB hard disk faster than expected, you can find drives in the 330MB or 410MB range. Graphic artists, desktop publishers, and others who work with a lot of large files may need drives in the 600MB range. A network manager should consider drives of 660MB and above.

The unformatted capacity of the hard disk represents the base storage capacity of the disk before it is formatted for use with a particular computer. The formatted capacity represents the capacity in megabytes of the hard disk after it has been formatted for use. The final formatted capacity can vary slightly due to differences in format structure.

The number of sectors per track that the drive formats will also vary.

Some higher-capacity drives, such as ESDI drives, allow you to vary this number slightly (and thereby change the capacity slightly). ESDI formats the drive at high-density (usually 35 sectors per track or higher) and is used on high-capacity drives.

Although it is a common practice to infer a drive's capacity from its model number, this is not always accurate. The model number and the formatted capacity are often close, and the difference between the two may only be a few percentage points. Sometimes the capacity is greater, as with BFP 8 640MB, which may format to 645MB. Sometimes it is less, as with the BFP 8 600MB, which may format to 584.7MB. Occasionally, the formatted capacity is significantly different from what you would expect. For example, BJK 410 might format to 345.8MB.

Data Formats

MFM was the original method of formatting data for use on hard drives. The MFM format uses 17 sectors per track with a data transfer rate of 5Mb per second and the Seagate ST-506 interface. The ST-506 interface, which is also known as the ST-506/412 interface, was developed by Seagate Technology and first used on the Seagate ST-412 drive.

RLL (run length limited) is an enhanced version of the MFM format that uses 25 or 26 sectors per track, which increases the capacity of a drive by 50%. The data transfer rate of an RLL-formatted drive is 7.5Mb per second. Like MFM drives, RLL-formatted drives use the ST-506 interface. Table 5-1 lists some typical hard disk drives with different interfaces.

TABLE 5-1 Typical Hard Drives

Size/Interface/Model	Formatted Capacity (MB)	Disks	Heads	Average Access Speed (ms)
2.5-inch				
No interface				
Areal MD 2050	50.2	1	2	<29
Areal BP-200	200	1	2	<29
PC XT/AT interface				
PrairieTek Prairie220	20	2	4	28
PrairieTek Prairie240	42.8	2	4	28
3.5-inch				
ESDI interface				
Brand BT91221E	100	3	5	16.5
Brand BT9220E	200	5	9	16.5

PC AT interface				
CMS LDNECMS-20	20	2	4	28
Quantum ProDrive 210AT	210	4	7	15
PC XT interface				
Seagate ST325X	21.4	2	4	45
Western Digital WD93048-X	43.2	2	4	70
SCSI interface				
Seagate ST325N	21.4	2	4	45
Hitachi DK312C-25	251	6	11	20
ST-506 (MFM format) interface				
CMS K20M25/30-OK	21.4	2	4	62
Seagate Swift 94355-100	83	5	9	16.5
ST-506 (RLL format) interface				
Seagate ST137R	32.7	2	4	40
Seagate Swift 94355-150	128	5	9	16.5
5.25-inch full-height				
ESDI interface				
Core HC40	40	2	4	9
Micropolis 1518-15	1,051	8	15	14
SCSI interface				
Micropolis 1373	72	3	4	23
Micropolis 1528-15	1,396	8	15	14
ST-506 (MFM format) interface				
Core AT 30	31.9	3	5	21
Priam 519	169.2	6	11	22
ST-506 (RLL format) interface				
Core AT30	48.7	3	5	21
Priam 519	244.4	6	11	22
5.25-inch half-height				
ESDI interface				
Core HC90	91	3	5	16
PC AT interface				
Comport 2041	43.7	2	4	29

SCSI interface				
Seagate ST224N	21.2	1	2	70
Micropolis 1684-7	340	4	7	14
ST-506 (MFM format) interface				
CMS HD20AT-S	21.4	2	4	65
Microscience HH-1090	80.1	4	7	28
ST-506 (RLL format) interface				
Seagate ST225R	21.17	1	2	70
Microscience HH-1120	122.4	4	7	28

Interleave

You can achieve a performance by adjusting your disk's interleave. Interleaving involves the method of storing data on a hard disk. If it is set up correctly, you can get a faster, more efficient transfer of information between computer and disk. To check or change your disk's interleave, you can use an interleave-adjustment utility program.

The disk's interleave ratio is a measure of how efficient the data is being read and transferred from disk to CPU. An interleave of 1:1 indicates that one sector is read and transferred for each sector that passes under the drive's read/write head. This is the ideal setting, resulting in the faster transfer of data.

Not all disk/controller/CPU combinations operate at this ratio. It takes time to read and transfer the data in the first sector, and the second sector may have passed by the read/write head before this is completed. Any further data transfer is held up until the disk makes a complete rotation and the second sector is again under the read/write head. This does not seem to be a large delay since the typical hard disk rotates 60 times a second, but in a computer it can be costly in terms of time.

With a 2:1 interleave, 2 sectors will pass by the read/write head for each sector read. The drive can read a full 17 sectors with two rotations of the disk. A slower system with a 3:1 interleave stores data in every third sector. The hard disk's interleave is programmed during low-level formatting, which places the markers that the operating system uses to keep track of stored data.

Most computer systems are fast enough to handle 1:1 interleaves, but not all hard disks are formatted that way. If your hard disk is not transferring information as efficiently as it could, you can use disk-utility software to check and modify the disk interleave. These programs run a series of tests to determine the best interleave. The program reads each disk track into memory, reformats the track with the new interleave, and returns the data to the hard disk. Changing the interleave can improve performance, but be sure to back up your hard disk before you begin.

Disk Crashes and Utilities

When the head of a hard drive touches the moving disk, you can lose the data on this portion of the disk. This is called a hard disk crash. You can use software known as *disk utilities* to recover data after a crash occurs. Disk utilities can also restore a disk when you have accidentally deleted a file or cross-linked files in the same clusters. However, they cannot rebuild a destroyed master boot record or get data back after a hardware problem. If this occurs and you do not have a backup of the data, or if the backup system fails along with the drive, an outside service can often recover data from a crashed disk.

Utilities like PC Tools (Fig 5-17) can also help after you have deleted files and want to bring them back. The reason a utility can do this is because, when DOS gets a command to delete a file, it does not actually erase the data off the disk. Instead, it changes the first letter of the file's name in the directory to a special symbol. Then, when you call for the file by its original name, the operating system will not recognize it. A utility program with an "unerase" or "undelete" function will prompt you for the deleted file name. It will then find it on the disk and rename it so it can be accessed.

The file access table (FAT) stored by DOS shows the way the files are arranged on the disk. When a disk is accidentally reformatted, the FAT is erased. Some utilities make a copy of the FAT, as well as other important

Figure 5-17 Disk utilities software (e.g., PC Tools) used for data recovery and disk optimization

information (such as bindery and trustee rights for a NetWare-formatted disk), and store it at the back of the disk. Reformatting does not erase this copy, and you can update the original FAT from the copy.

Disk Fragmentation. Most disk utilities allow you to defragment your disk. When DOS writes data to a disk, it will not always put parts of the same file in adjacent sectors. The process usually starts from the outside of the disk and moves inward. When you erase a file, DOS fills up the spaces that the erasure creates by moving in a section of a new file. This causes the fragmentation of files, and it takes the disk heads longer to read a file since they must take extra passes over the disk surface while they are reading the different fragments of the file.

Defragmenting reorganizes the disk surface so that parts of the same file are in adjacent sectors, which saves time when that file is read. Defragmenting also provides another benefit—you can more easily recover accidentally deleted files if they have previously been stored on disk in contiguous clusters.

Rather than using a defragmenting utility to straighten out the disk, you can back up your disk on tape, reformat the disk, and restore the data to the disk. As DOS sends the files to the tape, it collects the bytes for each file from their different locations on the disk and sends the file whole. When the system copies this data back onto the disk, it comes off the tape in whole files. This way, it returns to the disk with all the bytes belonging to individual files in adjacent sectors.

When you use disk utilities, you should always make a complete backup of the disk before you even put the utility software disk in. It gives you some insurance even when the software vendor guarantees (and not all of them do) that the program will not damage your data. If you lose power to the computer while doing the defragmentation, you could permanently lose your data.

Norton. You can use Advanced Norton Utilities 4.0 for file recovery and to provide system information (Fig 5-18). Like all DOS-based disk utilities, it will not work on a NetWare server disk, but you can use it with DOS-based network operating systems like 3Com's 3+. Norton Utilities runs from a command program (the Norton Integrator), which also provides on-line help for each utility.

The advanced version of Norton has a program called Speed Disk that rearranges the logical structure of the disk and that you can use to optimize the seek time and improve disk performance.

There is also a Format Recover utility that you can use to unformat an accidentally reformatted hard disk. A special maintenance mode intended

Figure 5-18 The Norton Utilities, with erase protection and recovery from accidental reformatting

for badly damaged disks, it bypasses the DOS logical organization to work at the cluster or sector level.

The program has a File Allocation Table Editor and Partition Table Editor for adding and removing partitions. There is a Directory Editor as well as an Absolute Sector mode for absolute physical sector access and verification.

Golden Bow. In this set of disk utilities, Vopt is a disk organizer package that allows you to defragment files. You can also use it for benchmark timing checks and system maintenance like flagging bad clusters. Vcache is a disk-caching program that you can use to cache up to 15MB of hard disk data in RAM. Since it is a write-through cache, all written data is recorded immediately onto the hard disk. Unlike a RAM disk, you will not lose your changes if the power is interrupted. Another utility called Vfeature Deluxe allows hard disk partitioning for large, bootable DOS partitions (up to a gigabyte). It supports nonstandard drives and can span two drives into a partition. It also does the formatting and has some security features. There is also a set of tools (Vtools) available for displaying, sorting, and deleting directories and files.

Mace. This program has three utilities for disk operations: Recovery, HotRod, and dbFix. Recovery is an unformat utility designed to be used if you accidentally reformat your disk. It saves a copy of the index tables. If the DOS index tables get deleted during an accidental format, you can use this very copy to restore the tables. Even if you have not installed Mace before an accidental format, you can still use the program to restore those files not in the root directory that are relatively continuous on the disk. If the data is in subdirectories, you can retrieve the names of the subdirectories from the names of the files in them. The program uses the DOS CD command to move to the subdirectories. Then you can use the Undelete command to restore the deleted files. HotRod is a defragmenting and cache utility for speeding up disk operations. It will also sort your files, providing RAM with faster response. The utility dbFix is for users of dBase, FoxBase, and Clipper. You can locate, repair, and recover files that are lost, unreadable, corrupted, or overwritten.

Hard Drive Trends

Recent years have seen many developments in the hard drive industry. A wide range of new products have come on the market that are smaller, faster, and better.

In the small drive arena, Areal Technology and PrairieTek have introduced 2.5-inch drives. PrairieTek's drives have an embedded IBM XT/AT-compatible hard drive controller with 20MB and 40MB capacities available. Areals' 2.5-inch drives use a single glass disk and are available with capacities of 50MB to 200MB.

In 1989, the 3.5-inch drive overtook the 5.25-inch in unit sales. There were 11 million 3.5-inch drives sold versus 8 million 5.25-inch drives. Most of these drives were in the 30–60MB range. Most new drives introduced by manufacturers use the 3.5-inch format. By using the smaller size, manufacturers are able to reduce production costs and still meet the 5.25-inch slot demand with brackets that mount a 3.5-inch drive in a 5.25-inch drive bay.

On the upper end of the capacity spectrum—over 100MBs—the 5.25-inch drive is still popular. Unless your application requires a 3.5-inch form factor, such as in a laptop or PS/2 model, the cost of the 5.25-inch technology is less than the 3.5-inch technology at higher capacities. Networks and multiuser systems always keep growing, which means greater amounts of storage. Drives with capacities of over a gigabyte are available in the 5.25-inch size.

The mechanism determines the drive's most important characteristics: capacity and speed. Drive mechanisms are available from Fujitsu, Hitachi, Hewlett-Packard, Maxtor, Micropolis, Quantum, Seagate, and Western Digital. Seagate has been a major source for PCs. Most vendors use only one mechanism for a given hard drive model; others may use different drive mechanisms at different times. Imprimis was a subdivision of Control Data Corporation that was purchased by Seagate in 1989, and Wren is one of Seagate's product lines. When one of these names appears in a hard drive's model name, the mechanism inside is from Seagate. Manufacturers also use model-name suffixes such as I (for Imprimis) and WD (for Western Digital).

Hard Drive Expansion Decisions

A hard disk is the biggest performance booster you can give to any MS-DOS-based machine. Most modern programs require one.

Choosing a hard drive is not an easy task. There are many different models, but there are a few things that you should look for. If you have an AT or a fast XT (1-MHz or better), you should get a drive with an access time of 28 ms or less. Slower machines can use 40-ms drives.

Generally, buy the largest hard disk you can afford. No matter how many megabytes of storage you have, you can run out. Even if you are good about cleaning out old files, modern software gobbles up disk space. You can easily fill a 20MB hard disk with three or four of today's programs. Table 5-1 shows a cross section of the types of drives that are available.

Adding Drives/Hard Cards. If you already have a hard drive, you can add another one. Most computers can handle two drives without problems. However, you may want to replace your current drive, since newer hard drives are bigger, faster, and cheaper.

You may hesitate to install a hard drive yourself, although it is not a difficult job. If you want an easier option, although a more expensive one, you may want to add a hard card to your system. All you have to do is find an empty slot in the PC and insert the card.

Plus Development makes hard cards that are more expensive than some others, but they are also faster. The Hardcard II 40 and 80 hold 40MB and 80MB of data. They can access this information at speeds below 28 ms. An advantage of these cards is that they will take up only one slot in your computer. Other hard cards require a little more space than a single slot due to the large size of their disk packages.

Quantum designed and manufactures the Impulse family. These cards are offered in 52–425MB sizes with effective access times as fast as 8 ms. An on-board disk cache can increase throughput as much as 50%. A special defect-free interface eliminates the need for defect mapping, and a patented airlock feature automatically locks the heads in a nondata landing zone for data integrity.

You can use the AT Series drives to build up 286, 386, and 486 AT-compatibles. The drives use an integrated controller that connects directly to a 40-pin connector on the motherboard or to a separate adapter. The AT Series ISA-150A is a 16-bit floppy/hard disk adapter. It can control two hard drives and two floppy drives.

Data Compression. This allows you to squeeze more information into the same disk. There are two ways of using data compression to get more room on your disk. The first is to use a program like PKZIP. This is a shareware program that is available on on-line services and bulletin-board systems. There are also companies that will sell you disks containing PKZIP and similar programs. You still have to pay the developer if you decide to use the programs, but they are generally inexpensive.

These programs work by taking your files and encoding them in a space-saving format. PKZIP can shrink a file down to about 50–66% of its original size. It works best on database files and spreadsheets. You cannot use these files while they are in their crushed-down state, and it takes a few minutes to restore them to full size when you need them. These programs are useful for storing files that you may need someday or software packages that you do not need every day.

A problem with data-compression programs is they are often difficult to use. However, there is some compression software that is designed for easier use. Two examples (also available on-line) are SHEZ and ArcMaster.

A second way of using data compression that is easier and faster is now becoming available. Boards and disks with dedicated data-compression chips allow you to pack your disks with half again as much information as you can now store. Previous products in this area did not live up to expectations. The newer generation of data-compression chips comes from companies like InfoChip Systems and Stac Electronics. These chips should be able to provide fast, transparent data compression.

A hard disk can fill up fast, and it may benefit you to install a data-compression card instead of deleting files you might need someday or installing a larger, expensive drive. These cards can increase your hard disk capacity up to three times its original capacity. Cards are available for DOS 3.1, 3.2, 3.3, 4.01, and 5.0 and Compaq DOS 3.31. Some even include disk caching.

Data-compression cards are easy to use. They plug into any open slot in your system, and the intercepts call to and from the drive controllers. You select the drives or disk partitions to be compressed or decompressed. These cards work with all types of storage devices, including hard disks, floppies, and RAM disks. They also offer data integrity—the information is decompressed without any changes. A directory displays uncompressed and compressed file sizes, along with each file's compression ratio. You can buy Micro Channel cards for IBM PS/2 models 50 and higher.

Buffers and Caches. A buffer on a disk drive or hard drive controller is RAM that stores the most recent information read off the hard drive. A memory cache is an intelligent buffer that is able to analyze the accesses to the hard drive. It will read data from the drive that the computer is likely to request. The hit-rate of a cache system is the percentage of times that the data the controller finds what it is looking for in RAM instead of having to read the data from the hard disk. Since transferring data from RAM is faster than reading data off the disk, this can greatly increase the speed of a hard drive system. The data transfer rate is the speed, measured in bits per second, that the drive transfers data to the computer system memory.

Adding Cache Memory. Getting more storage is only part of upgrading. You will also want more speed, and one way to improve speed is to use a disk cache. Any hard disk will perform better with a cache.

No matter what you do to speed up a disk, you still have moving parts. A mechanical system cannot compete with an electronic circuit. Caches put frequently used information into memory, where it can be found in a fraction of the time it takes to find it on a disk. Caching with disk-intensive programs like database managers can reduce the time spent reading and writing to disk by 90%.

There are two basic ways you can add caching to your computer. The first is to add a caching drive controller to your system. These controllers are more expensive, but they take care of managing the hard drive, and their dedicated RAM holds the most frequently used data for quick accessing.

The SmartCache controller from Distributed Processing Technology is an example of a full-length card. Any AT-compatible system with ESDI, MFM, or RLL hard drives will get a good performance boost with this controller, which comes with 512K of memory. Programs like dBase IV will run much faster with this card. If half a megabyte of cache is not enough, you can attach 2MB or 4MB daughter-cards to the main card. With the additional RAM, you can even run Windows 3.0 at a reasonable clip.

The second way to add caching is to use software caching, which has almost the same benefits as a caching drive controller. There are some basic caching tools in DOS. The Buffers parameter in the CONFIG.SYS file stores data in 512-byte sections. If you set

```
Buffers = 10
```

you are making a small cache of 5K.

If you have MS-DOS 3.3 or above, you can get a performance boost from Fastopen. It uses CONFIG.SYS to store the location of the most recently used directories in RAM, which makes changing directories faster. The increase in speed is not large, but it helps.

While the DOS commands can help, commercial caching programs are better at improving disk I/O. Multisoft's Super PC-Kwik and Golden Bow's Vcache will use either expanded, extended, or conventional memory. These programs are easy to use and provide high speeds from your drive. They will use some of the 640K of conventional memory.

RAM Disks. This involves using a program like the MS-DOS VDISK.SYS or RAMDRIVE.SYS, which makes a section of memory act like a disk drive. This is different from a cache in that a cache speeds up data moving to and from a hard disk. In a RAM disk, all the information stays in high-speed RAM as if it were on a disk. You would not want to keep an important spreadsheet in a RAM disk, since a momentary power failure would erase it.

You could put application programs or at least parts of them on a RAM disk. For instance, WordStar, like many other early programs, came in several parts, including a main program and other sections called overlay files. The overlays contain routines that are not used as often as the main program. To save memory, it is normal to leave these procedures on disk until you need them. By putting these files on a RAM disk, you can speed up WordStar by 200–300%. Other programs show similar increases using the same scheme.

If you have room for a large RAM disk of several megabytes, you can load entire programs into RAM. Quattro Pro, a Borland spreadsheet, performs well used in this way.

Intelligent Drives

There is a trend toward drives with hard drive controllers integrated directly into the electronics of the drive itself. You can connect these intelligent drives with a ribbon cable directly to the AT or XT bus of the computer, eliminating the need for a hard drive controller. By integrating the controller into the drive itself, manufacturers are offering simpler installation, since there are no problems with hard drive/controller compatibility. These trends are shown in Table 5-2.

SCSI Drives. The small computer systems interface is a hard disk interface that differs from conventional interfaces in that it is intelligent. Rather than requiring a hard drive controller to control the drive, SCSI drives require a host adapter that allows the computer to send commands to the drive. A SCSI drive contains an instruction set of commands, and up to seven SCSI devices can be used on a single computer.

SCSI (pronounced "scuzzy") is a standard for hard drives. This intro-

TABLE 5-2 Drive Interface Evolution

	Market Share (%)			
	1988	1990	1992	1994
ST506/412	60	40	20	10
Embedded AT	15	25	35	40
ESDI	5	10	10	10
SCSI	20	25	35	40

duction to SCSI will help you realize its usefulness. SCSI refers to the way peripherals are connected to the computer system and how they communicate with the system. It is often lumped together with other hard disk interfaces, but it is more than a simple hard disk interface.

SCSI provides a common bus for many types of peripherals, like CD-ROMs, optical memory devices, modems, and printers. The common bus lets you connect up to seven peripherals to one port on the back of the PC.

Some SCSI systems let you install additional internal hard drives into your system, giving you the option of several large storage devices. An SCSI hard disk drive system gives you high performance and automatic error correction. You also get an external port that allows daisy chaining of up to seven peripherals.

Usually when you connect peripherals to your system, you need controller boards for each device. A CD-ROM drive, a modem, and a printer would require three controller boards and three available expansion slots inside your PC. You also would have to be sure that each of these devices is compatible with your system and with each other. Any time you deal with multiple controller boards in the system, there are possible conflicts.

SCSI does away with the one board for one device requirement. With a SCSI interface, you need only one board, called a host adapter, from which you can connect the SCSI bus to the system bus. The peripherals attached to the SCSI must also be SCSI peripherals.

An SCSI hard drive provides some useful advantages, including the following:

1. It supports wide range of peripherals—disk drives of all sizes, capacities, performance; $\frac{1}{4}$-inch or $\frac{1}{2}$-inch tape, cartridge, reel, or DAT; optical disk, CD-ROM, and others.
2. Hardware/software is standard at the peripheral bus.
3. It is intelligent—allows block transfers.
4. It has a high data transfer rate range.
5. It has a parallel data path.

6. It allows connection of up to seven devices/adapters.
7. It coresides with MFM, IDE, and ESDI controllers.
8. It reduces system cost.

Most hard drives map the media defects out of the usable disk space, and, when the disk is installed in a system, the defects are recorded so the disk does not use this area. SCSI disk drives have the added ability to handle media defects that occur while operating. When the disk develops a bad sector, the drive will prevent data from being written to that sector and redirect the data to another location on the disk.

SCSI and ESDI. SCSI hard drives are a little like the enhanced small device interface. ESDI is only for hard disk drives. It does not allow the linking of different types of peripheral to one common controller board. ESDI allows two hard disks to run from the same controller. With a SCSI hard drive, bad sectors on the disk are skipped automatically. In ESDI, the drive manufacturer identifies the bad-sector locations, and the user runs a software program (which is compatible with the ESDI controller) to manage the bad sectors.

Most large-capacity drives are SCSI devices that attach to the PC's SCSI connector using an SCSI cable supplied with the drive. The other SCSI connector on the drive allows you to make a chain of SCSI devices. You can also use other SCSI peripherals, such as scanners and CD-ROM drives.

SCSI devices that are connected in a chain require termination and SCSI ID numbers. Termination refers to the need for a special resistor, called a terminator, at both the beginning and the end of a SCSI chain. Many drives have this resistor built into the internal electronics—they are "internally terminated." If you have two or more SCSI peripherals connected to a PC, you can attach an internally terminated drive only at the beginning or end of the chain. If your PC has an internal hard drive, you can attach an internally terminated drive only at the end of the chain. Some drives use a separate terminator plug that you attach to one of the drive's SCSI connectors. Other drives allow you to turn the internal termination on and off with a switch.

External and switchable termination is more flexible, and a switch is a little more convenient, since there is no terminator plug to lose.

In addition to proper termination, every peripheral on a SCSI chain must have an ID number, and no two peripherals can have the same number. You can set the SCSI ID number with a thumb switch or a rotary dial, a DIP switch, jumpers (usually metal prongs that are covered with a plastic sleeve), or through software. Switches are the most convenient, and you will find them on most large-capacity drives. You can usually override the SCSI ID setting with the utility software provided with some drives.

In the past, SCSI command sets have been given different interpretations and implementations, resulting in one manufacturer's device not being recognized by another's interface card. Both IBM and Compaq entered the SCSI market after many of these different implementations were in use.

Problem Areas. There are several areas to consider in using SCSI devices. Be aware that there are differences among the host adapters. The driver software must be able to support both the host adapter and the target device. Some manufacturers do not provide SCSI host adapters with their devices, and not all host adapters may work with the device. Other manufacturers provide host adapters with the SCSI devices they sell, which eliminates any compatibility problems.

You may need different SCSI commands for each target device, even if the target device and host adapter are the same types of products, like two hard drives manufactured by different vendors. This is the job of the device driver. It should be able to use the proper SCSI commands to operate the target device.

Outside of some potential configuration problems, you as the user will generally experience only the benefits of SCSI devices. They typically offer higher performance and reliability. The complexity of the interface is handled by the device driver, which either resides on the host adapter or is installed as part of the set-up procedure.

The main difference with SCSI is that the code necessary to control a device is moved out of the host, and an interface is established that is not hardware-specific. Before SCSI, most devices required a separate dedicated host controller. It was possible to find a controller that could be used with more than one device of the same type, but communication between a tape and a disk with only one host adapter was difficult or impossible. The device drivers in the host had to be able to coordinate their activity in such a way so that they did not conflict with each other. This was usually possible only when the hardware and software for the devices came from the same vendor.

SCSI makes it possible to have devices connected to the same adapter card that are not only of different types but are also from different vendors. The industry needs a standard or convention that allows the tape and disk software to coordinate their activity and use the adapter concurrently. Otherwise, we could have a situation where a disk and a tape are connected to the same adapter, but you cannot back up the disk on that tape because the tape and the disk software cannot be active at the same time.

Makers of host adapters provide several conventions. Adaptec uses a software product that works with its cards called ASPI (Advanced SCSI

Programming Interface). Columbia Data Products developed software for cards made by Western Digital called SDLP (Standard Device Level Protocol). These companies developed these products to resolve the conflict of more than one program needing to have access to the same card concurrently. When using ASPI or SDLP, the drivers for the disk or tape do not access the hardware directly. They communicate with an ASPI or SDLP driver, which coordinates requests and resolves any conflicts.

The Common Access Method (CAM) provides a more universal standard. This specification allows the same independence and flexibility as ASPI and SDLP, but it does it at the level of an industry-wide standard.

SCSI drives for the PC cost more to install due to the additional cost of the SCSI interface. In the 30–60MB range, the lowest-cost solution is MFM or RLL ST-506 technology in a drive kit, or a drive with an integrated controller. The Apple Macintosh is an exception, being completely SCSI due to the built-in SCSI type of interfaces on Macintosh computers. SCSI offers the easiest plug-in installation, when executed properly.

SCSI Adapters. The DTC3180 and DTC3280 from Data Technology are SCSI host adapters designed to increase the overall performance and connectivity of AT-compatible computers. These host adapters allow you to install up to seven additional SCSI peripherals using a single expansion slot. They will increase your performance about four times over standard AT hard drives.

These adapters use the SCSI specification and support the Common Command Set (CCS). They use dual 128-byte buffers to allow concurrent data transfers on the host bus and the SCSI bus.

The DTC3180 and DTC3280 have an on-board BIOS that supports bootable devices and automatically configures the system upon power-up. This eliminates the need to run a configuration program or add a driver each time an additional SCSI device is attached to the host adapter.

These adapters support up to seven SCSI devices and up to four 5.25-inch and 3.5-inch floppy disks. They can coreside with hard disk controllers and support removable hard disks.

The adapter board size is 3.8 inches x 6.0 inches. It uses 50-pin Centronics connectors. The current at +5 VDC is typically 0.58 amps.

Adaptec also offers adapters that provide a connection between the AT bus and SCSI bus. A typical kit includes:

1. An AT-to-SCSI host adapter with floppy controller.
2. A DOS software manager for support up to seven SCSI devices.
3. An OS/2 software manager.
4. Novell NetWare 386 and 286 software managers.

The data transfer rate is 2MB per second asynchronous on the SCSI bus and 5–10 MB per second on the AT bus.

Other kits are available from manufacturers such as Toshiba, Storage Dimensions, and Micropolis for Novell networks. These kits include the hard drive, controller, and driver software for installation. Many of these kits are drives packaged with a SCSI hard drive controller. These controllers come with the software drivers to install almost any SCSI drive for Novell applications. Another product for Novell hard drive installation is Disk Manager-N from OnTrack Computer Systems. This program replaces the Novell Compsurf program and allows a variety of drives to be formatted for use in Novell networks.

The SCSI Bus. The SCSI bus allows modular additions of peripherals using a single SCSI interface board. SCSI is the American National Standards Institute (ANSI) standard X3T9 for a peripheral bus and command set. It is also a high-performance peripheral interface permitting data to be distributed among peripherals independently of the CPU. This frees the CPU for more user-oriented activities.

The SCSI bus has 50 pins and 18 signals. An 8-bit data bus with parity uses 9 signals, and the other 9 signals coordinate device data transfers (see Table 5-3). Using a special I/O bus for a peripheral interface is new to PCs. An interface normally connects only two devices, as in the RS-232C, since it allows only one sender and one receiver to be connected. The SCSI bus is architecturally similar to computer buses in terms of signal organization, multiple-master capability, and operational phases.

Expanding with SCSI. The SCSI bus allows you to expand when you have reached the maximum capability of your initial system configuration. The key to using the SCSI bus as a basis for expansion is the realization that the scheme is cost-effective and easily implemented. It uses only one card slot, and the SCSI bus specification includes generic commands for specific peripheral devices. The intelligent SCSI controller allows peripheral-to-peripheral transfers without operating system involvement.

When purchased, a standard IBM PC configuration typically has 640K of memory, floppy and hard drives, a clock, and extended memory card, color monitor, keyboard, and printer. In a typical application such as word processing with a growing database, four or five card slots may already be occupied, allowing only one for expansion (Fig 5-19).

There is a progression in a typical PC user's needs as database and other applications increase. After using the system as purchased over a period of time, the user determines that the database exceeds the use of the connected hard drives and, if another hard drive subsystem is added, it will require use of the last remaining expansion slot. The SCSI bus and

TABLE 5-3 SCSI Bus Signals and Pin Assignments

Signal		Pin	Signal*		Pin
DBO	DATA BUS 0	2		GROUND	30
DB1	DATA BUS 1	4	ATN	ATTENTION	32
DB2	DATA BUS 2	6		GROUND	34
DB3	DATA BUS 3	8	BSY	BUSY	36
DB4	DATA BUS 4	10	ACK	ACKNOWLEDGE	38
DB5	DATA BUS 5	12	RST	RESET	40
DB6	DATA BUS 6	14	MSG	MESSAGE	42
DB7	DATA BUS 7	16	SEL	SELECT	44
DBP	BUS PARITY	18	CD	CMD DATA	46
	GROUND	20	REQ	REQUEST	48
	GROUND	22	I/O	I/O	50
	GROUND	24			
	TERM PWR	26	Reserved for optional terminator power (+5 volts)		

*Signal definitions:
ATN—Attention indicates initiator has message to send to target.
BSY—Busy acknowledges bus is busy.
ACK—Acknowledge with request complete asynchronous handshake for data bus transfers.
RST—Reset clears all activity on bus.
MSG—Message indicates bus is in message-transfer phase.
SEL—Select used during device selection phase.
CD—Command/Data defines type of information on bus—command/status or data.
REQ—Request with ACK, completes asynchronous handshake for data bus transfers.
I/O—Input/Output indicates data-flow direction on bus.

intelligent-peripherals approach allows the user to add another mass-storage subsystem using a SCSI bus controller in that expansion slot (Fig 5-20). However, this does not limit system expansion but, in fact, opens new paths for future growth. Installation of the SCSI bus controller and initial disk drive simplifies future expansion by giving the user two ports located at the rear of the drive. One port is used for the SCSI-IN cable, and the other is for the SCSI-OUT cable. The user can then add any peripheral device compatible with the SCSI bus controller with daisy-chained cables.

By going to the SCSI bus controller, the user gains the ability to integrate the entire database onto a single drive. When a backup system is required, the user can add an intelligent $\frac{1}{4}$-inch cartridge streaming tape system without the additional purchase of an expansion chassis or a tape controller, because the tape subsystem is daisy chained off the hard drive (Fig 5-21).

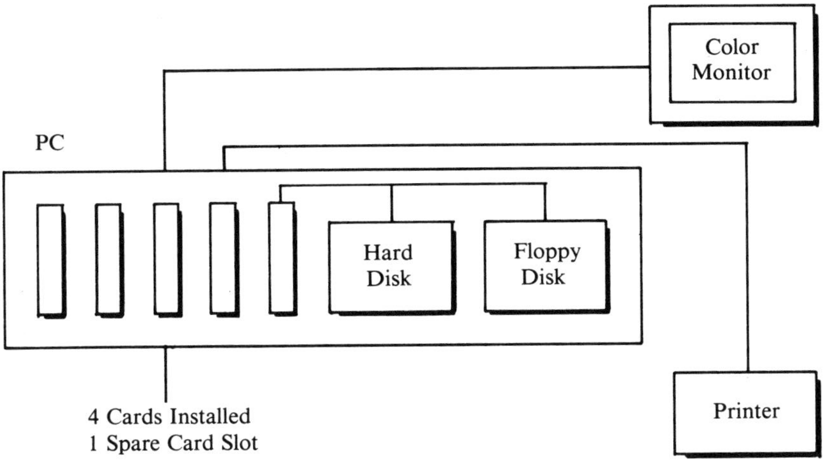

Figure 5-19 Typical P.C application—word processing with small database

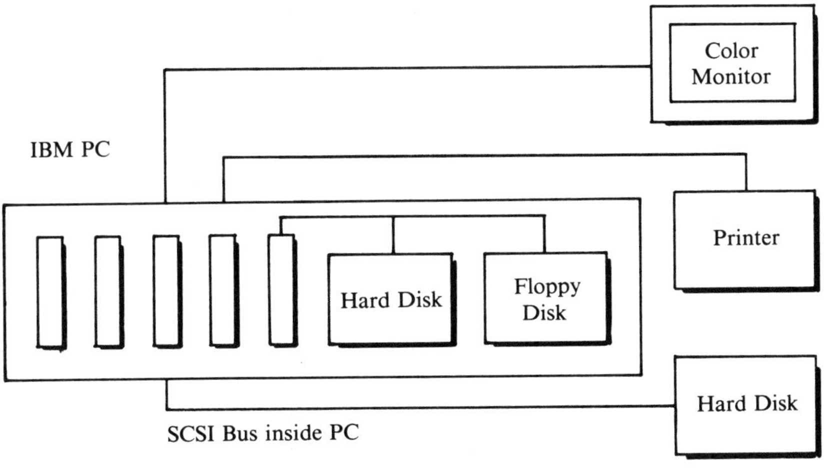

Figure 5-20 Hard disk installed on SCSI bus

Once the user has selected SCSI and has added additional mass storage, a $\frac{1}{4}$-inch cartridge tape subsystem can be integrated for convenient disk backup without the purchase of an additional expansion chassis or tape controller.

As applications multiply and the user's database grows, there is now a basis for additional expansion in any of the following directions: intelligent printer, additional tape subsystem, or greater mass data storage. The user can expand the system on an as-required basis through the use of the SCSI

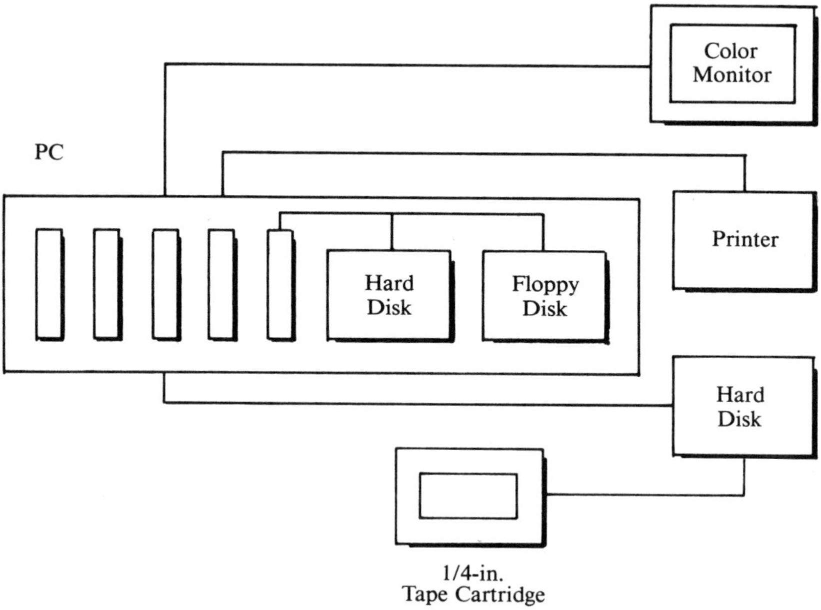

Figure 5-21 Adding a ¼-inch cartridge tape subsystem

bus scheme by daisy chaining additional devices (Fig 5-22). Each master device provides connection for up to a total of eight slave devices.

SCSI and the PC Bus. In a typical XT consisting of a 640K memory, floppy and hard drives, clock and extended memory card, monitor, and printer, four of the five backplane slots can be occupied. When the user outgrows this basic configuration and decides to expand using the SCSI bus and intelligent-peripherals approach, the SCSI bus controller becomes the controller for additional mass storage when it is installed in the remaining card slot.

Although SCSI and the PC backplane (internal bus) are both computer buses, their objectives differ. Backplane buses provide for transfers between different expansion module types with many functions and varying levels of intelligence. The SCSI bus specializes in bulk data transfers between peripherals and hosts. Since all SCSI bus devices are similar, the SCSI specification allows a response capability from each device using an independent command set.

When using the SCSI bus, the user needs to incorporate only one connection to the internal PC bus to handle all the system's peripheral devices. Increased system performance is obtained by using the SCSI standard, which has a 1.5MB per second data-transfer rate. At the core of this

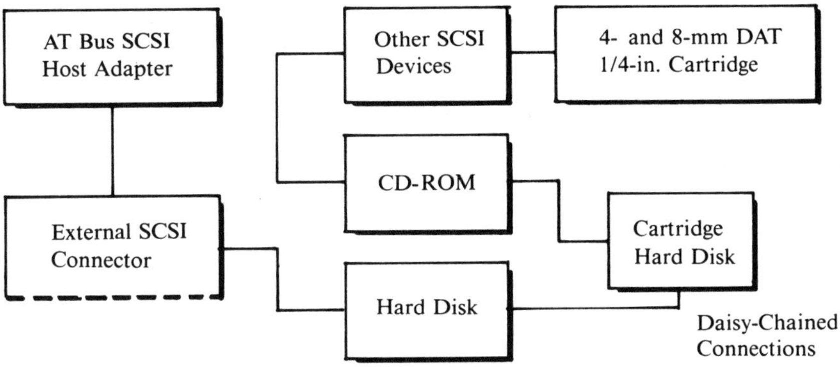

Figure 5-22 Using SCSI for a variety of devices

approach is the SCSI bus controller. The SCSI bus controller card uses a single card slot in the PC. The user can connect a number of components through the bus, such as hard drives, tape subsystems, printers, additional peripheral devices, and host PCs (Fig 5-22). The SCSI bus controller provides all the hardware and software (in ROM) necessary to configure these components.

In summary, the main features of the SCSI approach are:

1. Simple to install
2. Full support of DOS
3. On-board RAM data buffer
4. Daisy-chain cabling for device connection
5. On-board ROM to provide automatic booting

6

UPGRADING YOUR COMPUTER'S INPUT

A personal computer system is a modular system, and not all of the components need to come from a single source. You can match a compatible system unit, monitor, keyboard, expansion boards, and other components to suit your needs, applications, and budget. There is a large selection of PC-compatible hardware, and you will be faced with many choices, especially in the area of input devices. In this chapter, we will cover the wide variety of input devices available today.

KEYBOARDS

The keyboard has been and continues to be the main computer input, since manual keying is the primary method of getting new information into a computer. It is a low-cost component, and its flexibility and ease of connection will continue to make it the basic input component in most applications.

There is a wide selection of PC-compatible accessory or replacement keyboards, and these use several different technologies to detect a key depression. These include mechanical contact closures (Fig 6-1), change in capacitance, and change in magnetic coupling.

There are also several factors that may make one keyboard different from another. These include:

1. Layout and number of keys used
2. Key spacing

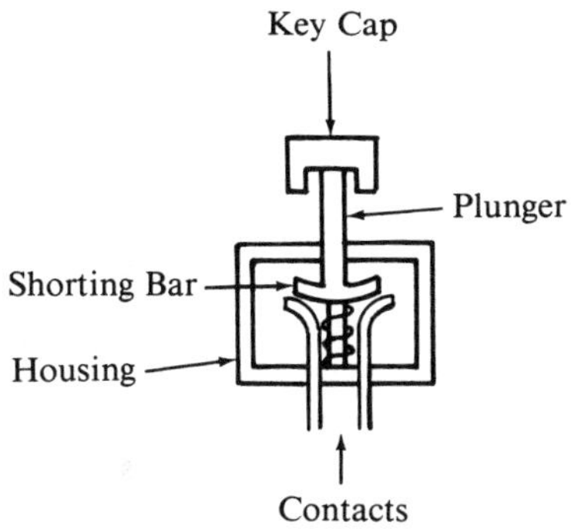

Figure 6-1 Typical mechanical key switch construction

3. Slope or shape of the keyboard
4. Shape of the key caps
5. Contact pressure required to depress a key as well as the sound when the key is depressed

Differences in the layout include separating keys such as Delete from other frequently used keys such as those for the return function, as well as making frequently used correction keys easy to reach. Many compatible keyboards offer tactile feedback and audible click, providing the feel of an electric typewriter keyboard and making the transition from typewriter to computer a little easier. Other differences can be more subtle, and individual preference will vary from user to user. Many of these units use long-life components, with many key switches rated for millions of repetitions.

In the common alphanumeric keyboard, each key depression causes a 7-bit code to be sent to the system memory (Fig 6-2). The program determines the code and sends it to the monitor or printer in the form of a character. The key may also have a fixed function such as Insert or Delete or the program that is running at that time may determine the key function. Some functions may also require multiple key depressions. It is also possible to accumulate consecutive characters into a buffer until a termination character is typed. This produces a character-string input and is common in many programming applications. The programmed function keys can also provide a separate unit, but usually the function keys are integrated with the main PC keyboard. The function keys are different from the other keys in that they have no predefined character meanings and are generally used for commands or menu options. The dedicated keys have permanent labels.

You can label the function keys with coded overlays on which the command names are printed. The function keys can also indicate pressure

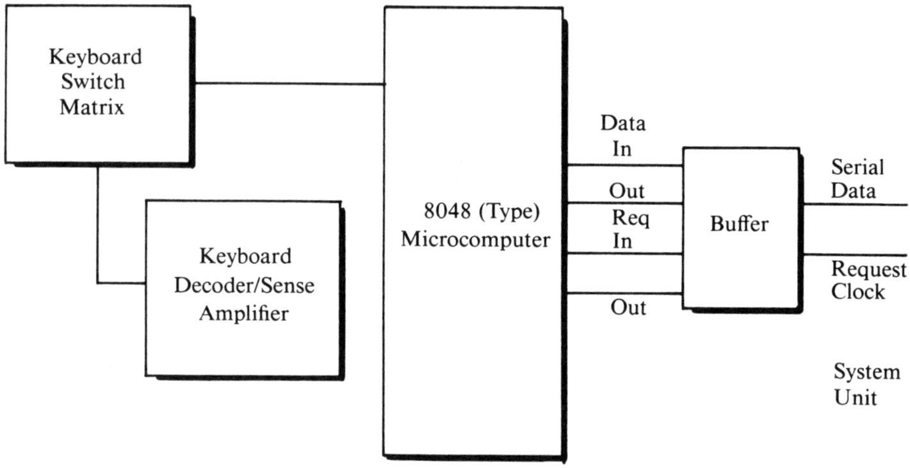

Figure 6-2 Typical keyboard circuitry—serial data sent to the system memory

releases in addition to depressions. This allows you to start an activity when a key is depressed and then to terminate the activity when the key is released.

The chord keyboard is a variation of the standard keyboard unit that has keys shaped like piano keys. You operate it by depressing several keys at the same time as though you are playing a chord. You can use this type of keyboard for music or command input. The use of five keys allows you to generate 31 chords. Learning the chords requires some training, but with some practice users can operate these devices rapidly. The chord keyboard is generally not suitable as a substitute for the standard type of alphanumeric keyboard, but you can use it as an auxiliary input device.

Keyboard Layouts

The common QWERTY keyboard layout evolved from the first mechanical typewriters and design and mechanical problems these early typewriters faced. Early keyboard layouts allowed higher typing speeds, but the machines would jam. Designers determined that a different layout of the alphabet would force typists to move their fingers greater distances, and this would reduce the possibility of mechanical jams.

Although the electronic keyboards of today do not have the mechanical limitations of the early typewriters, the QWERTY layout has stayed with us. While there are dedicated keys to access special functions, along with special characters and minor keyboard modifications to take advantage of machine capabilities, the main keyboard on most computers still uses the same QWERTY character layout that is found on other office machines.

Other keyboards have been proposed over the years to replace the inefficient QWERTY keyboard layout, such as the Malton layout developed by Lillian Malt in England. Some studies have shown the Malton arrangement to be twice as efficient as the QWERTY layout in typing 100 of the most commonly used English words. The Malton keyboard uses two round concave key assemblies—one for each hand. The keys are sloped to compensate for the differences in the lengths of the user's fingers. Although studies have shown this type of keyboard to be more efficient, it has not been accepted in the United States.

August Dvorak was another keyboard pioneer who was active in keyboard efficiency studies in the early 1930s. He conducted time-and-motion studies of typists, studying the frequency and order of letters appearing in the English language as well as the QWERTY keyboard and several other layouts. He patented an improved layout in 1936. Although the Dvorak layout was shown to improve productivity and reduce fatigue, the QWERTY was still used to train keyboard operators. In 1982, ANSI approved the Dvorak keyboard as an alternate to the QWERTY keyboard for alphanumeric office machines. Today, Dvorak layouts are available on a variety of office equipment.

Many PC desktop publishing packages are compatible with the Dvorak layout as well as others. There are also keyboards that are switchable between the Dvorak and the QWERTY. The Magic Keyboard from the Southern California Research Group is typical of these products. This type of product converts the keyboard into a switchable set of layouts. You can select between the available keyboard configurations or go back to QWERTY. You can choose the Dvorak, American Simplified, Alphabetical Order, Montgomery, One-Handed Left, One-Handed Right, and several variations of 10-key numeric and hexadecimal keypads. You can also order a custom programmable ROM (PROM) for a special layout.

Accessory Keyboards

Many different trades and commercial businesses use personal computers. These include skilled and semiskilled crafts, office and clerical functions such as word processing, secretarial services, technical authors, editors, and other writers. Sometimes, adding an accessory keyboard or keypad to a PC used in many of these applications can be helpful in upgrading both comfort and efficiency. There are a number of options available for PCs.

AutoKey. This is an auxiliary keypad with 20 keys available for keyboard sequences (macros). You can use it to store parts of the command set for software packages, thereby improving the accuracy of your input. Incorrect command sequences often cause time-consuming errors until the corrections are made. A keypad such as AutoKey assures that each code sequence is correct, eliminating a major cause of input errors. The AutoKey keypad is easy to install and is usually positioned at the top of the regular keyboard.

Keyport. This unit from Polytel is a flat-membrane touch pad with 300 programmable keys. The keys are set up as a 15 x 20 array on an $8\frac{1}{2}$-x-11-inch pad that attaches to the computer's game port adapter card. You can attach two pads to a single computer through the game port card.

The mylar membrane is screenprinted with a silver conductive grid and two resistive strips. When you press a printed key, the software senses the change in electrical resistance. The system software constantly polls the touch pad to detect any resistance change. It then interprets the resistance change as an individual key closure. A key can be defined as any string of keyboard keys and/or commands, except for those that would stop the operation of the current application. This includes Ctrl-Break and Ctrl-Alt-Del.

You program the keys by pressing the Alt key along with the desired key. A beep signals you that the unit is waiting for the desired sequence of commands or characters from the main keyboard or the Keyport. You can terminate the programming process by pressing the Alt key and the Keyport key again. You can program each of the 300 keys in this way. There is also system software that you can use for defining up to two Keyports at one time.

Keyboard Enhancers

In the early years of PCs, users often had to write their own programs or pay someone else to write them. Today, the variety of software for PCs is vast, but there are some specific needs that are not being met. Even though the variety and capabilities of off-the-shelf PC packages are extensive, some custom programming may be desirable. Keyboard enhancers such as Keyworks, SmartKey, ProKey, and SuperKey are a way to extend the use of each key with stored macros.

Keyworks. This is an example of a software enhancement product. It is accessible using a pop-down menu that is available with a single user-selected key. You can save as a configuration file the different attributes of the menu such as size, style, and color as well as the attributes of the macros. A typical configuration file follows:

F=5: Sets the foreground color to magenta.

B=2: Sets the background color to green.

M=50: Sets the maximum number of macros in memory to 50.

K=1,000: Sets the maximum number of keystrokes in memory to 1,000.

A keyboard enhancer such as Keyworks can provide a number of capabilities. You can save and retrieve sets of macros without leaving the application program. You can edit macros from the active application program. You can also save macros as ASCII files and edit them with a word processor.

You can create custom pop-down menus to control a single or multiple function or a group of functions. You can create screens to provide help, messages, and instructions, and you can set the style of the border and the color of the foreground and background.

The system can nest macros where they can call other macros. You can make up complex macro strings from much shorter macros. Macros can call themselves, forming a loop. A looping macro will call itself continuously until a Stop key is pressed—a function useful for filling a page with repetitive lines.

Macros can have fixed or variable-length pauses. A macro that contains a pause will stop during playback to let you input information from the keyboard. A variable-length pause lets you input keystrokes until you press a Stop or Return key. A fixed-length pause waits until you have completed a specific number of keystrokes.

SmartKey. Many computer applications are keystroke-intensive. You can use a program like SmartKey II Plus from Software Research Technologies to add a supershift facility to a PC, as well as other keyboarding enhancements. SmartKey was one of the first pop-up utilities and is a small program that takes up 2.25K of RAM. You use it to define a string of characters or commands. You can save key definitions on disk and reload them at any time. You can input repetitive characters when needed.

A key definition begins with pressing a Set-Up key. When SmartKey is first used, the Set-Up key is defined as the Escape key. You can keep this as the designated Set-Up key or choose another by using the installation program. Using the Set-Up key, you type a new identity for any other key. Then you hit the Set-Up key twice. Pressing the programmed key now results in a display of the programmed identity. You can redefine the key to another identity or return to its original identity by typing Set-Up, then the changes, and then Set-Up again.

The SmartKey Installation Option menu allows you to customize the program. You can define the Set-Up key as well as the maximum size of the translation table. You can redefine every key as one or more characters or commands. SmartKey includes a predefined Dvorak layout, which changes the keyboard to the Dvorak keyboard.

SmartKey and similar programs are useful in word processing and desktop publishing since they extend the definition of individual keys for lengthy insertions and commands.

OTHER INPUT DEVICES (POINTING DEVICES)

The purpose of a pointing device is to move the cursor quickly and efficiently around the screen in order to carry out various operations. In its simplest application, it replaces the arrow keys. A number of pointing devices use potentiometers. A set of rotary potentiometers can be mounted in a unit such as a joystick. Some designs use slide potentiometers, in which a linear movement replaces the rotation. The potentiometer output is converted and sent to the computer. The program can then manipulate and use these values.

Trackballs

Trackball controls use plastic balls, usually mounted with about one-half of the ball surface exposed from the top of an enclosure (Fig 6-3). You can rotate the ball freely, and usually with the palm of the hand. The computer detects the ball movements and uses them to move the screen cursor.

You can also use trackballs to select items displayed on a screen menu. Use the ball to move the cursor to the desired area of a menu. Pushing the

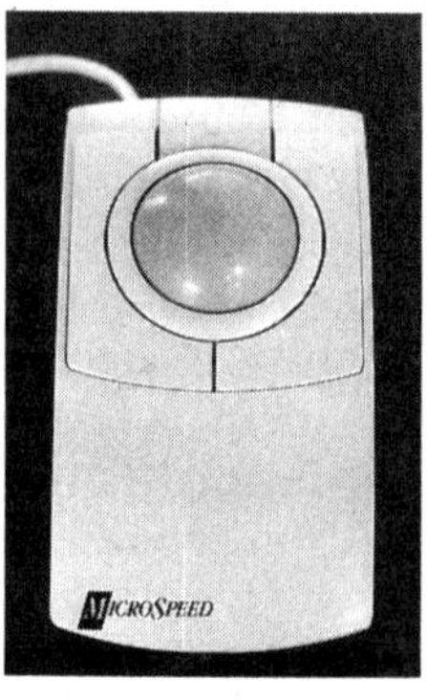

Figure 6-3 An example of a trackball input device

trackball button or a keyboard key (usually Return) makes the selection. The computer reads the cursor position at the time when the button or key is pressed and executes the command indicated.

In most trackballs (which are also called crystal balls), the ball's motion turns potentiometers, and the output is converted for use by the computer.

Thumbelina. This is a small trackball unit that provides trackball functions in a small package for PCs. You can attach it to your personal computer using a special snap mount that is included with the unit (Fig 6-4). When it is mounted this way, the unit takes up no space. You can remove it from the mount and use it in any comfortable position. You can use it during presentations, holding it in your hand and controlling the presentation while sitting or standing. Thumbelina is a full-function, three-button unit.

Light Pens

Light pens are indicating devices. They do not emit light to create lines on the screen, but they sense or detect the light from the picture elements on the screen. Some light pens do use a narrow focused light source, called a finder beam, which is directed at the screen to indicate what picture elements are in the pen's field of view.

The hand-held light pen is a pencil-sized plastic cylinder with a light sensor in one end. Figure 6-5 shows a typical light pen design. A cable connects one end to the computer. As you move the end with the light-sensitive tip to select a point on the screen, the pen sends a pulse when this screen area is bright. The pulse is then used to calculate the screen position.

You can correlate the signal from the light pen with a menu list to select a particular item being displayed. Most light pens also produce a second signal that you can generate by pushing a button on the pen.

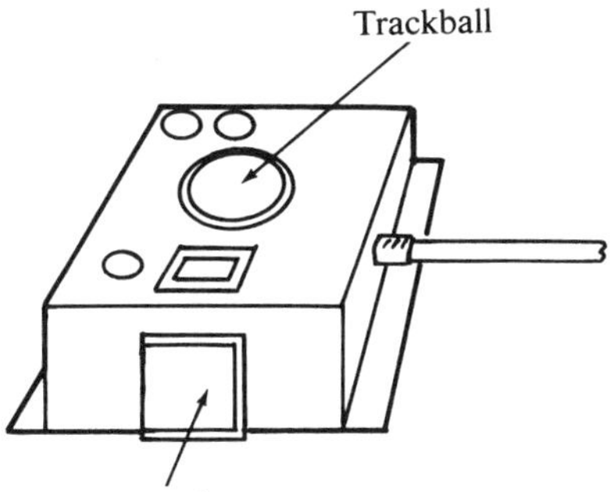

Figure 6-4 Thumbelina trackball

Lens Pen Tip Pen Body Fiber-optics Cable to Computer

Figure 6-5 Typical light pen design

Several factors can affect light pen performance. Many screens use bonded implosion shields over the display tube, leaving a gap between the outer glass surface and phosphor. This gap can cause accuracy problems when positioning the light pen. Unless it is properly adjusted, a light pen can detect false points such as adjacent characters or fail to detect the desired points. An add-on electromagnetic radiation screen can produce similar problems with light pens.

Joysticks

A joystick works like an aircraft control stick where the user controls the motion of a cursor on the screen by pushing it in the direction of the desired motion (Fig 6-6). The displacement-type of joystick actually moves, but another type—the force-actuated joystick—is fixed and the force from the user's hand is detected and used to move the cursor. These force-actuated or isometric joysticks use strain gauges on the shaft to measure the deflections caused by the force.

Figure 6-6 An example of a joystick input device

You can also rotate the joystick or push on the end of it to control other variables besides the basic movements (left, right, forward, or backward). Some systems use potentiometers to sense the movements, and some use springs to return the joystick to its center position.

In an absolute joystick, the travel of the joystick corresponds directly to the screen position. Moving the absolute joystick to its upper position will place the cursor at the top of the display. Moving it to its lower-left position will place the cursor at the lower-left corner of the display.

In the rate joystick, the motion of the joystick provides the direction of motion for the cursor. When you move the rate joystick to the left, the cursor moves left from its present position. If you move it to the lower-left, the cursor will move diagonally in that direction. If you return the joystick to center, then the cursor stops its motion. In some designs, by varying how far in any direction the rate joystick is moved, the user controls the speed of cursor movement.

An absolute/rate joystick is a hybrid that uses both techniques. You select the mode by using the switch on the joystick handle. In the absolute mode, a motion to the upper-left corner with the joystick will move the cursor to the upper-left corner of the display. Once the general area is reached, you can release the switch and position the cursor using the rate mode. It can be difficult to use a joystick to control the absolute position of a screen cursor accurately, since even a small hand movement is amplified in the position of the cursor. The cursor's movements can become erratic since the joystick does not allow fine positioning.

There is normally a small dead zone to allow for drift in the joystick's center position. The relationship of cursor velocity to joystick displacement is usually not linear, as shown in Figure 6-7.

A joyswitch is a variation of the joystick. This is a type of switch that

Figure 6-7 Nonlinear joystick velocity-displacement characteristic

can be moved in any of the following directions: up, down, left, right, and the four diagonal directions. A switch allows nine states. In each of the eight "on" states, the position of the screen cursor is changing at a constant rate in that direction.

Mouse Units

The mouse is another way to move information into a computer. It was developed by Douglas Engelbart at the Stanford Research Institute (SRI) in 1964. SRI experimented with a number of alternate man/machine interfaces between 1964 and 1965.

Many software products support the mouse. These programs use it for the selection of menu items, the specification of application parameters, the creation and movement of graphics, and the rapid placement of the cursor.

In many applications, the mouse is useful in making editorial changes, which generally follow a keyboarding operation. The quick specification of text, its movement, deletion, and duplication are all important and necessary operations in editing text.

The use of a mouse is common in desktop publishing applications. A mouse is ideal for drawing shapes, selecting menu items, and performing other tasks which can be done faster with a mouse than the keyboard.

The mouse takes the user's hands off the main keyboard and requires desktop space. These small units are designed to be moved with the hand on a desktop or mouse pad (Fig 6-8). The desktop units may use a rolling ball connected to internal encoders or potentiometers. Other types might use a light-emitting diode (LED) and a ruled metal surface. Movement of the unit causes the LED in the mouse to sense the ruled lines on the mouse pad.

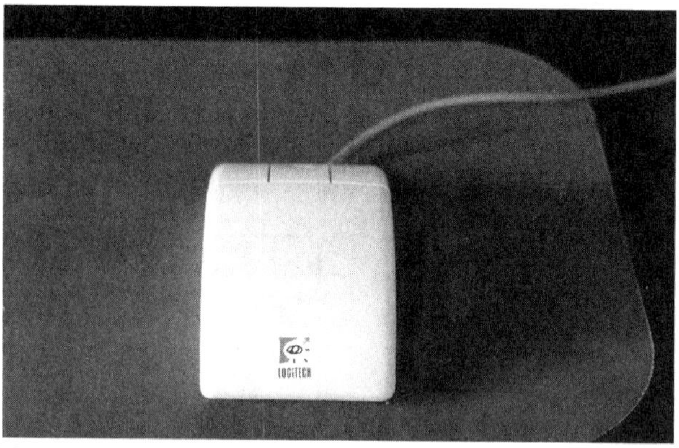

Figure 6-8 Roller-type mouse on rubber mouse pad

The system uses the voltage changes produced by the movements of the mouse to track the relative position. It converts the motion to binary values and the computer uses it to calculate the direction and magnitude of the mouse's movement. As you move the mouse on a flat surface, the computer maintains the current mouse position in memory. This position is incremented or decremented by the mouse's movements.

The mouse usually has one or more push buttons that are used to input commands. On most mice, the front of the device is lower because that is the way your hand naturally falls when you are using it. Mouse designs can differ in several ways, such as the number of buttons, the contour or shape, or the internal mechanism. Mice are also purposely lightweight since they are frequently lifted up and repositioned on the desktop. The buttons are often parallel to the desktop so that the mouse will not move accidentally when you press a button.

There are two basic types of tracking units—optical and mechanical. Within the mechanical category, there are five types—mechanical, opto-mechanical, optical-mechanical, acousto-mechanical, and analog. These tracking units have one to four buttons. The tracking can be affected by the rotation of the mouse. Resolution ranges from 20 to 2,000 counts per inch, and serial or parallel interfaces are available with relative or absolute position information in a variety of data formats and at different baud rates. Although there are six different techniques that can be used to perform the tracking function of a mouse, only three are in wide use: the optical, mechanical, and opto-mechanical.

Optical Mice. These are pure optical units that track position by counting the number of line (or dot) crossings on a special mouse pad, much as a bar code wand reads bar codes (Fig 6-9). There are no moving parts, so optical mice do not require maintenance. Tracking errors of less than 1 in 100 are possible throughout the life of the mouse. An optical mouse needs a special mouse pad for optimum performance. Some optical mice track motion relative to the orientation of the mouse pad. You cannot rotate the mouse more than 90 degrees in either direction. Other optical units track motion relative to the orientation of the mouse, which is similar to the tracking characteristics of mechanical mice.

Mechanical Mice. These units have a rotating ball that drives two orthogonal mechanical shaft encoders. This technique provides a low-cost mouse and lets you track motion on any surface, but these units have a limited lifetime due to the mechanical switching of the encoders. They also require periodic cleaning.

Opto-mechanical mice are similar in that they use a ball to drive two

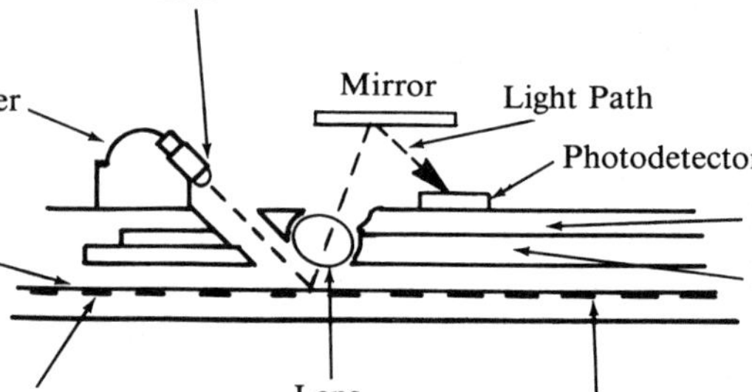

The optical mouse travels over a grid of lines on the mouse pad. A light-emitting diode (LED) produces a light beam which is either absorbed or reflected.

Figure 6-9 Optical mouse operation

orthogonal shaft encoders (Fig 6-10), but these encoders are optical rather than the mechanical switching type. This technique is also low in cost, but it has a longer life compared to the mechanical mouse. It lets you track on any surface, but periodic cleaning is required.

Optical-mechanical mice use an optically sensed spring-loaded plate to determine the direction and to optically count the line crossings on a special mouse pad. These units have characteristics that are very similar to optical mice.

Acousto-mechanical mice use strain gauges to determine direction and a piezoelectric transducer to determine the magnitude (Fig 6-11). There are no moving parts or maintenance, and the mouse can track motion on almost any surface. However, in this mouse, the resolution in counts per inch depends on the type of surface on which the mouse is used as well as the downward pressure placed on the mouse.

Analog mice use either a ball or two orthogonal metal rollers mounted orthogonally that drive the shaft of a potentiometer. These units have a limited lifetime and a limited amount of travel in any one direction due to the use of the potentiometer.

Generally, you will need some type of pad with nonoptical mice to reduce slipping and audible noise and to protect the desktop. This pad is often rigid. Most nonoptical mice do not work well unless they are horizontal.

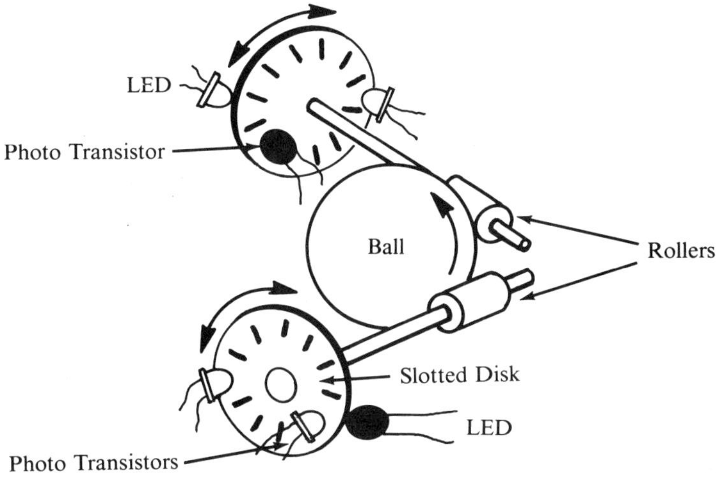

Figure 6-10 The opto-mechanical mouse mechanism (a rotating ball is connected to rollers that turn slotted disks. The disks turn between a LED and photo transistor combination.)

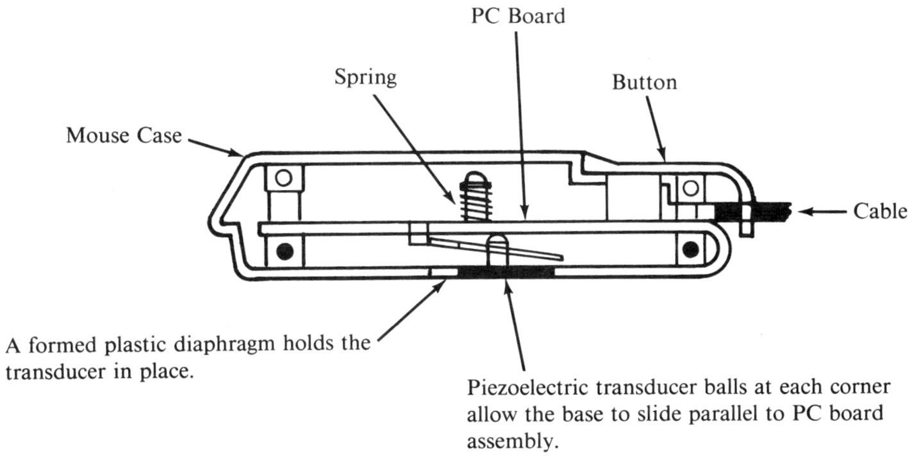

Figure 6-11 Acousto-mechanical mouse mechanism (Acousto-mechanical mice determine the direction by the change in resistance in a strain-gauge, which is returned to position by a spring. This provides a signal in proportion to the shear. The processor combines this data with velocity information from a piezoelectric transducer to indicate the movement of the mouse.)

Upgrade Concerns. The major concerns that occur with an upgrade to a mouse input device are:

- **Maintenance**—Optical mice have no moving parts, but mechanical, opto-mechanical, and analog mice require regular maintenance, and some mice have access holes for maintenance.
- **Slippage**—Optical mice will rarely miss a count, while mechanical mice can slip on the pad or desktop.
- **Audible noise**—Some types of mechanical mice that use a metal ball produce audible noise on some surfaces. This can increase over a period of time. It is sometimes possible to reduce this noise by running the mouse on a sheet of paper.
- **Jitter**—When a mouse is positioned between two grid points, a type of jitter effect called *teasing* may occur. The mouse may jump ahead or back by one count. This can also increase over time. Many devices use hysteresis to eliminate this problem.

Mouse Interfaces. The two basic type of interfaces for mice are parallel and serial ports. Parallel mice use a code for the motion, and the switch depressions are sent as a low voltage. Manufacturers use several 9-pin standards. Serial mice use RS-232 ports with a variety of protocols. Generally, these protocols relate the change in the mouse state (buttons or position) when the mouse changes state. The Mouse Systems serial protocol is typical. It is a 1,200-baud relative-position protocol and provides 48 updates per second with a maximum velocity of 50 inches per second. Information is transmitted only when there is a change of mouse state.

Logitech Mouse. This mouse uses optical-mechanical technology. It allows you to create pop-up menus for applications that are not mouse-supported. Software consists of an installation program to test the mouse, mouse drives that some application programs need in order to utilize a mouse, a menu generator program, and a mouse control program.

With the menu generator, you can use the mouse with applications that would not ordinarily support a mouse. Using this utility, you can create pop-up menus for the application and then select the menu items with the mouse.

The Logitech mouse also has a memory-resident program that controls mouse settings. You can change the sensitivity of the mouse to speed up or slow down the movement of the screen cursor, to change the mouse port parameters such as baud rate, and to change the mouse from a two- to a three-button mouse.

MousePen. This is an input device based on mouse technology that resembles and works like a pen (Fig 6-12). It fits in your hand and works on most surfaces, including a sheet of paper. You can use it on crowded desktops or in other cramped working spaces. Since it feels like a pen, it offers good control for applications like illustration and CAD.

The MousePen uses a dynamic resolution of 150 to 1,000 counts per inch which adjusts to your movements. You can move from one edge of the screen to the other by moving the MousePen about 3 inches. You can use it for precise control at 150 counts per inch. The compact size and lower power are advantages for laptop or notebook computer users. The MousePen Professional is compatible with the Microsoft mouse and Windows.

Cordless Mice. Mouse cables can be an inconvenience: They can limit the movement of the mouse or catch on desktop items as you move the mouse. A cordless mouse has the same basic shape and mechanical operation as a regular mouse, but, instead of a cord, the mouse uses a transmitter to send signals to a receiver plugged into your PC. Some cordless mice use infrared signals, while others use radio waves.

The Cordless Super Mouse uses infrared LED technology and operates like a TV or VCR remote control. There must be a clear line of sight between the mouse and receiver. The mouse must not be farther than 6 feet away from the receiver, which also acts as a mouse stand and battery charger for the mouse's two 8-hour batteries. One of the two batteries is always recharging while the other is powering the mouse.

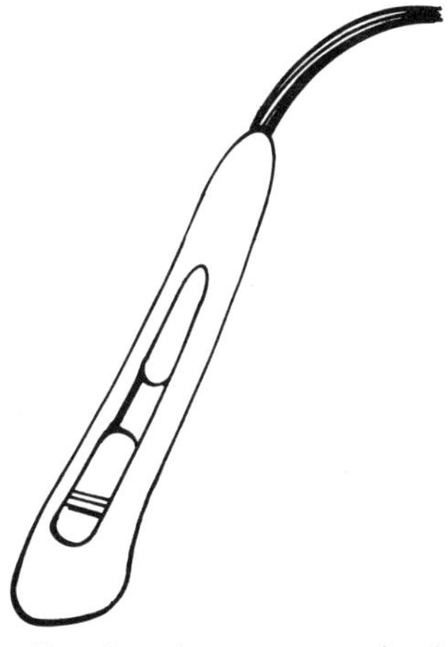

Figure 6-12 A MousePen, based on mouse technology

The Manager Mouse Cordless also uses infrared LED technology to communicate with the computer and runs on rechargeable batteries. When you move the mouse or click a button, the mouse converts this information into a series of infrared light pulses that are emitted by dual LEDs in the mouse. The receiver/charger unit detects the invisible infrared light pulses. The recharging jack is between the two LEDs. An overnight charge of 8 hours provides enough battery power for 8–10 hours of continuous use or about 2–3 days of average use. While the charger is connected, you can use the device like a conventional cabled mouse.

The MouseMan Cordless Radio Mouse is a low-frequency radio-controlled mouse. It has an operating range of 6 feet in a 360-degree circle around the receiver. It is similar to a cordless telephone in that you can place the receiver anywhere within its receiving range. There are eight frequency channels so, if you are operating within a meter of another MouseMan, you can change channels. The MouseMan runs on a lithium battery that lasts about a year since it runs at lower levels when the mouse is not active.

Touch Panels and Tablets

Touch panels allow you to indicate items on the screen by touching a finger to a menu selection instead of moving the screen cursor to the item. The touch panel mounts across the face of the display screen, and, when your finger touches the panel, this position is detected using one of several different technologies.

One type of high-resolution touch panel uses two layers of transparent material. One layer is coated with a thin conductor and the other is resistive. Finger pressure causes a voltage drop on the resistive substrate, which is used to calculate the coordinates of the pressure point.

Digitizing tablets use similar techniques. Graphic-pad digitizers use a flat tablet and a stylus pencil. The tablet provides a flat surface over which you move the stylus pencil. The computer monitors the position of the stylus. The stylus usually incorporates a pressure-sensitive switch that closes when you push down on it. The system uses this to indicate that you have made a stylus-position menu choice.

An electrical sensing system measures the stylus position. In one type, the tablet surface contains a grid of wires. The electromagnetic coupling between the electrical signals in the grid and in a wire coil in the stylus will change as you move the stylus. This produces an electrical signal in the stylus, and the system uses the strength of this signal to determine the position of the stylus on the tablet. In this way the digitizer senses the position of a pen, cursor, or some other pointer and sends this information to the computer as a coordinate on the pad. You can then digitize a drawing placed on the tablet by moving the stylus over each point or line to be recorded.

Other digitizer tablets use electrostatic or magnetostrictive techniques. An electrostatic tablet radiates an electric field that the pen senses. The frequency of the radiated field depends on where the pen touches the surface and can be used to indicate the tablet position. The tablet electronics convert the frequency changes into coordinates and sends them to the computer. Electrostatic digitizers can sense the pen position through most media with a low dielectric constant such as paper, plastic, or glass. Electrostatic systems can have problems digitizing accurately in close proximity to metal. They can also have problems digitizing partially conductive materials such as pencil lead or some felt-tip pen inks.

In a magnetostrictive tablet, the wires that keep track of the pen position are laid beneath the table. A magnetic pulse goes through the wires, producing a small strain wave that propagates across the tablet. A pick-up coil in the pen or cursor detects this wave. The position of the pen relates to the time between the start and the sensing of the pulse. Magnetostrictive tablets are not sensitive to conductive materials, but magnetic objects near the tablet surface can disturb the magnetic properties and degrade the operation. You must also periodically remagnetize these tablets with large magnets.

In an electromagnetic tablet, either the table or the pen sends out a small AC signal. A receiver circuit detects this signal and produces a digital signal that indicates the pen location. Electromagnetic digitizers are not affected by conductive or magnetic materials on their surface and generally require no periodic recalibration.

Felix. Felix is a miniature optical data tablet that uses sliding gates and light beams. There is a pointer connected to two plastic slides inside the base. A set of windows connected to these slides modulate two beams of light from LEDs. A built-in microprocessor senses and analyzes the movement of the light beams. When you increase finger motion, the microprocessor senses the change in speed and shifts into a high-speed mode to cover the finger motions.

Felix is a high-resolution, 300-dpi precision input and pointing tool for IBM PS/2 computers. Physically it is a 6-inch square, with a small handle that you grip like a pen. The handle moves within a 1-inch square space that represents the entire computer screen area. It is operated by finger rather than hand movement. While a mouse requires larger sweeping motions, with the Felix unit the hand remains stationary and finer motor skills are used. The maximum accuracy is 0.0015 inches and, with some practice, it is possible to manipulate a single pixel. Mouse motion is relative and does not maintain a one-to-one relationship to the screen. The movement of Felix and other fixed pointing devices match the screen closely.

Pointing Device Comparison

The ideal pointing device should be compatible with the requirements of both humans and machines. This includes the joints and muscles that have to operate the device. Not only is the required positioning precision for the specific task important, but the length of the task and its contribution to fatigue for the muscle group being used are also considerations. The two main muscle groups involved in operating these devices tend to be the forearm/wrist and the thumb/finger/wrist. The movement of the forearm/wrist group generally requires more energy and is more fatiguing than the movement of the thumb/finger/wrist group.

The mouse uses forearm/wrist motion except for switch activation, while the joystick uses only the motion of the thumb/finger/wrist group. The operation of a keyboard or keypad requires the repeated striking motion of the finger and wrist. The tablet makes use of forearm and wrist motions and closely approximates the activity of writing and drawing. The tablet has a high lineal resolution since the thumb/index-finger motions are used. For high-resolution applications like mapping where cost is not a primary consideration, the digitizing tablet provides the most convenient way for the user to enter x and y positions, since you hold the tablet stylus like a pencil and move it over the tablet face. With most tablets, the system can determine the position of the stylus whenever it is within $\frac{1}{2}$ inch or so of the tablet surface.

A keyboard- or computer-mounted device leaves the wrist and forearm in a known relationship to either the keyboard or the computer chassis, and the return hand motion tends to be minimal and direct. The return hand motion from either a tablet or mouse can vary and is not automatically repeatable. This can interrupt and delay the input or editing process.

For text editing, you may be able to position the cursor faster and with fewer errors with a joystick than you can with a mouse. Historically, joysticks have been used with computer games in PCs, and the mouse has become very popular for graphics applications.

If you use a joystick to place the cursor in the region of a spreadsheet data row or column, you can then use the rate mode to move it in a horizontal or vertical direction. This allows you to select a character within a cell or a line within a cell.

When selecting a pointing device, you should be concerned about resolution, repeatability, and size or range. These factors are important in mapping and detailed drawing, but they are less important when you are using the device to position a screen cursor, since you have the feedback of the screen cursor to guide hand movements. High resolution can be defined as the ability to detect more than one part in two thousand, usually 2048 x 2048 picture elements. Medium resolution refers to a resolution of half this number down to the upper edge of low resolution at 512 x 512 to 256 x 256 pixel displays. The cost of a pointing device usually depends on the level of resolution needed.

For medium-resolution applications where cost is a consideration, you could use either a mouse or an absolute joystick. You can always adjust a joystick with a rate mode to operate more coarsely.

For lower-resolution control applications, either a tablet, a mouse, or an absolute joystick would be suitable. The tablet allows a natural, absolute mapping of your motions onto the display space, with resolutions as high as 500–1,000 points per inch, and the fatigue factor is low. For applications where cost is more important, you might want either a mouse or a joystick. The mouse offers good speed and a resolution of 100–300 points per inch, but it does not allow a natural, absolute mapping, and the fatigue factor is higher. The mouse pen allows more natural positioning and with a lower fatigue factor. The joystick allows a higher speed and a resolution of 100–400 points per inch in the absolute mode and a 1,000–10,000 points per inch in the rate mode.

OPTICAL DATA INPUT

Optical scanning technology has been around since the IBM card readers sensed the arrangement of holes in the card. Early optical character recognition (OCR) used special tints and inks and was employed in large systems. The demand for fast, reliable data-entry devices has supported the development of OCR technology. OCR devices recognize human-readable characters, convert them into electronic signals, and process the signals into usable data using recognition and validation programs.

OCR typically involves reading typed or computer-printed material. The PC can process text that is captured this way using word processing and other programs. A uniform character is required, and characters must conform to one of a set of readable OCR fonts.

The speed for keyboard input ranges from 25 to 65 words per minute (wpm). An OCR device that can read 50 characters per second (cps) will produce about 500 wpm.

OCR was a part of many early mainframe-based systems. These systems used a fixed- or adjustable-field scanner with a resolution up to 200 dpi on an 8.5-x-11-inch input field (1728 x 2200 pixels). The display resolution was usually not sufficient to let you view more than a small portion of the image at one time, and scan times were generally several minutes.

OCR and Word Processing

The growth of word processing in the 1970s fueled the development of OCR. The dedicated word processing workstations of the time were costly and required a fair amount of user training. Most of the work performed on them was input data and documentation. Productivity gains of double and triple were common compared to typewriters. Although the benefits of OCR were well known, the restrictions and limitations of the technology at that time made their use costly and generally inefficient.

The scanning process cannot always capture formatting information, such as bold, italics, margins, and tabs. You have to add this information manually. Scanners can be sensitive to marks, spots, and other defects on original copy. Since the scanners can make errors, proofreading remains an important part of text production.

Since most scanners can read only a limited number of character sets, if the copy is not produced for a particular scanner then it may not be readable. Since scanners cannot read handwritten material, you cannot correct errors found on the originals until the errors have been read by the OCR device. You will then have to correct the errors during the editing process. The OCR device becomes a critical link in the system—if the OCR device fails to work properly, the process stops.

The availability of today's low-cost scanners makes OCR technology affordable and feasible on PCs. Digital images can be stored, retrieved, and transmitted the same as any other files, although the files are larger than the typical text files. Compressed data formats are available, and the basic scan-and-save capabilities of low-cost PC systems make them useful for many applications. With a 5 to 1 compression ratio, 1GB will hold about 10,000 page-format images of 100K each. The same 1GB will hold approximately 2,000 pages uncompressed. Enhancements include fast scanning, gray-scale, and color image support along with image processing hardware and software.

Machine-vision digitizing and recognition systems are used for such applications as automated inspection of parts. Advances in vision systems and artificial intelligence provide the fast image handling and processing required.

A typical scanning camera uses a 1,728-element linear charge-coupled device (CCD) array that moves across the image plane in steps to generate a digitized image. The camera has built-in compensation for any nonlinearities of the CCD-sensing elements. The system maintains images as segmented rectangular arrays of any size and shape. It defines multiple images simultaneously. When a portion of an image is displayed, it copies the displayed portion to display memory. Other applications for these scanners include the digitizing of topographical relief maps into a database.

The drive behind OCR has always been that it is faster and easier to convert the scanned text into computer usable ASCII characters than it is to keyboard the characters into the PC directly. In the past, most PC-based OCR programs required the user to train the software to recognize the type of font in use. There may also be some rearrangement of text that the program cannot link properly, and the user may need to assist the program in identifying areas with graphics and modify improperly interpreted characters. The current OCR software minimizes these types of problems.

OCR Operation

An OCR system must perform five basic functions:

1. Image detection
2. Character isolation
3. Character recognition
4. Data validation
5. Data transfer

For image detection, a scanner performs the optical-to-electrical conversion of the printed data. The scanner then isolates characters from extraneous information, such as borders, nonreadable data, and background images. It then classifies and matches the isolated characters to the proper character in a stored character set. Validation may take the form of a repetitive loop for reading, validating, and 1) confirming a successful data acquisition or 2) indicating a failure so the data can be rescanned or entered in another way. Then the data can be transferred to the host PC.

The hardware needed for the hand scanner includes the scanner interface on a single plug-in board. Larger scanners can have their own CPU and memory and attach to the host computer via an RS-232 port or parallel interface.

OCR text must be printed properly and must be within user-defined fonts. Characters should meet standards such as those established by ANSI or the International Standards Organization (ISO). OCR-A is an ANSI standard that establishes a machine-and-human-readable standard character set. The characters include letters and special symbols, in different sizes.

The ink on the material to be scanned should be nonreflective to provide the proper contrast. Photosensors have a high sensitivity in the near infrared spectrum where human eye sensitivity is weak.

You can use ink that is visible to the human eye but invisible to the optical character reader to mark positions and for descriptive material. This is called *nonread* or *blind* ink. The type of paper also affects the reflectance.

The OCR program does most data validation in the host computer. As unvalidated data is entered, the program judges its validity and sends a signal to the user to indicate if the data is valid.

Character Isolation and Recognition

In earlier OCR systems, character isolation and recognition was done with template matching. In this process, a diode array in the reader produces a two-dimensional image that is transmitted to the processor where a match is made with a known image. One problem with template matching is the large amount of memory required to hold all of the possible character templates for matching. Another problem is accuracy—the images are sensitive to differences in print quality, and distortion can occur from wanding performed at an angle.

Rather than using two-dimensional arrays that attempt to capture the image all at once, most hand scanners use a linear array of diodes in the wand. As you move the wand across the media, RAM stores a series of slices through a character. The computer reconstructs the complete image by assembling successive slices. Since fewer pixel signals need to be analyzed, this lowers both the communications bandwidth and processing requirements. Accuracy can be quite high, and an error rate as low as 1 in 10,000 characters is possible.

OmniPage. This program uses a form of page recognition instead of character recognition. Page recognition reads and processes documents while reducing the amount of human intervention. OmniPage scans the document as a bitmapped image and then separates the text from the graphics and converts it to ASCII format. It displays the ASCII characters in an editor where you can make changes. The program can handle single and multiple text columns as well as spreadsheet columns.

OCR and Scanners

OCR systems for PCs use two basic types of scanners: desktop document readers and portable hand-held readers. In the desktop units, the media either moves past the optical reader head, or the media is stationary and the scanner head moves (flatbed scanners). In the hand-held units, you pass the reader head over the characters or image to be read. Low-cost document readers are now available for desktop publishing applications. These low-cost readers interface with a host PC (Fig 6-13).

VIDEO INPUT UPGRADE OPTIONS

There are many types of systems available to improve the productivity of your PC system and we will discuss the common as well as innovative methods.

Video Digitizers

For image input with medium- to high-resolution color, video-based technologies are common. Applications include geographical, mining, remote-sensing, automated surveillance, and inspection where the final output is a color display or color area plot. Most video systems have certain characteristics in common. They use resolutions of 256 x 256, 512 x 512, or 1024 x 1024 pixels. Color and gray-scale capability ranges from 1 bit per pixel to 24 bits per pixel. Most high-resolution systems support 8 bits per pixel for display, giving 256 displayable colors. The use of 24 bits per pixel provides 256 levels of brightness for each of the three primary colors used, for a total palette of over 4 million color shades. Acquisition times are typically $\frac{1}{30}$ second, the same as the standard frame rate for television production.

Early video systems were expensive due to the high cost of conversion

Figure 6-13 Low-cost hand scanner for PCs

components and the memory required to store the image. Most video systems are used for pictorial imaging applications since they have relatively low resolution capabilities compared to other graphic devices.

In the three-dimensional (3D) area, there are programs for combining multiple simultaneous views and gray-scale information to generate accurate 3D shapes. These programs are used in some robotics and flexible manufacturing systems.

Laser Scanners

In applications where you need high resolution, you can use laser image digitizing. These systems can have input resolutions up to 2,000 lines per inch (0.0127 mm) for document sizes up to 25 x 36 inches. The digitizing and data transfer speeds can exceed 12 MHz (pixels per second), but most operate in the 3- to 5-MHz range. Large scanners can scan an 8.5-x-11-inch document in about 2 minutes at 3 MHz.

Laser scanners use a laser beam that is moved across the document with rotating mirrors. As the beam travels across the document, either a single- or multiple-element sensor receives the reflected light.

CCDs

Charge-coupled devices are an important part of today's scanners. They have evolved in recent years to their present level of capabilities and have improved along with large-scale integrated circuits and the reduction in size of memory chips. Scientists use CCD images to bring back photos from distant planets. Developments in the 1970s have led to such products as electronic still video cameras and camcorders. An array of CCD elements perform the actual scanning. Each element is a pixel, or picture element, with the light from the object image on it.

The CCD uses a photoconductive material similar to that used in the vidicon tubes in video cameras. The vidicon tube uses a single layer where the scanning beam defines the picture element. The solid-state CCD sensor has individual picture elements that are accessed by separate leads. This makes the solid-state sensor more expensive to manufacture.

In the vidicon tube, changes in the scan velocity and other problems affect performance. Solid-state sensors provide better positional accuracy. The CCD creates color by using a repetitive pattern of color filters (Fig 6-14). Using this color filter array (CFA), each pixel is covered with a color filter that allows only that color to pass.

The CCD uses charge coupling with the small areas of electrical charge that are created in the silicon semiconductor material. An electrical field

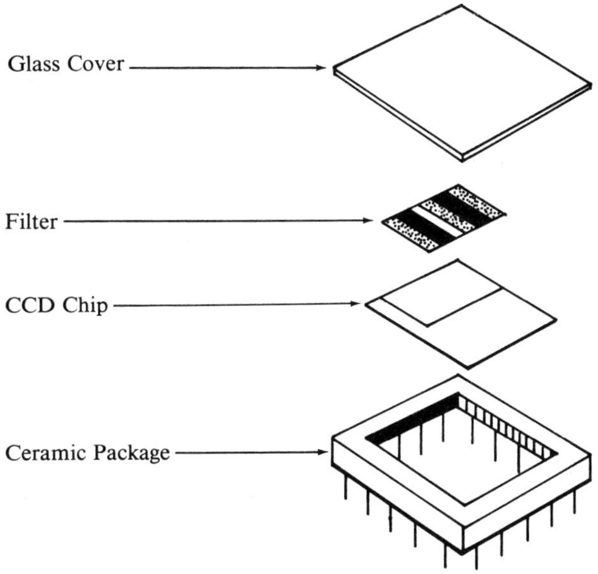

Figure 6-14 Components of a CCD

between a pair of gate electrodes located close to the surface of the silicon creates these areas (Fig 6-15).

The CCD elements are next to each other and, as the voltages on adjacent gate electrodes change, the individual charge packets beneath them pass from one element to the next. The CCDs act as shift registers since they transfer their charge to the next element while the amount of charge in each packet stays the same, even as it is being passed from one element to another.

When the silicon absorbs the light striking its surface, free electrons are generated. The number of free electrons generated is proportional to the light striking the surface. This light image is a reproduction of the original scene, and it generates a proportional electrical charge. The charge packets are transferred by charge coupling, and the value of each charge packet corresponds to a picture element or pixel. The actual CCD sensors are made up of a series of horizontal and vertical rows, creating an x-y array of elements.

CCD Characteristics. Monochrome sensors have higher speeds—since it is not necessary to have the three alternating systems of red, green, and blue, all of the pixels are available for the collection of photons. The more recent sensors transfer energy closer to the surface, so more energy can be collected. This also produces a higher-speed sensor. These sensors are designed primarily for high-definition television systems (HDTV).

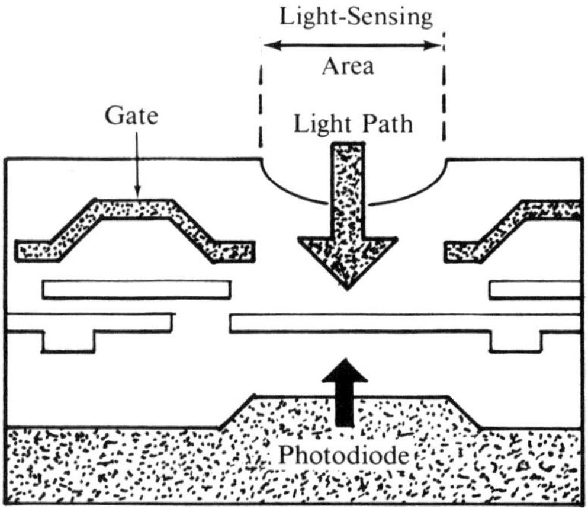

Figure 6-15 Cross section of CCD image sensor (Note the light path to the light-sensitive photodiode which acts as a gate electrode.)

CCDs provide higher reliability than vacuum picture tubes. They are a low-power device, but they can accept large amounts of light without damage or change to the photosensitive surfaces. CCDs generate electrical noise, but this noise is low enough to give good performance. Noise in an image appears as granular spots. Most noise in these systems does not come from the CCDs, but from adjacent circuits and connections in the system.

Digital Cameras

Digital cameras use linear or planar sensor chips in a camera-like fixture. The use of a lens allows remote viewing. One type of camera has a 1,728-element linear CCD array that is scanned mechanically in the film plane, behind a lens. The system then stores pixel data from the CCD array in memory.

Digital cameras have data rates from a few hundred pixels per second to 4 million pixels per second. They offer gray-scale imaging of up to 16 bits per pixel as well as color.

Low-performance cameras use pixel planar arrays of 256 x 128 or 256 x 256. This is the same type of chip used in home video camcorders. High-performance systems use 4,096-element linear arrays made up of two 2,048-element CCDs. A beam splitter optically combines the CCDs, and then they are scanned over a 4,096-line field, for a total resolution of 4096 x 4096.

You can use digital cameras like you would use a 35-mm still camera, with its compatible lenses and other photo equipment. The higher-performance units compare with laser scanners for high-resolution applications.

Raster-to-Vector Conversion

Raster-to-vector conversion programs allow the system to read the binary (bit-mapped) image and extract the data necessary to duplicate the original image. Think of this as viewing an image and writing down instructions to draw another image like it. The system stores the original binary image, which is analogous to a photograph in memory.

There are several techniques used for the interpretation of images for vectorizing purposes. A line-following system scans through the white areas of the image until a black pixel is found. This defines an edge since it is a transition between white and black. Then the system makes a series of explorations looking for continuations of the edge.

Another technique breaks the image into blocks. The system maintains data for each of the blocks if there is anything in the blocks. If the object or objects in the block are too complex to describe with a simple line, circle, or arc, the system breaks the block down into smaller components, and collects the same data. By repeating this procedure, it is possible to build a model of the image. This technique is useful in 3D object recognition for robot vision applications and parts handling.

Another approach used in robotics vision is based on spatial filtering. This is similar to electrical filtering, but it is performed in two or three dimensions in space rather than time.

Multielement Scanners

These scanners use multielement CCD arrays. Some units can handle large-format E-size drawings, which measure 34 x 44 inches. Some of the larger units have a fixed scan head and a drum on which the paper moves. Others use a flatbed for the document and move the sensor array.

The first multielement scanners were costly and designed for high-volume use, such as automated forms or invoice scanning. These systems were used for binary (black and white) imaging of high-contrast documents.

Scanner Parameters

Gray scale refers to the number of shades of gray the scanner is able to represent per dot, or pixel. A scanner which is able to represent only black and white has only two levels of gray. The more shades of gray a scanner is able to detect and record, the more closely the scanned reproduction matches the original.

Conventional halftone techniques for printing photographs use dots of different sizes to represent the shades. In a digital scanning device, the dots are all the same size. Shading is done by grouping dots into small units called *grains*. A grain can be made up of 4, 9, 16, 25, 36, or 64 dots in a square array. The smaller grain sizes provide more details. Gray scales are produced by partially filling the grain. A 2 x 2 grain has four possible fill slots, and it provides a five-step gray scale. An 8 x 8 grain can provide 33 gray levels, which means more shades but less detail. Line art does not use grains. Table 6-1 lists a number of monochrome scanners.

The resolution of a scanner refers to the scanner's sensitivity and is measured in dots, or pixels, per square inch. The maximum image size depends on the scanner's physical scanning range. Scanning speed refers to how quickly the scanner operates.

In a color scanner, the scanner detects and records the color information for each of the three basic colors—red, green, and blue. These three colors mix to produce other colors. Table 6-2 lists several color scanners. The IEEE-488 interface is available as an expansion board.

SCANNER TYPES

Scanners have evolved from the large, expensive, self-contained units to smaller, printer-size units (desktop scanners) and even low-cost hand-held units. Computer literature generally refers to the following types, although there is some overlap in classification (Fig 6-16).

Camera-based scanners use photographic technology to produce very high-resolution scans of two- or three-dimensional objects. The scanner head might resemble a 35 mm camera and can be mounted on a moving tower above a flat platform.

Feeder scanners resemble a single-sheet printer. Mostly used to scan letter-size documents, they can also handle larger and smaller sizes. You place the document in an input tray or manually feed it through the unit.

Flatbed scanners scan flat, two-dimensional objects such as documents and photographs. Some flatbed models offer a multiple-page feeder attachment for automatic multiple-page scanning.

Slide scanners are typically for high-resolution color scans of 35-mm slides. Most of these scanners support 256 gray-scale level output for gray-scale conversion of color or black and white slides.

Overhead scanners use a scanning platform with the scanning head fixed above the platform. The platform allows the scanning of small three-dimensional objects.

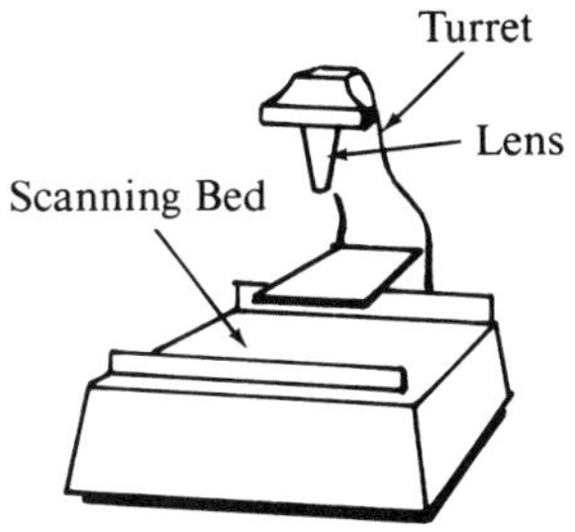

Camera scanner, also called a flatbed scanner by some

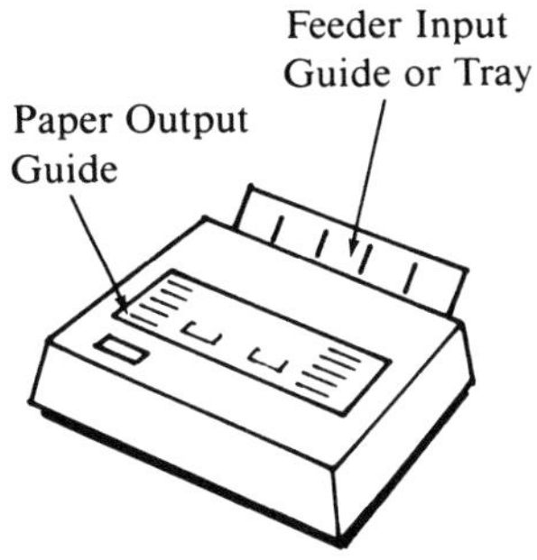

Feeder scanner, designed for letter-sized documents, manually fed using guide or tray

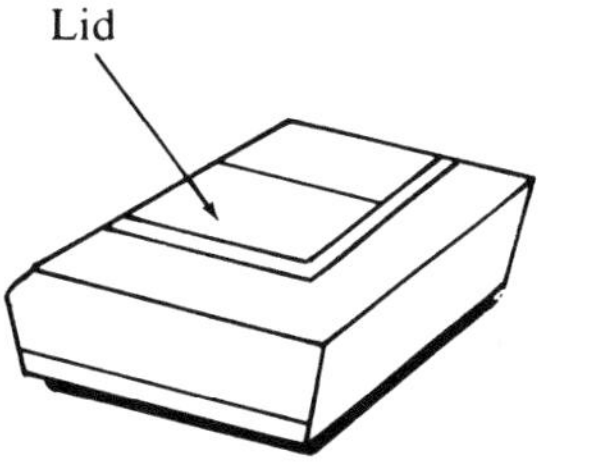

True flatbed scanner; document placed under the lid; multiple page feeders available

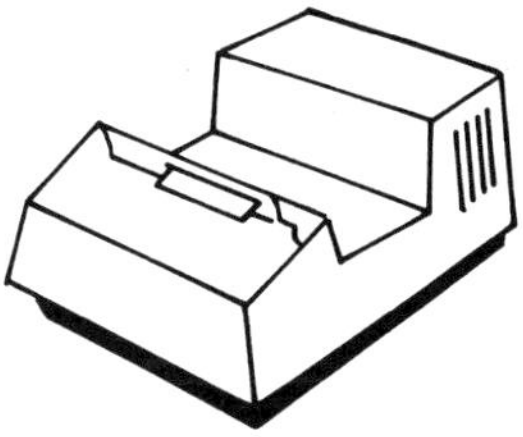

Slide scanner, designed for 35-mm color or black and white slides

Overhead scanner like a fixed camera scanner

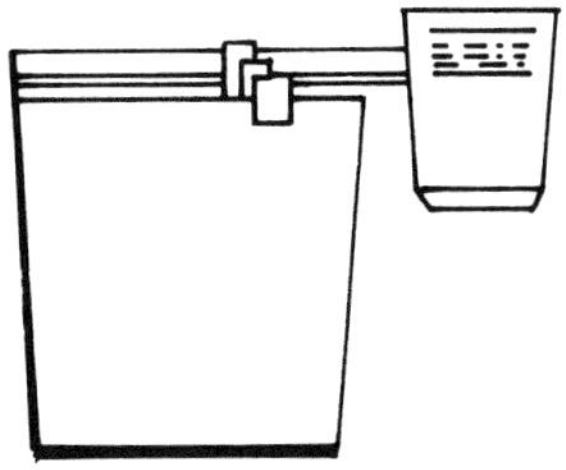

Platter attachment scanner, replaces the drawing head of the plotter; is able to scan large drawings

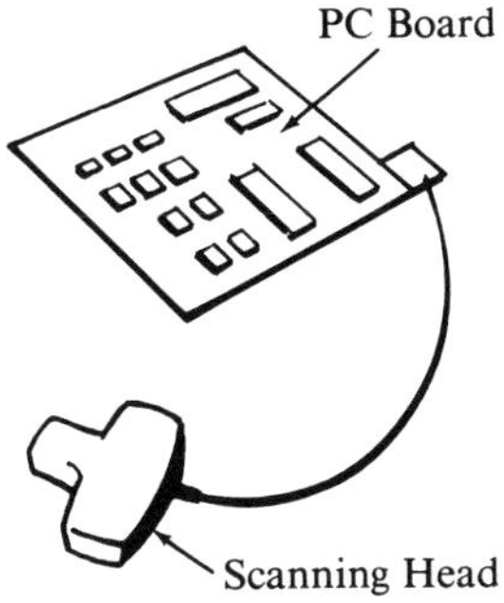

Printer attachment scanner; consists of a PC board and a scanning head that replaces the print head

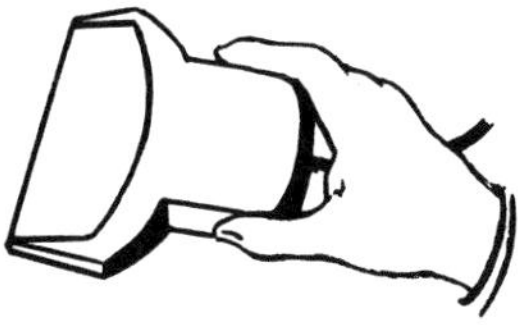

Hand-held scanner, usually about 4 inches wide; comes with imaging software for larger document

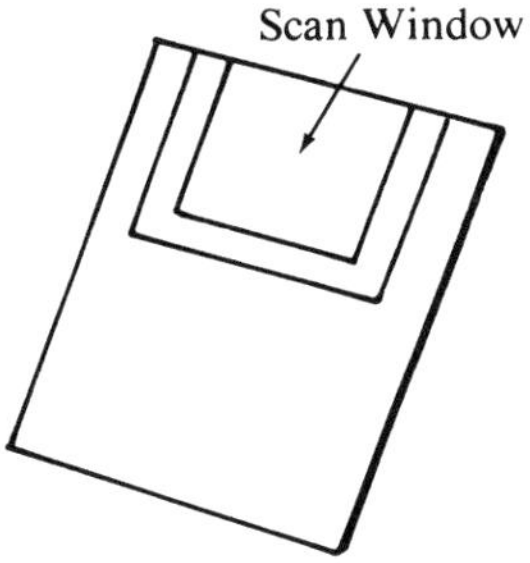

Color hand-held scanner, designed for color photos; needs separate red, green, and blue scans

Figure 6-16 Types of scanners

TABLE 6-1 Monochrome Scanners

Type/Model	Maximum Resolution	Maximum Gray-Scale Level	Scanning Speed	Maximum Image Size	Interface
Camera					
Eikonix/1000	4,096	256	1 min (letter)	unlimited	IEEE-488
Feeder					
Laser Connection IS-300	300	2 (16 dither)	12 s (letter)	11-in wide	PC Card SCSI
Microtek Lab MS-II	300	2 (64 dither)	9.9 s (letter)	8.5 x 14	Parallel SCSI PS/2
NewDEST PC Scan 2000 Series	300	256	9.4 s (letter)	8.5 x 14	SCSI
Flatbed					
Canon IXx12F	300	32	16 s (letter)	8.5 x 11	Serial Video Interface
Fujitsu M3094E	400	64	2.1 s (letter)	10.1 x 14.3	RS-232C
Hewlett Packard	300	256	10 s (letter)	8.5 x 11.7	Centronics
ScanJet Plus Microtek MSF-300G	300	256	9.9 s (letter)	8.5 x 14	Parallel, SCSI PS/2
Panasonic FX-RS506	400	16	9.8 s (letter)	8.5 x 14	IBM PC/AT, PS/2 Cards
Ricoh RS312	300	64	14 s (letter)	8.5 x 11.5	Bidirectional Parallel
TEC Image Scnr SX-3101	300	4 (16 dither)	21 s (legal size)	8.5 x 11	SCSI
Xerox/Datacopy 730GS	450	64	14 s (letter, 2 shades)	8.5 x 11.69	Centronics SCSI

TABLE 6-1 Monochrome Scanners (cont'd)

Type/Model	Maximum Resolution	Maximum Gray-Scale Level	Scanning Speed	Maximum Image Size	Interface
Hand-Held					
Diamond Flower	400	16 (32 dither)	0.87-in/s at 400 dpi	105 mm	IBM PC, PS/2 Cards
KYE International GS-4000	400	32	3 ms/line	12 x 14	IBM PC Card
Logitech ScanMan PC	400	16 (32 dither)	15 s (4.1 x 11)	4.w x 14l	IBM PC Card
Overhead					
Chinon DS-2000	200	2 (5 dither)	15.9 s (216 mm x 297 mm)	196 mm x 281 mm	RS-232C (IBM)
Chinon DS-3000	300	2 (16 dither)	24 s (216 mm x 297 mm)	196 mm x 281 mm	RS-232C (IBM)
Mirror Tech. VS200	200	2 (4 dither)	20–90 s (letter)	8.5 x 11	Serial
Mirror Tech. VS300	300	2 (16 dither)	30–90 s (letter)	8.5 x 11	Serial, SCSI (optional)
Truvel TX-3	300	256	0.83-in/s at 300 dpi	12 x 17	SCSI
Plotter Add-On					
Houston Instrument Scan-Cad	200	16	4.8-in/s max at 200 dpi	36 x 48	IBM PC Card

*Min = minute; s = second.

TABLE 6-2 Color Scanners

Manufacturer/Part No.	Maximum Resolution	Maximum Gray Scale Level	Color Resolution	Scanning Speed	Maximum Image Size	Interface
35mm Slide						
Bameyscan PC/AT	1,000	256	8 x 3 bits/pixel	3–4 min	35 mm slide	IBM PC Card
Eikonix 1435	2,800	4,096	12 x 3 bits/pixel	3 min	36 mm x 24 mm	IEEE-488
Flatbed						
Sharp JX-300	300	256	8 x 3 bits/pixel	45 ms/line max	8.5 x 11	IEEE-4888
Sharp JX-450	300	256	8 x 3 bits/pixel	30 ms/line max	11 x 17	IEEE-488
Overhead						
Truvel TZ-3BWC	300	256	8 x 3 bits/pixel	0.1-in/s mono; 0.8-in/s color	14.5 x 24	SCSI

Another type of scanner uses a device that replaces the drawing head of a plotter. This is called a **plotter add-on scanner** and is used for drafting applications since it can scan large-size drawings.

A similar add-on type of scanner replaces the print head in a dot matrix printer. Software included with this **printer add-on scanner** controls the movement of the scanner head and the document feed through the printer, allowing a line-by-line scan of documents and photos.

Monochrome hand-held scanners are small, low-cost, manually operated scanning units. Most hand-held models have a scanning width of about 4 inches and use imaging software for scanning larger documents.

Color hand-held scanners can provide full color or 256 gray-scale level scans. Combining information from separate red, green, and blue scans produces the color output.

Desktop Scanners

The general category known as desktop scanners is a popular add-on for personal computers. These products have evolved over the years. In the mid-1980s, desktop publishing pushed the development of desktop scanners for PCs. Some of the first products included those from Microtek, Datacopy, and DEST.

These early desktop scanners use a simple binary technology in which the scanned images (line art or photographs) are broken down into cells that are either black or white. In 1987, gray-scale techniques appeared. In gray-scale scanning, each cell in the scanned image is recorded as a shade of gray, providing you with more control over the quality of the scanned image before and during the editing process. The first machines to use this technology had 16 shades of gray, but scanners with 256 gray tones (8-bits-per-pixel) appeared shortly thereafter, and these became the gray-scale standard.

As desktop scanners evolved as an important peripheral for personal computers, their design and capabilities made them ideal for markets like desktop publishing, which can be broadly defined as electronic publishing or computer-aided publishing. Desktop publishing is the main application of desktop scanners. The products available have advanced rapidly from black and white to color scanning. There are differences in the capabilities of both the hardware and the software that controls the scanner. Some scanners are for color only, while others can handle color and gray-scale. Some are scanners for transparencies.

OCR is an important application of scanners with OCR software, which read printed or typed documents into a personal computer. While most scanners can be used for OCR, scanners with a built-in auto-document feeder are specifically suitable for OCR applications. The capabilities of OCR software have been improved for the entry of text from different sources, such as magazines, books, and other documents.

Scanned images are large users of disk space. If you use an uncompressed format, a 300-x-300-dpi setting produces 90,000 bits in 1 square inch, and a full-page scan exceeds 800KB.

There are also larger-size scanners that are capable of scanning documents up to 36 inches wide. While these will never be as popular as the smaller, lower-cost scanners, they represent some of the most advanced scanners.

Microtek. This manufacturer was one of the first firms to offer scanners. Its ScanMaker 600Z/ZS is a desktop scanner that you can use to scan 16.8 million colors and 256 shades of gray and black and white. It can capture images at up to 600 dpi. Once the image is captured, you can modify it with a graphics program called the PhotoStyler, which is a Windows 3.0 application that can be used to edit, retouch, and separate color images.

Microtek's ScanMaker 1850 can capture 24-bit color and 8-bit gray scale from 35-mm color or black and white slide images at resolutions as high as 1,850 dpi. You can scan the images in both portrait and landscape orientations. You can use the scans to produce color compositions and four-color separations. The unit comes with the PhotoStyler for retouching, editing, and color separating.

The Microtek MS-300A scanner, like most others, uses a CCD sensor array. It can scan photographs, line art, and graphics and text for OCR applications. This desktop scanner uses a roller feed to move the original past the image sensors. A standard page takes less than 10 seconds to pass by the image-sensing array.

Line art (black and white) and halftones (shades of gray) require different scanning modes, which are selected using the software that is provided. This utility, called VersaScan, allows you to control other parameters such as resolution, contrast, and brightness.

During imaging, the scanner produces a bitmap of the original image. As the scanner scans the document, logic circuits in the scanner determine how the image is to be interpreted. If the copy is black and white, a black area is given a logic *one*, which results in an area of dots, and a white area is given a logic *zero*, which results in an area with no dots. If a photograph is scanned, the various shades of gray are interpreted as a pattern of dots.

The MS-II scanner can handle multiple pages. It has a 50-page automatic document feeder, along with 300-dpi resolution and a sheet-fed design. You can use it for black-and-white graphics, including line art and halftone scanning.

The MS-II comes with Caere's OmniType, which is a version of Caere's OmniPage page-recognition software. OmniType is Windows 3.0-compatible and operates on 286, 386, and 486 computers with 4MB RAM.

Setting Up the Scan on the MS-II. The actual scanning operation is automatic after you set up the scanner. Like on a manually adjusted camera, you must adjust the scanner for the document. In the MS-II, this is done with the *scanner settings* screen. You use brightness and contrast adjustments to set a threshold value for the scanning process. These adjustments restrict the amount of light that reaches the scanner sensor. When the amount of light is below the threshold value, the data bit is represented as a black dot. When the amount of light is above the threshold value, the scanner produces a white dot. You can save settings and use them again. You can install settings that you use often to automatically load each time you run the program. You can use a scanning window to eliminate margins and other unneeded areas. This is shown in the center of the scanner settings screen.

Viewing Modes. In the MS-II, as each image is scanned into memory, you can view it in several viewing modes. In the Real Bits mode (the program default) each scanned bit is represented by one screen bit. Since there are generally three to four times as many scanned bits as screen bits, you can only display a part of the image at one time, unless the scan is very small.

In the Fat Bits mode, a 4 x 4 array of screen bits represents each scanned bit. A small window on the screen shows what the Fat Bits section looks like in the Real Bits mode. The Fat Bits mode magnifies the image enough to allow dot editing. You can turn individual dots on or off and paint or erase sections as desired.

Hand-Held Scanners

Many documents have artwork, pictures, and other graphics in addition to logos. You might create illustrations using a drawing or paint program. You might key in text using a word processor, or you might capture existing text and graphics using a scanner. Low-cost, hand-held scanners are now available that can handle many of these tasks. An example of a typical hand-held scanner is ScanMan (Fig 6-17).

ScanMan. This scanning unit has a 4-inch window, a control unit, and software. Since the scanning unit is just a little bigger than a mouse, it is handy and ready to be used when needed. You use the software like a desktop accessory, so it is accessible from any application. Setup is done from a menu. One of the settings is an adjustable time-out, which you can

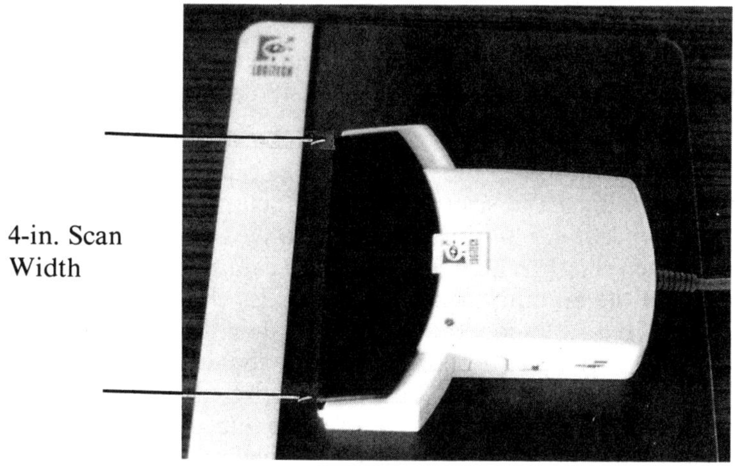

Figure 6-17 Typical hand-held scanner with 4-inch scan window shown on copy-holding pad

set from 1 to 30 seconds. The time-out begins when the scanner stops moving after scanning has started. You will usually display the image when scanning. The scanner is 4.2 inches wide, and the maximum length depends on the available memory.

ScanMan has scanning resolutions of 100, 200, 300, and 400 dpi and a mode switch for scanning either line art or photographs. You use the line-art setting for copy that contains no shades of gray and is made up of black lines on a white background. The photo mode provides shades of gray using groups of dots. Different-size dots are used to create the shades of gray in this scanner. Other scanners might change the concentration of dots to create shades. In either case, the process is called dithering. After you set the controls, you turn on the scanner by selecting Scan from a menu. Then you place the scanner over the copy, press the Start button, and move the unit in a straight line over the image.

You can save images in a number of graphics image formats including TIFF or TIFF Compressed. You can import the scanned images or paste them directly into application programs. Before saving the scanned image, you can view and edit it. After an image has been scanned, you can view it on the screen in one of four modes:

1. **Fit-in-Window** displays the entire scan, reduced and in proportion.
2. **Actual Size** displays the image in the same size as the original, with as much of the image showing as will fit in the window.
3. **Full Size** displays each scanned dot as a screen pixel. The size of the image depends on the resolution.

4. **Fat Bits** displays each scanned dot as a 4 x 4 square of pixels. The Fat Bits mode has editing tools for adding, deleting, copying, and moving pixels.

You can modify a scanned image by selecting the complete image or a portion of the image. You can move, delete, rotate, flip, mirror, or resize this area.

The Complete Half-Page Scanner/400. This is another low-cost hand-held scanner for the input of artwork, clippings, sketches, signatures, and other small graphics. The unit is about 5 inches long and about 5 inches wide. It can scan a 4-inch-wide image up to 14 inches long at a resolution of 200 dpi. You can piece these scans together to make full pages. You set the resolution to 200, 300, or 400 dpi, depending upon the intended use. You can save scanned images in data formats compatible with such programs as Ventura Publisher, Aldus PageMaker, Dr. HALO, PC Paintbrush, and Microsoft Windows Paint. There is a native file format called IMAGE. Scans saved in this format can be displayed, edited, deleted, or printed. The Complete Half-Page Scanner/400 and many other hand-held scanners can also support OCR.

As you scan an image with a hand scanner, you can view it and, if the scan is not satisfactory, you can repeat it. There is no need to input the page coordinates to the scanning software as required with some desktop scanners. The Complete Half-Page Scanner/400 comes with a special card that installs in a available expansion slot.

The software that comes with the scanner is called SmartScan. This is menu-driven software that supports scanning, editing, and saving images (Fig 6-18). A number of formats are available for importing images into desktop word processing, desktop publishing, and other applications (Fig 6-19). You can also export images to a graphics program for modification (Fig 6-20, 6-21, and 6-22).

You can set the scanning resolution to 200, 300, or 400 dpi. The working or display resolution can be 75, 100, 150, 200, 300, or 400 dpi. You can set the scan resolution higher than the display resolution on the screen, but, in most cases, these will be the same.

You position the scanner over the start of the copy, press the scanner button, and move it slowly down the surface of the copy. An image of the scan will appear on the display screen. If the scan is acceptable, you can edit and save it. If it is not acceptable, you can reject it, and repeat the process.

A Page option lets you merge several images. You can also translate images to or from the native IMAGE format and use the editing capabilities of SmartScan with images created in other programs.

```
                                   Monday 10/28 2:50 PM

Main Menu
-------------------------------------------------------------

          ++++   F1 ++++>Help ++++++++++++++++++
                 F2     >Scan
                 F3     >Image
                 F4     >Page
                 F5     >Convert
                 F6     >System Configuration

                 ESC    >Return to DOS

-------------------------------------------------------------
Press key or select function with arrow keys and <Enter>
```

Figure 6-18 Imaging software—main menu

Starting a Scan. When you turn on The Complete Half-Page Scanner/400, the screen is cleared and the CCD sensors come on. They will sense the light levels reflected from the paper as you move the scanner over the image. Controls on the side of the scanner adjust the gray scale and brightness. As you move the scanner, the image begins to appear on the screen.

You can use any keyboard key to turn the scanner off. Then a row of options appears at the bottom of the screen. These options let you set the scale and rotate, crop, erase, print, zoom, and pixel-edit the image. You can scan photographs using one of several different patterns, which are used to create textures that affect the gray-scale shading. The available settings range from high-contrast to a spiral pattern.

Truvel Flatbed Scanner. The Truvel TZ-3BWC is a camera-type flatbed scanner with resolution from 75 to 900 dpi (Fig 6-23). This type of scanner uses a moving tower to scan the copy that is placed on the bed. You can scan three-dimensional objects as well as flat documents and open books.

This type of scanner requires a tuning procedure before it is used. The tuning sets the aspect ratio so that scans are not distorted or out of proportion. The tuning for black-and-white scans is easier than that required for

```
                                              Monday 10/28 2:15 PM
----------------------------------------------------------------------
File Name for Image       >++++++++++++++++++++++++++++++++++<

Save as                    1
    1.     Image file
    2.     PC Paintbrush file
    3.     Dr. Halo file
    4.     Windows Paint file (1.0)
    5.     Windows Paint file (2.0)
    6.     Tiff file
    7.     Gen file



 F1> Help                   F10> Save and Exit        ESC > Exit
```

Figure 6-19 Save Image screen

color. The black-and-white tuning consists of a 15-minute warm-up, followed by a calibration check. Color tuning requires the tower to make several dozen passes over the target card and takes about 45 minutes. The system can save the tuning information in a file so it can be reused.

Making a Scan. The scanner uses a 15-minute timer to warm up the lights so that the scanning illumination is stable. The screen displays a timer showing the elapsed and remaining times. You set the type of scan (black-and-white or color) and the line-art or gray-scale level from a menu.

You must calibrate the scanner before scanning. This is done by placing a target card on the scan bed. The calibration procedure is similar to tuning. If the focus is out, then you need to adjust the tower. The scan bed is 12 x 17 inches, which is the maximum size of a scan. You must define the part of the scan-bed area that will be active. You can use a prescan to confirm that the scanning area is correct. Then you set the resolution to the full resolution of 300 dpi or to a certain percent by selecting from a menu. You can stretch or condense the image by setting the aspect ratio. The scanner then performs the scan and saves the file.

```
                                              Monday 10/28 2:10 PM
   Directory
-----------------------------------------------------------------------
     CAMERA1        WATER2
  +++CAR2++++       WATER3
     COAST3
     GOLF2
     HORSES
     MASK
     MONEYS
     PARTS1
     SNOWMAN
     SNOWFLAK
     TEST
-----------------------------------------------------------------------
 F1 > Help       F6 > Delete/Undelete     F9 > Print      ESC > Exit
 F2 > Display    F7 > Move                F10 > Save
```

Figure 6-20 Directory screen

VERBAL INPUT

Speech recognizers range from relatively low-cost versions that recognize a few hundred words to more expensive devices that recognize thousands of words. The words must be defined as discrete utterances preceded and followed by fixed pauses in some units.

Most word recognizers must be "trained" to the unique characteristics of an individual's speech. The system generally filters the word into several frequency bands, and then it matches patterns based on the relative loudness or pitch of the sound against a dictionary of recorded patterns. Training the recognized unit requires establishing a dictionary of patterns during which the user must speak the word several times. Automatic speech recognition is a more difficult task than automatic speech generation.

Voice methods offer the most natural form of computer/human inter-

```
                                                Monday 10/28 4:05 PM
Convert to IMAGE
-------------------------------------------------------------------------
                                        Type
  Filename                        T/X/G/P/H/M/B/F      Status
  ______________________          _______________      ______

  C:CARS.PCX                            P              IMAGE
  ++++++++++++++++++++++++++++++++++++++++++++++++++++++++++++++++++++




-------------------------------------------------------------------------
  F1 > Help       Shift F3 > Convert All      F7 > DOS Directory
  F2 > Display    F4 > Edit Document          F9 > Print     ESC > Exit
  F3 > Convert    F6 > Delete/Undelete        F10 > Save
```

Figure 6-21 Convert to Image screen

```
                                                Monday 10/28 4:19 PM
Convert from IMAGE
-------------------------------------------------------------------------
  ++CAMERA++
    CARTS2
    COAST2
    GOLF2
    HORSE
    MASK2
    MOONS
    MUSIC
    PARTS1
    SNOWMAN
    SNOWFLAK
    TEST2
-------------------------------------------------------------------------
Select a file to convert from IMAGE format into another format and press
<F3>

F1 > Help                 F10 > Exit
F3 > Convert              ESC > Exit
```

Figure 6-22 Convert from Image screen

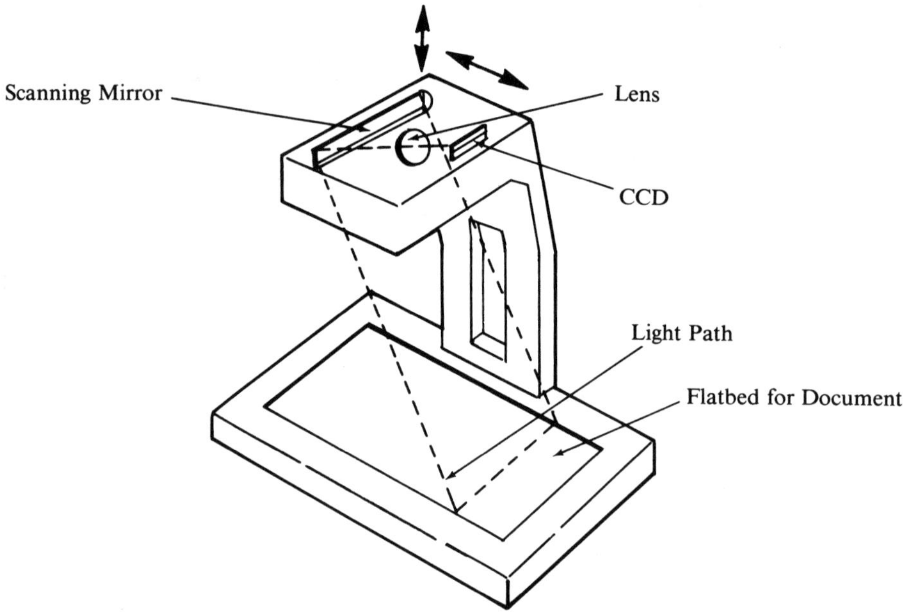

Figure 6-23 Typical flatbed scanner with lens, CCD light sensor, and scanning mirror

action. Its advantages include its speed and the freedom it gives for other tasks—not only is it much faster than keyboard entry, but it also frees the user's hands and eyes for other tasks. Direct speech input is also potentially more reliable than keyboard devices, since it eliminates any intermediate data-preparation and data-entry steps.

Applications include inventory control systems to increase productivity. Quality assurance inspection can be done quickly because voice input provides hands-free operation. In office and factory databases, voice input allows rapid data entry and retrieval as well as rapid report generation. In medical-records transcription, voice input can reduce terminology errors. Remote edits and downloads of data can be done in industrial control/automation applications.

Speech recognition generally requires the digitizing of waveforms and comparisons to stored-vocabulary reference patterns. There are two basic types of speech recognition systems. In **speaker-dependent** recognition, individual speech patterns are used, and the system must be trained to each operator. **Speaker-independent** systems compare a speaker's voice inputs with averaged voice-print patterns.

Speech-recognition systems convert the sound waveforms into a character equivalent of the contents of the spoken message. Speech recognition depends on the constraints placed upon the speaker. It must take into account the different voice qualities that speakers use in saying the same words. The system needs less information for speech recognition than for speech generation, since recognition can be performed by voice-print matching, where pitch and timbre are not as important.

Speech recognition is a pattern-recognition problem. The system must digitize the voice waveform and compare it to a stored reference pattern or vocabulary. The system forms word templates by several techniques, including filtering. It forms the template and then compares it to a series of templates or patterns stored in memory.

Speaker-dependent systems rely on the speech characteristics of the specific operator and can handle both isolated words and connected speech.

Speaker-independent systems do not store individual voice patterns and do not have to be trained to the individual operator. It compares the speaker's voice inputs with averaged voice-print patterns. The wide variations in pitch, intensity, and duration of human speech allow recognition of only isolated words or connected speech from a limited vocabulary. These systems are not as accurate or flexible as speaker-dependent systems.

Isolated-Word Recognition

Isolated-word recognition systems do not have the problems of continuous-speech recognition systems since all words are separated by pauses. These systems can be 99% accurate in recognizing words that are so isolated. Typically vocabularies contain 50 to 300 words.

These systems divide the acoustic signal into separate phonetic and spectral signals. The system then detects each of these and converts it separately into a bit pattern. It then matches these patterns with vocabulary words stored in memory.

The typical system includes a microphone input and visual or acoustic feedback of word entries (Fig 6-24). The operator trains the system by repeating the desired vocabulary words into a microphone so that templates can be made and stored. The isolated-word recognition utterances exist as predefined, known patterns. Most variations among pattern occurrences, other than those of duration or overall energy, are not important.

Continuous-Speech Recognition

Continuous-speech recognition involves the recognition of certain sets of words uttered without pauses. These systems use a hierarchical scheme where the parts of speech are recognized and grouped into larger

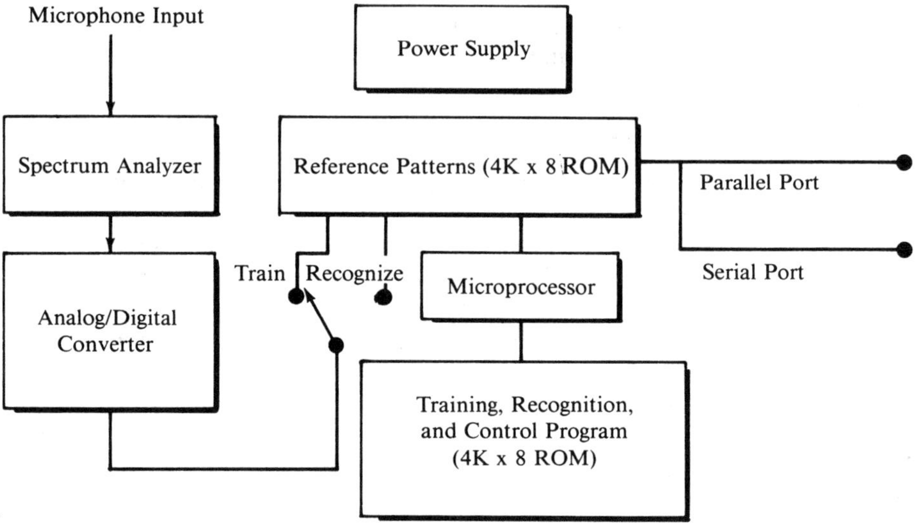

Figure 6-24 A typical block diagram of a voice-recognition module that, with the proper training, can recognize up to 100 spoken words

units. Most techniques are based upon information theory. One problem with continuous-speech recognition is that it is difficult to tell where one word ends and the other begins since the characteristic acoustic patterns of words vary depending on the context. As the vocabulary size increases, the matching becomes more difficult. The system may need to recognize all of the words in a sentence, but it may only need to interpret half of them correctly for the sentence to be understood. These systems can keep their program structure simple by using some task-specific knowledge. The system arranges alternate word sequences according to their frequency of use. Task-specific knowledge, based on rules, lexicon, and syntax, can be used to generate the words to complete the sequence.

Speech-Recognition Problems

Problems with speech recognition occur because a speaker rarely repeats words in the same manner and a listener does not always hear in the same way. Pronunciation, background noise, and speed vary in their contributions for both speaker and listener. The human mental function allows a person to weigh the words, appreciate the concept, or provide understanding for what a speaker is trying to convey. You need a knowledge of both the language and the context to recognize or understand a sentence.

The computer-based system must suit the application's needs and cost limitations. There are potential problems concerning user acceptance, acceptable error rates, lack of appropriate speech models, intelligibility of voice messages, procedures to correct recognition errors, and noisy operational environments.

Most speech-input systems have limited vocabularies. The inexpensive systems for PCs are speaker-dependent and are only capable of recognizing discrete-word speech from relatively small vocabularies. However, they do have relatively high acceptance and rejection accuracies. You can usually increase vocabularies by adding more memory, though operators have to pause between words on most systems.

Speech-Recognition Products

Commercial continuous-speech, speaker-dependent voice data-entry systems can operate at over 99% accuracy with high background noise. This noise can consist of conversation between workers, the sound of equipment, and the day-to-day variations in the user's tone of voice. These systems can recognize the voice patterns and vocabulary of selected users, using a standard vocabulary of 100 words, with options to 360 words at accuracies of 99% or greater. They are useful in commercial and industrial applications and require 1MB of floppy disk and 10MB of hard drive storage.

Most of the board-level products use speech-recognition chips that can recognize a certain vocabulary. General Instruments, Intel, IBM, and NEC manufacture speech-recognition chips. The chip sets include controller, feature extractor, and RAM. Intel's chip set is based on its digital signal-processor and microprocessor chips. In addition to chip sets, Intel offers boards and speech-transaction development systems. Other manufacturers such as Hitachi offer systems for word recognition in any language, with accuracy of over 99%. These systems interface with PCs and numerical-control machinery.

Although most manufacturers claim that their speech-recognition units achieve accuracies of between 97% and 99%, in many cases, the test procedures are not standard and the manufacturer carefully chooses the input database. Environmental factors such as noise, stress-related factors like fatigue, and applications issues tend to degrade recognition accuracy.

There is an integrated voice and Ethernet-compatible data network designed to work with the PC. This Comnet system allows you to phone the computer and leave or retrieve messages and request specific information. It uses voice digitizing and storage so the PC can recognize words for each application. You can transfer vocabulary files with Ethernet allowing you to have voice recognition on any PC in the network. The voice-recognition unit in conjunction with keyboard input can control most user application programs without modification.

Products are available for applications such as materials handling, quality control, machine-tool programming, inventory control, and data entry. Some of these products reduce the pause time between spoken words and allow voice input into computers at rates approaching 200 words per minute, which is faster than normal conversation.

Kurzweil AI's large-vocabulary voice-recognition products offer the advanced voice-recognition technology with a vocabulary of over 5,000 spoken words or phrases. VoiceReport creates printed reports by voice without manual transcription. Text creation and editing by voice is useful in business, medicine, engineering, legal, and government applications. For medical reporting, Kurzweil AI has developed systems for doctors across the country for generating patient reports. Kurzweil's VoiceMED products include: VoiceRAD for radiologists, VoiceEM for emergency medicine physicians, and VoicePATH for surgical pathologists.

Products like Cherry's VoiceScribe allow you to communicate with any IBM PC XT, PC AT, or compatible computer using voice entry. You can enter voice data to access, edit, and file data, virtually hands free. Features include:

1. The system can create a custom vocabulary for any application as you speak.
2. You can edit during operation.
3. The system responds to words or phrases within 0.2 to 2.0 seconds, which is close to real time.
4. You can combine vocabularies with other files to create new vocabularies.

Installation. You can have the Cherry VoiceScribe system up and running in about an hour. Software leads you through the start-up process and guides you in configuring your application. You repeat each command word several times, producing a pattern that is a combination of the repetitions. You can create up to 1,000 patterns—one for each word. Word-recognition accuracy is above 99% using the Doddington and Shalk test. The system will run on any PC/XT/AT-compatible with a full length card slot, one 5.25-inch floppy disk drive, a hard drive, and at least 256K of RAM.

CCSI Products. The Portable Transaction Voice computer, model PTVC-756, is a hand-held system that is XT-compatible. It has a built-in RS-232/422 interface and a weight of 2.15 pounds. It allows voice recognition of 500 words or phrases and has a 50-key alphanumeric keyboard with an LCD display.

The IntroVoice VI is a voice I/O system that provides voice recognition of 500 words with an accuracy of better than 98%. It also allows text-to-speech synthesis.

You can accurately record and collect computer data through the use of voice recognition. Both IntroVoice VI and PTVC 756 allow you to use simple verbal commands for entering and accessing information, resulting in more efficient processing of often complex and laborious data.

The IntroVoice system converts spoken words to commands and data. You can speak to your computer and run software. It allows voice input and voice output. It comes with an expansion card for MS/DOS computers and allows 500 words and over 98% accuracy.

The PTVC is a self-contained battery-powered data-entry device, with a built-in voice recognition and synthesis. You can use this hand-held microcomputer to collect and deliver information. A toolkit allows modification to existing text-to-speech rules and the addition of exceptions for any custom vocabulary.

Future Trends

Research into the conceptual structures of human processes will eventually have its effect on speech-processing technologies. This will result in more forgiving, mistake-tolerant machines and the development of informal ways to interact with machines. The computer interface of the future will integrate many technologies, including adaptive input devices for speech processing, interactive graphics, and natural language (Fig 6-25).

Artificial intelligence will play a major part in the success of these systems. Structured knowledge, learning, and problem solving are tasks for adaptive systems to accept, access, manipulate, and present information. The intelligent machine of the future will be able to carry on an intelligent conversation with a person and make judgments. It will also be able to program itself, listen, and obey spoken commands. It will also be able to see and interpret images.

CD-ROMs

Compact disk read-only memory is another method of getting information into a PC. CD-ROM technology is changing the way data is stored, delivered, accessed, and used. The capacity of a single 4.7-inch CD-ROM disk is equivalent to fourteen 40MB hard disks. CD-ROM drives are not fast, but they are twice as fast as early versions and small enough to fit in a floppy drive bay.

CD-ROMs hold large amounts of information—over 600MB. A

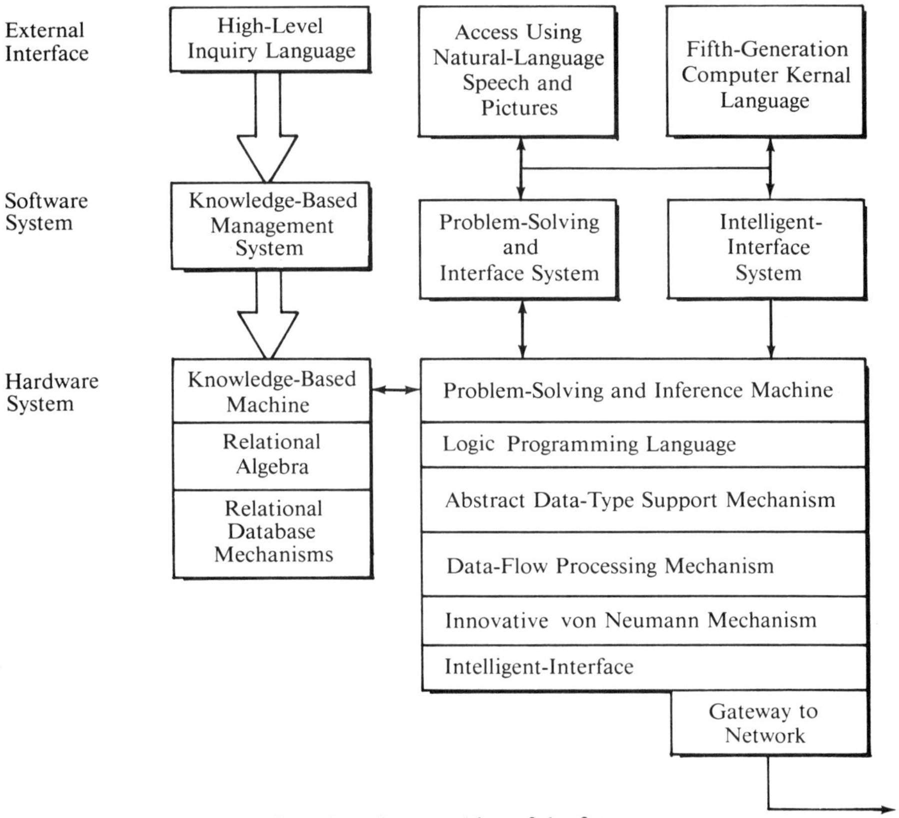

Figure 6-25 Intelligent interface machine of the future

CD-ROM can help you get your work done faster and more accurately. They are available for everything from financial databases to massive font collections. For example, you can use CD-ROM products like the Oxford English Dictionary and Microsoft Bookshelf to look up word spellings. These function as a CD-ROM reference library that is accessible from a word processor, database, or other application. There are general database products, such as Grolier's New Electronic Encyclopedia, as well as more specific products, such as Matthew Bender's Intellectual Property Law. Other databases available include the Ziff-Davis Computer Select and the UMI Washington Post on Disk. Animations are available on National Geographic's Mammals disk and Microsoft's Multimedia Bookshelf.

There are thousands of titles available and millions of installed drives. Some software products, such as Microsoft's multimedia extensions for Windows, are available only on CD-ROM. There are also multimedia disks that incorporate video and synchronized sound.

The third-generation drives have faster speeds and lower prices than earlier products. The newer products have an average access time of about 350 ms.

CD-ROM Technology

CD-ROM is a relatively new technology that has evolved from CD-audio. A single 4.7-inch plastic CD-ROM disk can hold 660MB of information. However, you cannot write on the disk or erase any portion of its contents. The cost of reproducing a disk from a master is generally less than $10 per copy.

The disk surface contains microscopic pits and lands which hold the information. A beam from a small laser in the CD-ROM player illuminates this ridged surface and reflects the stored information to a light-detecting photodiode, which interprets the surface irregularities. Nothing touches the surface of the disk.

CD-ROM players can read both CD-ROM and CD-audio disks. Both types of disks have the same appearance. However, the coding standards for the CD-ROM disks are significantly more stringent in order to assure the integrity of the stored information.

Formats

Today's CD-ROM drives are standardized—the drives meet the same specifications, and most units are similar. CD-ROM drives support the High Sierra and ISO 9660 standards, which document the basic rules for storing data. This allows you to play most newer disks in almost any CD-ROM drive.

The High Sierra format evolved from a 1986 meeting at the High Sierra Hotel in Lake Tahoe, Nevada. There was no international standard at that time, and the data format established at this meeting allowed CD-ROMs to be read by CD-ROM players from different manufacturers. It also became the basis for the international standard ISO 9660. The High Sierra data format is a subset of ISO 9660.

Although a CD-ROM can theoretically hold 680MB of data, most commercial disks do not exceed 600MB. Some drives can read the maximum possible amount of data on a CD-ROM (about 680MB).

Performance Factors

Important factors in a drive's performance include the average access time, throughput, and the size of the drive's buffer. The faster drives have an access time of 350 ms, with 64K buffers and a throughput of 150K per second. This is about three times slower than a floppy disk drive.

The newer drives provide faster access times, improved data transfer rates, and other improvements in performance and functionality. The average access time of 350 ms is important since the data transfer rate of a drive is fixed at 150K per second; therefore, the time it takes the head to seek out a particular piece of information is the main determinant of the drive's performance.

Another key performance feature is a continuous-read facility. This ensures that the maximum amount of data at the bus gets to the drive. Rather than fetching a sector and then waiting for a software command to get the next sector, continuous-read drives take the next few sectors and move them to the drive's cache. This results in a more even flow of data between the CD-ROM drive and the PC. Without the continuous-read capability, scrolling on the screen can appear to jump, and animated sequences will not appear to be continuous. If you use multimedia, the CD-ROM drive should have a continuous-read facility.

The newer CD-ROM drives are also designed to reduce dust errors. When the read head is dirty, it cannot decode the light reflected by the lands and pits on the disk's surface and the data becomes lost. You can overcome this problem with self-cleaning lenses and double-seal drive enclosures. Drives can also fail from a bad power supply, faulty lens assemblies, and other problems.

CD-ROM Packaging

CD-ROMs usually come packaged inside protective plastic boxes called *jewel cases.* The case provides protection for the disk during shipment and storage. Some CD-ROM drives use the disk directly from the jewel case, requiring you to replace the disk in the case the moment you remove it from the drive. In other drives, you place the CD-ROM in a plastic disk case, called a *caddy,* which has a built-in metal shutter. When you insert the caddy in the drive, the shutter slides to the side to reveal the disk to the drive's optical read head. The caddy provides protection for the disk until you can return it to its jewel case.

Most CD-ROM drives come with a mounting kit (if the unit is internal), cables, adapter, a caddy for holding disks in the drive, and Microsoft's MS-DOS CD-ROM Extensions (MSCDEX) Version 2.2. (In order to use the drive with DOS, you will need the Microsoft Extensions.) MSCDEX uses the network interrupt for communications between the device driver and DOS.

Upgrades

Upgrading to a CD-ROM drive is relatively easy. You plug the drive into the adapter, and you can even daisy chain multiple drives off of the first unit. Most new drives connect to standard SCSI adapters. Many earlier drives used proprietary SCSI adapters, and you could not daisy chain standard SCSI peripherals to these adapters as shown in Figure 6-26 or operate drives by different manufacturers from the same interface.

If LAN access is important, there are multidrive units, software, and high-speed controllers from both Online Computer Systems and Meridan Data that allow several users to access multiple drives simultaneously. There are also products like Pioneer's CD-ROM Changer, which has a cartridge that can hold six disks.

You can use most of these drives to play music. If you are equipped with phone and audio jacks and a remote control, you can play audio CDs. Some drives let you play audio CDs only via software control.

Chinon. The Chinon CDC-431 has an access time of 350 ms, an SCSI interface, a disk caddy, and a remote control unit. The Chinon does not use continuous read, and animation may not have a smooth flow. It has an LED display window, emergency eject, power and busy lights, and RCA and volume-controlled headphone jacks.

The remote control lets you skip between tracks, start, stop, pause, play random tracks, scan, and repeat either the last or all tracks played. You can play both music and data without having to use software to control the music.

Hitachi. The Hitachi CDR-1750S has a standard SCSI adapter, but a proprietary bus is used in the CDR-1700S. The CDR-1700S is much slower since it uses a 32K cache buffer, and the proprietary parallel interface it uses was developed earlier for XT machines. The CDR-1750S uses a 64K cache and an SCSI adapter.

The CDR-1700S causes animations to appear jerky and unrealistic. The device driver first reads the data, turns off an interrupt, and then waits for the next command. The faster drivers used in the CDR-1750S do not go through this procedure. Both the smaller cache size and the use of the Hitachi bus affect playback in the CDR-1700S.

The CDR-1750S comes with an SCSI card, a disk caddy and cables, several audio utilities, and Microsoft MSCDEX. It can perform continuous reads.

Both models use the same drive. The case is sealed to keep dust out, and there is an automatic lens-cleaning mechanism and a double-door

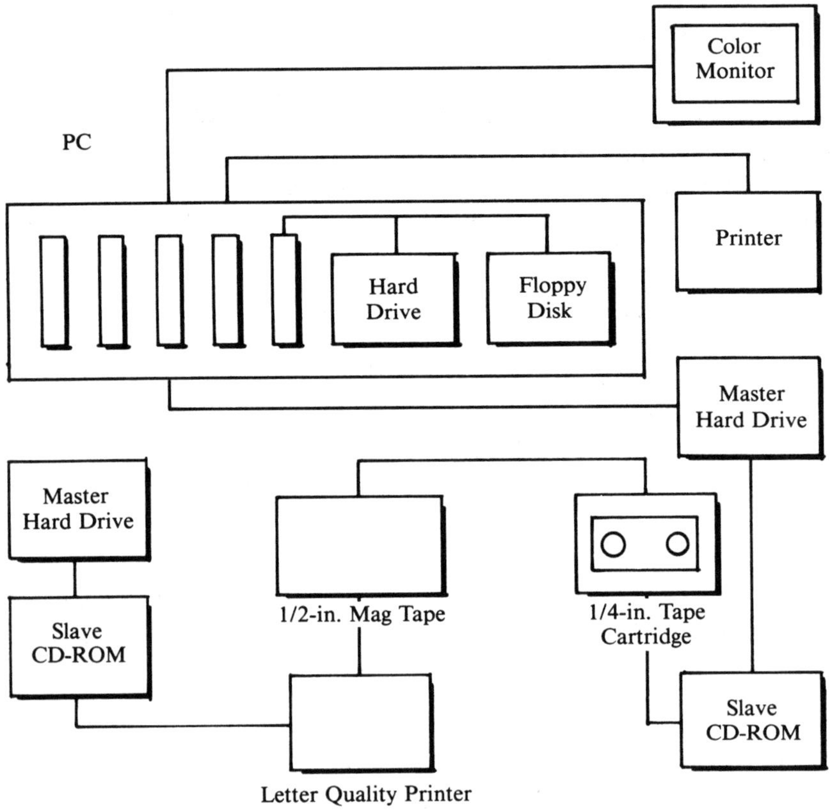

Figure 6-26 Daisy chaining CD-ROMs with standard SCSI adapters

system to reduce dust in the caddy area. There are disk-loaded, in-use, and power-on LEDs.

Texel. The Texel DM-5021 supports continuous reads, and animation displays run smoothly. There are no RCA jacks or emergency-eject mechanism. It uses an SCSI adapter card with drivers, and it comes with MSCDEX. You can use it to play audio CDs. The card can support other SCSI devices, and you can also get a parallel adapter plug that lets you run SCSI devices through your printer port.

Toshiba. The Toshiba TXM-3201A1 uses a standard SCSI adapter. The drive has a drive-activity light, an eject button, and two Centronics-style SCSI connectors. DIP switches set parity and run the test function. You can use the drive in an audio mode to play audio CDs, and the drive can be run in either a horizontal or vertical plane. The time it takes to eject a disk is a bit slow, and the volume control is not continuous since the drive uses a multiposition switch. The unit lacks a power-on light and RCA connectors.

The TXM-3201A1 includes a disk caddy and MSCDEX. It provides good performance, and, if used to play animations, the results should be smooth and natural. Dust protection is also good.

7

UPGRADING YOUR PRINTER

As you begin to rely on your computer more, you could find that your present printer no longer meets your needs. It might be too slow or noisy, or it might not provide the quality that has become expected today. Advances in printer technology continue, and printers have improved in many areas while prices have continued to drop.

The printer is a productivity and efficiency tool. Despite E-mail and LANs (products that might seem to reduce the need for printers), the need for printers continues to grow. As computer use grows, a wider variety of applications means more printer output (memos, purchase orders, acknowledgments, letters, bids, data sheets, mailings, shipping documents, accounting reports, and presentations). We use paper for most important documents, either as originals or hard-copy backup of important disk files. Printers need better technology as the need for more hard copy grows. Better, faster printers help us become more efficient and productive.

EVOLUTION OF THE PRINTER

During the 1970s, word processors replaced typewriters, and making revisions became easier. Daisy-wheel printers became the office standard because they provided letter-quality output from changeable print wheels (Fig 7-1). The quality and noise of these word processors were similar to the electronic typewriters of the time.

Figure 7-1 Internal view of daisy-wheel printer showing print wheel, hammer, and ribbon

Then, the personal computer appeared with word processing programs. The price of daisy-wheel printers dropped, but they were still slow and noisy.

As the use of spreadsheets and related graphics grew, daisy-wheel printers could not handle these new output requirements, and improved dot-matrix printers emerged to fill this void. Dot-matrix printers were four to five times faster and could print graphics (Fig 7-2). As manufacturers improved the dot-matrix printers by adding more pins and by increasing the number of passes to a printed line, these printers provided NLQ (near letter-quality) output. They also became competitive in price with daisy-wheel printers. NLQ improved and became acceptable for all but the most critical hard copy.

In 1984, the first low-cost laser printers appeared with the Hewlett-Packard (HP) LaserJet. These printers offered speed, efficiency, and versatility with excellent print quality. They were also quiet compared to both daisy-wheel and dot-matrix printers. Laser printers also had the capability to provide the type of fonts generally used only for typesetting.

Laser printers could print 5 to 12 pages per minute (ppm) and had the ability to produce camera-ready copy for newsletters and other mailings (Fig 7-3). They also made it possible to do mailings with cut sheets without the need for separating continuous-form paper or removing the tractor feed strips. You could also do printing directly on transparencies for overhead presentations.

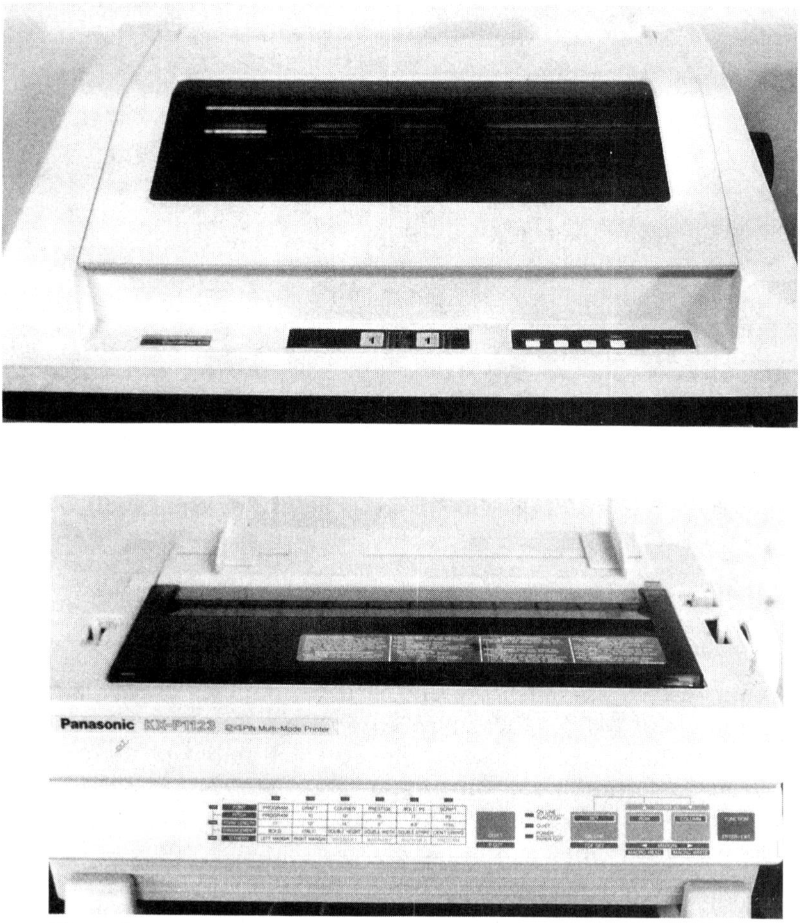

Figure 7-2 Dot-matrix printers

TYPES OF PRINTER MECHANISMS

A number of printing mechanisms have appeared over the years. Some never became very popular, but they were designed and marketed to fill special needs. Others like the dot-matrix-impact printers became so popular that they became known simply as dot-matrix printers.

Impact Printers (Dot-Matrix)

This popular type of printer is flexible and relatively inexpensive. It is a serial printer, meaning it generates one character at a time. It creates the

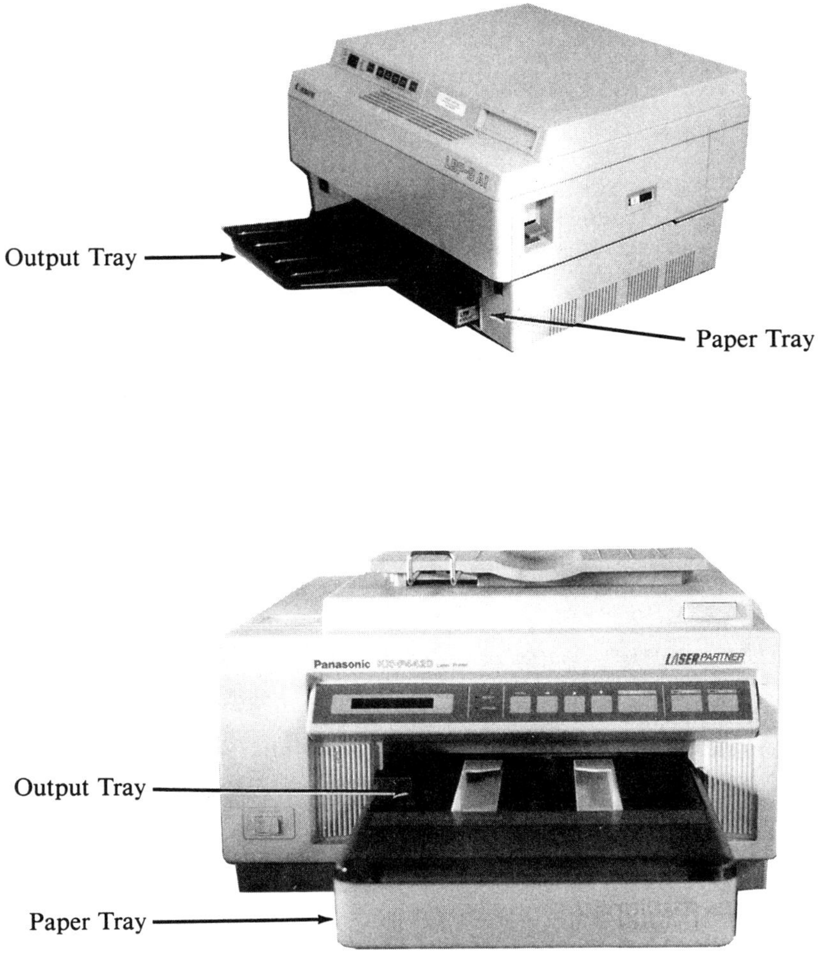

Figure 7-3 Laser printers

character by selectively moving a row of pins that print dots to form the desired character. The dot-matrix printing mechanism (called the print head) is fixed and does not rotate, and it prints using a vertical array of the wire pins. As the pins move in and out to form the characters, the print head moves across the paper (Fig 7-4).

Low-cost, low-resolution printers use 7–9 pins. Higher-cost, higher-resolution printers use 18–24 pins. ROM stores the characters to be printed and determines which pins in the array are to strike the ribbon and imprint the character on the paper. The more wire pins the unit has, the

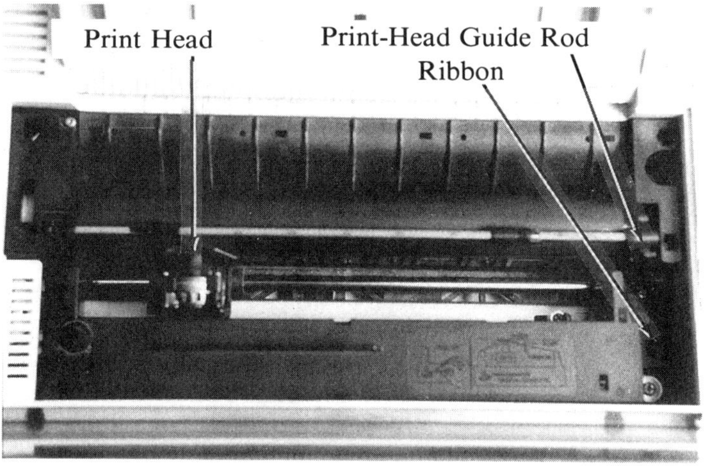

Figure 7-4 Internal view of dot-matrix printer showing print head, print-head guide rod, and ribbon

more closely the printing mechanism approximates the print quality of fully formed characters.

The impact process used is the traditional way to transfer ink to paper. It involves the pressing of the type element against an inked ribbon and onto the paper. In the dot-matrix impact printer, pressing the character-forming pins against the inked ribbon makes an impression of the character on the paper.

The dot-matrix impact printer consists of a print head with 7, 9, 18, or 24 solenoid-operated print wires (see Tables 7-1 to 7-5). A belt or cable moves the print head down the roller.

Two stepper motors drive the printer: one moves the belt or cable attached to the print head, while the other advances the paper (Fig 7-5). An internal microprocessor in the printer independently controls the two motors.

Pressure from a friction roller controls the paper. Tractors control pin-fed paper. The paper can be fanfold (with or without tractor holes), rolls, or single sheets. Optional roll-paper holders and single-sheet feeder assemblies are available for many machines. The inked ribbon is usually self-contained in a plastic cartridge and is easily replaced by opening the clear inspection lid over the print head and roller area.

Nonimpact Printers

Nonimpact printers do not use a ribbon, and depending on whether you are using plain or coated paper, there are various techniques for getting the data onto the paper. Printers that are popular for use with plain paper are:

TABLE 7-1 Narrow-Carriage 9-Pin Printers

Manufacturer/Model	Draft Speed	NLQ/LQ Speed	Graphics Resolution	Tractor Pin/Feed	Printer Emulation	Interface
Brother M-1109	100	25	216 x 240		IBM Graphics	Parallel/Serial
Citizen 120D	120	25	240 x 216	X	Epson FX IBM Proprinter	Parallel/Serial
Okidata ML182	120	30	240 x 72	X	Okidata	Parallel/Serial
Honeywell Compuprint 4/20	200	40	240 x 72	X	Epson FX100	Parallel/Serial
Epson FX-850	264	45	240 x 216	X	IBM Proprinter Epson	Parallel/Serial
Dataproducts 9030	300	33	240 x 72	X	IBM Proprinter Epson FX86/F286	Parallel/Serial
Fujitsu DX2300	324	54	360 x 180	X	Epson FX80/JX80 IBM Proprinter	Parallel/Serial

TABLE 7-2 Wide-Carriage 9-Pin Printers

Manufacturer/Model	Draft Speed	NLQ/LQ Speed	Graphics Resolution	Tractor Pin/Feed	Printer Emulation	Interface
Mannesmann Tally MT290	200	50	240 x 72	X	Epson FX IBM Graphics	Parallel/Serial
Okidata ML 193	200	40	240 x 216	X	Okidata IBM Proprinter	Parallel/Serial
Printek 2000	200	40	144 x 144	X	Epson FX Diablo	Parallel/Serial
Brother M-1709	240	33	216 x 240	X	Epson FX, IBM IBM Proprinter	Parallel/Serial
Epson T-750	240	40	240 x 72	X	Epson	Parallel/Serial
Dataproducts 9040	300	33	240 x 72	X	IBM Proprinter Epson FX-86/286	Parallel/Serial
Honeywell Compuprint 4/41	300	70	240 x 72	X	Epson FX/JX IBM	Parallel/Serial
Fujitsu DX2400	324	54	360 x 180	X	Epson FX/JX IBM	Parallel/Serial

TABLE 7-3 Wide-Carriage 18-Pin Printers

Manufacturer/Model	Draft Speed	NLQ/LQ Speed	Graphics Resolution	Tractor Pin/Feed	Printer Emulation	Interface
Honeywell Compuprint 4/62	250	120	144 x 144	X	Epson JX-80 IBM Graphics	Parallel/Serial
Mannesmann Tally MT230/18	300	150	240 x 144	X	Epson FX-105 IBM Proprinter	Parallel/Serial
Printek 930	300	80	144 x 144	Diablo	Parallel/Serial	
ALPS P2100	400	80	240 x 216	X	Epson FX-100	Parallel/Serial
Dataproducts 8070 Plus	400	100	165 x 82	X	IBM Graphics	Parallel/Serial
Honeywell Compuprint 4/66	480	75	144 x 144	Epson JX80 IBM Graphics	Parallel/Serial	
Seikosha SBP-10AI	800	104	240 x 72	X	Epson IBM Proprinter	Parallel/Serial

TABLE 7-4 Narrow-Carriage 24-Pin Printers

Manufacturer/Model	Draft Speed	NLQ/LQ Speed	Graphics Resolution	Tractor Pin/Feed	Printer Emulation	Interface
Epson Actionprinter L-1000	180	50	360 x 180	X	Epson	Parallel/Serial
Panasonic KX-P1124	192	63	360 x 360	X	Epson LQ-2500 IBM Proprinter	Parallel/Serial
NEC Pinwriter P5200	265	75	360 x 360		Epson LQ	Parallel/Serial
Dataproducts 9034	300	83	240 x 180	X	Epson LQ800/1000 Diablo 630	Parallel/Serial

TABLE 7-5 Wide-Carriage 24-Pin Printers

Manufacturer/Model	Draft Speed	NLQ/LQ Speed	Graphics Resolution	Tractor Pin/Feed	Printer Emulation	Interface
Fujitsu DL2400	216	60	360 x 180	X	Epson JX-80 IBM Graphics	Parallel/Serial
Mannesmann Tally MT222	220	72	360 x 360	X	Epson LQ1500/2500 Diablo 630, IBM Proprinter XL, NEC P	Parallel/Serial
Sanyo PR-241	228	63	360 x 180	X	IBM Graphics	Parallel/Serial
Digital Equipment LA210	240	40	132 x 72	X	Epson MX80 IBM Graphics	Parallel/Serial
Olympia NPC 136-24	240	40	360 x 180	X	Epson LQ2500 IBM Proprinter	Parallel/Serial
Fujitsu DL4400	264	73	360 x 180	X	IBM Proprinter Epson LQ-2500	Parallel/Serial
NEC Pinwriter P5300	265	75	360 x 360	X	Epson LQ Series	Parallel/Serial

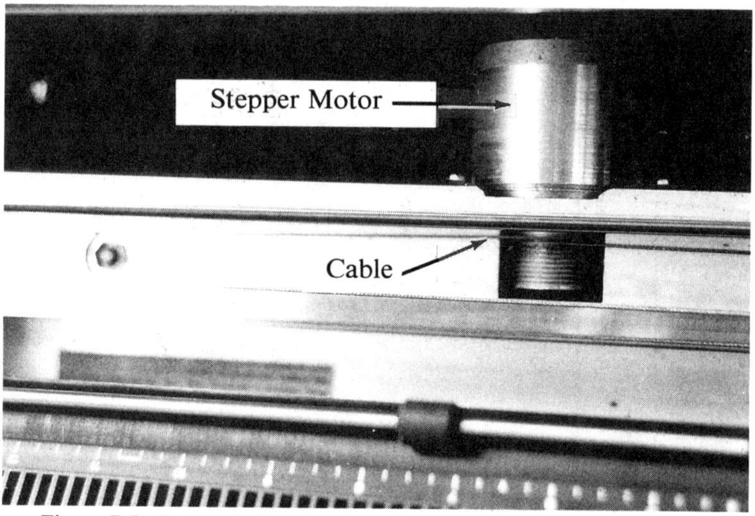

Figure 7-5 Internal view showing stepper motor and cable for moving print head

1. Inkjet printers, which spray tiny droplets of ink onto the paper in a matrix to form the image.
2. Laser printers, which use a laser to write images on a copier drum.
3. LCS and LED printers, which use liquid-crystal sensors or light-emitting diodes to write images on a copier drum.

Coated-paper printers include the following types:

1. Thermal printers, which use heated elements to write on thermally sensitive paper.
2. Electrosensitive printers, which use electric charges to burn off a thin metallic coating on a special conductive paper to reveal a black undercoat.
3. Electrostatic printers, which selectively charge the coated paper using a stylus and then pass the paper through a toner that is attracted to the charged area on the paper.

Nonimpact printers that create matrix images include the thermal-matrix printer. In this type, the print head moves across the paper and forms characters by heating specially treated paper with its heated pins.

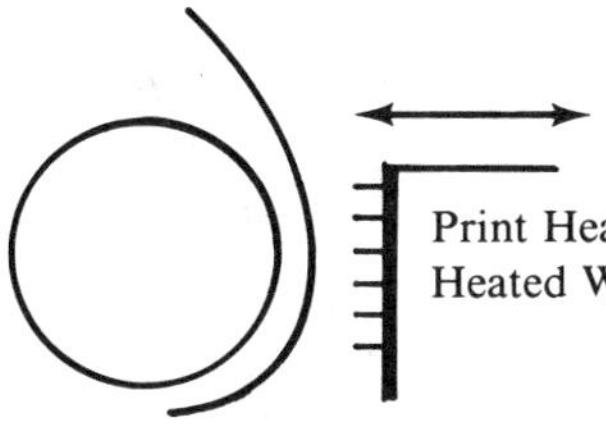

Figure 7-6 Thermal-matrix printing

Print rates are typically 20 to 120 cps. Figure 7-6 illustrates the thermal printing method. With this type of printer, the dot-matrix characters are printed one at a time, in serial fashion.

Electrosensitive-matrix printers use an aluminum-coated paper that changes color when a voltage is applied. The print head uses electrodes that are switched on when a dot is to be formed. An electric current travels through the paper to a metal plate behind the paper. The plate is at ground potential, and it completes the circuit path.

Serial Printers

Serial or character printers print one character at a time, similar to a typewriter. Some dot-matrix impact printers are serial printers.

Line Printers

Line printers are different from serial-printing dot-matrix units in that they form characters for a complete line, one line at a time, and are rated in terms of lines per minute (lpm). This makes them much faster than serial printers, which generate only one character at a time. These printers use a type-element array, such as a drum, chain, train, cylinder, belt, or band. Table 7-6 is a sampling of available line printers.

Some line-matrix printers use a shuttle comb or bank of print elements. Multihead matrix printers have multiple solenoid-operated print heads. Impact line printers, such as the band, drum, and chain types, use a hammer to force the paper (from behind) against the ribbon and a moving-type element. Drum printers (Fig 7-7) have a complete set of characters embossed against the circumference of a horizontally rotating steel drum. There is one full set of characters and one hammer for each print position. Characters to be printed are transferred to the printer memory one line at a time. The system scans the memory and couples it to the rotating drum.

TABLE 7-6 Wide-Carriage Line Printers with Tractor Feed

Manufacturer/Model	Graphics Resolution H x V dpi	Draft Print Speed	NLQ/LQ Print Speed	Buffer Size	Printer Emulation	Interface
Genicom 4410	210 x 144	400	66	2K	Epson Printronix	Parallel/Serial
Printronix P6040L	120 x 144	400	90	2K	Epson Printronix	Parallel/Serial
Dataproducts LM600	140 x 144	840	110	2K	HP PCL Printronix	Parallel/Serial
Dataproducts LM1200	140 x 144	1600	253	2K	HP PCL Printronix	Parallel/Serial

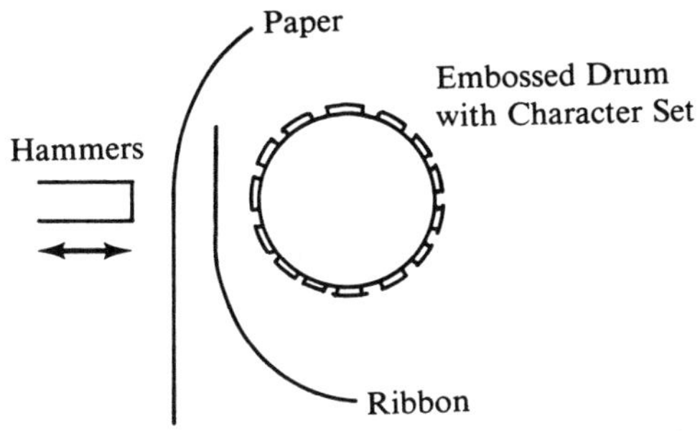

Figure 7-7 Drum-type of line printer

As the character to be printed rotates into position, the printer issues a *hammer-on* signal and the hammer strikes the paper, forcing it into the ribbon and drum. The print rate for this type of mechanism is determined by a combination of drum speed, character size, paper movement time, and data transfer rate. Many line printers use a single-hammer system and a platen or roller with a series of raised ridges.

The carriage movement, the motion of the hammer, and the revolution of the platen are synchronized due to the mechanical construction of the hammer, platen, and a dot sensor. Figure 7-8 shows the basic relationship between the hammer, the position of the printed dot, and the dot-sensor signal.

Page Printers

Some printers, such as laser and LED printers, print a whole page at a time. The mechanisms used are discussed later on in this chapter in the section on laser printers.

Printer Problems

There are unique problems in each of the printing techniques discussed. Line printers, for example, must be adjusted properly, or there will be smear or character misregistration. Vertically moving character sets, such as drums, can produce vertical misregistration or wavy lines. Horizontally moving character sets, such as bands and belts, can cause horizontal misregistration or uneven spacing between the characters in a line.

IMPORTANT FACTORS IN CHOOSING A PRINTER

The two most important factors you should consider when selecting a printer are probably speed and print quality. Speed is made up of the print

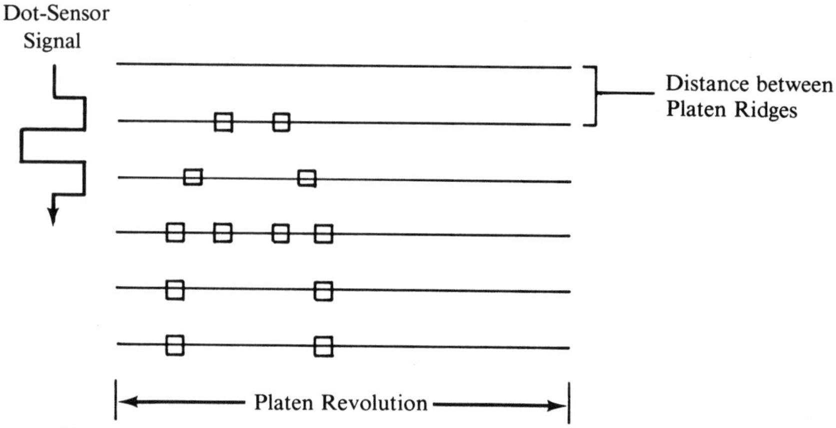

Figure 7-8 Line printing relationships

rate, throughput, and input data rate. In some printers, the print rate indicates how many characters the printer can place on the paper in a second and is measured in cps. In line printers, it refers to the number of lines printed per minute or lpm. In page printers (laser, LED types) the print rate is usually in terms of pages per minute or ppm. The input data rate relates to the interfacing of the printer with the computer.

The draft-mode speed of the dot-matrix printer is the fastest speed at which the printer can print text and is measured in cps. The NLQ/LQ speed is the speed of the printer in its best-quality print mode. Manufacturers might refer to this as near letter quality, letter quality, or correspondence quality.

The maximum resolution of a printer is measured in dpi. The figure given is the number of horizontal dots by vertical dots. The higher the numbers, the better the resolution of the printer.

Noise is an important consideration. Impact printers generally exhibit noise figures ranging from 50 adjusted decibels (dba), to as high as 75 dba. Dot-matrix printer heads make a buzzing sound, but this is usually something you can live with. You can always cover the unit with a noise-dampening cover.

Check the buffer or base-memory (RAM) size of the printer, which should be in kilobytes or megabytes. The printer uses this memory to store the information the computer is sending it to print. Also, the more memory a printer has, the more fonts it can handle for quicker access and faster printing. Most printers have expandable buffers, you can get a RAM upgrade via a proprietary expansion board or the addition of memory chips.

The printer interface is the type of connection that the computer uses to communicate with the printer. Parallel and serial ports are the two most

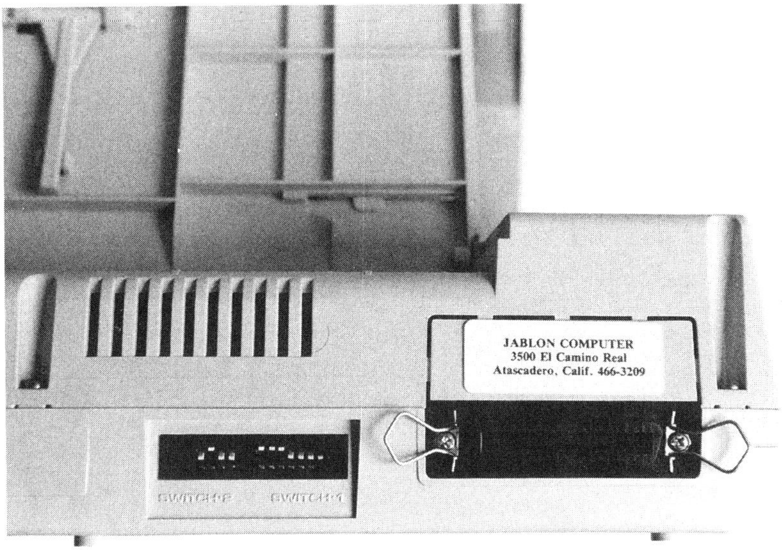

Figure 7-9 Rear view of dot-matrix printer showing Centronics parallel interface

common printer interfaces. Parallel refers to the Centronics parallel interface (Figs 7-9 and 7-10), and serial to refers to the standard RS-232-C interface (Fig 7-11). The connections at the computer end are shown in Figures 7-12, 7-13, and 7-14.

Many dot-matrix printers can handle tractor or pinfeed paper. Some also have friction feed capability to handle single sheets of paper. You can usually do color printing by adding a four-pass, four-color ribbon.

Printer emulations refer to the different printer languages that the printer can emulate. For example, a printer that can emulate an Epson FX-100 is compatible with any software that is designed to work with that printer. You can order some printers with a specific emulation, such as IBM or Epson compatibility.

DOT-MATRIX PRINTERS

Printer Controls

The following controls are found in most impact printers, and their proper operation is essential to most printer functions. The paper bail holds the paper against the platen. Marks on the bail help you position paper on the platen and locate the horizontal printing position.

The paper thickness lever adjusts the print head position to allow for

U1	U2	U3	U4	U5
1741	8259	8088	8087	714S30
5 62-pin slots			socket	U-6
				8288

U7	U8	U9	U10	U11
74LS 373		74LS 245	74LS 373	74LS 373	8284

U12	U13	U14	U15	U16	U17	U18	U19	U20	U21	U22	U23	U24	U25
74LS 245	74LS 245	74LS 245	74LS 244	74LS 244	74LS 244	74LS 373	74LS 670	RN1	SW1	RN2	74LS 244	74LS 322	SW2
		U27										U26	
												74LS 175	

Spare socket U28	U29	U30	U31	U32	U33	U34	U35	U36
	9264	9264	MK36A 70N-4	9264	9264	8253	8237	8255

U37	0	U38	U39	U40	U41	U42	U43	U44	U45
4164		4164	4164	4164	4164	4164	4164	4164	4164
U53	1	U54	U55	U56	U57	U58	U59	U60	U61
4164		4164	4164	4164	4164	4164	4164	4164	4164
U69	2	U70	U71	U72	U73	U74	U75	U76	U77
4164		4164	4164	4164	4164	4164	4164	4164	4164
U85	3	U86	U87	U88	U89	U90	U91	U92	U93
4164		4164	4164	4164	4164	4164	4164	4164	4164
RAM banks									

(next to RAM banks)

U46	U47	U48	U49	U50	U51	U52
All 74LS 138	138	138	08	02	04	08
U62	U63	U64	U65	U66	U67	U68
74LS 138	138	20	138	138	74	RN3
U78	U79	U80	U81	U82	U83	U84
74LS RN4	158	125	00	74	04	10
U94	U95		U96	U97	U98	U99
74LS 04			74	08	175	04

Figure 7-10 Centronics parallel interface reference

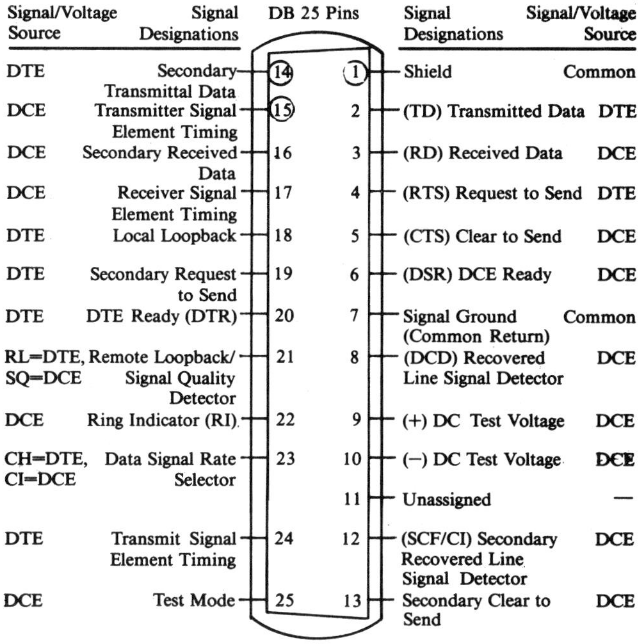

Figure 7-11 RS-232 interface reference

different paper thickness and multipage forms. The lever should be close to the platen for normal printing and farther away from the platen for thicker sheets and multicopy forms.

The paper release lever controls paper-holding tension. In the forward position, paper is tight against the platen. In the backward position, the paper is free for positioning or removal. The platen knob allows manual control of the platen for paper insertion and for changing the paper's vertical position.

Maintaining Printers

Most printers need only a little preventive maintenance. You can clean the surfaces and platen with a damp cloth. Be careful to not use cleaners with solvents or excessive water. To help maintain proper operating temperatures inside the printer, avoid operating the printer in extreme temperatures, such as those found in direct sunlight, and keep them away from direct airflow from room heaters and air conditioners. Keep paper clips, coffee, matches, cold drinks, and other small objects and liquids away from the printer.

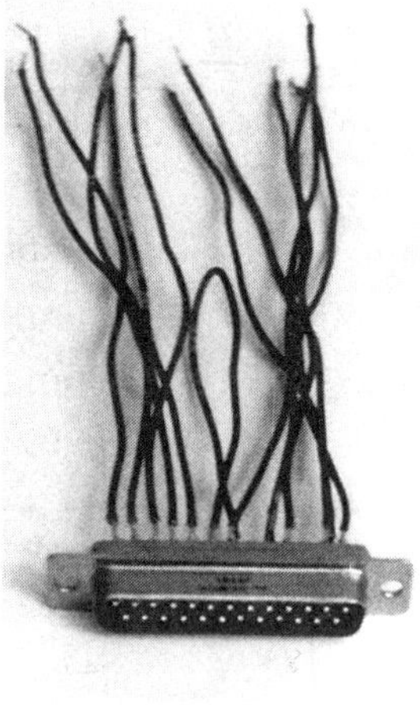

Figure 7-12 DB 25 connector used in serial interfaces (printer end) and parallel interfaces (computer end)

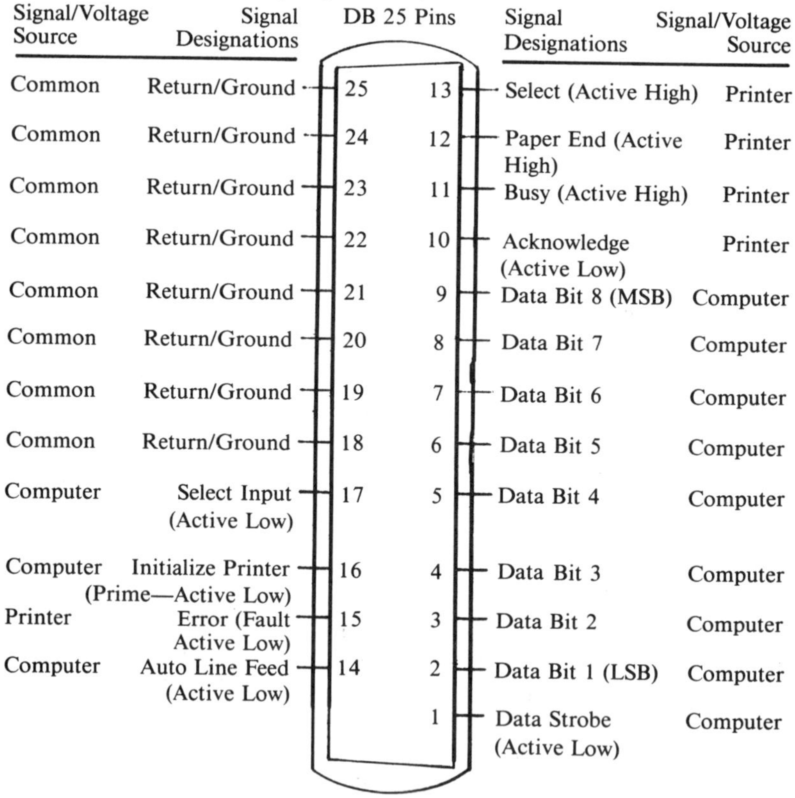

Figure 7-13 IBM PC-style parallel interface

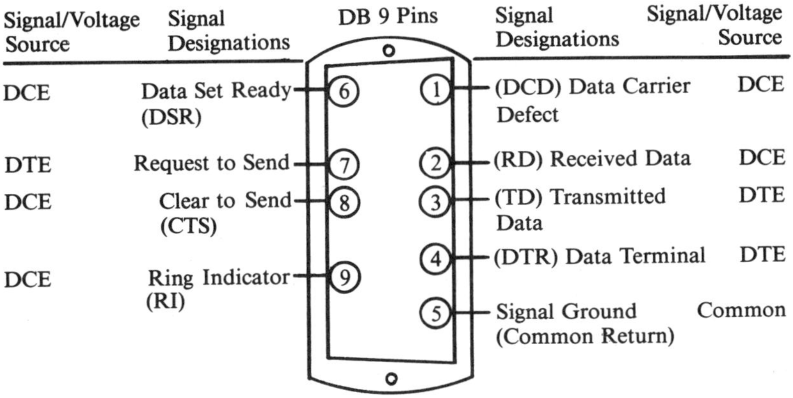

Figure 7-14 IBM AT-style RS-232 interface

Select the right paper for the job. Always make sure to position the paper squarely in the tray and set it tightly around the platen. Also, make sure the paper thickness lever is in correct position. To remove paper from the printer, use the form-feed switch or turn the platen knob.

Samples of printouts you made when the printer and/or the ribbon was new can help you know when to replace both the print head and ribbon cartridge. Use only quality ribbon cartridges in your printer. Other cartridges might not give the same performance and could even damage your printer. Store print heads and ribbon cartridges in their containers, in the same environment as the printer.

The platen and paper rollers are made of rubber and require periodic cleaning to cleanse and renew their surfaces for more positive friction drive. You should periodically clean the platen, paper rollers, and pressure rollers. You will need to remove the platen for access to these. Use soft tissues or cloth wipers and a commercial platen cleaner. Be careful not to get platen cleaner in the unit.

Some printers use a plastic or metal guide to hold paper flat as the print head moves across the paper. The guide moves with the print head. Usually, you have to remove the ribbon cartridge to get at the guide. If the guide is held in place by spring clips, you might be able to grasp it firmly on each end and pull straight up to remove it. You can clean the guide using soft tissue or a soft cloth, Fantastik, Formula 409, or other commercial product.

Do not use alcohol to clean the platen or other rubber parts since it hardens the surface. Periodic wiping of the exterior of the printer with a soft, damp cloth will keep up its appearance. You should periodically wipe and dust the interior to remove large accumulations of paper dust and other foreign matter. It is best to lubricate the printer when it is being reassembled—place a drop of light machine oil on each bearing surface after it has been wiped clean with a soft cloth.

Examples of Dot-Matrix Printers

Epson. The Epson LQ-570 printer produces drafts at 315 cps at 15 characters per inch (cpi). The LQ-870 prints drafts at 413 cps at 15 cpi. The wide-carriage LQ-1170 also prints drafts at up to 413 cps. All three printers come with scalable fonts and enhanced graphics and use Epson ESC/P2, a printer control language designed to produce two scalable fonts ranging in size from 8 to 32 points. There are 12 built-in fonts, 360 x 360 graphics, and print enhancements (such as shadow, italic, and outline) for custom documents. These printers include ESC/P2 drivers for Microsoft and WordPerfect software.

There are four feed paths—top, front, rear, and bottom—so you can run a variety of paper types and sizes, including continuous four-part forms, labels, envelopes, and letterhead. Automatic paper handling allows you to load and stack both single sheets and continuous paper.

You control font selection and paper handling on the front control panel.

The Epson LQ-570 prints NLQ documents at up to 105 cps at 15 cpi. The column width is 80 picas. It accepts No. 6 and No. 10 envelopes, single sheets, continuous paper, labels, and forms and has four paper paths.

The Epson narrow-carriage FX-850 and the wide-carriage FX-1050 use 9-pin printing. These will print up to 264 cps at 12 cpi in high-speed draft mode or 54 cps at 12 cpi in NLQ mode, so you can produce a typical business letter in less than 20 seconds. The graphics resolution is 240 x 216 dpi. Both printers use the Epson standard code for printers.

The 24-pin LQ-200 printer offers seven bit-mapped, NLQ fonts and front-panel controls. In addition to top and rear paper loading, the LQ-200 also has bottom loading. There are also type-style enhancements like double-high/double-wide characters, shadow, and outline.

The LX-810 is a 9-pin dot-matrix printer. It prints 240 cps in draft mode and 48 cps in NLQ mode. The LX-810 has a built-in 4K buffer.

NEC. NEC dot-matrix printers include the Pinwriter P6200 (narrow carriage) and P6300 (wide carriage). They have optional color capabilities and built-in and optional typefaces. A memory buffer of 80K frees your system while the printer produces up to forty pages.

These 24-wire printers have a rear feed, and the push tractor allows you to feed continuous forms without having to remove them when you want to print single sheets. You can use a bottom feed slot when printing continuous labels, envelopes, multipart forms, and card stock. There is also a tear-off bar for printing invoices and sales orders.

The P9300 is a 24-wire printer that you can use for single sheets, cut-sheet pages, six-part forms, envelopes, labels, and even card stock. The P9300 prints at speeds up to 400 cps and produces NLQ printing at over four ppm. You can have color capabilities with the simple change of a ribbon. The P9300 provides characters sets for nineteen different languages.

Okidata. The Okidata Microline 320 and 321 9-pin printers run at 300 cps in draft mode and 250 cps in utility mode (designed for invoices, shipping documents, and receipts). For NLQ documents, you can print at 63 cps. A direct-access panel on the front is used to select type size, print quality, and form feed.

The Microline 380 is a 24-pin printer with built-in, resident fonts and different character pitches. There is a paper park that lets you insert and print single sheets without removing your continuous-form paper. The push tractor for rear feed and power-assisted paper loading for top feed make it easier to insert paper stock. There is an optional pull tractor for bottom feeding of multipart forms, card stock, and labels. If you use a lot of single sheets, there is an optional cut-sheet feeder to handle the paper. The Microline 380 prints in NLQ mode at 60 cps and in utility mode at 180 cps.

The pull tractors on the narrow-carriage models (320, 390, 380, and 182) and the wide-carriage models (321, 391, and 393) allow bottom feeding of paper. You can use these printers for thick forms, heavy card stock, and labels as well as regular paper stock. The narrow-carriage tractors will accept forms from 3 to 10 inches wide; and the wide-carriage 321, 391, and 393 tractors accept media from 3 to 16 inches in width. All the tractors use an acoustic cover.

INKJET PRINTERS

There are 50 nozzles in an inkjet cartridge. Each of these nozzles is about half the diameter of a human hair. An ink bubble forms when a resistive heater is turned. This can occur at up to 3,600 times a second for each nozzle. As the bubble grows to its maximum size, the ink is ejected out of the nozzle. Since the ink cartridges contain print nozzles, every time you add a new cartridge, they are automatically replaced. An average cartridge can produce over 120 million drops of ink. It will take up to 25 individual bubbles to make the dot on an "i."

The cartridges require some special precautions. Always use fresh cartridges, and keep unused print cartridges sealed in their containers. When replacing print cartridges, install the new print cartridge promptly.

Avoid turning the printer off with the print cartridge out of the *park* or *home* position (at the right side of the carriage path). When in the park position, a cap seals the print-cartridge nozzles from exposure to air, preventing the ink from drying in the nozzles. Do not allow the cartridge contacts and nozzles to touch anything, including your fingers. Oils on your skin and dust can affect print quality. Always store print cartridges at room temperature.

Printouts may begin missing one or more rows of dots when the following problems exist:

1. The print cartridge has passed its expiration date.
2. The cartridge is not pressed firmly against the carriage contacts.
3. The cartridge ink reservoir is low or empty.
4. The contacts on the cartridge or printer carriage are dirty.
5. There are bubbles in the cartridge.

Lexmark ExecJet

The Lexmark ExecJet printer offers an upgrade from a hard-wire dot-matrix printer because it is quiet and fast. This wide-carriage, 64-nozzle, letter-quality inkjet printer is designed for IBM PCs, PS/2s and compatibles. It is engineered for low-to-medium usage with versatile paper handling. It has a wide carriage, tractor, automatic sheet feed, optional second bin, and a front manual-feed slot capable of handling documents up to 17 inches wide. You can use it for envelopes, labels, and transparencies.

It has 360 x 360-dpi resolution for text and graphics, quality and draft modes, and 18 resident fonts as well as font cards. With most applications, you will use about one ink cartridge a month. The cartridges have a shelf life of two years.

Hewlett-Packard DeskJet

HP's DeskJet 500 printer produces 300-dpi output like most laser printers. It runs at 3 ppm and is a good solution if you need quality printing, but do not do enough printing to justify the expense of a laser printer. The DeskJet has other laser-like features. It is quiet, so you can be near it while it is running and still conduct a phone conversation. It can handle up to 100 sheets of letter- or legal-size paper with its paper tray.

The DeskJet uses a variation of Hewlett-Packard's printer control language (PCL) for its command language, so it can work with software programs written to drive a HP's LaserJet. The printer has built-in Courier, Gothic, or CG Times fonts, and you can add font cartridges or download fonts to a RAM cartridge. There is a driver that lets Windows programs access scalable Courier, CG Times, Univers, and Symbol typefaces. You can also use the DeskJet 500 with Windows print enhancers like Adobe Type Manager, Facelift, or Superprint.

LASER PRINTERS

The laser (light amplification by stimulated emission of radiation) has become a widely used tool in today's world (Figure 7-15 shows a typical laser printer). In a laser, the frequency and phase of light are fixed, and the beam of light generated is coherent (sharply defined) and intense. The laser can use a gas, liquid, or solid to produce the light beam. The semiconductor laser is the type of solid laser used in printers. It is driven by simple control signals, has a compact size, and consumes less power than other types of lasers.

During printing, the drum is constantly rotating, making several complete rotations per printed page (Fig 7-16). Before forming the image, a rubber cleaning blade cleans off the remaining toner from the previous rotation of the drum. After the drum is cleaned, it is conditioned. The conditioning process consists of the application of a uniform negative charge on the entire surface of the drum.

During the writing operation, the laser beam creates an electrostatic image on the photosensitive drum. This image then develops into a visible image. During the developing process, the electrostatic charge causes toner to be attracted or repelled from charged areas on the drum (Fig 7-17). This forms a visible toner image on the drum. During the transfer operation, the printer applies a positive charge to the back of the paper. This causes the

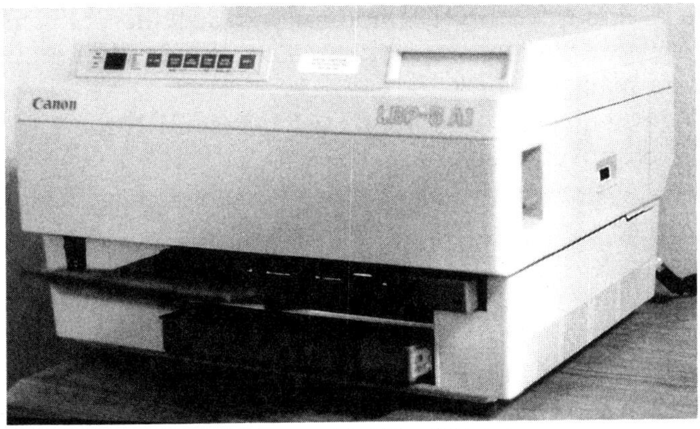

Figure 7-15 Canon laser printer with 300 x 300 dpi

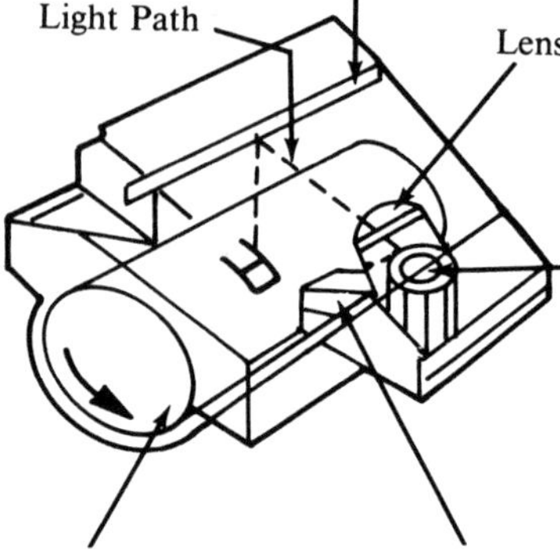

Figure 7-16 Important internal components of the laser printer

negatively charged toner on the drum's surface to be attracted to the page, forming a visible toner image on the page. Before the paper reaches the fusing station, a weak electrostatic attraction and a slight physical adhesion holds the toner on the paper. At the fusing station, heat and pressure melt and fuse the toner into the paper to produce a permanent image on the paper.

The early laser printers functioned in larger offices with high-volume printing. These were usually network systems supporting a number of users, reducing the cost on a per-user basis to a reasonable level.

Some applications, such as large spreadsheets, may not be suitable for laser printers, since paper sizes are fixed by the paper-cassette size. Laser printers are desirable in the following situations:

1. Where output quality is important in documents such as external letters, presentations, reports, newsletters, advertising materials, and camera-ready copy.
2. Where the quantity of output needed is sufficient to justify the additional cost over alternative printers.
3. Where special output styles are needed such as documents with multiple fonts.

You can upgrade laser printers in the following ways:

1. You can use additional paper cassettes for different types of paper (letterhead, second sheet, forms) or different sizes of paper (letter, legal, envelopes).

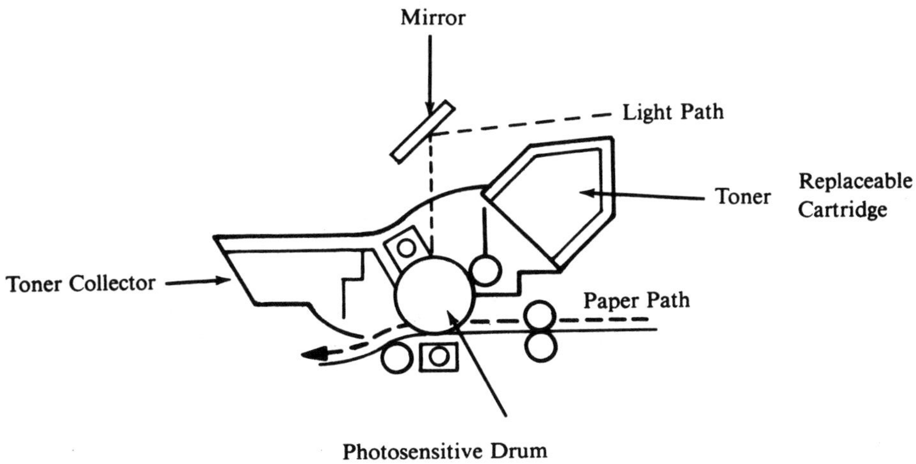

Figure 7-17 Laser printer cartridge

2. You can use additional RAM for fonts or graphics.
3. You can use additional font cards or font cartridges for multiple type styles or sizes.
4. You can use new versions of software that take advantage of a laser printer's power and add downloaded fonts, forms generation, or desktop publishing.

Tables 7-7 through 7-9 list some laser printers available today, from low-speed printers to high-speed models. Included are their resolutions, print speeds, and other features.

Printer Tips

One of the most common causes of poor print quality, faded print, streaking, or spotting is a dirty cartridge or printer. This usually means a build-up of toner and paper fibers on sensitive areas. When the toner level is getting low, the print appears lighter, and white streaks may begin to appear. You can redistribute the toner by removing the cartridge and shaking it several times from end to end and then rocking it from side to side. Reinsert the cartridge and continue to use it until the print begins to fade again. The toner supply is then probably exhausted, and you should replace the cartridge. You can get increased life from a toner cartridge by operating your printer with the print density adjustment dial set on a higher number for lighter print.

When stored properly, an unused toner cartridge still sealed within

TABLE 7-7 Low-Speed Laser Printers

Manufacturer/Model	Resolution (dpi)	Print Speed (ppm)	Base Memory	Maximum Memory	Emulations/ Compatibility*
AEG Olympia Laserstar 6	300 x 300	6	1.5MB	2MB	A,B,C,D,H
ALPS America LPX600N	300 x 300	6	512K	2MB	A,B,E,G,H
Acer Technologies Acer LP-76	300 x 300	6	512K	1.5MB	F
Codonics LPS	300 x 300	6	1.5MB	5.5MB	A,B,C,D,E,F,G,J
Mannesmann Tally MT905	300 x 300	6	512K	4.5MB	A,B,F,H
Okidata Laserline 6	300 x 300	6	128K	512K	E
Packard Bell PB9500	300 x 300	6	1.5MB	4.5MB	F
Personal Comp. LaserImage 1030	300 x 300	6	512K	5MB	A,B,C,F,G,J
Printer Systems Intelligent 106	300 x 300	6	512K	3MB	F,G
Ricoh Corp. PC Laser 6000/PS	300 x 300	6	2MB	4MB	F,J
Sharp Electronics JX-9500 Laser Printer	300 x 300	6	512K	2MB	A,B,F,G,H
TEC LB-1305B	300 x 300	6	512K	1/2/4MB	A,B,F,H
Tandy LP1000	300 x 300	6	1.5MB		F,G
Texas Instruments OmniLaser 2106	300 x 300	6	2MB		A,C,E,J
BGL LaserLeader	300 x 300	8	512K	2.5MB	A,B,E,F
Blaser Star II	300 x 300	8	512K	5MB	A,B,D,E,F
Brother HL-8E	300 x 300	8	1MB	3MB	A,C,D,E,F,G,H
Canon LBP-8	300 x 300	8	1.5MB	4.5MB	A
General Tech. GBT 6636	300 x 300	8	512K	4MB	F
Genicom 6142	400 x 400	8	1MB	3MB	A,C,D,F,G
Hewlett-Packard 33440A LaserJet Series II	300 x 300	8	512K	4.5MB	D,E,F
Hewlett-Packard 33447A LaserJet IID	300 x 300	8	640K	4.6MB	F
Imagen 2308/S ImageServer XP	300 x 300	8	2MB	6MB	A,B,L
Imagen ImageStation/S	300 x 300	8	1.5MB		A,C
Laser Connection QMS KISSplus (1MB)	300 x 300	8	1MB		A,B,C,D,E,F,G,H,J,K

TABLE 7-7 Low-Speed Laser Printers (cont'd)

Manufacturer/Model	Resolution (dpi)	Print Speed (ppm)	Base Memory	Maximum Memory	Emulations/ Compatibility*
Laser Connection QMS-PS810/1012117	300 x 300	8	2MB	3MB	A,C,D,E,F,J
Mita Copstar LP-2080	300 x 300	8	512K	4.5MB	A,B,C,F,G,J
NewGen Systems TurboPS/300	300 x 300	8	2MB	5MB	A,B,D,E,F,J

*KEY:

A = Diablo 630
B = Epson
C = Hewlett-Packard GL
D = Hewlett-Packard LaserJet
E = Hewlett-Packard Plus
F = Hewlett-Packard LaserJet II
G = IBM Graphics
H = IBM Proprinter
I = NEC Spinwriter
J = PostScript
K = Qume
L = Tekronix

TABLE 7-8 Low- to Medium-Speed Laser Printers

Manufacturer/Model	Resolution (dpi)	Print Speed (ppm)	Base Memory	Maximum Memory	Emulations/ Compatibility*
C. Itoh LIPS II	300 x 300	10	512K	2MB	A,B,D,H
Kyocera F-1000A	300 x 300	10	512K	1.2MB	B,F,G,K,I
Mannesmann Tally MT910	300 x 300	10	512K	2.5MB	A,B,E,H,K
Qume LaserTEN Plus	300 x 300	10	512K	640K	A,B,D,E,G,H,K
Xerox 4045 Laser CP Model 50	300 x 300	10	512K	1.5MB	A
Panasonic KX-P KX-P4450	300 x 300	11	512K	1.5MB	A,B,E,H
BGL Tech. LaserLeader Mark I	300 x 300	12	4MB	6MB	L
Fujitsu RX7200	300 x 300	12	640K	4.6MB	A,B,C,E,H
Minolta SP 130	300 x 300	12	1.5MB	2MB	A,B,E
Olivetti PG 1230	300 x 300	12	512K	2MB	A,B,E,G
Printronix L1012	300 x 300	12	512K		A,B,E
Toshiba PageLaser 12	300 x 300	12	512K	2MB	A,E,G

*KEY:

A = Diablo 630
B = Epson
C = Hewlett-Packard GL
D = Hewlett-Packard LaserJet
E = Hewlett-Packard Plus
F = Hewlett-Packard LaserJet II
G = IBM Graphics
H = IBM Proprinter
I = NEC Spinwriter
J = PostScript
K = Qume
L = Tekronix

TABLE 7-9 Medium- to High-Speed Laser Printers

Manufacturer/Model	Resolution (dpi)	Print Speed (ppm)	Base Memory	Maximum Memory	Emulations/ Compatibility*
Talaris Systems 1590-LN	300 x 300	15	3.5MB		L
Texas Instruments OmniLaser 2015	300 x 300	15	512K		A,D,E
Pentax Tech Laserfold 240	240 x 240	16	32K		B
Fujitsu RX7300E	300 x 300	18	2.5MB	2.5MB	A,B,C,E,H,K
Kyocera F-3010	300 x 300	18	1.5MB	2MB	A,B,F,G,I,K
Printer Systems Intelliprint 218	300 x 300	18	3MB	11MB	F,G
BGL Tech. LaserLeader Mark II	300 x 300	20	2.5MB	8MB	C,E,F,L
Imagen 3320 ImageServer XP	300 x 300	20	3MB	6MB	A,B,L
CSS Lab. OA Writer 223	300 x 300	22	4MB	8MB	B,C,D,E,F,G
Fujitsu RX7400E	300 x 300	22	2.5MB	2.5MB	A,B,D,H,K
Office Automat. Sys. LaserPro 2200	300 x 300	22	1.5MB		A,B,D,E,G,H,I,K
QMS/QMS Lasergrafix 2200	300 x 300	22	7MB		A,C,K,L
Talaris Sys. Printstation	300 x 300	24	6MB		A,C,F,L
BGL Tech. LaserLeader Mark III	300 x 300	26	4MB	8MB	C,D,E,F,J,L

*KEY:

A = Diablo 630
B = Epson
C = Hewlett-Packard GL
D = Hewlett-Packard LaserJet
E = Hewlett-Packard Plus
F = Hewlett-Packard LaserJet II
G = IBM Graphics
H = IBM Proprinter
I = NEC Spinwriter
J = PostScript
K = Qume
L = Tekronix

the foil bag and inside the carton will stay fresh for about 2.5 years. The shelf life of an opened toner cartridge is less. Some tips on the proper care and handling of toner cartridges include:

1. Do not stand the cartridge on end or turn it upside down.
2. Do not touch the protective flap covering the photosensitive drum on the bottom of the cartridge.
3. Do not open the light-blocking and drum-protection shutters.
4. Do not expose the cartridge to sunlight or other bright light sources over 1,500 lux.
5. Do not use the cartridge for at least one hour after moving from a cool to a warm area.
6. Do not expose the cartridge to heat ducts or other sources of heat.

Hewlett-Packard LaserJet Printers

The first low-cost laser printers for personal computers appeared in 1984 with Hewlett-Packard's LaserJet printer. The LaserJet uses the Canon engine, which was developed for low-cost plain-paper copiers. It has a disposable cartridge that contains the toner and developer. The laser-printer engine uses this cartridge in combination with a semiconductor laser, rotating multifaceted mirror, and focusing optics.

The LaserJet printer uses this engine as its core, along with the interface electronics needed to support the use of a personal computer. This is done with an RS-232C serial cable, and the computer transmits data at rates of up to 9,600 baud. When the data reaches the LaserJet, it is sent through character-generation circuits that generate the dot patterns for the characters. This includes the standard ASCII character set and those characters needed in some European languages. You can access additional sets of characters with proportionally spaced fonts by plugging in special ROM cartridges.

The printer changes the dot patterns representing characters and other graphic symbols into signals that control the laser beam. A six-faceted mirror reflects the beam and directs it to write the desired character on the drum. An electrostatic process develops the image on plain paper at the rate of 8 ppm.

The LaserJet uses a print mode for document printing and two graphic modes—portrait and landscape. The print mode supports 300 dpi, the highest resolution that can be used on the printer. The graphic resolution depends on the display resolution of the computer, which can range from 75 to 300 dpi.

LaserJet Plus. In the latter part of 1985, Hewlett-Packard introduced an enhanced version of the LaserJet with more memory—512K. HP did not discontinue the LaserJet, but made upgrade kits available to upgrade existing machines with the new features. User-available memory is 395K, six times that of the LaserJet. The additional memory allows support for downloadable fonts and full-page raster graphics at 150 dpi. The addition of a Centronics parallel interface does much to reduce the amount of time needed for printing graphics. A reset button is added to the control panel, and seven additional internal fonts are available.

LaserJet II. The HP LaserJet Series II was introduced in 1986 and provided a number of improvements, including a lower price, smaller size, and 30% less weight, along with a 200-sheet input bin and a 16-character liquid crystal display (LCD) control panel. There are 6 resident fonts and 2 font-cartridge slots. Plug-in memory expansion boards were made available. The LaserJet II, with the newer Canon LBP-SX laser beam engine, has parallel and serial ports and allows multiple fonts on a page. HP again upgraded the LaserJet series, which uses HP's PCL, to accommodate more features.

LaserJet III. The HP LaserJet III appeared in 1990. This printer supports PostScript, and a personality cartridge is available for LaserJet II printers that allows them to process PostScript files. PostScript is Adobe System's page-description language that is used to define the complete layout of the page to be printed. The PostScript cartridge slips into the font cartridge slot of the printer and provides 35 Adobe typefaces, while you can download other typefaces from the computer.

LaserJet III uses the printer command language HP PCL Version 5, which is compatible with previous LaserJets. It provides support for the additional fonts with more sizes. There is also better page-layout capability and faster printing of graphics. HP PCL 5 uses AGFA Compugraphic's Intellifont for font scaling. Type can originate from 8 internal typefaces, disk, and cartridge. Scaling can range from 0.25 point to 999.75 points in quarter-point steps. HP PCL 5 also has HP-GL/2, which is HP's plotter language for vector graphics.

Software is available for special font and graphics effects, including reverse, oblique, shadow, and mirror printing of fonts. You can use various pattern-filling effects for shades of gray for both character and object filling.

The LaserJet III uses an imaging technology that enhances the effective output resolution and smooths the jagged edges that can be found in 300-dpi printing. This results in text and graphics with smoother edges, sharper points, and cleaner line crossings. It does this with smaller dots that are made by modulating the intensity of the laser beam. The beam modulation produces lower amounts of energy on the photosensitive drum, resulting in less toner and smaller dots. Then, a special integrated circuit analyzes the dot patterns as they are formed and reforms the patterns if needed to improve the printing of edges, corners, and intersections.

PCL 5 provides many of the benefits of PostScript, but operates much faster. It also provides backward compatibility with older software. The LaserJet III can scale fonts, printing letters in any size up to 13 inches high. It comes with CG Times and Univers outlines built in, and you can get other font outlines in cartridge or disk formats.

PCL 5 allows rotation of any font, even when it has been sent to the printer in the form of a bitmap instead of an outline. It also makes a printer more efficient at printing graphics, especially those that include boxes, bars, and borders. With PCL 5 and graphics compression, the LaserJet III's standard 1MB of RAM is enough for most users. You can add up to 5MB of RAM to the LaserJet III and turn it into a PostScript printer with a cartridge. HP also has the LaserJet III PostScript printer that includes 3MB of RAM, the PostScript cartridge, and an AppleTalk interface.

Another variation is the LaserJet IIID, built around the same print engine as the LaserJet III. It can automatically print on both sides of a sheet of paper, and it has two 200-sheet paper trays. It is able to switch from one to the other when the paper runs out, or it can print form letters automatically mixing letterhead and second pages. There is an optional envelope feeder that lets you print envelopes or alternate envelopes with letters.

The LaserJet IIIP is a 4-ppm laser printer. It uses the same case and print engine as the IIP.

NEC

The NEC Model 90 is a laser PostScript printer with 300 x 300-dpi resolution. It uses a 6 ppm engine and provides Adobe PostScript compatibility, as well as compatibility with IBM and Macintosh systems. The Model 90 comes with a software kit with WYSIWYG screen fonts for both Macintosh and Microsoft Windows environments.

Epson

The EPL-7000 and EPL-7500 are laser printers from Epson. The 6-ppm EPL-7000 comes with 14 resident fonts, including Courier, Courier bold, and Courier italic. It has 512K of standard RAM, upgradable to a maximum of 6MB, and a 250-sheet paper tray. You can upgrade RAM by adding memory directly to the controller and by using Epson's memory expansion boards.

The EPL-7000 offers two-channel printer sharing. Two users, when connected to the serial and parallel ports, can have concurrent, independent printer use, without changing control-panel switches.

The Epson EPL-7500 is a RISC-based (reduced instruction set computer) Adobe PostScript laser printer that you can use for both Macintosh- and MS-DOS-based applications. The 6 ppm printer comes with 35 resident fonts, including Times, Helvetica, Palatino, Zapf Chancery, Courier, and New Century Schoolbook. Also included are 2MB of RAM, a 250-sheet paper tray, and HP LaserJet Series II emulation.

LCS AND LED PRINTERS

Liquid-crystal sensor (LCS) and LED printers are similar to laser printers and achieve the same type of laser-quality output. These printers use the light from a liquid crystal or LED to form the image. The use of the LCS or LED print head is different from laser systems, which use rotating mirrors and lenses. The print head is solid-state, with no moving parts, which allows a simpler design than laser printers. However, laser printer technology has been around longer and is likely to remain popular.

Okidata LED page printers come with a 200-page letter tray, and you can use a variety of paper stocks with it. It prints pages face down in the correct paper order, saving collating time.

There are optional legal-size trays for longer forms and documents. You can add a second tray and print up to 200 additional pages of letterhead and second sheets without interruption. The second tray requires a special mechanism.

Page memory is shared among graphics, forms, and soft fonts. Okidata LED page printers have 512K total memory. You will need to add additional memory to your page printer if you are using full-page graphics, a scanner, or many large headline fonts in the same document. You can increase the memory to 4.5MB on Okidata 800s and 820s, up to 4MB on the 840s, and up to 2.5MB on the OL400.

The Okidata OL400 is a 4-ppm LED printer. It uses a solid-state LED print head and has no moving parts. The OL400 has a 200-sheet capacity in addition to manual feed and takes labels, envelopes, and transparencies. The OL400 has support of more than 600 software packages and has HP II-compatible emulation. It can operate with text, graphics, and imaging software, and you can download fonts, forms, and scanned images. It has 17 built-in fonts for headlines, boldface, and italics in four typefaces, including Swiss and Dutch. There is an optional font card slot.

The OL800 is an LED page printer that you can upgrade to an OL820 for faster font scaling or to an OL840 Adobe PostScript printer for Apple and IBM systems. The OL800 provides 8 ppm with 300-dpi graphics. It has 26 resident fonts and 4 typefaces with 512K memory built in. You can upgrade it to 4.5MB RAM. It can print on a variety of paper, card, label, transparency, and envelope stock. It comes with a 200-page letter tray and dual-bin capability. Legal, executive, A-4 size, and envelope trays are available. You can also add a second tray mechanism, and a tray to print up to 200 letterhead with 200 second sheets without interruption. With a multiport option, the OL800 will provide equal access to up to three PCs in a shared environment. It has HP, IBM Proprinter, and Diablo 630 emulations.

The OL820 uses on-the-fly hardware font scaling from 4 points to 3.5 inches for 13 resident PostScript fonts. It uses a proprietary font chip to automatically scale fonts to the required size as the document is printing. You can use the OL820 for printing envelopes, transparencies, and card stock. You can expand its 512K memory to 4.5MB, and you can add 22 bitstream PostScript-compatible fonts.

The OL830 offers Adobe PostScript, HP Series II, and Diablo 630 emulations. It has 2MB of RAM, parallel interface, and Adobe Type Manager with 17 Adobe PostScript fonts. The fonts include Courier, Times Roman, Helvetica, Helvetica Narrow, and Symbol. You can also use a font card or downloadable fonts. It has a 200-sheet tray capability, and you have the flexibility of using letterhead and second sheets, letter- and legal-size, or letterhead and envelopes. You can expand the OL830 with an additional 2MB of RAM, up to 18 additional resident fonts, and Serial/Apple Talk interfaces. For automatic switching between emulations, you can use the OL830 with Printer Control Panel from LaserTools. This software package detects whether your output requires HP LaserJet II, PostScript, or Diablo and switches the printer as needed.

You can use the OL840 in both MS-DOS and Apple operating environments, and it works with UNIX-, XENIX-, and Sun-based workstations. The OL840 offers 35 Adobe PostScript scalable fonts and 26 bitmap fonts. It has Adobe PostScript download font handling, gray-pattern fill, 360-degree font rotation, and drop shadowing. It prints 8 ppm and handles single sheets, mailing labels, and transparencies.

Tables 7-10 and 7-11 list some LCS and LED printers, along with their features. A printer's speed is gauged by the number of pages it is able to print per minute. LCS, LED, and laser printers are able to emulate printer standards such as PostScript. A printer's resolution refers to the number of dots it can print in a square inch area.

The tables also indicate the maximum amount of memory the printer is able to support with RAM upgrades. Base memory refers to the amount of RAM the printer is equipped with.

TABLE 7-10 LCS Printers

Manufacturer/Model	Resolution (dpi)	Print Speed (ppm)	Base Memory	Maximum Memory	Emulations/ Compatibility*
Qume Crystal Print WP	300 x 300	6	128K		A,B,E,H
Taxan KE-300	300 x 300	8	3MB	5MB	D,E,J
Fujitsu RX7100	300 x 300	5	640K	4.6MB	A,B,C,E,H
EC Info. Sys. LC 860 Plus	300 x 300	8	1.3MB		E
NEC LC 89x1	300 x 300	8	3MB		A,D,J
General Bus. Tech. GBT 6615	300 x 300	15	1MB		F
Kentek Info. Sys. K-2+	300 x 300	15	4MB		A,E,L
Rosetta Tech. RT4115 Page Printer	300 x 300	15	2.5MB		A,F,L

*KEY:

A = Diablo 630	G = IBM Graphics
B = Epson	H = IBM Proprinter
C = Hewlett-Packard GL	I = NEC Spinwriter
D = Hewlett-Packard LaserJet	J = PostScript
E = Hewlett-Packard Plus	K = Qume
F = Hewlett-Packard LaserJet II	L = Tekronix

TABLE 7-11 LED Printers

Manufacturer/Model	Resolution (dpi)	Print Speed (ppm)	Base Memory	Maximum Memory	Emulations/ Compatibility*
General Bus. Tech. GBT 6624	300 x 300	24	1MB		F
Kentek Info. Sys. K-4 Duplex	300 x 300	24	7MB		A,E,F,L
Printronix L2324	300 x 300	24	4MB		D,E
Rosetta Tech RT4224 Page Printer	300 x 300	24	3.5MB		A,L

*KEY:

A = Diablo 630	G = IBM Graphics
B = Epson	H = IBM Proprinter
C = Hewlett-Packard GL	I = NEC Spinwriter
D = Hewlett-Packard LaserJet	J = PostScript
E = Hewlett-Packard Plus	K = Qume
F = Hewlett-Packard LaserJet II	L = Tekronix

8

UPGRADING WITH POWER, OPTICAL, AND TAPE BACKUP SYSTEMS

WHY YOU NEED POWER BACKUP

A number of factors can cause PC downtime. The reliability of hardware and the quality of software are certainly important in keeping a PC functioning and available. However, another important—yet often neglected—factor is the quality and reliability of your computer's electrical power. The quality of the hardware and software is controlled to a large extent by the manufacturing process and correct usage of the products, but the quality of the electrical supply depends on factors that are often beyond your control.

Your utility company may generate high-quality electric power, but that power can be corrupted by special occurrences like lightning or the grid switching that the utility practices during high-demand peak periods. These transients interrupt the continuous flow of power to your computer. During these periods (which can be relatively short), the power that reaches your computer may not meet the electrical requirements of the system.

Additional power contamination may be due to influences internal to the building. When other equipment is turned on, the initial starting-power requirements can temporarily cause transient voltages and surges, resulting in data errors and equipment damage. Most studies show that power disturbances occur on the average of two times a week for a typical commercial facility and that most disturbances are generated within the building.

POWER PROBLEMS

Computers are sensitive to several types of power disturbances (Fig 8-1). Power transients can force too much power into the computer or deprive the computer of the necessary power. The first type of transient includes surges and spikes, while the second includes sags, brownouts, and blackouts. All disturbances can cause malfunctions in computers. Power disturbances can affect a system differently depending on their duration and which part of the system was being used when the disturbances occurred. The following types of disturbances cause problems in electronic equipment.

1. **Spikes:** also known as impulses; they show up as overvoltages superimposed on the line voltage. They can last between 0.05 and 100.0 microseconds.
2. **Sags:** cycle-to-cycle decreases in the power-line voltage below 80% of the nominal value, usually lasting less than several seconds. Sags occur frequently at the wall-socket level and account for the majority of total power-line disturbances. Sags are a major cause of data loss.
3. **Surges:** cycle-to-cycle increases in the power-line voltage above 110% of the nominal value lasting less than several seconds. Surges cause most of the hardware damage in computers.
4. **Outage:** results in a zero-voltage condition. Outages account for about 15% of the total number of power-line disturbances that occur at the wall-socket level.
5. **Noise and oscillations:** usually decay within one cycle of the line voltage and have a frequency range from 400 Hz to 5 kHz.

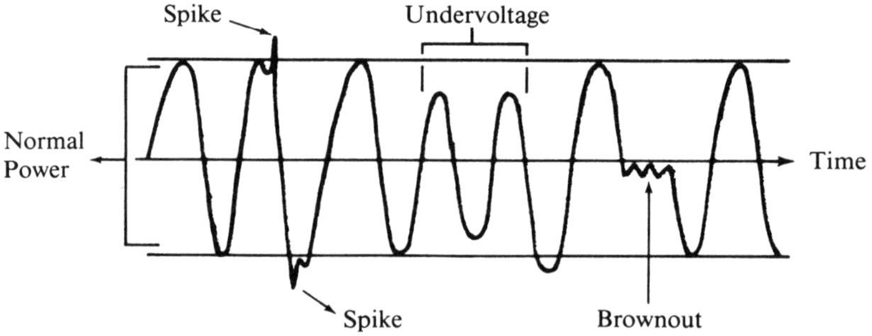

Figure 8-1 Power-line problems

Power Spikes

Since spikes are rapid excursions of voltage with a large amplitude, they can propagate through the system and cause sensitive components to break down. Although spikes are high-magnitude events, they only last for split seconds (0.05 to 100.0 microseconds), but they can still disrupt computer operations and even damage equipment. The most disastrous effect of spikes can be actual hardware damage. High-voltage impulses can actually melt holes in delicate microchip circuit traces. Sometimes this damage is immediately apparent, but other times it is latent, not appearing until days or weeks after the event. Less catastrophic effects include corrupted printing and processing errors.

Power Sags

Sags are the opposite of surges. They are multicycle undervoltage conditions and can be a serious threat to computers. If the voltage supply to the computer is inadequate, it can cause the computer to lock up. Sags can also slow the speed of disk drives, causing read errors or disk crashes.

Sags, depending on their duration, can result in different types of problems in computers. If the sag lasts longer than one or two cycles, it can cause the computer power supply to detect a low voltage on its output, resulting in computer shutdown. You must then reboot the computer.

If the sag lasts for a cycle and its duration is approximately equal to the holdup time of the power supply in the computer, the problem can be more critical. The power-supply voltage of the computer will decrease near the end of sag and then increase. This transient condition can cause the reversal of 1s and 0s in memory. These changes will be transferred to disk storage as bugs or data errors and can result in program hang-ups.

A long sag becomes a brownout. These long-term undervoltages can last for minutes or even hours and are often caused by utilities when peak demand exceeds generating capacity.

Brownouts can cause computer malfunctions and hardware damage the same way that shorter sags do. They deprive the logic circuits and disk drives of the voltage they need to operate properly.

Power Surges

Undervoltage problems cause more damage than surges, but the surge that follows a sag can cause serious damage. A surge is an overvoltage or increase in the AC-line voltage. While a spike is more of an instantaneous or short-term overvoltage, surges last longer than one cycle ($\frac{1}{60}$ second). Surges are more dangerous because of their duration rather than their magnitude. Long or frequent surges can damage computer hardware.

Insurance-company data shows that 40% of transient problems are surge-related. Surges stress computer components, particularly in the power supply, and can cause premature component failure.

Outages

Blackouts are extended zero-voltage conditions lasting for minutes, hours, or even days. They become more frequent as the power distribution grid is overtaxed. Blackouts can result from ground faults, accidents, lightning strikes, or other acts of nature.

A system crash is the most obvious effect of outages. Disk drives and other system components can also sustain damage when power is suddenly lost. When the power goes out completely, if it goes out quickly enough, it is like a system shutdown and there will be no damage to the computer. When the power returns to normal, it does it in a series of surges, producing an effect called hammering. Hammering can cause the hard disk drive head to fall down onto the surface of the disk and then lift up and drop down again with each surge. Serious damage can occur to both the head and hard disk.

Noise and Oscillations

Noise is used for various kinds of high-frequency impulses that ride on the normal power waveform. It can range from a small fraction of a volt to several volts in amplitude. One common problem is radio frequency (RF) noise. RF noise consists of high-frequency signals that travel on electrical wires or cables.

Lightning, radio transmissions, and computer power supplies can generate RF noise, which can create erratic behavior in any electronic circuit. Noise can cause computer processing errors, incorrect data transfer, and printer errors.

Electrical noise can enter the computer through power and other cables and can be interference from fluorescent lights and other equipment. Noise can cause fluctuations in the voltage and cause data to be lost or corrupted.

If the amplitude of oscillations is less than 50% of the nominal voltage over a period of time, the power supply can break down. If it does not break down, then the oscillations will appear on the output of the power supply and have the same effects as sags on the power supply lines to integrated circuits.

Power Disturbance Causes

Many things can cause spikes. The most important cause is lightning, which can strike on or near a power line—or even miles away—causing large jumps in voltage. Other causes of spikes include switching large electrical loads on or off, utility switching, and static discharges.

Surges can occur when some device on the line that has been drawing a large amount of power suddenly stops or is shut off. Surges can also occur when utilities switch large loads off the line. Also, equipment that is between the service entrance and the computer can affect the power quality. Air conditioners turning on and off can cause surges on power lines.

Ground faults, undersized power systems, and sudden start-ups of large electrical loads are all typical causes of voltage sags. Lightning is also a major cause of sags when the power system is recovering.

Fluorescent lights generate electrical noise that, if it gets through to the machine, can cause erratic performance. Other devices that can cause problems include copiers and printers.

PROTECTING YOUR POWER SUPPLY

All computers use some form of filtering to reduce transients and electrical noise. Metal enclosures are also used for their shielding properties (Figs 8-2 and 8-3). Computer logic circuits require clean, continuous power; and filtering, along with shielding, allow the computer to operate under normal conditions. However, transients on the AC power line may swamp the filter and the shielding if they have enough energy.

Types of Protection

There are various ways available to protect your computer, ranging from low-cost surge suppressors to expensive intelligent power systems (IPS).

Surge Suppressors. Surge suppressors are a common power-protection device and the least effective of the available protection devices. Figures 8-4 and 8-5 show two types of surge suppressors, which are also called spike suppressors.

Surge suppressors reduce the voltage of a surge by using a device like a varistor to limit the maximum voltage. The voltages they can suppress are limited to about 200–300 volts. Varistors are relatively slow devices, so short spikes of higher voltages can get through to your computer. About 90% of the surge suppressors sold use varistors.

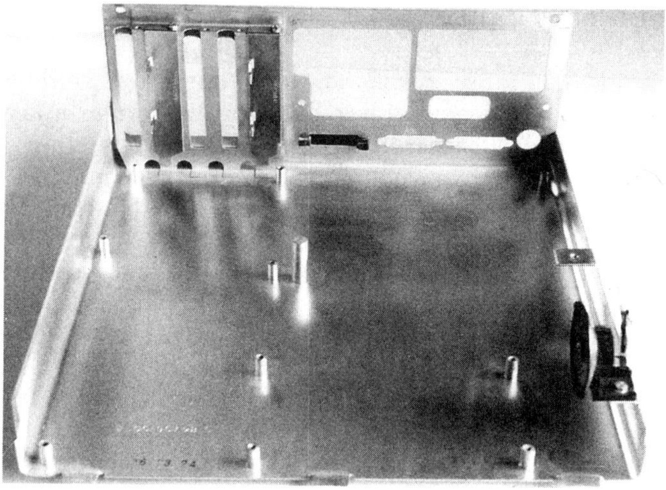

Figure 8-2 Metal enclosure used for system board

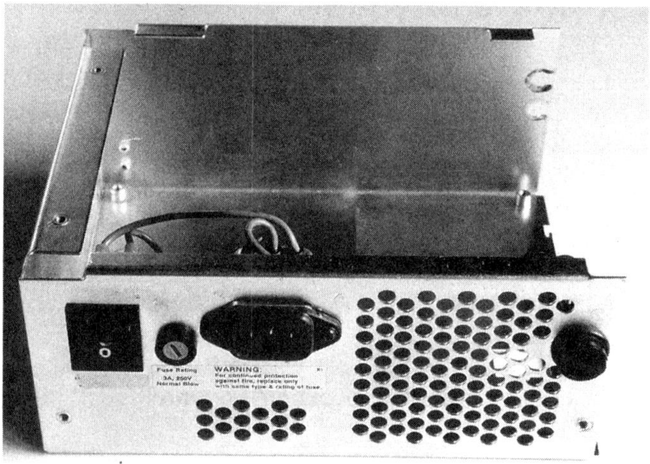

Figure 8-3 Metal enclosure used for power supply

Some surge suppressors use gas tubes instead of varistors. Gas tubes can handle large amounts of energy and can even provide some protection for lightning effects. Series inductors are also used to limit the effects of surges.

Standby Power Systems (SPS). The main problem with surge suppressors is that they have no power reserve that can be applied when there is an undervoltage. This type of power problem requires a standby or uninterruptible power system.

Figure 8-4 Single-outlet plug-in type of surge suppressor

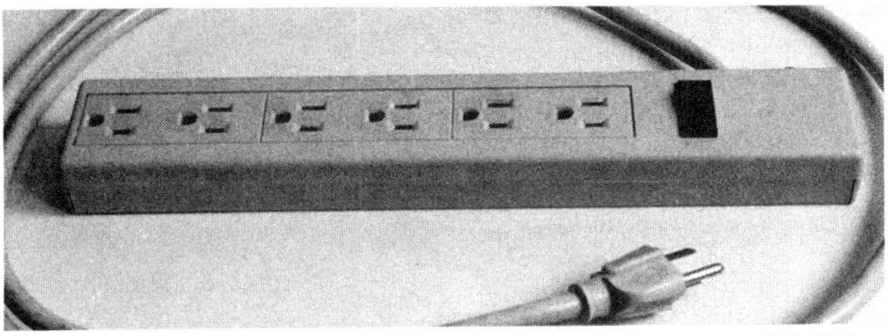

Figure 8-5 Multiple-outlet strip type of surge suppressor with lighted on-off switch

An SPS, also called an off-line system, has a battery to power the computer when a power sag, brownout, or blackout occurs. You plug the SPS into the wall outlet and the computer into the SPS. If the power should drop below a critical level, the SPS will switch from AC-line power to its battery backup.

An important factor during switching is the switching time. This is the time it takes the system to switch from line to battery power. If the switching time is too long, the hardware may not react to it, but the data might. This is especially true on a network where information is traveling over some distance. The maximum allowable switching time under these conditions is about 1 ms. Most SPSs have switching times from 1 to 4 ms. Table 8-1 lists a number of standby power units with ratings and transfer times.

Uninterruptible Power Systems (UPS). An uninterruptible power system is also known as an on-line system. While an SPS connects you to AC-line power until it detects a problem, the UPS provides the power from its own battery, which is being continuously charged from the

TABLE 8-1 Standby Power Backup Units

Manufacturer/Model	Power Rating	Full-Load Backup Time (in minutes)	Half-Load Backup Time (in minutes)	Transfer Time
APC UPS 110SE*	110 VA (90 W)†	28 (85 VA)	25 (60 VA)	2 ms
Perma Power* SPS-250	250 VA (200 W)	8	15–20	4 ms
Durant Tech. BPS 300	300 VA	10	30 (180 VA)	<1 ms
Sota SPS 300VA	300 VA	5	15	4 ms
APC 330XT	300 VA (200 W)	12 (270 VA)	16 (160 VA)	1–3 ms
PARA Sys. MM300SS	300 W	80	20	1 ms
APC 450AT	450 VA (300 W)	7	30 (160 VA)	1–3 ms
Perma Power SPS386	450 VA	8	25 (60% Load)	<1 ms
Durant Tech. BPS 550	500 VA	8	25 (300 VA)	<1 ms
SL Waber Linkbacker LB500	500 VA (400 W)	5	30	2 ms
DataShield T.2+520	520 VA	15 (Typical)		<1 ms
SCOA UPS-700SE	700 VA	5	10	<2 ms
APC 800RT	800 VA (600 W)	6	20 (450 VA)	2–4 ms
Durant Tech. BPS 800	800 VA	8	25	<1 ms
Meirick 1000	1,000 VA (800 W)	7	14	2–3.5 ms
APC 1200VX	1,200 VA (800 W)	15	38	2–4 ms
Perma Power SPS-1200	1,200 VA	8	25 (60% Load)	<1 ms
SL Waber Linebacker	1,250 VA (1,000 W)	6	12	2 ms
Sola SPS/R 1500 VA	1,500 VA	6	15	1 ms
ELGAR IPS 1600	1,600 W	15	41	<4 ms

*Fits under monitor.

†VA=volt-amps; W=watts.

line (Fig 8-6). There is no switching time, and the line conditioning is built into the system. If a blackout should occur, the UPS will provide power long enough to allow you to save your work or finish your printing. You can then shut down your computer as you normally would. Some units have an alarm that goes off when a power problem is detected.

Some of the earlier UPS units generated excessive heat that reduced the lifetime of internal components. Most of today's units use oversize components and run much cooler; however, you do need to replace the battery periodically. Most batteries will last from 3 to 5 years. You should replace the battery when the backup time drops to about 60% of the backup time when the unit was new. If you are not using the unit, you should charge it every 6 months to maintain the battery. On some units, the interface signals other equipment that a power failure has occurred. Figure 8-7 shows the layout of a typical UPS unit, and Table 8-2 lists some typical UPS units.

TABLE 8-2 Uninterruptable Power Sources

Manufacturer/Model	Power Rating	Full-Load Backup Time (in minutes)	Half-Load Backup Time (in minutes)
Alpha Tech. 300R(E)	300 VA	30	72
Clary PC-1240	400 VA	4	12
Durant Tech. UPS 400	400 VA	4	10
Unison PS 4.5*	450 VA	6	15
Alpha Tech. 650FR(E)	650 VA	19	45
Best MD750VA	750 VA	11	37

*Fits under monitor.

Intelligent Power Systems. The IPS is similar to a UPS, but it has software that performs an orderly shutdown of the system, saving and closing files without any loss of data. When the power comes back on, the software starts the system back up and reopens to the files you were working in when the power shut down—all accomplished with no loss of data.

The big advantage of an IPS over a UPS is that you can leave a system or network powered by an IPS unattended. A UPS's battery can give you time to make an orderly computer system shutdown, but you must be available to perform the shutdown before the battery energy runs out. An IPS will shut down the network automatically.

Sizing Your System for Power Backup

Choosing the UPS or SPS that is right for you is straightforward—you need to ask yourself some basic questions about your power protection

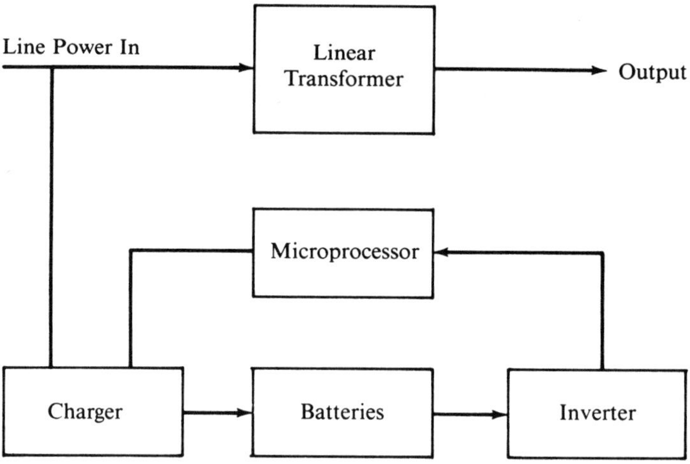

Figure 8-6 UPS operation (A microprocessor-based waveform analyzer examines the input signal. If a problem is observed, the inverter is switched in to support the load.)

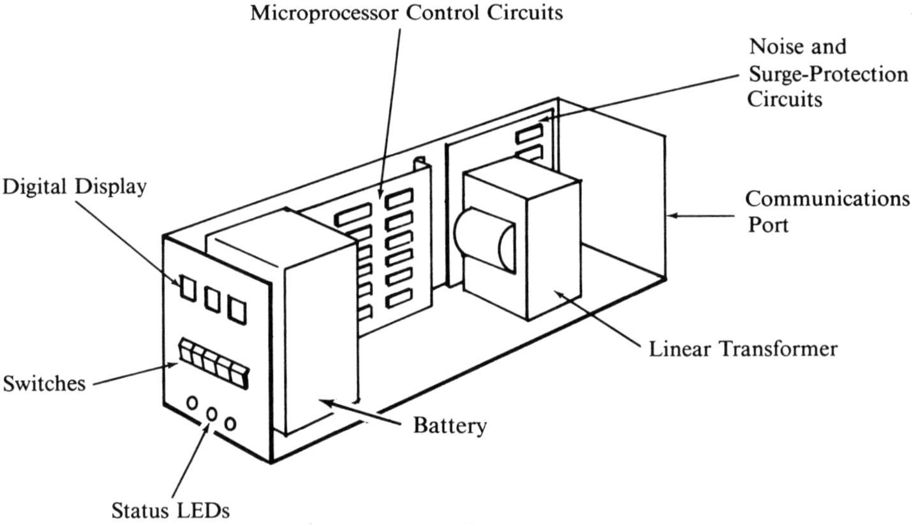

Figure 8-7 Typical UPS layout

needs and then make your selection from the options available for your model. The following guidelines will get you started.

First, decide how big your UPS or SPS has to be to protect your loads. Make a list of all equipment to be protected by the UPS. Remember to include monitors, terminals, external data storage devices, and any other critical peripheral. Check the nameplate on the back of each device for each voltage and amperage requirement. Multiply the two numbers to calculate the volt-amps (VA) requirement for each device. For example, a monitor that draws 0.5 amps at 120 volts requires 60 VA. Some devices list their power consumption figure in watts. To convert this to VA, multiply the number of watts by 1.4. Then add the VA requirements for all of your system components, and remember that 1,000 VA = 1 KVA.

Be sure to allow enough capacity for future growth. For example, to allow for a 20% growth factor, multiply your VA requirement by 1.2. This will be the total VA requirement needed to handle growth.

UPS and SPS Examples

Tripp Lite UPS. The UNISON is an on-line UPS designed to protect your computer system from blackouts, brownouts, surges, and line noise that can corrupt data and damage your equipment. This UPS is a dual-converter design that takes advantage of recent innovations in power-converter design, magnetic core materials, and output waveform regulation. This allows reduced size and weight, increased efficiency, higher peak current ratings, and improved waveform accuracy. This system uses a special high-frequency power conversion and control technique to provide continuous, on-line power protection.

There are 600-VA and 800-VA modules that include a LAN interface for Novell, 3Com, and other networks. The LAN unit contains an interface port (DB-9 connector) that works with software and cabling for unattended shutdown. When a power failure occurs, the network will automatically power itself down, preventing data and file management problems.

The BC series UPS has extra-large batteries for longer battery life and backup times, brownout protection at 103 volts, spike suppression, line noise filtering, and phase-synchronized 2-ms switching. Instead of switching to battery power during low-voltage (brownout) conditions, there is a built-in voltage regulator that automatically adjusts the output to 120 VAC. This keeps you running during brownouts without draining the battery.

EFI. The SysGarde 505 and LanGarde 505 battery backup units are 505 VA standby units for temporary power and surge suppression. The SysGarde unit provides 20 minutes of holding time for a halfload and 5–7 minutes for a full load. The LanGarde 505 is Novell-certified and compatible with all versions of NetWare.

TAPE BACKUP SYSTEMS

Among the upgrade options available are more powerful processors like high-performance 386 and 486 chips; improved user-friendly operating systems; and fast, high-capacity hard disk subsystems. Other product areas that have seen significant technology advances include tape backup systems.

Not so long ago, the only tape standard that existed was $\frac{1}{2}$-inch 9-track tape. These open-reel backup systems were standard in mini- and main-frame systems. However, in the microcomputer arena, this technology never became popular, and a more suitable tape backup standard emerged in the form of $\frac{1}{4}$-inch cartridge tape.

1/4-Inch Tape Cartridge

The $\frac{1}{4}$-inch tape cartridge is the most common method of tape backup. There are two standard sizes—the DC600 cartridge and the smaller DC2000 minicartridge. DC600 drives generally use a controller board, and DC2000 drives tend to be based on a floppy controller. Figure 8-8 shows the essential parts of a tape cartridge, and Figure 8-9 shows the construction of a tape drive. Tables 8-3 through 8-7 show the available $\frac{1}{4}$-inch cartridge tape backup systems for various formats, both internal and external.

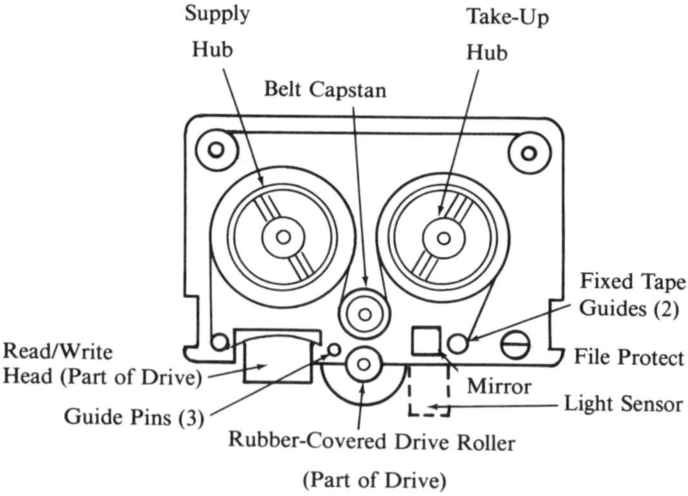

Figure 8-8 Tape cartridge

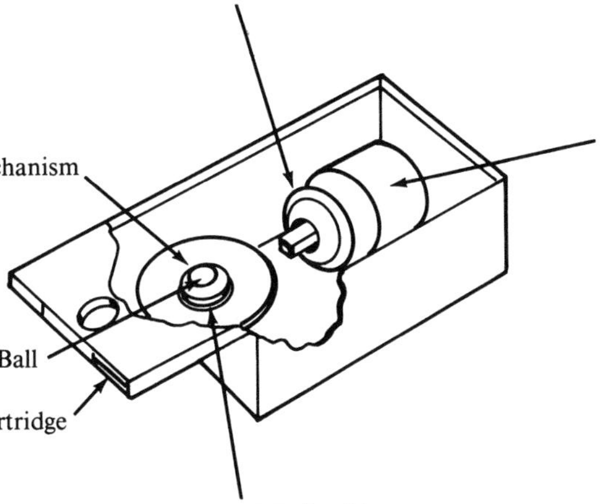

Figure 8-9 Drive for removable cartridge backup

Although $\frac{1}{4}$-inch cartridge tape has become the backup medium of choice for microcomputers, several factors may limit its future success. First, there is the tape-to-disk capacity imbalance. The popular $\frac{1}{4}$-inch cartridge tape subsystems have a maximum single-tape capacity of 150MB, but high-capacity, hard disk systems offer capacities of over 700MB and are still growing. The tape manufacturers are responding: 3M is pushing 320MB cartridge media, and the Quarter Inch Cartridge (QIC) Committee is pushing a 1GB $\frac{1}{4}$-inch system.

The second problem for $\frac{1}{4}$-inch cartridges involves high-level tape formats and tape interchangeability. There is little, if any, interchangeability possible since tape backup subsystem manufacturers use different tape formats during data backup. This situation is similar to that which existed during the early days of microcomputers, before the introduction of the IBM PC, when a number of floppy disk formats existed. Some major tape backup manufacturers are heading for format standardization.

1/8-Inch Digital Cassette

The $\frac{1}{8}$-inch digital cassette tapes are similar in structure to standard audio cassettes. The $\frac{1}{8}$-inch cassette drives compete primarily with the $\frac{1}{4}$-inch DC2000 cartridges in capacity, but they utilize an SCSI or QIC interface instead of a floppy drive interface. Tables 8-8 through 8-10 list various systems available in this format.

TABLE 8-3 Tape Backup—1/4-Inch Data Cartridge (Internal)

Manufacturer/Model	Capacity (MB)	Interface*	XT Bus	AT Bus	PS/2 Bus	Data Transfer Rate†
3.5-in Internal						
Tecmar QT-60i/PS	60	QIC-02			X	90K/sec
Genoa Galaxy 31150MC	150	QIC-02			X	112.5K/sec
5.25-in Internal						
Emerald Systems RAP 060-2000	60	SCSI		X		90K/sec
Genoa Galaxy Galaxy 3160	60	QIC-02	X	X		86K/sec
Maynard Elect. MaynStream 60Q-10605	60	QIC-02	X	X		86K/sec
Sysgen 310	60	QIC-36	X	X	X	90K/sec
Wangtek 5099EK	60	QIC-36	X	X		90K/sec
Tecmar QT-90i	90	QIC-02	X	X		90K/sec
Irwin 615OU	250	QIC-36	X	X	X	720Kbps
Tallgrass TG-1500/2i	250	QIC-36			X	QIC-150
Colorado Memory	500	QIC-02	X	X	X	QIC-112/113

*Tape backups may include a controller board, the controller may be offered as an option, or the tape drive may not require a controller board. The interface of the drive or tape backup refers to the type of connection and communications protocol that the device uses to communicate with the host computer.

†The speed at which data is transferred from the tape backup to the controller board.

TABLE 8-4 Tape Backup—1/4-Inch Data Cartridge (External)

Manufacturer/Model	Capacity (MB)	Interface*	XT Bus	AT Bus	PS/2 Bus	Data Transfer Rate†
Cipher Data 5400	60	QIC-02	X	X	X	87K/sec
Emerald Systems RAP 060-9000	60	SCSI		X		90K/sec
Maynard Elect. MaynStream 60-10503		QIC-02			X	86K/sec
Sysgen 315	60	QIC-36	X	X	X	90K/sec
Wangtek S5099EK	60	QIC-36	X	X		90K/sec
Tecmar QT-90e	90	QIC-02	X	X	X	90K/sec
Genoa Galaxy Galaxy 31150Z/MC	150	QIC-02			X	112.5K/sec
Irwin 6150E	250	QIC-36	X	X	X	720Kbps
Tallgrass TG-1500/2e	250	QIC-36			X	90K/sec
Colorado Memory	500	QFA-500e	X	X	X	112.5K/sec

*Tape backups may include a controller board, the controller may be offered as an option, or the tape drive may not require a controller board. The interface of the drive or tape backup refers to the type of connection and communications protocol that the device uses to communicate with the host computer.

†The speed at which data is transferred from the tape backup to the controller board.

TABLE 8-5 Tape Backup—1/4-Inch Minicartridge (3.5-Inch Internal)

Manufacturer/Model	Capacity (MB)	Interface*	XT Bus	AT Bus	PS/2 Bus	Data Transfer Rate†
Irwin 220	29	Floppy			X	250Kbps
Alloy Tape System/2	40	Floppy			X	500Kbps
Archive ArchiveXL 3550	40	Floppy			X	500Kbps
CMS Enhancements	40	Floppy		X		500Kbps
Everex Excel II 40fi	40	Floppy			X	500Kbps
Tecmar QT-40i/PS	40	Floppy			X	500Kbps
Wangtek FAD 3500C3	40	Floppy	X			250Kbps
Mountain Filesafe TD4740	44	Floppy			X	500Kbps
Tallgrass TG 1140	60	Floppy	X	X		250 or 500Kbps

*Tape backups may include a controller board, the controller may be offered as an option, or the tape drive may not require a controller board. The interface of the drive or tape backup refers to the type of connection and communications protocol that the device uses to communicate with the host computer.

†The speed at which data is transferred from the tape backup to the controller board.

TABLE 8-6 Tape Backup—1/4-Inch Data Cartridge (5.25-Inch Internal)

Manufacturer/Model	Capacity (MB)	Interface*	XT Bus	AT Bus	PS/2 Bus	Data Transfer Rate†
Irwin 120	29	Floppy	X			250Kbps
Alloy Retriever/40	40	Floppy		X		500Kbps
Archive XL 3560	40	Floppy			X	500Kbps
CMS Enhancements 40INTAT	40	Floppy		X		500Kbps
Everex Excel 40AT	40	Floppy		X		500Kbps
Wangtek FAD	40	Floppy	X			250Kbps
Colorado Memory	120	Floppy	X	X	X	250 or 500Kbps

*Tape backups may include a controller board, the controller may be offered as an option, or the tape drive may not require a controller board. The interface of the drive or tape backup refers to the type of connection and communications protocol that the device uses to communicate with the host computer.

†The speed at which data is transferred from the tape backup to the controller board.

TABLE 8-7 Tape Backup—1/4-Inch Data Cartridge (External)

Manufacturer/Model	Capacity (MB)	Interface*	XT Bus	AT Bus	PS/2 Bus	Data Transfer Rate†
Irwin 420	29	Floppy	X			250Kbps
Tecmar QT-Mac40	38	SCSI			X	750Kbps
ADIC 400	40	Floppy	X	X		250 or 500Kbps
Alloy Retriever 40e	40	Floppy		X		500Kbps
Procomm PLT40-250	40	Floppy	X			250Kbps
Sysgen Bridge-Tape	44	Floppy	X	X	X	250 or 500Kbps
ADPI Easi Tape	60	RS-232	X	X		38.4K BAUD
Tallgrass TG 4000	60	SCSI			X	750Kbps
Colorado Memory	120	Floppy	X	X	X	250 or 500Kbps

*Tape backups may include a controller board, the controller may be offered as an option, or the tape drive may not require a controller board. The interface of the drive or tape backup refers to the type of connection and communications protocol that the device uses to communicate with the host computer.

†The speed at which data is transferred from the tape backup to the controller board.

TABLE 8-8 1/8-Inch Digital Cassette (3.5-Inch Internal)

Manufacturer/Model	Capacity (MB)	Interface*	XT Bus	AT Bus	PS/2 Bus	Data Transfer Rate†
Emerald Systems RAP060-13017	60	SCSI			X	86K/sec
Maynard Elect. MaynStream 150-11408	150	SCSI			X	116K/sec
TEAC MT-2ST/N50	155	SCSI		X		116K/sec

*Tape backups may include a controller board, the controller may be offered as an option, or the tape drive may not require a controller board. The interface of the drive or tape backup refers to the type of connection and communications protocol that the device uses to communicate with the host computer.

†The speed at which data is transferred from the tape backup to the controller board.

TABLE 8-9 1/8-Inch Digital Cassette (5.25-Inch Internal)

Manufacturer/Model	Capacity (MB)	Interface*	XT Bus	AT Bus	PS/2 Bus	Data Transfer Rate†
Maynard Elect. MaynStream 20-10105	20	QIC-02	X	X		86K/sec
Digital Storage Sys.	60	QIC-02		X		90K/sec
Emerald Systems RAP060-2010	60	SCSI		X		86K/sec
Sysgen 210	60	QIC-36	X	X	X	90K/sec
TEAC MT-2ST/45B	60	QIC-36		X		86.3K/sec
Digital Storage ARC 7151	150	QIC-02		X		90K/sec

*Tape backups may include a controller board, the controller may be offered as an option, or the tape drive may not require a controller board. The interface of the drive or tape backup refers to the type of connection and communications protocol that the device uses to communicate with the host computer.

†The speed at which data is transferred from the tape backup to the controller board.

TABLE 8-10 1/8-Inch Digital Cassette (External)

Manufacturer/Model	Capacity (MB)	Interface*	XT Bus	AT Bus	PS/2 Bus	Data Transfer Rate†
Maynard Elect. MaynStream 20-10103	20	QIC-02			X	86K/sec
Emerald Systems RAP060-13010	60	SCSI		X		86K/sec
Procomm HiPerformance T60	60	SCSI			X	86K/sec
Sysgen 215	60	QIC-36	X	X	X	90K/sec

*Tape backups may include a controller board, the controller may be offered as an option, or the tape drive may not require a controller board. The interface of the drive or tape backup refers to the type of connection and communications protocol that the device uses to communicate with the host computer.

†The speed at which data is transferred from the tape backup to the controller board.

8-mm Helical-Scan Data Cartridges

The 8-mm helical-scan data cartridges are capable of storing up to 2.3GB of data on a single tape. The 8-mm helical-scan technology includes those devices that store information on standard video cassette recorder (VCR) tapes. Table 8-11 lists examples of helical-scan tape backups available.

Digital Audio Tape

DAT is the most recent technology for tape backup. Using helical-scan technology, DAT is capable of 1.3GB of backup capacity on a 4-mm cassette (see Table 8-11 for an example of this format). The selection of DAT over $\frac{1}{4}$-inch tape depends on a few key factors:

1. Does the higher-density recording provide improved data integrity?
2. Will the actual data access speed exceed that of $\frac{1}{4}$-inch tape?
3. Is the end-user cost per megabyte less than $\frac{1}{4}$-inch tape?

If the answers favor DAT technology, $\frac{1}{4}$-inch cartridge technology should be replaced.

1/2-Inch Reel-to-Reel

The $\frac{1}{2}$-inch reel-to-reel backups are used primarily for their high level of format compatibility and data portability. You can access the data on a reel-to-reel on a vast variety of equipment, from microcomputers to minis to mainframes.

Share of Market

Over the last 5 years, the use of $\frac{1}{2}$-, $\frac{1}{4}$-, and $\frac{1}{8}$-inch tape drives has been minor compared to the growth of the helical-scan types. Figure 8-10 shows the growth rates in the different types of available tape drives.

Tape Drive Speeds

Tape drives tend to have low access speeds for off-line data storage and retrieval. Table 8-12 shows the access speeds of 1.2-inch and $\frac{1}{4}$-inch cartridge drives and 4-mm DAT and 8-mm helical-scan tape drives. Transfer rates for rewritable optical drives are faster than those for most tape cartridge drives. These are discussed later in this chapter.

TABLE 8-11 Helical-Scan Tape Backup

Manufacturer/Model	Capacity (MB)	Interface*	XT Bus	AT Bus	PS/2 Bus	Data Transfer Rate†
4-mm DAT—5.25-inch Internal						
Summus GigaTape 1.2	1,200	SCSI		X		170K/sec
8-mm Cartridge						
Maynard Elect. MaynStream 2200HS	2,200	SCSI			X	235K/sec
Mountain Filesafe 2100	2,200	SCSI		X		246K/sec
Summus GigaTape 442	2,300	SCSI		X		246K/sec
Video Cassette						
Digi-Data Gigastore 5.4	2,500	PERTEC	X	X		250K/sec

*Tape backups may include a controller board, the controller may be offered as an option, or the tape drive may not require a controller board. The interface of the drive or tape backup refers to the type of connection and communications protocol that the device uses to communicate with the host computer.

†The speed at which data is transferred from the tape backup to the controller board.

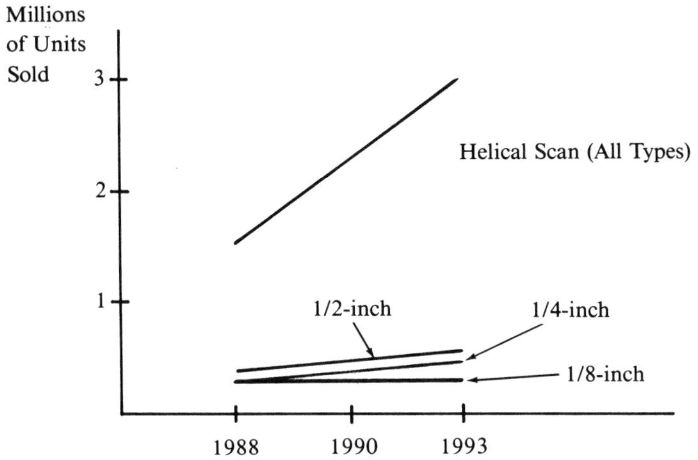

Figure 8-10 Trends in tape drives

TABLE 8-12 Tape Drive Access Speeds

Drive Type	Access Speed (seconds)
$\frac{1}{4}$-inch cartridge	30–40
$\frac{1}{2}$-inch cartridge	24–44
Helical-scan types	20

Examples of Tape Drives

Maynard. The ArchiveXL minicartridge systems come with easy-to-use QIC-system backup utility software. The software is easy to learn and use since it is fully menu-driven. You can use the system to back up all files, selected files, or changed files. An automatic backup allows you to back up files you have selected at some predetermined time. You can save several backups on one tape, or a single backup can span multiple tapes.

Drives are available with 40MB and 80MB capacities, and you can expand them to 60MB and 120MB by using extended-length tapes. Data-compression software can expand the capacities of these drives to 124MB and 250MB on media small enough to fit in your pocket. Minicartridge media costs less than the equivalent capacity on floppy disks.

You can use ArchiveXL tape backup systems with IBM PC, XT, AT, and PS/2 computer systems. The Archive XL controller (ISA/EISA) is available for internal ArchiveXL drives used in a dual floppy system, or for external drive users who want to share their ArchiveXL drive between multiple XT/ATs.

Iomega. Iomega's Bernoulli Box provides another method of data backup as well as extended storage for MS-DOS PCs, PS/2s, and compatibles. The Bernoulli 10MB, 20MB, 44MB, and 90MB magnetic-disk cartridges are designed for mass extended storage. A 90MB cartridge contains the storage capacity of 240 floppy disks or 21,000 pages. When a disk cartridge is full, you can replace it with another, at a cost of only a few dollars per megabyte. A 90MB cartridge weights 6 ounces and can be easily stored or shipped to another location. Shipping a full cartridge is usually cheaper than using a modem. Bernoulli disk cartridges can withstand more than 1,000 Gs of shock force without data loss, and you can lock up data that must be kept confidential.

OPTICAL BACKUP SYSTEMS

CD-ROMs

CD-ROMs are a type of optical, laser-based technology similar to audio CD players. A single CD can store over 600 MB of information. CD-ROM drives have read-only capability. However, while CD-ROMs are useful for disseminating large amounts of information, there are other optical mass-storage devices that you can use for backing up files as well.

WORM Drives

Write-once-read-many (WORM) drives were the first type of optical backup technology to become widely available. With a WORM drive, you can write to it once, but you cannot change or erase what is already written. You can use WORM drives for backing up large amounts of data that you will not need to change or edit. WORM drives are used primarily for archiving data and use a cartridge that you can take out and store. Scanned images and files that you need to store for a long time can be written on the cartridges and stored until needed. While paper records can deteriorate, data stored in digital format will print out at the original quality in the future.

Available WORM drives (both internal and external) are listed in Tables 8-13 and 8-14, along with their pertinent characteristics.

TABLE 8-13 WORM Optical Drives (5.25-Inch Full-Height Internal)

Manufacturer/Model	Capacity (MB)	Interface	Average Access Time† (ms)	Cartridge Capacity per Side (MB)	Cartridge Size (inches)
N/Hance Systems 15,000 525PC	242	PO AT BUS	135.0	121	5.25
Toshiba WM-D070	600	SCSI	400.0	300	5.25
Storage Dimensions Laserstor PS-8001	754	SCSI	108.0	377	5.25
Panasonic LF-5014	940	SCSI	90.0	470	5.25
N/Hance Systems 5120SCE	1,200	SCSI	135.0	600	5.25
Pentax LS-S501	652	SCSI	56.7	326	5.25
Laser Magnetic Storage Laser Drive 510	654	SCSI	75.0	327	5.25

†The amount of time that it takes the drive, on the average, to move a track and read data.

TABLE 8-14 WORM Optical Drives (External)

Manufacturer/Model	Capacity (MB)	Interface	Average Access Time† (ms)	Cartridge Capacity per Side (MB)	Cartridge Size (inches)
N/Hance Sys. 525PCE	242	PC AT BUS	135	121	5.25
Micro Design Int. LB-400	400	SCSI	190	200	5.25
Pioneer DD-S5001	654	SCSI	60	327	5.25
Storage Dimensions Laserstor PC800	754	SCSI	108	377	5.25
Micro Design Int. LB-800	800	SCSI	108	400	5.25
Panasonic LF-5010	940	SCSI	90	470	5.25
N/Hance Systems 5120SC	1,200	SCSI	135	600	5.25
Storage Dimensions Laserstor LS1600AT	1,572	SCSI	108	393	5.25
Laser Magnetic Storage LaserDrive 1200E	2,000	SCSI	150	1,000	12.0
N/Hance Systems 5120GBX/2	2,400	PC AT BUS	90	600	5.25
Micro Design Int. LB-5000	5,000	SCSI	160	2,500	12

†The amount of time that it takes the drive, on the average, to move a track and read data.

Rewritable Optical Disks

Unlike WORM drives, you can *write to* as well as *read from* rewritable optical disks, also called "erasable optical drives." You can use this type of optical disk like a hard disk, although optical drives have slower access times than hard drives. However, the technology is still new and more expensive than WORM drives. Rewritable and WORM drives are similar, but the media are different in that one can be written to and the other cannot. Examples of this type of system are given in Tables 8-15 and 8-16.

TABLE 8-15 Rewritable Optical Drives (5.25-Inch Full-Height Internal)

Manufacturer/Model	Capacity (MB)	Interface	Average Access Time† (ms)	Cartridge Capacity per Side	Cartridge Size (inches)
Ricoh RO-5030E	595	SCSI	71	297	5.25
Mitsubishi Elect. MW-5D1	600	SCSI	80	300	5.25
Hitachi OD112-1	644	SCSI	75	322	5.25
Sony SMO-D501	650	SCSI	95	325	5.25

†The amount of time that it takes the drive, on the average, to move a track and read data.

TABLE 8-16 Rewritable Optical Drives (External)

Manufacturer/Model	Capacity (MB)	Interface	Average Access Time† (ms)	Cartridge Capacity per Side	Cartridge Size (inches)
Summus LightDisk	594	SCSI	90	297	5.25
Mitsubishi Elect. MW-5U1	600	SCSI	80	300	5.25
Alphatronix PC+Inspire	650	SCSI	83	325	5.25
Hewlett-Packard HP6300 Mod 650/A	650	SCSI	95	325	5.25
Sony SMO S501	650	SCSI	95	325	5.25
AGA (Advanced Graphic App) DISCUS DR650	652	SCSI	61	326	5.25
Laserdrive Ltd. Model 810	810	SCSI	175	405	5.25
Alphatronix PC+Inspire	1,300	SCSI	83	325	5.25
Sony WDD-3000	2,100	SCSI	500	1,050	12.00

†The amount of time that it takes the drive, on the average, to move a track and read data.

Rewritable Optical Media. There are three methods that are used to produce rewritable optical media: magneto optic, phase change, and dye polymer. Most early drives used magneto-optic techniques. Phase-change media represents the second generation of rewritable media, and dye-polymer media is the latest development.

Magneto-Optic Technology. This technology uses a magneto-optic recording layer consisting of an amorphous alloy of rare earth elements. To record data, the laser beam strikes a spot on the sensitive layer and causes the spot's magnetic field to change polarity. A lower power beam of the same laser then reads the information as binary codes. The rewriting sequence uses three steps: erase, write new data onto the disk, and verify the new data.

The main advantage of magneto-optic media is long life. Magneto-optic media has been operated at 7 million write-erase cycles without data degradation. In contrast to the phase-change and dye-polymer technologies discussed in the next sections, data written using magneto-optic technology is permanent unless intentionally erased, and there is no actual physical change to the media. Most magneto-optic media manufacturers claim a media life of 10 years.

Phase-Change Technology. This provides another approach to rewritable optical media. In the phase-change technique, a laser beam changes the structure of a light-sensitive layer from a stable amorphous state to a crystalline state. The surface reflectivity changes from low to high, and the laser beam reads this change. To erase data, the laser beam changes the light-sensitive layer back to the stable amorphous state. Phase-change media will last about as long as magneto-optic media. However, unlike magneto-optic media, phase-change media permits direct overwriting without having to erase before rewriting. It is also less expensive than magneto-optic media, but is higher in cost than dye-polymer media.

Dye-Polymer Technology. Dye polymer is a process in which the laser beam's heat changes the topology of the disk surface. The laser beam creates a slight ripple or rise on the surface of the sensitive layer. This defect scatters the light, resulting in less reflection than the pure surface. To erase data, the beam reduces the defect. This is the least expensive method of producing rewritable optical media. However, media life is relatively low—only a few hundred thousand write-erase cycles. Manufacturers have been concentrating more on magneto-optic technology than on dye-polymer technology.

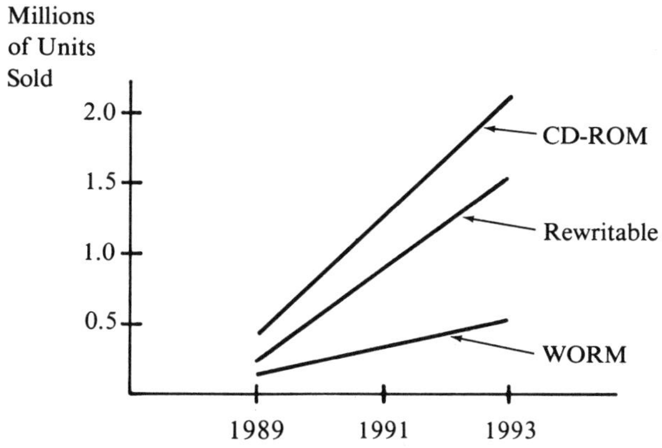

Figure 8-11 Trends in optical drives

Which System Is Right for You?

Both WORM and rewritable drives use moveable disk cartridges that can be stored, and rewritable subsystems are being used for on-line storage of CAD/CAM files with up to 5GB of data storage. Both systems offer high-capacity storage, typically ranging from 600MB to several gigabytes. Rewritable drives have a faster access time than WORM drives—65 ms—while WORM drives take about 50% longer.

If you do not need rewritability, write-once optical disks provide a cost advantage over rewritable optical. Rewritable drives can cost twice as much as write-once drives per megabyte. However, standards for rewritable optical drives are more advanced than those for write-once drives.

Figure 8-11 shows the growth rates in the three types of optical drives.

Optical Drive Jukeboxes

These are large systems that contain multiple rewritable, WORM, or CD-ROM optic drives and mechanically interchange media from a stack of disks, similar in method to audio jukeboxes.

9

UPGRADING WITH FAX AND MODEM UNITS

FAX

Fax communication is an efficient way to share visual information. You can use a fax board to send reasonable facsimiles of drawings, illustrations, layouts, or entire publications. Some specialized publications are using fax technology instead of sending hard copies. Even international subscribers can receive their copies only a few minutes after the publication has been put together.

In 1992, there was an installed base of more than 8 million fax machines worldwide, with 2.5 million of those in the United States. Most predictions like those in Figure 9-1 indicate that fax will become as common as the telephone by the year 2000.

Interest in this office-productivity tool has been fueled by two factors:

- Fax technology has drastically reduced acceptable deadlines. In the early 1970s, most businesses functioned successfully by taking three to five days to transfer information through the mail. With the advent of overnight mail in the late 1970s, the acceptable waiting period for information shortened from three days to overnight. Since fax has become available, even overnight is not acceptable—instant access has become the norm.
- Office automation has moved toward a more integrated environment under the control of a network. Recent advances allow the fax to become a key part of this environment.

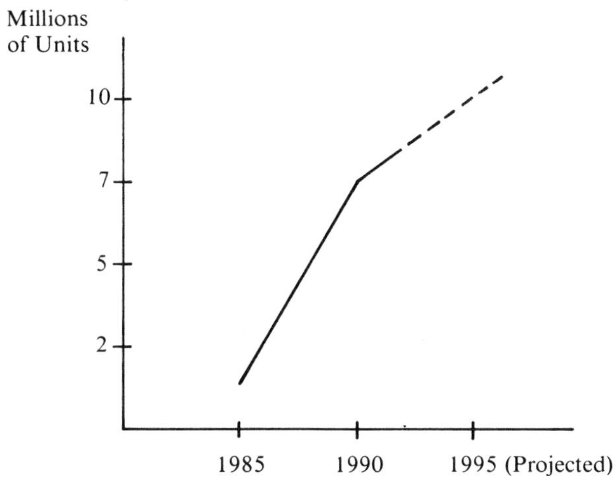

Figure 9-1 Fax growth

Computer/fax interface products allow transmission directly from a mainframe, minicomputer or PC to a fax machine or to another computer. With these interface devices, you can also send messages from the PC to multiple fax machines with the push of one button. Many users are discovering the potential of these products as I/O nodes for their telecommunications and data processing networks.

Fax accessories include products such as surge suppressors and fax care kits. They allow you to extend the life of the machine, protect data, and increase the fax unit's capabilities.

With the need for immediate communications and integrated office automation in both business and personal communications, facsimile and related products will continue to grow in importance into the next century.

Fax Standards

Facsimile transmissions must conform to standards established by the Comite Consultatif International Telephonique et Telegraphique (International Telegraph and Telephone Consultative Committee or CCITT). The standards have followed the technology.

- **Group I.** The first group of CCITT standards appeared in 1968. These were used for the Group I facsimile devices, which transmit the contents of a standard-size page (8.27 x 11.69-inch outline) on a telephone line using an analog signal. The page is divided into 1,144 scan lines and transmitted at the rate of 180 scan lines per minute, or one page every 6.35 minutes.

- **Group II.** In 1976, the transmission rate went up to 300 scan lines per minute, and the transmission of gray-scale images was added in the Group II machines.
- **Group III.** When Group III facsimile appeared in 1980, it included both dedicated fax machines and PC boards that can page in a minute or less. The Group III page is made up of 1,083 scan lines of 1,728 pixels, which results in a resolution of 204 dpi horizontally and 96 dpi vertically. A high-resolution mode increases the vertical resolution to 196 dpi. Group III facsimile machines use a data compression technique called "Modified Huffman." This technique reduces the scan-line data required by describing it in changes from white to black, or black to white.
- **Group IV.** These facsimile machines appeared in 1984. These machines can transmit a standard page in less than 10 seconds, at resolutions of 200 x 200, 240 x 240, 300 x 300, or 400 x 400 dpi. A Group IV facsimile requires a data line rather than a voice-grade telephone line like other fax machines.

Trends

The fax industry is still maturing from the early stages of product trials and tests toward a more general, overall acceptance. In the future, we can expect to see major firms offering fax units equipped with a variety of features at continually deceasing costs.

Fax technology has been going in two directions. There are high-end products for mid- to large-size corporations, where fax traffic is rapidly increasing, and low-end products for the home office and the small business owner.

Fax is not new to most large corporations. These users have come to expect machines equipped with features like sequential and relayed broadcasting, enhanced autodialing capabilities, and confidential mailbox access codes. Large users will be the first to accept and utilize newer products, such as plain-paper fax and Group IV units. As prices come down, there will be more acceptance by the general fax consumer market—the home office/small business market is expected to purchase about 70% of all fax units. This type of business generally has between 3 and 99 employees.

Fax is a product that has been changing rapidly due to technology advancements. Many of the businesses that already have one of the earlier fax units may need to upgrade to a more feature-rich machine. As more advanced fax technology, such as digital transmission, has emerged, Group III devices are replacing Group II and I fax machines, which take three and six minutes to transmit a page. More than 90% of all fax machines installed throughout the world today are Group III machines. Most of the fax machines in use have a resolution of 200 dpi. (This is less than the accepted 300 dpi used for most desktop publishing.) Group III machines incorporate some digital features and offer transmission speeds of less than one minute per page, with many offering speeds from 10 to 20 seconds. Group IV machines work only with dedicated communications lines such as Integrated Services Digital Networks (ISDN) and private data networks and are the highest-priced machines. Group IV will gradually be replaced by a Group V standard.

Using fax can be less expensive for high-volume users than mailing, since telephone rates are much less than postage rates for these users. Low-volume users tend to pay telephone transmission charges that equal or exceed those of the postal system.

Most of the fax machines that have been sold over the years use heat-sensitive paper, which is not as desirable as plain paper because of its glossy feel and a lack of image stability. However, just as copier technology progressed from thermal to plain paper, fax technology is evolving, and plain-paper fax represents the future. Because the technology is still relatively new, plain-paper fax machines cost more and are justifiable only to large users. Thermal units can meet the majority of users' needs and budgets. Tables 9-1 and 9-2 list typical thermal- and plain-paper units.

Fax Features

Call scheduling is the software option of scheduling a fax transmission to be sent at a specific time. Some faxes include **graphics editing software** that allows the creating and editing of graphic faxes. The **maximum resolution** of the fax board or fax modem refers to the number of pixels (horizontal by vertical) that the board/modem is capable of sending and receiving. The greater the resolution, the better the clarity of the picture.

A **transaction log** is a report detailing the faxes sent and received and the status of those transmissions (including errors). **Background operation** refers to the fax board/fax modem's ability to send or receive fax transmissions while simultaneously performing other tasks. The boards/modems generally feature a microprocessor to operate the fax functions transparently in the background. **Polling** is the ability to call another fax device and ask or "poll" if that fax device has any faxes addressed to the caller. This is extremely useful for intracompany fax routing. **Broadcasting** is the capability of sending a fax to a multitude of locations automatically. This feature is often called "mass faxing."

TABLE 9-1 Thermal-Paper Fax Machines

Manufacturer/Model	Maximum Resolution	Broadcasting	Group IV	Group III	Group II	Group I	Timed Dialing
Canon FAX-730	203 x 196	X		X	X		X
Fujitsu 150	203 x 196			X	X		X
Murata F-45	203 x 392			X	X		X
Ricoh FAX15	203 x 196			X	X	X	

TABLE 9-2 Plain-Paper Fax Machines—9,600 bps

Manufacturer/Model	Maximum Resolution	Broadcasting	Group IV	Group III	Group II	Group I	Timed Dialing
Canon FAX-350	203 x 392	X		X	X		X
Olivetti FX 2100	296 x 203	X		X	X		X

Fax on a PC

Many PCs have the basic elements of a fax machine—scanner/modem/printer. Although the fax modem differs from the usual Hayes-compatible asynchronous modem found on most PCs, you can generally use the scanner and printer (see Table 9-3 for fax modems and boards that are available).

A PC fax board can provide fax formatting, transmission, and reception. You can utilize the other components of the PC to provide many capabilities beyond most stand-alone fax machines. A PC fax board is usually less expensive than a stand-alone fax machine since it does not duplicate the scanner and printer that you may already have on your system. Also, it can process text and graphics from floppy or hard disks and convert fax transmissions into data formats that you can quickly edit or reformat. Using the PC printer gives you output on plain paper instead of the more expensive and glossy thermal paper.

Examples of Fax Products

MicroFax. The MicroFax board from Datacopy uses a Hayes-compatible 1,200-baud modem and installs in an expansion slot of IBM-compatible computers. It supports a number of displays, printers, and scanners.

The user interface consists of three menus:

1. Commands
2. Logs and Files
3. Set Up

You begin a session by selecting the phone numbers and files you want to transmit. Phone numbers are stored in a file called a phone book. You can change, add, delete, and search for a phone book listing.

Text files can be from a word processor or program listing, or they can be edited with MicroFax's editor. Text files should be in ASCII format, with no more than 80 characters per line and 66 lines per page. Any word-processing format data, such as bold or tabs, will be lost. You can alter the format of the transmitted information by using the Text to Fax Setup dialog box. The box contains settings for redefining the character width (from 20 to 5 characters per inch), the character height (normal or double), the page length, and the margins.

After you have received a text-based fax document, you can reconvert

TABLE 9-3 Fax Modems and Boards

Manufacturer/Model	Maximum Resolution	Background Operation	Call Schedule	Broadcasting Polling	Transaction Log	Computer Compatibility*
4,800 bps External						
Everex EverFax	100 x 200		X	X	X	PC
9,600 bps External						
American Data	203 x 196	X	X	X	X	PC
Fujitsu dexNET200	200 x 200					RS-232
The Complete CFAX/P	196 x 204		X	X	X	RS-232
4,800 bps Internal						
American Data Tech. Smart FAX48	203 x 196	X	X	X	X	PC
The Complete PC CFAX	196 x 204	X	X	X	X	PC
9,600 bps Internal						
American Data Technology SmartFAXplus	203 x 196	X	X	X	X	PC
Pacific Image Communications PIC SuperFax MCA	203 x 196	X	X	X	X	Micro Channel
Ricoh ImageCard	200 x 100	X	X	X	PC	
SpectralFAX Faxcard	200 x 200	X	X	X	X	PC
The Complete CFAX19600	196 x 204	X	X	X	X	PC

it into ASCII form only through the use of OCR technology. OCR software analyzes character shapes and constructs an ASCII file from its findings. Datacopy offers optional software with its scanner for this purpose. Datacopy also provides a utility program to convert from a number of graphic formats to and from fax format.

You can send any file, regardless of its size, type, or content, between computers that are both equipped with a MicroFax card. MicroFax-to-MicroFax communication uses a binary file transfer (BFT) process, communicating error-free at 9,600 baud. You can indicate destinations that utilize the MicroFax and BFT in the phone book by adding "MF" after the phone number.

Sending a Fax. MicroFax supports transmission with Group III-compatible facsimile machines. Initiating a fax session begins by selecting Call from the command menu. Then you select the phone numbers from a displayed list of available numbers.

Next, set the time of the transmission. You can send the fax immediately, or you can set a future time or date when you want the transmission to occur. MicroFax will use the computer's clock for setting the time and date. The Activity Journal will list the files that have been sent. The latest transmission will appear at the end of the list.

Receiving a Fax. You can accept faxes in a background mode, enabling you to use the PC in another application while the MicroFax card handles the reception without interrupting you. After the fax has been received, the MicroFax board will signal you for an acknowledgment.

The received fax documents are listed in the Received Log. It will list the file name, phone number of the originating device, time and date received, and the length of the call.

Other Features. A polling feature lets the MicroFax unit call another Group III-compatible facsimile device. If this device has documents either in its memory or document feeder, polling can capture these documents and have them sent to the MicroFax unit. You can use polling during off-peak times when telephone rates are low to collect documents from remote locations that are waiting to be sent.

Logs are used to handle fax activity. A Received Log, Call Schedule, and Activity Journal help with receiving calls from remote points, programming calls for transmission, and recording both successful and unsuccessful calls.

Utilities include SnapFax for screen capture and transmission to remote sources or for printing. Note Pad is a small text editor that can be used for creating memos, letters, and cover sheets for fax transmissions.

Nightwatch displays a flashing screen to prevent others from turning off the computer. It automatically prints incoming documents when they are received.

SatisFAXtion. This fax board does not require you to stop working to send or receive a fax. When you want to fax, it is as easy as printing with the WYPIWYF (way you print is the way you fax) software. When you are ready to send a document, you do not have to exit your application. The entire process is invisible and completed in seconds.

Broadcasting a fax to several destinations is convenient. Select the numbers to which you want to send faxes, and the board and software will take over while you complete another task on the screen.

SatisFAXtion includes a 2,400-bps data modem with advanced MNP5 for 4,800-bps data communications. There is a built-in scanner port for the Intel Hand Scanner. Configuration takes place in software.

There is also a NET SatisFAXtion software package for LANs. This package also incorporates WYPIWYF and allows all users to send and receive faxes from their PCs. It supports both DOS and Windows, and it can handle multiple SatisFAXtion boards, supporting up to 1,000 users per fax server on the most popular networks.

The network version supports HP LaserJet II emulation, including font cartridges A–Z, and it provides fax management facilities, such as queue management, transaction reporting, accounting, real-time status monitoring, and security.

JT Fax. You can add power and flexibility to your PC with the Hayes JT Fax 9600B. You can use it to send and receive fax documents, store faxes for later use, and send them to your printers. It is compatible with a wide range of word processing packages, printers, and scanners.

It provides a fast PC-based fax with 9,600 bps transmission. You can use these faster units to communicate with Group III facsimile machines or PC-based faxes at remote locations. This product comes with a Smartmodem 2400 module and Smartcom EZ software, so you can use it for both fax and data communications.

VoiceFax. Fax is available with voice recognition for unattended fax operation. This allows one to call a computer, listen to a computer-generated message, and key in the required information to obtain a faxed document without an operator's assistance.

VoiceFax is a cost-effective means of dispensing information. It lets a caller select from 500 documents in ASCII, Paradox, DBF, and WKS file formats. You can limit the number of calls or documents available to each caller per day or restrict incoming calls to a particular area code. VoiceFax monitors and records the on-line usage, providing demographic data.

VoiceFax requires a 386 or 486 with 4MB RAM, an 80MB hard disk, VGA graphics, a voice-recognition board, a fax board, and two dedicated phone lines. It also supports multiple fax boards for multiple transmissions.

MODEMS

The word "modem" is a contraction of "modulator/demodulator." Modems use modulation techniques to translate digital data signals into a signal form suitable for transmission over a particular medium, usually telephone lines (Fig 9-2). They use demodulation to retranslate the transmitted signals into the original digital data pattern once they reach their destination. You can connect your computer to a telephone line using a modem.

While true modems use modulation/demodulation, if we extend the definition of modem to include *all* devices that allow communications between data units over media that would not normally allow data transmission, then a modem may or may not transmit data through modulation and demodulation. Short-haul modems can use techniques such as "current drive" and "return to zero." In some applications, these modem-like devices can have advantages over true modems. Therefore, we will include these in our discussion of modems.

Modulation and Demodulation

The modulation process allows a device to generate an analog carrier signal and vary a characteristic of this signal, such as the amplitude, as a

Figure 9-2 Modem operation (A message to be transmitted is sent to the modem, which modulates it for the phone lines. At the other end, the modem demodulates it and sends it to the PC where it can be displayed or printed.)

function of the digital data signal. Demodulation reverses the process and allows the original data signal to be recovered.

A simple modem might use only two variations of a characteristic. A frequency-modulating modem might use one frequency or tone to represent spaces (0s) and another frequency for marks (1s).

The most common modem modulation techniques are amplitude modulation (AM), phase modulation (PM), and frequency modulation (FM). Some modems use these techniques in different combinations. Most modems use PM and FM since they are better suited to the requirements of data communications than AM.

AM Modems. AM modems use a change in the amplitude of the carrier signal in relation to the data signal (Fig 9-3). The number of amplitude levels is a function of the amount of information that each level can transmit. With two levels, each level can transmit either a 0 or 1; with four levels, each level can transmit either 00, 01, 10, or 11. This allows four-level modems to transmit twice as much information in the same time span as two-level modems.

Some modems use AM in combination with another technique to increase the speed of data transmission. For example, a carrier signal modulated with two phases can transmit a maximum of one data bit per cycle (0 or 1). If that carrier signal is also modulated with two amplitudes, we get quadrature amplitude modulation (QAM), and the number of data bits per cycle increases to two (00, 01, 10, or 11).

AM is inexpensive, but it has several drawbacks. One problem is a relatively wide bandwidth requirement, which allows AM to be used only for very low-speed data transmissions. AM also has a low noise tolerance, which can cause data errors that are unacceptable in data transmissions.

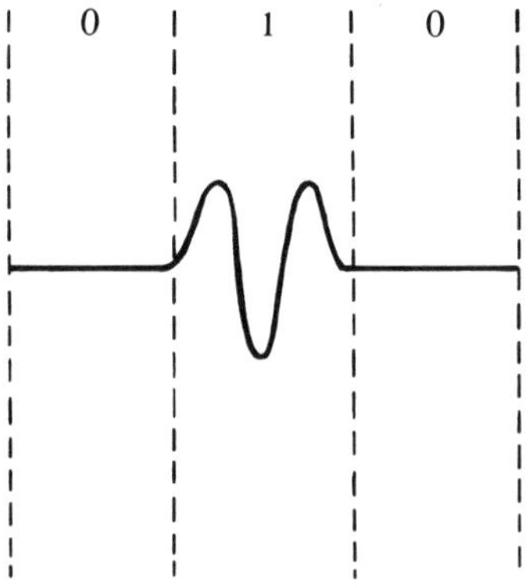

Figure 9-3 Amplitude modulation technique

PM Modulation. PM has good noise immunity, but, like AM, it uses a lot of bandwidth. PM can be done with a shift between two phases, with each phase shift representing a single data bit. This technique is commonly called phase shift keying (PSK). A more complex implementation of PM might use four or more phase shifts to transmit data, and each phase shift transmits two or more data bits. This method reduces the required bandwidth and permits higher data rates. Shifts of 90, 180, 270, and 360, for example, could be used to transmit 00, 01, 10, or 11.

The receiving modems in PM detect each phase shift by reference to a fixed phase, which typically is the last phase. The modems must detect each shift as it occurs to provide high data rates. The modems must also be synchronized with each other for the best performance. This last requirement forces PM modems to use synchronous data transmission, which is their primary use.

The detection and decoding circuitry results in high implementation costs for PM, but these have been coming down recently as integrated circuit costs drop.

FM Modems. FM uses a lower bandwidth and has a much lower implementation cost. FM modems do not need to be synchronized, and the circuitry is much simpler. They typically use frequency shift keying (FSK), where the carrier shifts between two frequencies or tones.

FSK modems are usually phase-coherent, so each new frequency follows the phase of the previous frequency. There is no forced phase shift and no frequency components generated from such a shift. The receiving modem needs to work with only the two data-carrying tones. The data rates are higher since phase-coherent modems can detect the tones within a half cycle.

Some modems use an on-off scheme to transmit data. They turn the carrier signal on or off to transmit 0 and 1.

Classes of Modems

Modems and modem-like devices can be classified as follows:

1. Short-haul modems
2. Long-haul modems
3. Medium-distance modems
4. Data-over-voice (DOV) modems
5. Acoustic couplers
6. Modem eliminators
7. Line drivers

Short-Haul Modems. These modems typically operate at distances of up to 10 miles and are in widespread use for data transmission within metropolitan areas, in campus environments, and within building complexes. When short distances are involved, short-haul modems are often a better choice than long-haul modems because they are less expensive and provide higher data rates. Their high data rates provide for more efficient use of existing leased lines.

A common data rate for short-haul modems is 9,600 bps, but some short-hauls can operate at much higher rates (256 Kbps). Most short-hauls, which are also known as local data sets, operate on privately owned metallic circuits or leased lines. The distances at which they operate are limited by the transmission speed and the diameter of the wires over which they transmit.

Short-haul modems do not usually require DC continuity. The communication line for a short-haul is isolated from the modem with a transformer. This helps to protect the modem from damage and disturbances by transient signals such as lightning on the lines. Short-hauls also provide high reliability and lower bit-error rates.

Most short-haul modems are not true modems. They do not have a carrier signal that they modulate. These modems are actually line drivers, sending the digital signal directly over the channel and acting as a signal conditioner. Since the integrity of the digital signal is a function of speed and distance, these short-hauls have a limited range.

Short-haul modems are inexpensive and can be quite small. Units are available that measure less than 4 inches in length, weigh only a few ounces, and plug directly into an RS-232 connector.

Long-Haul Modems. These modems allow you to transmit data over large distances—cross-country or transoceanic. Long-haul modems usually modulate a voice-frequency carrier signal with the digital data pattern. Problems that occur in these long lines include amplitude and phase delays. Long-haul modems are designed to "correct" for these delays.

Long-haul modems can be divided into two subtypes, depending on the type of lines they use. Most long-hauls designed for PCs use the public switched (DDD) network. Some businesses use dedicated leased telephone lines (Bell System Type 3002 voice channels) for economy. There are special modems for these leased lines.

DDD modems are the units most commonly used, and they are the devices most people have in mind when they use the term "modem." DDD modems are typically Bell-compatible and will operate with either Bell System modems or other Bell-compatible models. All DDD modems require FCC certification (United States) or DOC registration (Canada) for direct connection to the DDD network.

Modems that operate on dedicated leased lines do not need certification, but they may require line conditioning for the best operation on dedicated leased lines. Conditioning will control the frequency response and other line characteristics to reduce errors at high speeds.

In the past, leased-line, long-haul modems generally operated at higher speeds than DDD modems. When most DDD modems were operating at relatively low data rates of 1,200 bps, speeds of 4,800 bps and above were typical of leased-line long-hauls. Now, however, higher-speed DDD modems operating at 2,400 bps and more are more common.

The microprocessors in long-haul modems have resulted in improved reliability and flexibility. Most long-hauls give you complete menu-driven control from the keyboard. Features such as autodialers that store multiple numbers and menu-driven log-in sequences make operation easy.

Many vendors offer long-haul modems and, as a result of price/performance competition and technological advances, the price of these modems has dropped substantially over the years. Besides becoming more affordable, long-hauls are becoming smaller, faster, and more versatile.

There is a wide variety of long-haul modems available on the market. While you are choosing the one that is best for you, you should also realize that long-hauls are not the answer for all applications. Short-haul modems can be a more appropriate and cost-effective alternative if they can be used for your particular application.

Medium-Distance Modems. These modems are newer devices and are available from only a few manufacturers. They fall between short-hauls and long-hauls in terms of capabilities and price. Like short-hauls, they can replace long-hauls in some applications. They provide data communications between points beyond the capabilities of short-hauls, but they can operate at the higher data rates of short-hauls.

Medium-distance modems can operate at distances of up to 200 miles and are often used on leased lines served by multiple central offices. They are true modems since they generate a carrier signal and modulate it. The price is lower than long-hauls due to the elimination of some of the long-distance circuits used in long-hauls.

Data-over-Voice Modems. DOVs are also a recent development in modems. They are sometimes called local-area data transports (LADTs). They allow simultaneous voice and high-speed data communications on a single pair of conductors for distances of up to several miles.

DOVs are true modems since they generate carrier frequencies and modulate them with the digital data pattern. Frequency allocation and a filtering system prevent the voice and data channels from interfering with each other. These units are not designed for use on the DDD network or leased lines.

With DOVs, a telephone network can form the basis of a LAN. Each telephone outlet is a potential modem site, and there is no need to pull additional cables. Some DOV models install with standard modular jacks, simplifying the installation and relocation of equipment.

Other Modems. In addition to the standard long-haul, short-haul, medium-distance, and DOV modems, there are other types of modems and modem-like devices that are used in more specialized applications where conventional modems are not practical or cost-effective. Acoustic couplers, for example, are suitable for portable applications. These devices use a wireless, acoustical connection through the telephone handset. In general, acoustic couplers do not operate at speeds greater than 600 bps, which is a disadvantage. They are also subject to interference from acoustical noise surrounding the headset. They are lower in cost than conventional long-haul modems.

Modem eliminators can be a substitute for conventional modems when the distances are less than 200 feet.

Line drivers, like modem eliminators, are useful as alternatives to conventional modems in very local applications. These devices usually require DC continuity and run on customer-owned twisted wire pairs or coaxial cable. The line is not isolated from the equipment, which makes line drivers susceptible to damage and interference from transient signals. Some short-haul modems are actually line drivers.

The type of modem or modem-like device that is best for an application depends on a number of factors. The capabilities of each type are as important as how much money is available and which features are essential.

Multiplexing

A multiplexer can also provide substantial savings in line and modem costs. The two basic techniques of multiplexing are frequency division and time division. In frequency-division multiplexing, the communications channel is split into different frequencies and the data from the different sources is transmitted together. In time-division multiplexing, data from each source is put on a time schedule, and only one data signal is transmitted at a time. Time-division multiplexing can allocate time on either a fixed or changeable statistical basis.

Trends

For the last decade, modems have been trending toward smaller, faster, and less expensive machines. Most of the modems in the early 1970s operated at 300 bps (about 30 characters per second). In the late 1970s, modem speeds increased to 1,200 bps. In the mid-1980s, the industry saw a major shift from 1,200 bps to 2,400 bps and, in the late 1980s, to 9,600 bps, with some leveling projected through the 1990s (Fig 9-4). The newer 9,600-bps modems also run at 2,400-, 1,200-, and 300-bps speeds, maintaining compatibility with the older modems in use.

The 300- and 1,200-bps modems followed the Bell/AT&T 103 and 212A protocols. The 2,400-bps units adopted the CCITT V.22 bps standard. For 9,600-bps transmissions, there was a CCITT V.32 standard in place that was drafted by the CCITT in 1984 for dial-up 9,600-bps modems. Standardization allows 9,600-bps modems from different manufacturers to be compatible and to communicate with each other. However, the technology was complex and expensive to produce, and the first V.32 modems were unsatisfactory in performance and cost. The initial use of this standard gained limited acceptance, and several modem manufacturers developed their own standards. Most of the resulting products operated like pseudo-duplex modems. Examples include the PEP modems from

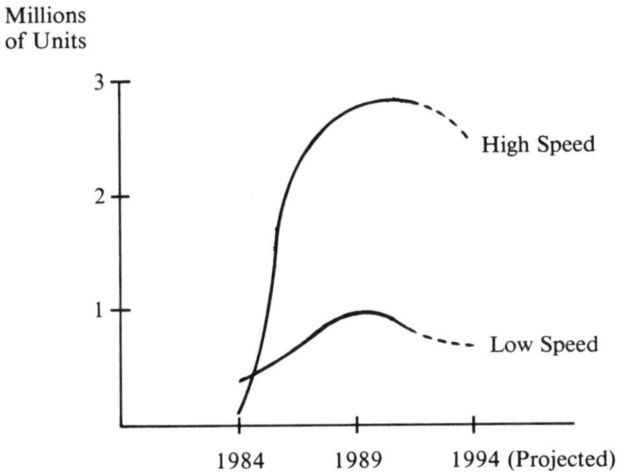

Figure 9-4 Modem trends: 1984–1994

Telebit and Ven-Tel, the US Robotics HST asymmetrical modem, the Hayes V-Series 9600, and the Microcom Networking Protocol (MNP) Class 6 modems from Microcom and Micro-Tech. These modems are not full duplex modems with a simultaneous transmit and receive facility.

Then, a series of newer-generation V.32 modems were introduced. These units provided the performance that was needed at a lower cost, and the V.32 standard became accepted. V.32-compatible full-duplex 9,600-bps modems became available at reasonable prices. The faster a modem can send data through a phone line, the less will be spent on phone bills. In most applications, increased speed means greater efficiency and productivity.

Modems have also become more intelligent, performing functions like storing and dialing phone numbers, changing their option settings, and performing self-test routines. Other recent improvements include error correction, data compression, speed conversion, remote configuration, and callback security.

As error correction, data compression, and speed conversion have become popular in modems, the majority of modems follow the MNP standard. MNP is an industry-standard error-correction protocol for modems. MNP standards of Class 3 and higher send data between two modems synchronously, speeding up the transfer of data over asynchronous communications. MNP Class 5 adds data compression and advanced error handling. These features allow modems to operate virtually error-free—even over noisy phone lines—and to function at almost twice their rated speed.

Remote configuration and callback security are also recent features. Remote configuration allows a user with a modem at one location to issue configuration commands to a modem at another location. Callback security prevents unauthorized access to on-line systems. It allows the modem to receive a call from a user and then hang up and call the user back at a predetermined phone number.

In the 1990s, while much interest will be on LAN technologies and digital networking, modems will continue to fill many traditional roles as well as new ones. V.32 modems will be used as LAN bridges and in modem servers. Dial-up modems are also getting increased use in synchronous applications that include remote 3270 access. V.32 modems are being used on four-wire leased lines with dial backup capability. Statistical multiplexers, which allow several users to use a single phone line, also allow modems to be used more efficiently.

There are 14,400-bps and 19,200-bps models as well as new features and network interfaces that make modems more versatile.

High-Speed Modems

Modern communications are essential in today's business world. High-speed modems represent one of the growth areas in communications. For example, Intel's 9600EX provides up to sixteen times the speed of a 2,400-bps modem. The 9600EX is an external, full-duplex modem for systems with asynchronous communications support, such as the IBM PC, XT, AT, PS/2, and compatibles. The 9600EX offers full compatibility with international standards of modem communications. It provides V.32 modulation and uses advanced V.42 data compression to compress data as much as four times. This increases the effective throughput to as much as 38.4Kbps. In order to improve data transmission over noisy lines, the 9600EX supports the V.42 Link Access Procedure for Modems (LAP-M) and the MNP, Classes 1-5. Automatic speed selection allows communications with 9,600-bps, 4,800-bps, 1,200-bps, and 300-bps modems.

Hayes Modems

In the area of PC data communications, Hayes modems and software were some of the first products to offer standard performance specifications. Today's internal and external models offer automatic dialing capability for unattended operation as well as storage for frequently called numbers. Figures 9-5 and 9-6 show the growth trends in these two types of modems. Standard features include call progress monitoring to provide information on the status of calls.

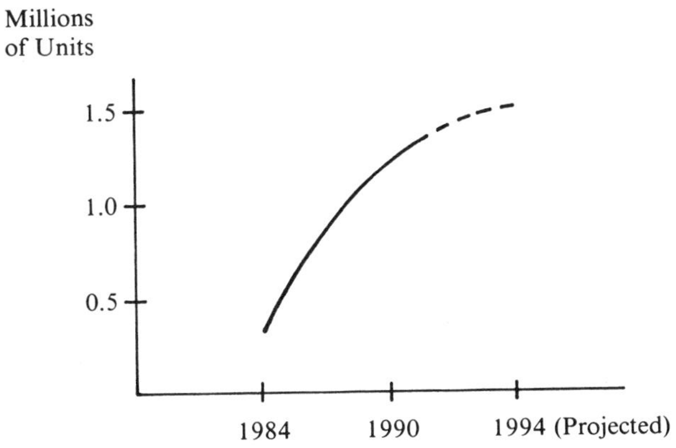

Figure 9-5 Internal modem growth

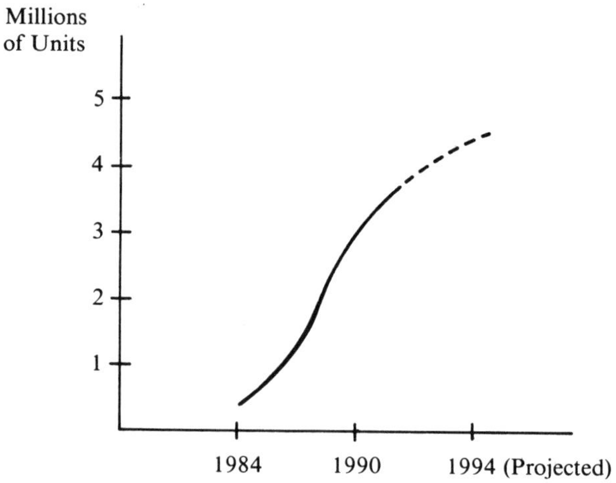

Figure 9-6 External modem growth

Examples of Modems

There is a wide variety of modems on the market from which you can choose, depending on the requirements of your application. Tables 9-4 through 9-7 list a sampling of modems available today.

Smartmodem. The Smartmodem 2400P provides the standard features and functions of a Hayes Smartmodem 2400 with the added convenience of an internal card, one designed specifically for IBM's Micro Channel PCs. Like all Hayes Smartmodem 2400 products, this modem gives you Hayes AutoSync, which allows you to communicate synchronously with a host computer without having to buy additional emulation cards.

Ven-Tel Modems. These units are 100% Hayes-compatible. For high-speed communications, Ven-Tel offers the 9600 Plus series modems. These allow secure, high-speed communications over both dial-up and leased lines at speeds of up to 38.4 Kbps. Ven-Tel designs these modems to meet CCITT V.32 specifications and to support MNP Classes 2–5 and V.42bis. These modems have three levels of security to restrict remote-user access. They are compatible with most PC systems and communications software.

MODEM COMMUNICATIONS

You can access a great deal of information with a modem, including databases of business histories, services for home shopping, banking,

TABLE 9-4 External Modems—2,400 bps

Manufacturer/Model	MNP Compatibility Level									Computer Interface*	Hayes-Compatible†
	1	2	3	4	5	6	7	8	9		
ATI Technologies 2400etc/e	X	X	X	X	X					RS-232C	X
Anchor 24E5	X	X	X	X	X					RS-232C	X
Ark Ark2.4K Plus SS				X						RS-232C	X
Cardinal 2400MNP	X	X	X	X	X					RS-232C	X
Computer Peripherals					X					RS-232C	X
Data Race Action 24 (24-1001)				X	X					RS-232C	X
DataTrek 624					X					RS-232C	X
E-Tech Bullet E2400	X	X	X	X						RS-232C	X
GVC SM-24M					X					RS-232C	X
Goldstar GSM 2400M					X					RS-232C	X
Incomm Midget 24ME	X	X	X	X						RS-232C	X
Longshine Technology 8824MNP					X					RS-232C	X
Memotec 224 Series II		X	X	X						RS-232C	
Microcom AX/2400c	X	X	X	X	X					RS-232C	X
MultiTech Systems MultiModem 224E MT224EH		X	X	X	X					RS-232C	X
NEC 12432C	X	X	X	X	X					RS-232C	X
Novation 2400 XE				X	X					RS-232C	X
Telcor 2424MA	X	X	X	X	X					RS-232C	X
Telenetics Model TC921S-24	X	X	X	X	X					RS-232C	X
Tri-Data OZ Guardian 2496	X	X	X	X	X					RS-232C	X
Ven-Tel 2400 Plus (2400-33)		X	X	X						RS-232C	X
Western Datacom 424 Class 5		X	X	X	X					RS-232C	X

*The type of connection port used for external modems, or the computer compatibility of internal modems.

†If the modem is Hayes-compatible, then it recognizes the standard Hayes set of AT modem commands and will work with Hayes-compatible software.

TABLE 9-5 External Modems—9,600 bps

Manufacturer/Model	MNP Compatibility Level									Computer Interface*	Hayes-Compatible†
	1	2	3	4	5	6	7	8	9		
Ark ARK DL 424-A10 S.A.	X	X		X	X	X				RS-232C	X
Data Race Action 32 (24-1003)						X				RS-232C	X
E-Tech Bullet E9696M	X	X		X	X	X				RS-232C	X
Memotec Dial Access 296		X		X	X	X				RS-232C	
Microcom QX/3296c	X	X		X	X	X				RS-232C	X
Telcor Systems 2938MA	X	X		X	X	X	X			RS-232C	X
Western Datacom 432 Line Backer		X		X	X	X				RS-232C	X

*The type of connection port used for external modems, or the computer compatibility of internal modems.

†If the modem is Hayes-compatible, then it recognizes the standard Hayes set of AT modem commands and will work with Hayes-compatible software.

TABLE 9-6 External Modems—15,000 and 19,200 bps

Manufacturer/Model	MNP Compatibility Level									Computer Interface*	Hayes-Compatible†
	1	2	3	4	5	6	7	8	9		
Microcom QX 15,000 bps	X	X		X	X	X		X	X	RS-232C	X
Telebit TrailBlazer Plus 19,200 bps					X	X				RS-232C	X

*The type of connection port used for external modems, or the computer compatibility of internal modems.

†If the modem is Hayes-compatible, then it recognizes the standard Hayes set of AT modem commands and will work with Hayes-compatible software.

TABLE 9-7 Internal Modems—2,400 bps

	MNP Compatibility Level										
Manufacturer/Model	1	2	3	4	5	6	7	8	9	Computer Interface*	Hayes-Compatible†
ATI Tech.	X	X		X	X	X				IBM PC	X
Cardinal 2450MNP	X	X		X	X	X				IBM PC	X
Data Race PC-Race 24					X	X				IBM PC	X
E-Tech Bullet PC2400M	X	X		X	X	X				IBM PC	X
Goldstar GSM 2400 PC						X				IBM PC	X
Incomm Turbo PS 24M	X	X		X	X					Micro Channel	X
MultiTech MultiModem224EC				X	X	X				IBM PC	X
Novation 2400					X	X				IBM PC	X

*The type of connection port used for external modems, or the computer compatibility of internal modems.

†If the modem is Hayes-compatible, then it recognizes the standard Hayes set of AT modem commands and will work with Hayes-compatible software.

investing, travel booking, and thousands of bulletin-board systems for freeware and potential contacts.

With a modem *and* a communications package, you can:

1. Exchange data and software with remote PCs.
2. Link office buildings with high-speed modems.
3. Use special-interest bulletin boards and on-line services (Fig 9-7).
4. Send faxes via on-line services.
5. Research companies, patents, and other data.
6. Use a script language to perform news and information searches.
7. Obtain freeware and shareware directly to your system.
8. Exchange electronic mail with others.
9. Use your PC in remote-host mode, so you can exchange information.
10. Play interactive on-line games with others at remote locations.

Although you will generally not be aware of the modem itself, you will be closely tied to your communications software, so you should have one that fits your needs.

Windows and Communications

A number of packages attempt to provide an edge by using Windows. The visual approach has some advantages over basic character-based programs. The Windows packages make it easier to cut and paste text to and from on-line sessions. They also let you work on another program while

Figure 9-7 A typical on-line service

you are transferring files. Some provide Dynamic Data Exchange (DDE) links to other Windows applications for automating communications—you could pass on-line news stories to your word processor.

Some packages use icons that you click on to select different services like CompuServe. Generally, you set up the icons for the services and options that you need. You might find the icon-based interfaces of some programs like DynaComm and MicroPhone easier to set up than others, and some may prefer a simpler window program like Crosstalk for Windows.

There are also newer, easier-to-use versions of some of the older character-based programs. Heavy users of modem communications may find Crosstalk Mk.4 suitable. A scaled-down version, Crosstalk Communicator, is suitable for beginners. HyperAccess/5 and Procomm Plus fall in between the two Crosstalk programs in capability and ease of use.

In addition to ease of use, the following features are important:

1. Error-checking, which allows you to move files at high speed without losing data.
2. Messaging features such as a dialing directory.
3. Multitasking features like background transfers which are useful if you send large files.
4. Script languages, which you can use for creating unattended applications.
5. Terminal emulations for logging on to minicomputers and mainframes.
6. Remote operations, which let you dial in to an unattended PC and swap files.

Buying Communications Software

When selecting a communications package, you will want a package that is easy to use. You also want a package with good messaging and file-transfer support (Table 9-8). Other items that may be important to you are multitasking, session automation, remote options, and the specific emulations offered.

A good package offers a friendly, intuitive, customizable user interface. This means well-designed menus, dialing directories, hot keys, and mouse support. The package should have preset scripts that you can easily modify for the most common services. The installation should be simple, and the documentation should be clear and well organized. Technical support from the vendor can also be an important variable.

TABLE 9-8 Modem Communications Packages

Package	RAM	Mouse or Windows Support	Messaging	File Transfer Protocols*
Crosstalk Mk.4	320K		I,C,O,H,S	K,X,Y,CO,Z,P
Crosstalk Communicator	320K		I,O	K,X,Y,CO,Z
Crosstalk for Windows	320K	W,M	C,O	K,X,CO,Z,P
DynaComm	150K	W,M	C,O,H	K,X,CO,Z,P
HyperAccess/5	350K		I,C,O,H,Q	K,X,Y,CO,Z,P,D
MicroPhone II	256K	W,M	I,C,O,H,S,Q	X,Y
Procomm Plus	192K	M	I,C,O,H,S,Q	K,X,Y,CO,Z
Qmodem SST	320K		I,C,O,H,S,Q	X,Y,Z
Smartcom III	512K		C,O	K,X,Y,D
Smartcom Exec	512K	M	C,O	K,X,Y,Z
Telemate 7	500K	M	I,C,O,H,S,Q	K,X,Y,CO,Z,P
Unicom	120K	W,M	I,H,S,Q	K,X,Y,CO,Z

*Key:

C = Cut and paste from buffer
CO = CompuServe B
H = Hot key to external word processor
I = Interactive dialing directory
K = Kermit
M = Mouse support
O = On-line text editor
R = RAM required
S = Split-screen chat mode
Q = Queue dialing
W = Windows application
X = XMODEM/XMODEM CRC
Y = YMODEM-G
Z = ZMODEM

If the package has a well-designed dialing directory, then you can easily view and modify entries. If you want to use bulletin boards and other multinumbered services, you can use a queue dialer to dial the next number if the first is busy. An autocapture buffer makes it easy to scroll through text and to cut and paste text.

Other useful features include print and capture commands and an on-screen timer. There should be a reasonable amount of status feedback during file transfers along with a well-functioning editor or, at least, the ability to export or import files to your word processor easily. When you swap files with other PCs or services, an error-checking protocol can check every byte that is sent with those that are received. Most packages offer XMODEM, but if you use a faster protocol, such as YMODEM or ZMODEM, you can save connection time and costs.

If you need to swap large files often, you may want to run other applications while a file transfers in the background. Under these conditions, system performance should not be hampered, and there should be enough RAM left to run today's more powerful applications. Some programs will let you run several sessions at once using multiple modems or a multitasking X.25 network. This will allow you to get price quotes from two services at the same time.

You will need enough power and flexibility in the script language as well as other tools for automating the communication procedures.

1. Keystroke macros allow you to send text strings or launch scripts.
2. A learn mode will allow you to record log-on procedures and then run them as scripts.
3. A script editor will let you select commands from a menu.
4. A debugger or trace facility will help you troubleshoot a script.
5. DDE allows you to automate file transfers among Windows programs.

Most packages have some remote capabilities and offer a remote-host function so callers can call in and swap files while the PC is unattended. The remote modes should have password protection to screen out unauthorized users. You should be able to define access by directory as well as drive.

The more common emulations are TTY, VT-100/102/52, ANSI (IBM PC), and IBM 3101. These will allow you to log on to most of the popular service or bulletin boards. If you are going to communicate with a variety of larger computers, you will need more of the less common emulations.

Examples of Communications Programs

Crosstalk Mk.4. This PC communications program can be used for both simple applications like accessing a bulletin board and more complex applications such as a multisession terminal emulation or a PC-to-host file transfer. Crosstalk Mk.4 has on-line, context-sensitive help. You can select from three interfaces, twenty-one terminal emulations, and eleven file-transfer protocols. Crosstalk Mk.4 works with most intelligent modems, and you can access most of the leading network asynchronous communications servers (ACSs). An application script language lets you automate repetitive tasks and customize your menus.

The original Crosstalk version had an interface that was difficult to use. Version 2.0 used an improved interface similar to Procomm's dialing directory. Crosstalk Mk.4 has a user-customized dialing directory (Fig 9-8). A set of Alt-key combinations brings up utilities and scripts. You can modify the directory to display other items, such as the phone number and the last time a number was called. Logging on is simple—you just point to an entry and press Enter. Setup is done with Alt-S. You can use other Alt-key combinations for file transfers and changing parameters. In addition to

Name	Description	Speed Modules
ANSWER	Answer a call (unconfigured)	2400 MODEM, ANSI
AT&T	AT&T Mail	2400 MODEM, CONTROL, DEC
CSERVE	CompuServe (Direct)	2400 MODEM, CONTROL, DEC.CS
DIRECT	Direct (hardwired) connection	2400 MODEM, ANSI
EASYCALL	Use this to make a call	2400 MODEM, ANSI
LEXIS	LEXIS/NEXIS through Telenet	2400 MODEM, CONTROL, DEC
++MCIMAIL	MCI MAIL direct++++++++++++++++++++++	2400 MODEM, CONTROL, DEC+++
NEWSNET	Newsnet through Telenet	2400 MODEM, CONTROL, DEC
NORMAL	Crosstalk Mk.4 Normal Setup	2400 MODEM, ANSI

++Enter++	++Ins++	++Alt-S++	++Del++
call MCIMAIL	create new entry	setup MCIMAIL	delete MCIMAIL
++Alt-M++	++Alt-E++	++Alt-Y++	++Alt-Q++
utility scripts	edit text file	preferences	go to DOS

Figure 9-8 Crosstalk type of dialing directory

the dialing directory, you can use the old pop-up menu, the Crosstalk XVI interface, or a command line. Mk.4 can handle all major file-transfer protocols, including the IND$FILE protocol used on IBM mainframes.

Mk.4's script language, CASL, has over 400 commands to handle everything from windowing to complex math. It offers unlimited variables, a debugger, and seven data types. You can assign commands and scripts to function keys and create customized utilities. You can also work on other applications while you are transferring files. This can require about 320K, but, if you drop some of the unneeded features, you can reduce the requirement to about 90K. The package lets you run up to fifteen simultaneous sessions with either multiple modems or Tymnet's X.PC.

Crosstalk Communicator. This is a simplified version of Crosstalk Mk.4 designed for beginners. It does not allow background transfers and has fewer transfer protocols and only a few emulations. It does not have a synchronous mode or allow multiple sessions. The on-line menu is bigger with more preset scripts for logging on to on-line services. There is also password protection and the same CASL script language used in Mk.4.

The dialing directory is similar to Mk.4, and there are just as many parameters to select. The main differences are the protocols and emulations. There are no Crosstalk and IND$FILE protocols and only six emulations.

Crosstalk for Windows. This Windows package has Crosstalk's CASL language, but it does not take full advantage of Windows. You select options from pull-down menus, but there are no icons. You customize twelve buttons that you can use to launch scripts. The installation is simple, and there is an on-line tutorial. It is easy to set up, but there is no dialing directory. You open a file menu, and then select a phone-book entry and click it to dial. The entries are short and without comments.

There are six commands to control DDE links to other Windows applications. File transfers can run in the background, and you can cut and paste with the built-in notepad.

DynaComm. This Windows package has a script language that supports DDE and Windows screen objects. You have tiled and stacked windows with icons for on-line services. However, DynaComm has limited protocols.

The main program has nineteen utilities and scripts. There is a learn mode along with a tutorial and a few games. You cannot launch on-line service from icons or add icons for your own scripts. Dialing a number is a little slower than Crosstalk for Windows:

1. You click on an icon to get to the main screen.
2. Move to the file menu.
3. Pick an option to open a file.
4. Go to the settings file.
5. Move to the phone menu and click on dial.

The package has scripts for seven on-line services that use icons. The icons take you part way, and then you must go back to typing commands. Some icons can be a little confusing.

There is a small editor for cutting and pasting. File transfers with large files of over 300K can cause lockup problems, and you have to break the file into smaller chunks.

The script language is comparable to Crosstalk for Windows, but it is more suitable for Windows applications because you can script icons and dialog boxes more easily. There are thirteen emulations.

HyperAccess/5. This is an easy-to-use package with more features than expected in beginners' software. It uses good script language, and there is a fairly complete list of emulations and protocols. It also provides data compression and virus detection.

A first-letter type of menu is used on the top of the opening screen, and a dialing directory is on the lower part (Fig 9-9). You can select a number and dial the modem with three keystrokes. There is also a menu of speed keys on the bottom of the screen.

It is easy to cut and paste with this package. You can use the built-in editor or your own word processor. There is also an easy-to-use learn mode, but there is a lack of prewritten scripts for on-line services. The virus scanner looks for the signatures of sixty-eight viruses, but it will not work on compressed files. There are emulations for IBM, Wang, and DEC terminals. The script language is comparable to Procomm's, but it is easier to use.

MicroPhone II. This Macintosh program has been converted to Windows with much of the same interface (many icons with simple menus). There is no support for DDE. The opening screen has icons for CompuServe, BI, Dow Jones, GEnie, and MCI Mail. After you set them up, you click on an icon to launch a script that logs you on. The scripts are not ready-made—you have to go through several menus to set them up. There are on-line text buttons that provide a custom, mousable interface. There is no on-line status. Cutting and pasting are easy, but there is no built-in editor.

MicroPhone II provides three protocols: XMODEM, YMODEM, and YMODEM-G. There are four terminal emulations: VT-100, VT-52, ANSI, and TTY. There is no support for scrollable lists and only a few tools for creating dialog boxes. The learn mode does not record pauses, so you need to enter them manually. The built-in script editor lets you put scripts together from menus. If you attempt to use a menu during a session, you may get a message like

```
MODEM NOT RESPONDING
```

which occurs if you open a menu while the modem is hanging up.

Mirror III. This program allows background transfers and has many terminal emulations. However, some users have found problems with the interface, and there have been some bugs during screen changes.

The dialing directory is similar to Procomm, but a status screen similar to Crosstalk XVI is used to change global parameters and launch scripts. The program slows down and seems to stall when you log off.

In order to use the ZMODEM protocol, you install it from a separate shareware disk. The background mode takes 470K to run, but you can reduce it to 185K if you drop features like the dialing directory.

Mirror III's script language is comparable to Procomm Plus. Remote

```
System settings

Select:  Xmodem   Ymodem   Zmodem   Kermit   HyperProtocol

Name of system              :   MCI Mail (2400 bps)
Telephone number            : 9,543-1560
Rate (50-115200 bps or baud)        : 2400
Duplex (Full, Half)                 : Full
Bits per character (5-8)            : 7
Parity (None, Odd, Even, Mark, Space : Even
Stop bits (1,2)                     : 1
Emulation                           : TTY
Logon script                        : MCI
 ASCII protocols           --Set test sending/receiving details
File transfer protocols    --Set file transfer protocol details
Hardware                   --Set port, modem and printing details
Colors                     --Set display colors
Miscellaneous              --Set other details.
```

Figure 9-9 Setting up a dialing entry on HyperAccess/5

callers are treated with menus and authorized users can use a DOS shell, but you cannot restrict callers to specified directories.

Procomm Plus. This is an upgrade of the popular Procomm shareware program. Version 2.0 has the ZMODEM protocol and mouse support. It also has a better editor and script language than its predecessor. There are a total of thirty-two terminal emulations. There have been some problems with some of the DEC emulations, and the documentation is still more like a shareware program.

Procomm Plus is one of the easiest programs to use, with its intuitive dialing directory that includes the date of last call. There is also a pop-up notepad. Alt-key combinations let you go through the setup parameters quickly, and function keys call scripts and external programs. There are prewritten scripts for CompuServe and Dow Jones. You can use a mouse to dial numbers and pick choices from menus.

The program requires 295K with all of the features. You can reduce this to 192K if you drop some features such as the editor and the DOS gateway. You can cut and paste file names between Procomm and a remote system, and you can mark on-line text and move it to an editor with word wrap and split-screen displays. The new emulations include DEC VT-220 and VT-320 and IBM 3161.

You can use the enhanced script language to add other emulations. There are more than ninety new commands, including some commands for file and string manipulation and others for support of floating variables and arithmetic operators.

Qmodem SST. This shareware package is similar to Procomm Plus. The program has a good dialing directory and editor, and the setup sequence automatically tests and optimizes many brands of high-speed modems. The documentation is weak, but the on-line help is good. There are no prewritten scripts or background mode.

The interactive dialing directory has queue dialing for polling busy numbers, and the pop-up notecards are handy. The editor works like WordStar making cut-and-paste operations easy. Missing are Kermit and CompuServe B protocols, and there is no support for IBM 3101.

The script language has sixty-eight commands and is similar to Procomm. There is true windowing and a debugger, and you can execute DOS commands from scripts. Qmodem is useful if you want to set up a simple, easy-to-maintain bulletin board.

Smartcom III. This program is included with some V-Series Hayes modems. It is less powerful than Crosstalk Mk.4, and the Hayes Smartcom Exec is easier to use. Smartcom III does not use a true dialing directory. The communications settings are divided into two groups: the activity settings deal with phone numbers, emulations, and file transfers; the connection settings deal with parameters like modem speeds and port numbers. The documentation is weak, and it can be difficult to tie a log-in script to a phone number.

There is a complete menu of options, and the file manager is good. There are no hot keys, so the keyboard is busy at times. You cannot change parameters or protocols while on-line.

The script language is similar to Procomm's. You can use the script editor to parse together commands from menus. A remote mode provides passwords, but callers cannot access DOS. The emulations are limited, and there is no ZMODEM protocol.

Smartcom Exec. This is a smaller version of Smartcom III designed for beginners and replaces Smartcom II. It is easier to use than Smartcom III and does not allow multiple sessions, data compression, and encryption. The background and remote modes as well as the emulations are the same as Smartcom III. The script language is also similar. The main differences are the easy-to-use mouse interface, better documentation, and the ZMODEM protocol. The Interrupted ZMODEM protocol is useful in that it allows the modem to continue a file transfer after a line noise interruption. Smartcom Exec does not use a true dialing directory and is limited in emulations, but it is a good starter program.

The interface is similar to Smartcom III, but it is more streamlined and intuitive. You can set up only one protocol per on-line system. There are no prewritten scripts, but you can get some through a Hayes bulletin board system (BBS).

Telemate. This shareware program has a character-based windowing interface and a pop-up clipboard for cutting and pasting. The emulations are limited, and there is no remote mode.

It does have an easy-to-use interface since you access all functions, including the dialing directory, with pull-down menus. The editor is very functional, and the file viewer and the other modules work well in this windowing environment. You can zoom in, move, and resize the windows as you move data between them. You can also work in these windows during file transfers, but you cannot work with other programs since there is no background mode.

The script language is well structured and is similar to Pascal. The documentation is good, but there is no capability for a trace or debug. You can use a number of data types with unlimited string and integer variables. The program takes about 500K of RAM, but you can reduce this by dropping some features.

Unicon. This is a shareware Windows program with the Procomm type of dialing directory. It is easy to use with its pull-down menus, and you can use Windows utilities such as the Calculator, Calendar, and Notepad. You can use the buttons on the bottom of the screen for operations like dialing and loading. You can customize some buttons to launch scripts or other programs. There is no DDE support. The number of protocols supported is as adequate as any other program, but Unicon supports only three emulations: TTY, ANSI, and VT-100.

The script language is limited mostly to logging in. You can record keystrokes to build macros, but there is no true learn mode. You can set scripts to launch using buttons. The overall design is friendly and straightforward.

10

UPGRADING YOUR SYSTEM WITH SOFTWARE

There are a number of ways you can upgrade your system with software. In this chapter, we will cover operating systems, Windows, and other programs for use with Windows.

MS-DOS 5.0 UPGRADE

An easy way to give your personal computer new life is to add the MS-DOS 5.0 upgrade for the operating system (Fig 10-1). It gives your applications more memory to use. On PCs with 80286 processors and higher, most of the MS-DOS 5.0 Upgrade loads into extended memory, freeing at least 45K of conventional memory for DOS applications. You can stop crowding your computer's memory and make more room for applications, eliminating the need to decide between operating-system functions and applications with large memory requirements. MS-DOS 5.0 moves most of the operating system to high memory above 640K in 1MB 80286 systems and beyond.

In 386-series PCs, you can also load device drivers, terminate-and-stay-resident (TSR) programs, and network software into upper memory, freeing additional memory for large applications and files. The memory management features for DOS applications make MS-DOS 5.0 useful for computers running Microsoft Windows.

The MS-DOS 5.0 upgrade makes PCs, including 8088 computers, easier to use and allows them to be more productive. It has an easy-to-use

Figure 10-1 The MS-DOS 5 Upgrade

graphical shell, with on-line help that makes file management very intuitive. Task swapping lets you run multiple applications at the same time. A full-screen text editor lets you view what you are editing as you edit it. There are also undelete and unformat commands that make it possible to undo MS-DOS errors right from the operating system.

When you relocate device drivers and other programs above 640K, you will have more space for applications and will be able to manipulate programs and data faster and more easily. This is especially true when you are using the improved shell of MS-DOS 5.0. The mouse-driven menus and an on-line help program allow even novice users to run applications and perform operations such as unformatting an inadvertently formatted hard disk.

MS-DOS 5.0 makes it easier to locate and sort files with an enhanced DIR directory command. You can also change all file attributes with an enhanced ATTRIB command. If you want to write small programs, there is a built-in full-screen text editor and a QBasic Interpreter.

MS-DOS 5.0 is easy to install and works on most desktop systems equipped with previous DOS versions. IBM also has a full upgrade package for prior users of PCDOS that can automatically upgrade your prior PCDOS to MS-DOS 5.0 and allow you to save your old operating system. The IBM package contains all the features and functions of IBM DOS 5.0 at a reduced upgrade price.

DOS 5.0 Memory Management

You need more conventional memory to run programs like Microsoft Windows. MS-DOS 5.0 has two features to help in this area. You can load 45K of the DOS kernel (the core of the operating system) into an area of memory known as the high memory area (HMA). The HMA is the first

64K of extended memory located just above the 1MB memory boundary. If you have at least a 286-based PC and at least 64K of extended memory, you can take advantage of this feature. MS-DOS 5.0 needs only about 60K of RAM; therefore, when you load 45K of RAM into HMA, you will have only 18K left in conventional memory. This makes MS-DOS 5.0 a smaller program than past versions; MS-DOS 3.3 needed 66K and MS-DOS 4.0 took between 76K and 82K.

You also have access to the area of memory between 640K and 1MB. In prior MS-DOS versions, this area of memory has been reserved for add-in adapters like video and disk controllers, leaving some blocks of this upper memory unused. MS-DOS 5.0 frees these unused blocks for device drivers and TSRs.

When you use extended memory, you need a memory manager to keep track of what programs are using the different parts of extended memory. A memory manager can also permit extended memory to emulate expanded memory. An extended memory manager like EMM386 can provide access to the upper memory block, but you must have a 386-based PC or higher to use this feature. If you purchase another memory management program such as the Quarterdeck QEMM or Qualitas 386/Max to handle the upper memory area, MS-DOS 5.0 will not interfere. When you install MS-DOS 5.0, it does not automatically install EMM386. You need to modify your CONFIG.SYS to use EMM386.

Since MS-DOS 5.0 frees conventional memory, it is the best version of DOS to run with Windows. There can be some problems getting Windows to run smoothly with older DOS versions if you need a lot of TSRs and drivers. With MS-DOS 5.0, Windows will run better since you can place the TSRs and drivers into the HMA, making more memory available for applications.

Installation

MS-DOS 5.0 is easy to install and is designed to upgrade machines that currently have MS-DOS. When you install MS-DOS 5.0, the program looks for an older version of MS-DOS. It will not install unless it finds MS-DOS 4.0, 3.3, or any of the earlier versions. Unlike upgrading in the past, this version does not require you to clear your system by removing all programs and files, loading the new DOS, and then reloading all your data again. MS-DOS 5.0 lets you install over all your existing programs.

You insert a disk into the A drive and type

```
A:Install
```

The program will take you through a step-by-step installation procedure.

You can also create an Uninstall disk in case you decide to go back to your old DOS version.

Network users can also install MS-DOS 5.0 with relative ease compared to earlier versions. After MS-DOS 5.0 is installed on the server, the individual users type `Setup` and complete the installation procedure just as a nonnetworked user does.

MS-DOS 5.0 and Windows

MS-DOS 5.0 can also provide a smoother transition if you are not yet ready for Windows. There are new features like the DOS shell, which is a good Windows introduction. The shell provides more of a graphical user interface (GUI) than the previous DOS Shell found in MS-DOS 4.0.

Pull-down menus contain commands for many of the file-management and disk-maintenance tasks that were previously performed from the DOS command line. You can create directories, copy files, and view files either by using a mouse to point and click on commands listed in the file menu or by using an Alt-key combination with a set of disk utilities that lets you format and copy disks from the shell.

The shell allows you to use a task swapper so you can move between two DOS applications without having to exit one program first. You cannot cut and paste between two applications, but you have the convenience of having two applications open at once. The shell eliminates the DOS command line and provides the "point-and-click" feel of a graphical-based system.

There is also a full-screen editor that replaces the old Edlin utility. With Edlin, creating and using batch files involved learning the Edlin editing commands. MS-DOS 5.O's text editor is like having a word processor for DOS files. It uses pull-down menus and mouse support.

Other new utilities are undelete and unformat. If you accidentally delete a file or format a hard or floppy disk, these commands provide some safety, but you must use them as soon as possible after the error occurs.

The documentation that comes with MS-DOS 5.0 includes examples of the new features which can help users at all skill levels. There is also an on-line help program.

MS-DOS 5.0 Options and Compatibility

Some users should probably not upgrade to MS-DOS 5.0. If you already have a memory manager and are not interested in on-line help, MS-DOS 5.0 may not be the best choice for you. Also, the older versions like MS-DOS 3.3 support hard drive partitions of 32MB. Later versions of

MS-DOS, such as 4.0 and now 5.0, support larger hard drive partitions. If you use software that supports partitions of 32MB, upgrading and enlarging these partitions may make your software incompatible. This could force you to upgrade your software, and you may not be ready to. Most current software is compatible with MS-DOS 5.0.

There is a way out for compatibility problems. If you run an older software package with MS-DOS 5.0, the program usually looks for a specific DOS version number before executing. Every time you load MS-DOS 5.0, a device driver that is included in the CONFIG.SYS file called "SETVER.EXE" places into memory a table listing software programs and the number of the MS-DOS version each program looks for. You can modify the version table if a particular program is not included to prevent any compatibility problems.

DR-DOS

DR-DOS is a major improvement over older MS-DOS versions. It provides new levels of performance and integration beyond that of DOS versions prior to DOS 5.0. DR-DOS is a product of Digital Research, the creators of the CP/M operating system. It uses a menu-driven install program to ease the task of changing operating systems. Menus also help you customize the memory manager and other features. The install program gives you the option of replacing all existing MS-DOS utility files or creating a new directory for DR-DOS's use.

Memory Management

DR-DOS 5.0 provides memory relocation for 386 and 486 processors, such as QEMM and 386-to-the-Max; but it also provides these features to owners of ATs. HIDOS.SYS is a DR-DOS device driver that moves the DR-DOS kernel (or core of the system) out of the base 640K and into extended memory. To run HIDOS.SYS, an AT-compatible needs 64K or more of extended memory. DOS relocation with HIDOS.SYS gives users of even the oldest AT-compatibles about 40K more base RAM. Newer ATs with a Chips and Technologies NeAt chipset can also use HIDOS.SYS to relocate device drivers, TSRs, and network drivers into unused sections of the reserved memory between 640K and 1MB. HIDOS.SYS allows manual or automatic selection of memory areas for relocation, and you can have up to 704K of RAM with Hercules, MDA, or CGA video cards for nongraphics software.

EMM386.SYS is the DR-DOS device driver that provides 386/486 memory-mapping features similar to those found in QEMM or 386-to-the-

Max. It allows manual or auto mapping of upper memory for use as EMS 4.0 memory, ROM shadowing, and relocation of the DR-DOS kernel. It can be used with Paradox 386, Lotus 1-2-3 Version 3.X, and other DOS programs that use extended memory.

Microsoft Windows 3.0 is not compatible with DR-DOS's EMS driver. You can use DR-DOS's extensions to CONFIG.SYS, so you can choose either the DR-DOS or Windows version of an EMS driver when starting up.

MEM.EXE is like the command found in MS-DOS 4. It displays statistics on the first megabyte of memory, including ROM locations in the reserved 640K-to-1MB range. It has several options, including a display of the first megabyte of memory (Fig 10-2). More detailed displays can provide the locations of DOS and any device drivers.

The *DR-DOS User Guide* and *Field Notes* are better than most user guides. You can also use the help function to look up commands and syntax. You activate the help function by adding a /H to the command. In most cases, the commands are easier to understand and more flexible than their MS-DOS equivalent.

The CONFIG.SYS File

DR-DOS has some enhancements like branching options in the CONFIG.SYS file where device drivers can customize your system. Using DR-DOS, you can label parts of the CONFIG.SYS file with labels like those found in .BAT files. A new command "?" allows you to select the options. DR-DOS also has an Echo command similar to that found in .BAT files to provide you with additional information.

Other additions to CONFIG.SYS include History, which allows you to recall past DOS commands, and Cache, a disk cache program for either extended or expanded memory.

Edlin, the original line editor of MS-DOS, has been replaced in DR-DOS by a full-screen Editor. This program is like WordStar in its control-key command structure. Help screens include a context-sensitive quick reference to get you up to speed with WordStar. You can use Editor to change AUTOEXEC.BAT, other .BAT files, CONFIG.SYS, and other files. Block moves, saves, and deletions are simplified with Editor.

File Management

Digital Research's GEM operating environment was never very popular except with users of a few programs like Ventura Publisher. The GEM environment is a Macintosh-type user interface. Some of the file-manage-

```
---------------------------------- Conventional memory ----------------------------------
0h       10000h    20000h     30000h      40000h      50000h      60000h      70000
0K       64K        128K      192K        256K         320K       384K        448K



512K    576K     640K       704K      768K        832K     896K         960K    1MB

80000h 90000h   A0000h    B0000h    C0000h     D0000h  E0000h      F0000h 100000h
------------------------------------------------- Upper memory --------------------------

655,360 bytes (640K)--conventional memory

533,440 bytes (520K)--largest available block

4,194,304 bytes (4,096K)--extended memory

4,194,304 bytes (4,096K)--extended memory used

         0 bytes (0K)--extended memory available
```

Figure 10-2 DR-DOS memory-map screen

ment features of GEM are used in Viewmax, which is the visual file manager included in some versions of DR-DOS 5 (Fig 10-3). Some OEM versions of DR-DOS do not use it. Install lets the user invoke Viewmax automatically at boot time. The use of icons and menus make Viewmax easy to learn. As a file and directory manager, it is faster than Windows 3.0's File Manager. You can mark multiple files for moving or deletion with Viewmax, and it works fast with either mouse or keyboard. Viewmax also allows you to launch applications and to set start-up options.

DR-DOS 5 has no compatibility problems with most programs like Novell NetWare and Btrieve. There have been some problems with LANtastic and Norton's Safe Format, Version 5. Unless you use one of the few incompatible programs, the increased performance of DR-DOS makes it a good upgrade.

MS-DOS 5.0 also provides memory management and other useful utilities. While details of the two DOS products differ, users with a 286 CPU or better who do not switch to either DR-DOS 5 or MS-DOS 5.0 are missing a relatively easy way to give their systems more performance.

WINDOWS

There are a number of different computer-related activities in most applications. The trend is to integrate the capabilities of today's products for

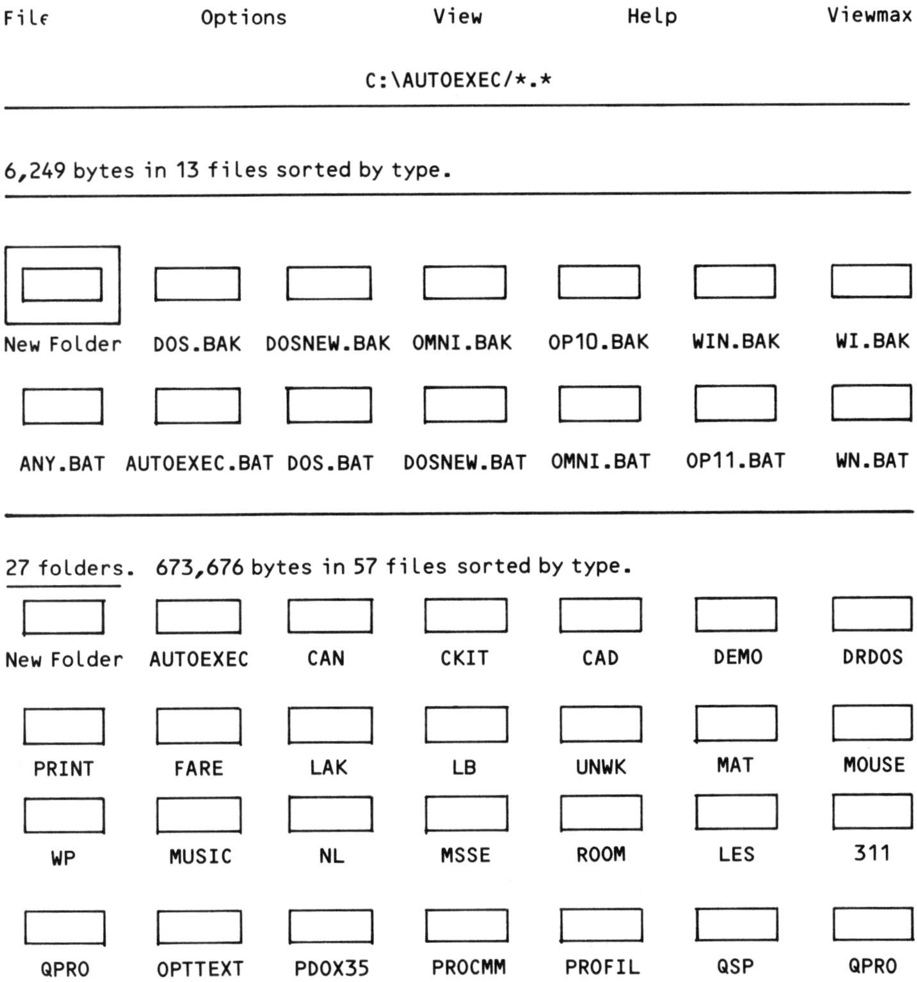

Figure 10-3 DR-DOS Viewmax display

specific software applications. Before this becomes a reality, the problems of moving, editing, manipulating, and combining text, data, graphics, and scanned images must be addressed.

The ease of file movement depends largely on the disk operating system and the file export/import capabilities of the applications software. Most programs that deal with text and graphics employ user interfaces that are friendlier than the raw disk operating system that runs the application. Conventional DOS commands tend to be difficult to remember and are often inconvenient and awkward to use during an application session. You can use a layer of interfacing software to remove many of these problems.

This is the idea behind products like Microsoft Windows (Fig 10-4). Windows is an extension of DOS that allows easier access to DOS commands with simple English-like commands. It also allows simultaneous operation of more than one software application. However, its *major* characteristic is the use of graphical screen windows. Windows uses icons for representation. In this and in other ways, Windows is much like the Macintosh (Fig 10-5).

Windows includes system-supported desk accessories along with either mouse or keyboard activation. The windows can act like drop-down menus, and the program also uses a clipboard and control panel.

Windows acts like a system administrator since it can control the flow of text and graphical information from several sources. Some programs are specifically written to run with Windows, such as PageMaker PC which *requires* the Windows environment.

The use of Windows can provide you with a number of advantages. You will have an easy-to-use DOS shell, which enhances the general functionality of the application. Windows handles the interface between an application and various system resources, such as printers and port assignments. It also manages the system memory, allowing it to work with several applications. It automatically loads the application as it is needed, while keeping the other applications ready to load. Windows allows you to view the complete processing environment or use the whole screen for one application.

Windows is really designed to use a mouse, although you can use the keyboard to perform all functions. You can move the mouse quickly around the screen and make selections by clicking the mouse button.

When you start Windows, it shows an Executive window that lists the files on disk and uses icons to represent the attached disk drives. The common DOS functions, such as changing directories, formatting disks,

Figure 10-4 Microsoft Windows—an extension of DOS with simple English-like commands

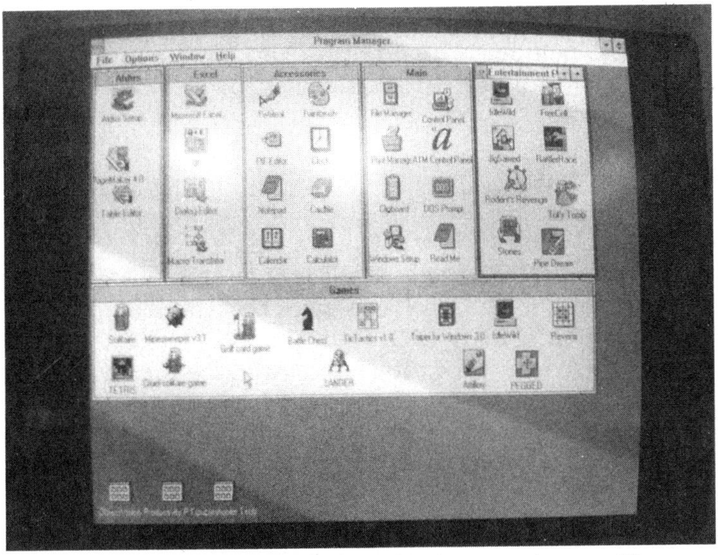

Figure 10-5 Main screen of Windows showing extensive use of icons

and renaming files, are accessible from drop-down menus in this window. You start applications by moving the mouse arrow to them and then clicking the mouse button.

A typical window can have many parts, but the use of icons makes these parts easy to comprehend. You can resize the window to cover any part of the screen. As you open additional windows, they are tiled (one on top of the other), so you always have a partial view of the earlier windows that were opened.

You can scroll horizontally and vertically through the contents of a window using scroll bars along the bottom and right sides. If you need to reposition a window, you move the mouse pointer to the middle of the title bar and click the mouse button. The pointer will change to an icon that you can drag to a new location.

A Zoom command allows windows to be enlarged to fill the whole screen and then reduced to their original size. You select the Zoom command from the System menu, which is a part of each window. You can also use the Icon command in the System menu to convert the window into an icon at the bottom of the screen.

You can use Windows to control the flow of information between software and hardware as well as for the installation, selection, and setup of printers. Windows has a built-in spooler which you can use to hold files going to the printer. It does this in the background without major interruptions.

Windows uses program information files (PIF) for setting up menus. A utility disk is included with PIFs for the most popular applications. Other applications can use default settings, or you can create a custom PIF.

The Clipboard

You can move information from window to window using a clipboard, which acts as a holding area for text or graphics that are cut from or copied from an application. You can check the contents of the clipboard by running CLIPBRD.EXE from the MS-DOS Executive window. You can place the contents of the clipboard in a window by selecting the insertion point with the mouse and then selecting Paste from the System menu.

OS/2

Many of today's applications have memory requirements that are not adequately met by the 640K limitation of MS-DOS. The more powerful personal computers have larger memories that can handle these software applications and also support multitasking.

When IBM introduced its PS/2 computer line with its more powerful hardware, a new operating system called OS/2 also became available. OS/2 can run on a native OS/2 mode, which can access up to 16MB of system memory on a 286 system or 64 terabytes on a 386 system. It can also run on an MS-DOS mode, which can access up to 640K. This allows you to run older software that has not been written for OS/2.

OS/2 is menu-driven and designed to be used with a mouse. The main menu allows you to choose between OS/2 or MS-DOS. You can also use it to install programs, add program titles, start programs, switch between different programs (multitasking), and update information about programs.

OS/2 is more user-friendly than the earlier versions of MS-DOS, and it has a built-in help system. Help is available for those items that are listed on displays and for some system messages.

You may find it easier to move to OS/2 2.0 since it runs Windows and you do not have to choose between the two. OS/2's memory protection keeps one runaway application from crashing the whole system. With MS-DOS and DOS-based Windows, if a program crashes, you could lose an entire system. In OS/2, a crash will take out the application, but everything else keeps running. OS/2 makes sense for transaction-processing operations that need quick turnaround and real-time, true multitasking with a minimum of crashing problems.

Installing Programs

Programs that have been installed in OS/2 can be started by pointing to a list. A program is added to the list using the OS/2 command prompt. The following screen example for adding a program illustrates the type of user interface in OS/2.

```
ADD A PROGRAM TITLE

TYPE THE INFORMATION BELOW.

PRESS THE ENTER KEY TO SAVE.

PROGRAM TITLE.............

PROGRAM PATHNAME..........
```

The program title can be up to thirty characters long. The pathname follows the DOS format, starting with the drive, then the directory, and then the filename.

You install DOS programs using the DOS command prompt. You will get the usual DOS drive prompt, and the program is installed using standard DOS procedures.

Running Programs

OS/2 programs run from the Start-a-Program list. While a program is running, the system adds its name to the Switch-to-a-Running-Program list. When you stop a program, you are returned to either OS/2 command prompt or the Program Selector, depending upon how the program was launched. You can switch between running programs at any time, either by returning to the Program Selector (Ctrl—Esc) and selecting another program, or by pressing Alt—Esc to display the next program on the Switch-to-a-Running Program list. DOS programs are started and switched using the instructions that came with them. They do not provide any new benefits under OS/2.

OS/2 Commands

Many OS/2 commands are similar to their DOS counterparts. For example, the OS/2 command to copy a file called Text from drive A to drive C is

```
COPY A:Text C:
```

just like DOS. There are also new commands, such as

```
REPLACE
```

which can be used to copy files from a source to a target. There are some refinements in the command structure, since you can now use AND OR logic statements for combining commands.

IBM's disagreements with Microsoft Corporation regarding OS/2 and Windows development have confused many as to future direction and support for the different versions of the operating system. First there was OS/2 Version 1.3, then IBM's 2.0, and then Microsoft's 3.0, or portable OS/2. Some users will do better with Windows, while MS-DOS 5.0, with more memory and graphical features, may be better for others. Under a 1990 agreement, IBM and Microsoft agreed to support five operating environments: DOS, Windows, 16-bit OS/2 1.0, 32-bit OS/2 2.0, and portable OS/2 3.0. OS/2 has the potential to offer a more robust, more sophisticated operating environment than MS-DOS or Windows. It could become the operating system of the 1990s.

OS/2 2.0 is better suited for mission-critical applications in client/server environments than Windows, which is DOS with a GUI front end. It does not have the capabilities of OS/2 in multitasking.

Presentation Manager

This is the graphics interface used in OS/2. It is based on Windows 2.0 and is a part of Windows 286 and Windows 386. Presentation Manager provides a graphical environment where multiple applications can be open at the same time. The GUI can be applied to all application programs. This means that the applications can be more compatible and that they should have a similar look and feel.

The system memory is more manageable than DOS, and the screen is managed with windows that can be moved, sized, and tiled for easy recall. A mouse quickly activates program selections and options. The mouse saves time compared to keying in commands. You can also use the mouse for creating graphics and moving graphic elements.

Both text and graphics are displayed in a closer approximation of the final printed copy. A number of drivers are available for upgraded peripherals such as large screens, special display adapters, printers, and input devices.

OS/2 2.0 is the full 32-bit version that needs more memory. OS/2 1.3

is a smaller, faster 16-bit version that can run on 286 and SX machines. It does not need the large amounts of memory used by other versions. OS/2 1.3 can run one DOS and two OS/2 applications with about 2MB of memory. There is improved performance for packages that were previously memory-limited. Improvements of up to 25% are possible. The hard disk requirement is only 10MB.

OS/2 1.3 includes Adobe Type Manager with the Presentation Manager user interface, yielding three scalable PostScript font families that look the same on the screen and printer. Most of OS/2's previous printing problems have been solved with a Print Manager that makes it easier to install and configure printers and allows OS/2 to use more devices.

OS/2 1.3 offers more advanced multitasking capabilities than Windows and requires about the same amount of memory.

OS/2 Extended

OS/2 Extended Edition (EE) has more multitasking capabilities than OS/2. There is no need to save one program before moving to another since you can open and use as many OS/2 windows as you need with Presentation Manager.

OS/2 EE 1.3 performs system functions faster than earlier OS/2 versions, especially in memory-constrained environments. When applications overextend the system memory, it results in more disk activity while data is swapped between disk and memory.

For most applications, OS/2 EE 1.3 can provide performance enhancements that are two to three times faster than OS/2 EE 1.2 when loading programs from LAN servers to LAN requesters. This faster access can provide higher productivity in server environments. Version 1.3 reduces the minimum RAM requirement from 3.5MB to 3MB.

OS/2 EE 1.3 includes Adobe Type Manager with the IBM core set of fonts. This provides high-quality typographic text in a wide range of sizes and styles for supported printers and displays. There are over 600 different Adobe typefaces available on OS/2 EE.

Using the OS/2 EE 1.3's Communications Manager, you can maintain multiple communications sessions while continuing to run other applications. The Communications Manager module has a number of communications and network management capabilities. It can act like IBM's Systems Network Architecture (SNA) LAN gateway and can handle host file transfers, 3270 and Asyc terminal emulation, and 5250 Workstations. A LAN Requester allows each workstation running the OS/2 EE to access LAN resources.

OS/2 EE 1.3 also provides support for relational databases. Using the

Database Manager, you can create, access, and edit relational databases based on the IBM Structured Query Language (SQL). The Database Manager supports Ethernet DIX V2.0 and IEEE 802.3-based networks as well as all 386-based PS/2 models.

USING WINDOWS APPLICATIONS

The Windows software package can transform the way you use your PC. Windows gives you the ability to run more than one application at a time and to transfer information between applications. It allows you to use more of your PC's power. The graphical interface provides more of an intuitive environment for the PC, and the graphical environment allows you to streamline operations on your PC. Windows gives you more control over the way your software works, allowing you to operate with more power and not be hampered by previous restrictions. Windows 3.0 expands the use of memory in the PC. It goes beyond the older DOS limitation of 640K and addresses extended memory.

Simple icon-based commands replace the usual DOS commands. You can work more quickly and move around using several programs at once. You use a clipboard to cut, copy, and paste between applications. You can also set up automatic links with a DDE feature. The File Manager, speeds up file and directory management tasks, such as creating directories and copying, moving, or searching for files.

Windows makes it is easier to start up and work with software applications. Since you can run more than one application at a time, it is easier to transfer information between them or organize and manage files. For example, you can switch from a database application to a spreadsheet and then to your word processor with a few moves of your mouse without taking the time to quit one application and restart another.

When you work with two or more applications, even if they are not designed specifically for Windows, you can transfer information from one to the other. This type of information sharing allows you to combine the work done in several different application programs into a single, unified document. As you are working with an application, you can pause at any time to take care of other tasks.

Windows comes with a number of accessory programs to help with task management. These accessories include a clock, an appointment calendar, a calculator, a notepad, a card file and a macro recorder. Windows includes the following applications: Write, Paintbrush, Terminal, Program Manager, File Manager, and Task List. There are also two computer games designed to give you some practice working with Windows.

NewWave. Hewlett-Packard designed NewWave for Windows to make DOS and Microsoft Windows applications easier to use. This can improve productivity since it provides an environment where you can control all your DOS and Windows programs as well as files into icons. You click on an icon, and both the file and its program open simultaneously. With NewWave, you do not have to jump between the Windows Program Manager and File Manager. There is no need to type DOS commands or use subdirectories to find files.

The NewWave Agent utility is an automatic macro maker and helps you save time on repetitive tasks. You complete a task once while the NewWave Agent records your activity. You can then have this activity repeated when you need it. NewWave also makes it easier to share information on a network. You just drag your document with the network server icon and the network users can access your files.

Windows Applications

These programs are specifically designed to take advantage of Windows' features and to work with other Windows applications. All Windows applications require Windows in order to run.

ABC Flowcharter. This program by Roykore allows you to create flowcharts. You can point and click to draw shapes, and, as you begin typing, the text will automatically fill each shape. If you rearrange shapes, the lines will automatically reroute. You can enhance the chart with different colors, patterns, border styles, and fonts. Links can be made to subcharts, or notes can be attached for additional detail.

ACCPAC Simply Accounting. This package includes a primer of basic accounting principles and a tutorial with sample data and sample charts of accounts for different applications. The menu structure is easy to learn and consistent. There is automatic transaction posting instead of more time-consuming month- and year-end closing routines. It also has pop-up customer, vendor, employee, job, account, and inventory lists for quick reference during transaction entry; and there is full integration among functions.

The integrated package includes General Ledger, Accounts Receivable, Accounts Payable, Payroll, Inventory Control, and Project Costing. You can use it to keep your books; track income and expenses; and print checks, W2s, and financial statements. To enter data, you fill out the forms that appear on screen; this includes checks and invoices that look realistic.

Adobe Illustrator. This product is designed for single-page design and layouts. Version 3.0 is easy to learn and use and has several new tools and enhanced capabilities compared to earlier versions. Version 3.0 has better text handling for graphic design and illustration. It can handle most facets of page layout. You can use it for technical illustration, freehand sketching, and automatic tracing of scanned images. There is also a blending tool to create airbrush effects or animated sequences. It requires 2MB of RAM.

Adobe Streamline. This program converts a high-resolution bit-mapped image into a PostScript language file or another format. You can use the image as is, modify it with a drawing program, or export it to a page-layout program. You can use Adobe Streamline with line art, photographs, and free-form and hand-drawn sketches. You can modify gray-scale art, such as that used in halftone photographs, and control the contrast for up to 16 levels of gray. If you need to create color images, you can select your tints and colors, preview or edit them in Adobe Illustrator or another drawing program, and then print them on a PostScript color printer.

Adobe Type Manager. This software is designed to clean up characters on your monitor so that what you see on your monitor screen looks the same as the output from your laser printer. It comes with 13 scalable font programs, and you can use other PostScript Type 1 font software, including more than 650 faces in the Adobe Type Library. If you do not use a laser printer, Adobe Type Manager will also smooth out text printed on a dot-matrix printer, resulting in dot-matrix output that approximates laser output.

After Dark. This program protects an unattended computer from burn-in damage to the screen. It prevents permanent damage to the screen phosphor by automatically displaying animated art. There are over 30 animations available, including tropical fish, ticking clocks, and bouncing balls. You can even set a password so only you can change the screen. A task manager also monitors system communications and network activity to maximize performance while running After Dark.

Aldus PageMaker. This desktop publishing package is designed for writing, page design, and graphic production. Version 4.0 has more than 75 new features and enhancements to create professional-looking publications.

The PageMaker desktop publishing program is compatible with Windows, OS/2 Presentation Manager, and Apple Macintosh. You can transfer files in mixed computing environments or switch systems without learning new software. You can write and edit text using the Story Editor, which has about the same capabilities as a stand-alone word processor. You can create designs quickly using tools that integrate text and graphics.

PageMaker 4.0 supports long documents and has extensive text-handling capabilities. It has professional typographic controls for most publishing applications.

PageMaker 3.0 for the OS/2 Presentation Manager supports the features of the OS/2 operating system. It has the ability to perform multiple tasks and to have a number of PageMaker publications open at one time. You can also import a variety of software formats including mainframe graphics.

Aldus Persuasion. This package automatically formats outline text into visuals for presentations. It allows you to concentrate on the content of the presentation instead of the design. Persuasion has word processing, drawing, and charting tools. You can customize one of the 36 design templates and create or import logos, technical diagrams, and illustrations.

Persuasion allows you to produce charts and tables from a spreadsheet, or you can enter data directly into Persuasion's datasheet. You can also create and edit organizational charts using the outline capabilities.

You can use this program for automatic slide layout, color or black-and-white overhead transparencies, and paper copies. There are also animated screen effects like dissolving and wiping.

Ami Pro. This visual word processor lets you work with pictures, symbols, and colors as well as words. Documents are enhanced with frames, graphics, colors, and charts. It is user-friendly, and its functions and features fit well in the Windows environment.

Ami Pro can handle a wide range of business documents, from simple letters to reports and newsletters. There is a Revision Marking/Document Compare feature, so you always know which revision you are working on. It also has scientific and equation processing, enabling you to set up complex formulas in the document. A click-and-drag outline feature helps to manage, control, and rearrange long documents. You can also keep chapters of book-length manuscripts separate and then compile them later. Ami Pro uses the same SmartIcons which are found in all Lotus Windows products.

ToolBook. This software package allows you to build custom applications for Windows without using traditional computer programming languages. With ToolBook, you can build applications piece by piece. You create graphical objects as you would with a drawing program.

You can use ToolBook to change or create your own self-tailored Windows applications. A ToolBook application can be a simple collection of information, a front end for other applications, or a self-contained application.

Object Vision. This program also lets you create interactive Windows applications without programming. These can be used for a variety of tasks. You can:

1. Estimate costs
2. Generate quotations
3. Compute insurance premiums
4. Compute depreciation
5. Calculate payroll deductions
6. Qualify applicants for loans
7. Automate questionnaires

You design your own screens with simple building blocks, drawing images on the screen. Relationships are set up between variables, and you can customize the application for special needs or procedures. You can connect your ObjectVision application to database files in Paradox, Btrieve, dBASE, and ASCII formats.

CorelDraw. This is a graphics package for the PC. You can use it to produce headlines, reports, logos, forms, signs, invitations, flyers, advertisements, greeting cards, newsletters, technical drawings, brochures, overhead transparencies, T-shirts, and other drawing products.

This program is easy to learn and use, and it provides a selection of over 150 fonts. You have exact control over the way the output looks, which makes this package useful for technical illustrations. This precise manipulation of objects makes it easy to produce most types of graphic materials.

It has autotracing, blending, calligraphic pen strokes, definable fills, enveloping, extrusion, fountain fills, import/export filters, masking, and perspective. It comes with a 1.5-hour tutorial video.

Correct Grammar. This sentence checker from WordStar should catch 95% of your grammar, style, usage, and spelling errors. Correct Grammar has been programmed to understand the rules of English grammar. It also makes specific suggestions on how you can improve your writing. You can use it to organize your ideas and improve your clarity and precision.

The Correct Grammar sentence checker works with all Windows applications. It could be used for a letter in Word for Windows, a sidebar in a PageMaker newsletter, a note in an Excel spreadsheet, or a slide in PowerPoint.

Lotus 1-2-3. This popular program is available for Windows with advanced spreadsheet technology, presentation capabilities, and full compatibility. Lotus 1-2-3 for Windows uses SmartIcons that allow you to complete all spreadsheet operations by clicking the mouse. This version is designed for Windows with pull-down menus and dialog boxes. It provides Windows fonts and colors and can be used for multiple documents and applications. It is compatible with all 1-2-3 files, styles, and macros. The slash commands are also available with the slash key.

There is a Datalens facility to query external databases, eliminating the need to rekey data. A Solver utility allows you to analyze and solve business problems. The Software Developer's Kit helps you to build applications.

Microsoft Mail. This is a communication program that is easy to set up on most PC or AppleTalk-based networks. You do not need specialized hardware or a dedicated server. An intuitive interface and on-line help allow you to move quickly through most tasks. Mail is designed to simplify and speed up communication. Addressing, sending enclosures, sorting messages, moving mail to folders, and updating directories are some of the tasks that you can do with a mouse. You can access mail while you are in another program with one command.

Microsoft Office. This program for Windows contains the following four applications for Windows: Word, Excel, PowerPoint, and Mail. The combination is designed to increase overall office productivity. The program uses a client version of Microsoft Mail. Some features are streamlined and easier to access. Word is a powerful word processor, and, with Windows, it is easier to use. PowerPoint is designed to create high-quality business presentations.

Microsoft Excel. This spreadsheet program allows you to complete complex tasks by clicking your mouse. Excel is a graphical spreadsheet that combines power with ease of use. There are a number of analytical tools for creating better charts and for generating output that looks like the display on the screen.

You can use a toolbar selection to format data and reports, create formulas, and organize your data. The toolbar allows you to perform routine operations without having to go to the menu or learn a command.

You can point and click to link several spreadsheets and combine worksheets with different formats into a summary worksheet to review the most important data. A single click hides the details and produces summarized reports. A double click takes you back to the complete worksheet. You can solve multiple-variable equations for a what-if type of analysis, or you can specify the solution and Excel will provide the problem.

Excel gives you the ability to create reports and presentations with automatic charting. It has 3-D charts and drawing tools that you can access with the click of a mouse.

Excel can read and write Lotus 1-2-3 files. The help feature demonstrates the equivalent Excel command when you type a 1-2-3 command.

With Excel and the Windows 3.0 graphical environment, you can:

1. View and size multiple worksheets on the screen
2. Run worksheets at the same time you run other applications
3. Link and embed data from worksheets to word processing documents

This can all be done with minimal memory requirements.

PhoneNET Talk. This software system lets MS-DOS and Windows PCs make the connection with a wide range of printers and servers. PhoneNET Talk is based on AppleTalk which has been used by millions of microcomputers. It supports network adapters for Ethernet, Token Ring, and LocalTalk. Features include Dynamic Mode Addressing and Name Binding, which make it easier to set up or reconfigure the network. It allows your PC to use PostScript printers and is supported by most file servers, including those from Novell, Sun, AT&T, DEC, and Apple. In addition to working with a variety of file servers, printers, and other network services, it is useful in mixed networking environments.

Instant ORGcharting. This program is designed to make organizational charts or tree diagrams. Instant ORGcharting for Windows creates, edits, and prints these charts and diagrams. It is easy to use—to make a chart, you type in the names, titles, and other information, and the program automatically creates a chart. You point and click to add, delete, or modify, and the program redraws a new chart. It provides a large number of chart and branch styles, and you can add colors, patterns, borders, logos, or more text.

Microsoft Money. You can use this program to write checks, set budgets, and track expenses. It gives you a quick and flexible way to enter, report, and view financial information. When you use it to write checks, it will fill them in for you as you write and print them from your accounts.

You can track expenses in the account book by categories and subcategories. You can track bank deposits, withdrawals, and loan payments in detail. A mouse click compresses each transaction into a single line so that it is easy to read. Reconciliation is automatic with a SmartReconcile facility that you can use to identify and correct errors. You can schedule future transactions so that the system will notify you when automatic deposits and payments are due. Reports, instant summaries, and budgets are available with a toolbar that gives you one-step access to the most frequently used commands.

Microsoft PowerPoint. This program helps you to create overhead and 35-mm slide presentations. It works with Windows to simplify the process of creating presentations. With PowerPoint you can create slides or overheads directly on your screen, and the screen shows exactly what your output will look like.

The program manages text, drawing, and charting in a special presentation format, and you can access all of your slides from one file and view the complete presentation. There are 40 color and black-and-white templates. PowerPoint has word processing tools with spell checking, data charting, and drawing.

The first step in using PowerPoint is to list and organize your topics. Then, you can write supporting points for each topic with the built-in word processor. Next, you can make graphs and charts using the drawing tools or import graphics from other applications. Then, you can rehearse your presentation by running your slide show on your screen.

Microsoft Project. This is a project-management program designed for planning. Project for Windows is easy to use and flexible. You can view and present your projects in a number of ways:

1. You can use GANTT charts to display time scales.
2. You can use PERT (network) charts to show the project work flow.
3. You can view multiple project files to see how the resources are allocated.
4. You can use resource histograms to balance the work load.
5. You can create calendars to plan schedules.

Microsoft Publisher. Today's business world requires more professional-looking documents. Publisher for Windows provides page layout, text, and graphics tools to create professional-looking publications such as newsletters, business forms, and other documents.

Starting a document requires answering a few simple questions while the program builds the document to your specifications. A built-in word processor lets you enter text directly into your publication. It automatically wraps text around graphics or other blocks of text. When you lay out a page, you can import pictures with a mouse. The program includes a library of clip art along with Bitstream Facelift fonts for Windows.

Microsoft Schedule+. This program is designed for Microsoft Mail 3.0 users. It provides calendars so you can organize your work schedules and set up reminders to flag events. You can also access and check coworkers' calendars so that you can know when they are available to set up meetings.

Microsoft Word. This is a WYSIWYG word processor for Windows. The program runs on an 80286 processor or higher with 640K memory, EGA monitor, Windows 2.11 or higher, and a hard disk.

It uses the graphical abilities of Windows—fonts and graphics appear on the screen exactly as they will print. You can edit on the screen before printing and combine text, graphics, images, and data in a single document. You can transfer numbers, text, and pictures from other applications directly into your document.

There are templates for routine jobs, and the integrated file conversions make it easier to import and export files.

Basic editing operations on Word for Windows are done with the mouse, including selecting text, cutting and pasting, inserting boilerplate, and managing windows. For cutting (or copying) and pasting, you select the text and click on Edit. To select a block using a mouse, you click and drag. If you want to use the keyboard to edit, you hold down the Shift key and use the cursor keys for moving. Then you choose Cut or Copy and click the mouse at the desired location. The text will be deleted or copied to the clipboard. Then you can select Paste at the desired location, and the text will be pasted from the clipboard. There is an Undo command that you can use to reverse the last operation.

Word for Windows has a glossary text feature that you can use to create or insert boilerplate text. This glossary for boilerplate is similar to that used for the non-Windows version of Word, but you cannot use it to create or run macros. For these procedures, you use the Macro menu.

Creating headers and footers is also a little different. Rather then typing in the text and then selecting and formatting it, you first choose the Header/Footer command. You select Header or Footer, click on the Options if you need to set positioning and page numbers, and click OK. A box will appear at the top or bottom of your file. You then type your header or footer text in the box.

The Search and Replace commands pop up dialog boxes; then you enter the same search and replace information you would in Word. The Go To command works like Word's Jump command, allowing you to jump to a specified page or bookmark. To create a bookmark, you select Insert Bookmark, type in a name, and click OK. Then, when you leave your file, you type the name of the bookmark to mark your place and use the F5 key to get back to the same spot when you reopen the file.

A new Ribbon function makes it easier to perform formatting tasks. The Ribbon appears near the top of the screen. It controls basic text formatting. If you are doing more complex changes, you use the Format menu. First, you select the text you need to format. Then, to select a font, you click on the box with the current font's name and select a new font from the list box with the mouse. You can change the size of the text by clicking on the points box and selecting a size. The Ribbon controls character appearance. You click on a B for boldfacing, and there are other buttons for italics, small caps, underlining (which can be continuous, word-by-word, or double underlining), superscript, and subscript.

To create different windows on the same file, you need to use New window. If you want multiple windows containing different files, you use File New or File Open. Window Arrange All will automatically size and position the windows. You size a window by clicking on a side or corner of its border or on the corner icon. Then you drag the window to the desired size. You move a window by clicking in its title bar and dragging the window frame.

A new Document Summaries command lets you create, view, or alter the summary at any time. There is a Summary dialog box with additional information, including word count and file open time.

Microsoft Works. This is an integrated all-in-one program for word processing, business analysis, database management, charting, and illustration. You can use it to:

1. Compose and edit documents
2. Analyze financial information
3. Develop budgets and forecasts
4. Maintain lists and forecasts
5. Create reports
6. Produce mailing labels
7. Personalize form letters
8. Design forms

Using the word processing program, you can create documents and combine spreadsheet graphics, drawings, and text on a page. The spreadsheet program allows you to analyze numbers, manage finances, and chart information. The database uses database forms that you can customize. You can draw diagrams, logos, and pictures using the drawing tools and then copy and paste them into the word processor. WorksWizards helps you through the process of creating custom documents such as address books and mailing labels.

Norton Desktop. This program gives you easier access and maneuverability in the Windows environment by integrating the Windows Program Manager and File Manager. This lets you copy, move, view, and delete a file or application by clicking and dragging icons on the desktop.

Desktop also comes with a set of tools to safeguard your data and help you work with more efficiency. These tools include Backup, UnErase, and SuperFind. Desktop is also easy to learn and use.

Professional Write Plus. This a Windows word processor for the business professional who does not want to take the time to learn complex software. It gives you the tools you need to create memos, letters, and reports quickly and easily.

The documents appear on the screen the same as they will in print. You can include information from other software such as graphs and spreadsheets using DDE. The program has a grammar checker, spelling checker, and thesaurus as well as an E-mail interface for communicating.

Professional Write Plus sticks to the Windows menu command structures. It has features for quickly creating business documents such as a customizable icon bar where you can display up to twelve icons to speed up operations.

With this word processing program, you can also do things like invert graphic images, and it has an extensive list of file conversion routines. It also includes an integrated version of the Grammatik grammar checker. Like Ami Pro, the pull-down menus use dialog boxes with graphical examples. Both programs use a customizable icon bar, but the icons do not have Ami Pro 1.2's 3-D appearance. Neither program allows you to open more than one window without loading another copy of the program. Professional Write Plus is easier to use than Word for Windows.

You can set the program to automatically move files to other applications. For example, every time it sees a file with an XLS extension, it will load the file in Excel. Message Handling Service (MHS) is part of the X.400 international standard. MHS compatibility allows you to exchange mail with MHS packages, like WordPerfect Office.

Professional Write Plus is not the first word processor with built-in E-mail features; MultiMate was first. Professional Write Plus is one of the first to provide most of the features needed for E-mail. This includes features like distribution lists, reply, copy, printing, and attachments. It does not use message folders or blind copies and return receipts.

The E-mail module in Professional Write Plus is integrated with its word processor. Therefore, to send the current document, you select a pull-down menu option, choose a mailing list, and answer prompts related to style, graphics, and text. It is also easy to move received documents to the main editing screen. Most E-mail packages have Windows, so you can load both your E-mail and word processing packages and cut and paste between them.

Professional Write Plus would be a good choice if you want to save some of your PC power or if you want to add E-mail to LAN stations with a simpler installation process.

WinConnect. This program allows you to connect your laptop to your desktop computer using Windows. The laptop drives appear as additional drives on your desktop machine, and you can access the files you want quickly, even from a Windows application.

WinConnect acts as a disk sharer that works in the background of Windows. You can update the files on your laptop from your desktop machine. The package includes a File Enhancer that lets you copy, move, and delete files and create directories. There is a 25-foot cable to make the connections.

WordPerfect for Windows. If you are a WordPerfect user, this program is a good choice if you want to upgrade to Windows without a lot of relearning. With a few keystrokes, you can remap the keyboard to respond to standard WordPerfect commands. Its interface of dialog boxes, menus, and screen layouts gives you a sculpted look.

Features include a button bar with icons that can extend along either side of the screen. The button bar can simultaneously show commands in the form of icons or text or both.

Adding commands is easy since you can move commands by clicking the mouse and dragging the item to the button bar. You can fill the button bar with the commands you need, eliminating the need to use pull-down menus.

WordPerfect for Windows has all the regular WordPerfect functions: integrated text and graphics, tables, styles, spreadsheet links, and equations. It does not go beyond version 5.1 in functions. WordPerfect for Windows will read and write 5.1 files directly with no conversion steps.

WordPerfect for Windows comes with a file management program that you can use to locate and organize programs, documents, and graphic images. You can use small windows on the screen to simultaneously display directories, subdirectories, files, and file contents. You can run this utility from WordPerfect or from the Windows desktop. WordPerfect for Windows also lets you print using either the standard Windows printer drivers or WordPerfect's own drivers, which are faster.

WordStar for Windows. WordStar for Windows is designed for those who have used WordStar, WordStar 2000, or WordStar Legacy. This version is similar to the short-lived WordStar Legacy, but it has an enhancement user interface. There is a two-level style bar across the top of the screen and an optional toolbox on the left side of the screen. These provide access to most program functions. The program has most of the same features as other products, but it has fewer menus, which makes it a little easier to learn and to use.

You can enter text in draft mode, and it will wrap it to fit within the boundaries of your screen, unlike some other Windows programs. In the WYSIWYG mode, you can zoom in and out as you edit, changing the magnification level from 25% to 200% with keyboard hot keys. This program includes Bitstream's FaceLife, which keeps the font edges sharp.

WordStar for Windows can be configured to use WordStar or WordStar 2000 keystrokes. The program's pull-down menus display the active set. The program includes an integrated version of the CorrectGrammar style checker, which is accessible through the Utilities menu and can be used with other Windows applications. The thesaurus has a more complete set of words and definitions than most other products.

There are drawing tools based on Micrografx Designer and extensive page-layout capabilities. The typographic controls include leading, kerning, and tracking to 1/1,000 of an em. The program can also sort odd from even pages and print them in separate batches. Other programs require you to import text into PageMaker or Ventura Professional to do this.

This popular word processor now has the visual effects and ease-of-use possible in the Windows environment. You can control an entire page of text, layout, graphics, and tables. The use of Dynamic Data Exchange (DDE) allows you to move information from other programs.

SOURCE LIST

COMPANY	ADDRESS AND TELEPHONE

Chapter 1: The IBM PC Family

Acer Technologies Corp.	401 Charcot Ave. San Jose, CA 95131 800-538-1542
ACMA Computers, Inc.	117 Fourier Ave. Fremont, CA 94539 800-666-8898
Advanced Digital Corp.	5432 Production Dr. Huntington Beach, CA 92649 800-SEE-POWR
Advanced Logic Research	9401 Jeronimo Irvine, CA 92718 800-444-4ALR
Alphanumeric Intl.	3360 E. Firestone Blvd. Santa Fe Springs, CA 90670 213-921-8689
Altos Computer Systems	2641 Orchard Parkway San Jose, CA 95134 800-258-6787

AMAX Engineering Corp.	47315 Mission Falls Court Fremont, CA 94539 415-651-8886
Amdek Corp.	3471 N. First St. San Jose, CA 95134 800-722-6335
American Computer Prod.	2960 N. First St. San Jose, CA 95134 408-434-0850
American Mitac Corp.	410 E. Plumeria Dr. San Jose, CA 95134 800-648-2287
American Research Corp.	1101 Monterey Pass Rd. Monterey Park, CA 91754 800-443-4519
Amstrad, Inc.	1915 Westridge Dr. Irving, TX 75038 800-777-0395
Arche Tech., Inc.	48881 Kato Rd. Fremont, CA 94539 800-422-4674
Area Electronics Sys.	330 E. Orangethorpe Ave. Placentia, CA 92670 714-993-0300
AST Research	2121 Alton Ave. Irvine, CA 92714 714-863-1333
AT&T Information Systems	100 Southgate Parkway Morristown, NJ 07960 800-247-1212
BIOS (Distribution Plus)	7313 Grove Rd. Frederick, MD 21701 800-777-6050
Bi-Tech Enterprises, Inc.	10 Carlough Rd. Bohemia, NY 11716 516-567-8155
BSM/Business Solution In Micro	1355 Glenville Richardson, TX 75081 800-888-DISK
Blackship Computer Sys.	4031 Clipper Court Fremont, CA 14538 800-431-6249

Bristol Research Corp.	1000 Brioso Dr. Costa Mesa, CA 92627 714-642-3373
Business MicroSystems	531 S. Plymouth Ct. Chicago, IL 60605 800-282-0286
Canon USA Inc.	One Canon Plaza Lake Success, NY 10042 516-488-6700
Charles River Computer	246 E. 44th St. New York, NY 10017 800-333-3CRC
Clone Tech., Inc.	13522 W. 107th St. Lenexa, KS 66215 913-469-0400
Commax Technologies, Inc.	2031 Concourse Dr. San Jose, CA 95131 408-435-5000
The Computer Store	67 East Evelyn Ave. Mountain View, CA 94041 415-968-3466
Compaq Computer Corp.	P.O. Box 692000 Houston, TX 77269-2000 800-231-0900
CompuAdd	12303 Technology Blvd. Austin, TX 78727 800-627-1967
Computer Products United, Inc.	12803 Schabarum Ave. Irwindale, CA 91706 800-824-2936
Continental Technology	300 McGaw Dr. Edison, NJ 08837 800-USA-CTI1
Cordata Technologies	1055 W. Victoria St. Compton, CA 90220 800-621-6746
Core International	7171 North Federal Hwy. Boca Raton, FL 33487 407-997-6055
Corona Data Systems	275 E. Hillcrest Dr. Thousand Oaks, CA 91360 805-495-5800

CSC Computer Systems	229 West Grand Ave. Bensenville, IL 60106 800-284-7746
CSS Laboratories	1641 McGraw Ave. Irvine, CA 92714 714-852-8161
Data General	4400 Computer Dr. Westboro, MA 01580 800-DATA-GEN
Datamedia Corp.	11 Trafalgar Sq. Nashua, NH 03063 800-DMC-INFO
Dataworld Inc.	3733 San Gabriel River Pkwy. Pico Rivera, CA 90660 800-722-7702
Delta Computer Corp.	300 N. Continental Blvd. El Segundo, CA 90245 213-322-4222
Diablo Systems	P.O. Box 5030 Fremont, CA 94537 415-498-7000
Diversified Technology	112 E. State St. Ridgeland, MS 39158-0748 800-443-2667
DTK Computer, Inc.	15711 E. Valley Blvd. City of Industry, CA 91744 818-333-7533
Dyna Computer Inc.	3081 N. First St. San Jose, CA 95134 408-943-0100
Eltech Research Inc.	1725 McCandless Dr. Milpitas, CA 95035 408-942-0990
Epson America, Inc.	2780 Lomita Blvd. Torrance, CA 90505 800-421-5426
Ericsson Information Sys.	Greenwich Office Park 1 P.O. Box 2522 Greenwich, CT 06836 202-661-1666
Everest Computer Corp.	1153 Tasman Dr. Sunnyvale, CA 94089 408-734-2604

Everex Systems, Inc.	48431 Milmont Dr. Fremont, CA 94538 800-821-0806
Fivestar Computers	1621 W. Crosby, Suite 112 Carrollton, TX 75006 800-752-5555
Fortron/Source	6818-G Patterson Pass Rd. Livermore, CA 94550 415-373-1008
Fountain Tech., Inc.	12K Worlds Fair Dr. Somerset, NJ 08873 201-563-4800
Franklin Telcom	733 Lakefield Rd. Westlake Village, CA 91361 805-373-8688
GCH Systems, Inc.	201 Ravendale Ave. Mountain View, CA 94043 800-366-4560
Goldstar Technology	1130 East Arques Ave. Sunnyvale, CA 94086 408-737-8575
Hercules Computer Tech.	921 Parker St. Berkeley, CA 94710 415-540-6000
Hewlett-Packard Corp.	19310 Pruneridge Ave. Cupertino, CA 95014 800-752-0900
HITech International	712 Charcot Ave. San Jose, CA 95131 408-435-8827
Hyundai Electronics America	166 Baypointe Parkway San Jose, CA 95134 408-473-9220
IBM	Old Orchard Rd. Armonk, NY 10504 914-765-1900
Intel Corp.	5200 NE Elam Young Pkwy. Hillsboro, OR 97124 800-538-3373
Intelligent Data Systems	6319 E. Alondra Blvd. Paramount, CA 90723 800-325-2455

ITT Information Systems	2041 Lundry Dr. Dallas, TX 95131 800-321-7659
JC Information Systems	61 Whitney Place Fremont, CA 94539 415-659-8440
Kaypro Corp.	533 Stevens Ave. Solana Beach, CA 92075 619-481-4300
Laser Digital, Inc.	1024 Morse Ave. Sunnyvale, CA 94086 800-826-4225
Leading Edge Hardware	225 Turnpike St. Canton, MA 02021 800-343-6833
Mark Computer Products	470 Washington St. Norwood, MA 02062 800-762-6245
Maxar	710 Lakeway, Suite 285 Sunnyvale, CA 94086 408-733-0810
Maxum Systems, Inc.	36 E. 19th St. New York, NY 10003 800-235-5016
MCED	Williamsport Industrial Williamsport, PA 17701 717-327-9575
Micro Express, Inc.	2114 South Grand Ave. Santa Ana, CA 92705 800-642-7621
Mini-Micro Business Sys.	2050 Ringwood Ave. San Jose, CA 95131 408-434-6859
Mitsuba Corp.	650 Terrace Dr. San Dimas, CA 91773 800-648-7822
Mitsubishi Electronics	991 Knox St. Torrance, CA 90502 213-515-3993
NEC Information Systems	1414 Massachusetts Ave. Boxborough, MA 01719 800-343-4418

Northgate Computer Sys.	13895 Industrial Park Blvd. Plymouth, MN 55441 800-548-1993
Octagon Technologies	18 E. 16th St. New York, NY 10003 800-726-1775
Olivetti USA	765 U.S. Highway 202 Somerville, NJ 08876 800-447-4700
Orlentec Corp. of America	748 Monterey Pass Rd. Monterey Park, CA 91754 800-654-3559
OSICOM Tech., Inc.	198 Green Pond Rd. Rockaway, NJ 07866 800-922-0881
Panasonic Industrial Corp.	2 Panasonic Way Secaucus, NJ 07094 800-742-8086
Pan-United Corp.	1967 Rte. 27, #12 Edison, NJ 08817 800-433-3006
PC Craft, Inc.	530 E. Jamie Ave. La Habra, CA 90631 714-870-6691
PC Designs	2500 North Hemlock Circle Broken Arrow, OK 74012 918-251-5550
PC Network	625 Academy Dr. Northbrook, IL 60062 312-205-1525
Polywell Computers, Inc.	61-C Airport Blvd. South San Francisco, CA 94080 800-999-1278
Precision Systems Group	7660-20 Phillips Highway Jacksonville, FL 32256 800-326-4774
Proteus Technology Corp.	75 Kingsland Ave. Clifton, NJ 07014 800-782-8387
Racore Computer Prod.	170 Knowles Dr. Los Gatos, CA 95030 800-325-1833

Samsung Information Sys.	77 Tasman Dr. San Jose, Ca 95134 408-434-5400
Sanyo Business Sys. Corp.	51 Joseph St. Moonachie, NJ 07074 201-440-9300
Spear Technology	710A Landwehr Rd. Northbrook, IL 60062 800-282-1212
Star Industries, Inc.	7655 East Redfield Rd., #10 Scottsdale, AZ 85260 800-STAR-286
Supercom Ind., Inc.	3001 Hadley Rd. S. Plainfield, NJ 07080 201-757-7999
Syntrex Inc.	246 Industrial Way Eatontown, NJ 07724 800-242-7152
Systems Integration Asso.	222 E. Pearson St. Chicago, IL 60611 312-440-1275
Tandon Computer Corp.	301 Science Dr. Moorpark, CA 93021 805-523-0340
Tandy Corp.	1800 One Tandy Center Fort Worth, TX 76102 817-390-3700
Tatung Co. of America	2850 E. Presideo St. Long Beach, CA 90810 213-979-7055
TeleVideo Systems Inc.	550 E. Brokaw Rd. San Jose, CA 95161 408-954-8333
Texas Instruments	P.O. Box 809063 Dallas, TX 75380-9063 512-250-7111
Transamerican Computer	4503 Irvington Ave. Jacksonville, FL 32210 904-384-9545
Tussey Computer Products Ltd.	3075 Research Dr. State College, PA 16827 800-468-9044

Twinhead Corp.	30 Chapin Rd. Pinebrook, NJ 07058 201-808-1688
Ultra-Comp	11988 Dorsett Rd. Maryland Heights, MO 63043 800-435-2266
Victor Tech., Inc.	395 Phoenixville Pike Malvern, PA 19355 215-251-5000
VIPC Computers Corp.	384 Jackson, #1 Hayward, CA 94544 800-222-5657
VNS America Corp.	910 Boston Post Rd. Marlboro, MA 01752 800-444-SIVA
Wells American	3243 Sunset Blvd. West Columbia, SC 29169 803-706-7800
Wyse Technology	3471 N. First St. San Jose, CA 95134 800-GET-WYSE
Zenith Data Systems Corp.	1661 Feehanville Dr. Mt. Prospect, IL 60056 800-842-9000
Zeos International Ltd.	530 5th Ave. N.W. St. Paul, MN 55112 800-423-5891

Chapter 2: Upgrading the System Unit

Cyrix Corp.	1850 N. Greenville Ave. Richardson, TX 75081 214-234-8388
Elite Micro Technology	18557 E. Gale Ave. City of Industry, CA 91748 818-912-1368
Integrated Information	2540 Mission College Blvd. Suite 105 Santa Clara, CA 95054 408-727-1885
Intel Corp.	5200 N.E. Elam Young Pkwy. Hillsboro, OR 97124 800-538-3373

International Keytech Corp.	354 Paseo Sonrisa Walnut, CA 91789 714-598-6219
Jameco Electronics	1355 Shoreway Rd. Belmont, CA 94002 415-592-8097
MicroLogic	7905 S.W. Cirrus Dr. Beaverton, OR 97005 503-627-0369
MicroWay	Research Park, Box 79 Kingston, MA 02364 508-746-7341
Technoland	2960 Gordon Ave. Santa Clara, CA 95051 800-788-1338
Weitek Corp.	1060 E. Arques Ave. Sunnyvale, CA 94086 408-738-8400

Chapter 3: Memory Upgrades

Above Software Inc.	3 Hutton Centre, Suite 950 Santa Ana, CA 92707 800-344-0116
Acculogic	18023-E Skypark Circle Irvine, CA 92714 800-234-7811
All Computers Inc.	1220 Yonge St., Second Floor Toronto, Ontario M4T 1W1 416-960-0111
Atlas Technology	3900 Montclair Rd. Birmingham, AL 35213 800-326-9555
Better Software	55 New York Ave. Framingham, MA 01701 508-879-0744
Biologic	7950 Blue Gray Circle Manassas, VA 22110 703-368-2949
Black & White	P.O. Box 1040 New York, NY 10024 212-787-6633

Bloc Publishing Corp.	800 S.W. 37th Ave. Miami, FL 33134 305-445-0903
Boca Research Inc.	6401 Congress Ave. Boca Raton, FL 33487 407-997-6227
Compaq Computer Corp.	P.O. Box 692000 Houston, TX 77269-2000 713-370-0670
Compu.D International	6741 Van Nuys Blvd. Van Nuys, CA 91405 818-781-3282
Corvus Systems Inc.	160 Great Oaks Blvd. San Jose, CA 95119 800-426-7887
Fort's Software	P.O. Box 396 Manhatten, KS 66502 913-537-2897
Intel Corp.	5200 N.E. Elam Young Pkwy. Hillsboro, OR 97124 800-538-3373
Merrill & Bryan Enterprises	9770 Carroll Center Rd., Suite C San Diego, CA 92126 619-689-8611
Newer Technology	7803 E. Osie Wichita, KS 67207 800-678-3726
Nordra Technologies Inc.	P.O. Box 645 Andover, NJ 07821 201-786-6878
Qualitas	7101 Wisconsin Ave. Bethesda, MD 20814 301-907-6700
Quarterdeck Office Systems	150 Pico Blvd. Santa Monica, CA 90405 213-392-9701
Rybs Electronics Inc.	2590 Central Ave. Boulder, CO 80301 303-444-6073
Softlogic Solutions Inc.	1 Perimeter Rd. Manchester, NH 03203 603-627-9900

Softnet Communications Inc.	15 Hillcrest Dr. Great Neck, NY 11021 800-627-7060
Software Co.	83-65 Daniels St. Briarwood, NY 11435 718-262-8787
SOTA Technology Inc.	559 Weddell Dr. Sunnyvale, CA 94089 800-933-7682
STB Systems Inc.	1651 N. Glenville Richardson, TX 75081 214-234-8750
Syntax Computer, Inc.	5680 Bandini Blvd. Bell, CA 90201 213-262-1300
Vericomp	P.O. Box 23360 San Diego, CA 92123 619-277-0400

Chapter 4: Video Systems

AMDEK	1901 Zanker Rd. San Jose, CA 95112 408-436-8570
AOC International	10991 North West Airworld Dr. Kansas City, MO 64153 800-443-7516
Artist Graphics III	2675 Patton Rd. St Paul, MN 55113 800-627-8478
AST Research	2121 Alton Ave. Irvine, CA 92714 714-863-1333
ATI Technologies	3761 Victoria Park Ave. Scarborough, Ontario CN M1W 3S2 416-756-0718
CCSI/Voice Connexion	8258 Kingslee Rd. Bloomington, MN 55438 612-944-1334
Cherry Electrical Products	3600 Sunset Ave. Waukegan, IL 60087 312-360-3500

Colorgraphic	5388 New Peachtree Rd. Atlanta, GA 30366 404-455-3921
Conrac Display Products	1724 South Mountain Ave. Duarte, CA 91010 818-303-0095
Cornerstone Technology	1883 Ringwood Ave. San Jose, CA 95131 800-562-2552
CTX International	161 Commerce Way Walnut, CA 91789 714-595-6146
DTP Systems	48431 Milmont Dr. Fremont, CA 94538 800-821-0806
E-Machines	9305 S.W. Gemini Dr. Beaverton, OR 97005 503-646-6699
Electrohome	809 Wellington St. N. Kitchener, Ontario CN N2G 4J6 519-744-7111
Elite Business Applications	4201 Remo Crescent Dr. Bensalem, PA 19020 800-942-0018
EXIM	1376 Gramercy Place Gardena, CA 90249 213-516-7018
Goldstar Technology	1130 East Arques Ave. Sunnyvale, CA 94086 408-737-8575
Hewlett-Packard Corp.	3000 Hanover St. Palo Alto, CA 94304 800-531-5205
Hitachi	6 Pearl Court Allendale, NJ 07401 201-825-8000
Hyundai Electronics America	166 Baypoint Parkway San Jose, CA 95134 800-234-3553
IDEK America	204 South Olive St. Rolla, MO 65401 314-364-7500

Intecolor	2150 Boggs Deleuth, GA 30136 404-623-9145
Leading Edge	225 Turnpike Canton, MA 02021 617-828-8150
Magnavox	I-40 & Strawplains Pike Knoxville, TN 37914 615-521-4316
Micro Display Systems	755 E. 31st St. Hastings, MN 55033 800-328-9524
Mitsuba	650 Terrace Dr. San Dimas, CA 91773 800-MIT-SUBA
Mitsubishi Electronics	991 Knox St. Torrance, CA 90502 213-515-3993
Moniterm	5740 Green Circle Dr. Minnetonka, MN 55343 612-935-4151
Monitronix	929 Eastwind Dr., Suite 220 Westerville, OH 43081 800-365-5646
NANAQ USA Corp.	23510 Telo Ave., Suite 5 Torrance, CA 90505 213-325-5202
NEC Home Electronics	1255 Michael Dr. Wood Dale, IL 60191 312-860-9500
NSA Hitachi	800 South St. Waltham, MA 02154 617-893-5700
Nutmeg Systems	25 South Ave. New Canaan, CT 06840 800-777-8439
Packard Bell	9425 Canoga Ave. Chatsworth, CA 91311 818-773-4400
Paradise	150 North Hill Dr. Brisbane, CA 94005 404-239-3000

PCPC	4710 Eisenhower Ave., Suite A4 Tampa, FL 33634 813-884-3092
Princeton Graphic Systems	601 Ewing St., Bldg. A Princeton, NJ 08540 609-683-1660
RasterOps	10161 Bubb Rd. Cupertino, CA 95014 408-446-4090
Relisys	320 South Milpitas Blvd. Milpitas, CA 95035 408-945-0587
Samsung Electronics America	301 Mayhill St. Saddle Brook, NJ 07662 201-587-9600
Seiko Instruments	1130 Ringwood Court San Jose, CA 95131 800-255-7617
Sota Technology	559 Weddell Dr. Sunnyvale, CA 94089 800-933-7682
Tatung Company of America	2850 El Presidio St. Long Beach, CA 90810 800-544-3888
Taxan USA Corp.	161 Nortech Parkway San Jose, CA 95134 800-421-2929
Toshiba America, Inc.	One Parkway N., Suite 500 Deerfield, IL 60015 800-457-7777
Ventek Corp.	31336 Via Colinas, Suite 102 Westlake Village, CA 91362 818-991-3868
Wyse Technology	3571 N. First St. San Jose, CA 95134 800-GET-WYSE
Xtron	19 Rector St., 35th Floor New York, NY 10006 800-854-4450
Zenith Data Systems	1000 Milwaukee Ave. Glenview, IL 60056 312-699-4800

Chapter 5: Upgrading Disk Drives

Adaptec	691 South Milpitas Blvd. Milpitas, CA 95035 408-945-8600
Areal Technology, Inc.	2890 N. First St. San Jose, CA 95314 408-954-0360
Brand Technologies	9559 Irondale Ave. Chatsworth, CA 91311 818-407-4040
CMS Enhancements, Inc.	1372 Valencia Ave. Tustin, CA 92680 714-259-9555
Comport	3096 Orchard Dr. San Jose, CA 95134 408-437-2404
Core International	7171 North Federal Highway Boca Raton, FL 33487 407-997-6055
Fujitsu America, Inc.	3055 Orchard Dr. San Jose, CA 95134 800-626-4686
Hitachi America	2000 Sierra Point Pkwy. Brisbane, CA 94005-1819 415-589-8300
Kalok Corp.	1287 Anvilwood Ave. Sunnyvale, CA 94089 408-747-1315
Kyocera Electronics, Inc.	8611 Balboa San Diego, CA 92123 619-576-2669
Micropolis	21211 Nordhoff Chatsworth, CA 91311 818-709-3300
Microscience International	777 Halamar Ave. Sunnyvale, CA 95086 400-730-5965
Mitsubishi Electronics	991 Knox St. Torrance, CA 90502 800-556-1234

NEC Technologies	1255 Michael Dr. Wood Dale, IL 60191-1094 800-447-4700
PrairieTek Corp.	2120 Miller Dr., Suite E Longmont, CO 80501 800-825-2511
Priam Corp.	20 West Montague Express San Jose, CA 95134 800-227-2917
Procom Technology	205 McCormick Costa Mesa, CA 92626 714-549-9449
PTI (Peripheral Technology)	685 E. Cochran St. Simi Valley, CA 93065 805-581-1000
Quantum Corp.	1804 McCarthy Blvd. Milipitas, CA 95035 408-432-1100
Quarterdeck Office Systems	1918 Main St. Santa Monica, CA 90405 800-845-6621
Seagate Technologies	920 Disc Dr. Scotts Valley, CA 95066 408-438-6550
Storage Dimensions	2145 Hamilton Ave. San Jose, CA 95125 408-879-0300
Toshiba America, Inc.	9740 Irvine Blvd. Irvine, CA 92718 800-457-7777
Western Digital	2445 McCabe Way Irvine, CA 92714 800-854-7525

Chapter 6: Upgrading Your Computer's Input

Affinity Microsystems	1050 Walnut St. Boulder, CO 80302 800-367-6771
Altra	1200 Skyline Dr. Laramie, WY 82070 800-726-6153

BSA Computer Corp.	1213 Trend Dr. Carrollton, TX 75006 800-683-9272
The Complete PC	1983 Concourse Dr. San Jose, CA 95131 408-434-9600
Computer Research Specialists	24621 Del Prado Dana Point, CA 92629 714-493-4120
Design Technology	1050-R Pioneer Way El Cajon, CA 92020 619-440-7666
Genovation, Inc.	17741 Mitchell North Irvine, CA 92714 714-833-3355
Ideal Scanner	11810 Parklawn Dr. Rockville, MD 20852 301-468-0123
Key Tronic	P. O. Box 14678 Spokane, WA 99214-0687 800-262-6006
Logitech	6505 Kaiser Dr. Fremont, CA 94039-7210 415-795-8500
Mextel Inc.	159 Beeline Dr. Bensenville, IL 60106 312-595-4146
Microsoft Corp.	10700 Northrup Way Bellevue, WA 98009 800-426-9400
Microtek	16901 South Western Ave. Gardena, CA 90247 213-321-2121
Mouse Systems Corp.	2336H Walsh Ave. Santa Clara, CA 95051 408-988-0211
Northgate Computer Systems	13895 Industrial Park Blvd. Plymouth, MN 55441 612-553-0111
Polytel	1250 Oakmead Parkway Sunnyvale, CA 94086 800-245-6655

Scantron	1361 Valencia Ave. Tustin, CA 92680-6463 714-259-8887
Southern California Research	P. O. Box 2231 Goleta, CA 93118 805-685-1931
Technoland	2960 Gordon Ave. Santa Clara, CA 95051 800-788-1338
Torrington Co.	59 Field St. Torrington, CT 06790-4942 203-482-9511
Truvel Corp.	8943 Fulbright Ave. Chatsworth, CA 91311 818-407-1031

Chapter 7: Upgrading Your Printer

Advanced Matrix Technology	765 Slynn Rd. Camarillo, CA 93010 800-992-2264
ALPA America	3553 N. First St. San Jose, CA 95134 800-825-2577
Apple Computer	20525 Mariani Ave. Cupertino, CA 95014 800-247-1212
Axonix Corp.	2257 S. 1100 East, Suite 2C Salt Lake City, UT 84106 801-466-9797
Blue Chip International, Inc.	7305 W. Boston St. Chandler, AZ 85226 602-961-1485
Brother International Corp.	200 Cottontail Lane Somerset, NJ 08875-6714 800-284-4357
C. Itoh Electronics, Inc.	2505 McCabe Way Irvine, CA 92714 800-227-0315
Citizen America Corp.	2401 Colorado Ave., Suite 190 Santa Monica, CA 90404 800-556-1234

Commodore	1200 Wilson Dr. West Chester, PA 19380 215-431-9100
Copal USA Inc.	2291 205th St., Suite 190 Torrance, CA 90501 800-441-7263
Data General Corp.	4400 Computer Dr. Westboro, MA 01580 508-366-8911
Dataproducts Corp.	6200 Canoga Ave. Woodland Hills, CA 91365 818-887-8000
Datasouth Computer Corp.	4216 Stuart Andrew Blvd. Charlotte, NC 28217 800-222-4528
Digital Equipment Corp.	200 Baker Ave. Concord, MA 01742 617-264-1111
Epson America	23530 Hawthorne Blvd. Torrance, CA 90505 800-421-5426
Facit, Inc.	400 Commerical St. Manchester, NH 03108 800-722-1717
Florida Digital, Inc.	295-F North Dr. Melbourne, FL 32935 407-242-2842
Fujitsu America, Inc.	3055 Orchard Dr. San Jose, CA 95134 800-626-4686
Genicom Corp.	One Genicom Dr. Waynesboro, VA 22980 800-4-GENICOM
Hewlett-Packard Corp.	8010 Foothills Blvd. Roseville, CA 95678 916-786-8000
Honeywell Bull	71 Stevenson St., 15th Fl. San Francisco, CA 94105 415-974-4340
IBM Corp.	900 King Dr. Rye Brook, NY 10573 900-IBM-2468

INFOSCRIBE	11507 Sunset Hills Rd. Reston, VA 22090 800-233-4442
Mannesmann Tall Corp.	8301 South 180th St. Kent, WA 98032 800-843-1347
NEC Information Systems, Inc.	1414 Massachusetts Ave. Boxborough, MA 01719 800-343-4418
Okidata	532 Fellowship Rd. Mount Laurel, NJ 08054 800-OKI-DATA
Olympia	3140 Route 22, Box 22 Somerville, NJ 08876 800-333-3843
Output Technology Corp.	East 9922 Montgomery Spokane, WA 99206 800-422-4850
Panasonic Industrial Co.	2 Panasonic Way Secaucus, NJ 07094 201-348-5200
Printek, Inc.	1517 Townline Rd. Benton Harbor, MI 49022 800-368-4636
Printronix	17500 Cartwright Rd. Irvine, CA 92714 800-826-3874
Sanyo Business Systems	51 Joseph St. Moonachie, NJ 07074 800-524-0047
Seikosha America, Inc.	1111 Macarthur Blvd. Mahwah, NJ 07430 800-338-2609
Star Micronics, Inc.	200 Park Ave. New York, NY 10166 212-986-6770
Toshiba America, Inc.	9740 Irvine Blvd. Irvine, CA 92718 714-583-3000

Chapter 8: Upgrading with Power, Optical, and Tape Backup Systems

Backup Power Systems

Alpha Technologies Inc.	3767 Alpha Way Bellingham, WA 98226 206-647-2360
American Power Conversion	P.O. Box 3723, Columbia St. Peace Dale, RI 02883 800-443-4519
Best Power Technology, Inc.	P.O. Box 280, Route 1 Necedah, WI 54646 800-356-5794
Clary Corp.	320 West Clary Ave. San Gabriel, CA 91776 818-287-6111
Computer Accessories Corp.	6610 Nancy Ridge Dr. San Diego, CA 92121 619-457-5500
DataShield	269 Mount Herman Rd. Scotts Valley, CA 95066 408-438-0946
Durant Technologies, Inc.	5627 West Howard Ave. Niles, IL 60648 312-647-6707
Elgar Corp.	9250 Brown Deer Rd. San Diego, CA 92121 800-73-ELGAR
Kaglo Electronics Corp.	6584 Ruch Rd.—E. Ellen Twp. Bethlehem, PA 18017 800-524-0400
Meirick	P.O. Box 298 Frisco, CO 80443 303-668-3251
Para Systems, Inc.	1455 Lemay Dr. Frisco, CO 80443 800-238-7272
Perma Power	5601 West Howard Ave. Chicago, IL 60648 800-323-4255
SCOA Systems	2100 Golf Rd. Rolling Meadows, IL 60008 800-777-7262

SL Waber	520 Fellowship Rd. Mt. Laurel, NJ 08054 800-634-1485
Safe Power Systems	528 W. 21st St. Tempe, AZ 85282 800-325-5848
Sola Electric	1717 Busse Rd. Elk Grove Village, IL 60007 800-626-6269
Superior Electric Co.	383 Middle St. Bristol, CT 06010 800-446-6161
Tripp Lite	500 N. Orleans Chicago, IL 60610 312-329-1777
Unison Technologies, Inc.	23456 Madero Mission Viejo, CA 92691 714-855-8700

Optical Drives

Advanced Graphics Applications	90 Fifth Ave. New York, NY 10011 212-337-4200
Amdek Corp.	3471 N. First St. San Jose, CA 95134 800-82-AMDEK
Chinon America	660 Maple Ave. Torrance, CA 90503 800-441-0222
Hewlett-Packard Corp.	700 71st St. Greeley, CO 80634 303-350-4388
Hitachi America	401 W. Artesia Blvd. Compton, CA 90220 800-262-1502
Laserdrive Limited	1101 Space Park Dr. Santa Clara, CA 95054 408-970-3600
Laser Magnetic Storage Int.	4425 Arrows West Dr. Colorado Springs, CO 80907 800-777-5674
Micro Design International	6985 University Blvd. Winter Park, FL 32792 407-677-8333

Mitsubishi Electronics	991 Knox St. Torrance, CA 90502 213-217-5732
NEC Home Electronics (USA)	1255 Michael Dr. Wood Dale, IL 60191 312-860-5739
N/Hance Systems, Inc.	908R Providence Hwy. Dedham, MA 02026 800-BUY-WORM
Panasonic	Two Panasonic Way Secaucus, NJ 07094 201-348-7000
Pentax Teknologies	880 Interlocken Parkway Broomfield, CO 80020 303-460-1600
Pioneer Communications of America	600 East Crescent Ave. Upper Saddle River, NJ 07458 800-421-6450
Ricoh Corp.	5 Dedrick Place West Caldwell, NJ 07006 201-882-2000
Sony Corp.	Sony Dr. Park Ridge, NJ 07656 201-930-6790
Storage Dimensions	2145 Hamilton Ave. San Jose, CA 95125 408-879-0300
Summus Computer Systems	P.O. Box 219270 Houston, TX 77218 800-255-9638
Toshiba America	9740 Irvine Blvd. Irvine, CA 92718 800-456-DISC
Trimarchi, Inc.	P.O. Box 560 State College, PA 16804 800-356-6638

Tape Backup Systems

Acknowledge Inc.	100 Pennsylvania Ave. Framingham, MA 01701 800-533-1776

ADIC	14737 NE 87th St. Redmond, WA 98073 800-336-1233
Alloy Computer Products	100 Pennsylvania Ave. Framingham, MA 01701 508-875-6100
Alpha Microsystems	3501 W. Sunflower Ave. Santa Ana, CA 92799 800-548-4848
Alphatronix	P.O. Box 13687 Durham, NC 27709 919-544-0001
Analog & Digital Peripherals	251 S. Mulberry St. Troy, OH 45373 513-339-2241
Archive Corp.	1650 Sunflower Ave. Costa Mesa, CA 92626 800-237-4929
Bell Technologies	330 Warren Ave. Fremont, CA 94539 800-FOR-UNIX
Braemar Corp.	1140 Rupp Dr. Burnsville, MN 55337 612-890-5135
Cipher Data Products	10101 Old Grove Rd. San Diego, CA 92138 800-424-7437
CMS Enhancements	1372 Valencia Ave. Tustin, CA 92680 714-259-9555
Colorado Memory Systems	800 S. Taft Ave. Loveland, CO 80537 303-669-8000
The Complete PC	521 Cottonwood Dr. Milipitas, CA 15035 408-434-0145
Digi-Data Corp.	8580 Dorsey Run Rd. Jessup, MD 20794 301-498-0200
Digital Storage Systems	1234 Sherman Dr. Longmont, CO 80501 800-225-3953

Emerald Systems	4757 Morena Blvd. San Diego, CA 92117 800-553-4030
Everex Systems, Inc.	48431 Milmont Dr. Fremont, CA 94538 800-821-0806
Genoa Systems Corp.	75 East Trimble Rd. San Jose, CA 95131 408-432-9090
Interpreter, Inc.	11455 W. 48th Ave. Wheat Ridge, CO 80033 800-232-4687
Irwin Magnetics	2101 Commonwealth Blvd. Ann Arbor, MI 48105 800-421-1879
Maynard Electronics	460 E. Semoran Blvd. Casselberry, FL 32707 800-821-8782
Mountain Computer	240 Hacienda Ave. Campbell, CA 95008 800-458-0300
Parallel Peripherals	200 Hanscom Dr., #325 Bedford, MA 01730 617-274-0775
Priam	20 W. Montague Expressway San Jose, CA 95134 800-227-2917
Procom Technology	200 McCormick Ave. Costa Mesa, CA 92626 714-549-9449
Summus Computer Systems	P.O. Box 219270 Houston, TX 77218 800-255-9638
Sysgen, Inc.	556 Gibraltar Dr. Milpitas, CA 95035 408-263-4411
Tallgrass Technologies	11100 W. 82nd St. Overland Park, KS 66214 800-825-4727
TEAC Corp.	7733 Telegraph Rd. Montebello, CA 90640 213-726-0303

Wangtek	41 Moreland Rd. Simi Valley, CA 93065 805-583-5255

Chapter 9: Upgrading with Fax and Modem Units

Fax Boards and Fax Modems

American Data Technology, Inc.	44 West Bellevue Dr. Pasadena, CA 91105 818-578-1339
Apple Computer	20330 Stevens Creek Blvd. Cupertino, CA 95014 408-996-1010
ATI Technologies Inc.	3761 Victoria Park Ave. Scarborough, Ontario CN M1W 3S2 416-756-0718
Best Data Products, Inc.	5907 Noble Ave. Van Nuys, CA 91411 800-632-2378
Chinon America, Inc.	660 Maple Ave. Torrance, CA 90503 800-441-0222
Cypress Research Corp.	648 Broadway New York, NY 10021 212-475-7782
Data Race, Inc.	12758 Cimarron Path San Antonio, TX 78249 512-692-3909
Deico Electronics, Inc.	2800 Bayview Dr. Fremont, CA 94537 415-651-7800
Everex Systems	48431 Milmont Dr. Fremont, CA 94538 800-821-0806
Fujitsu Bus. Communications	3190 Miraloma Ave. Anaheim, CA 92806 800-654-0715
Gammalink	2452 Embarcadero Way Palo Alto, CA 94303 415-856-7421
Microtek Labs., Inc.	16901 South Western Ave. Gardena, CA 90247 800-654-4160

OAZ Communications, Inc.	1362 Bordeaux Dr. Sunnyvale, CA 94089 408-745-1750
Pacific Image Communications	1111 South Arroyo Parkway Pasadena, CA 91105 818-441-0104
Product R & D Corp.	1194 Pacific St. San Luis Obispo, CA 93401 800-234-5584
Quadram Corp.	One Quad Way Norcross, GA 30093-2919 404-923-6666
Ricoh Corp.	5 Dedrick Place West Caldwell, NJ 07006 201-882-2000
Savin Corp.	9 West Broad St. Stamford, CT 06904 203-967-5000
SpectraFAX Corp.	209 South Airport Rd. Naples, FL 33942 813-643-5060

Fax Machines

Brother International Corp.	200 Cottontail Lane Somerset, NJ 08875-6714 800-284-4357
Canon USA Inc.	One Canon Plaza Lake Success, NY 10042 516-488-6700
Epson America, Inc.	2780 Lomita Blvd. Torrance, CA 90505 800-922-8911
Fujitsu Bus. Communications	3190 Miraloma Ave. Anaheim, CA 92806 800-654-0715
Konica Business Machines	500 Day Hill Rd. Windsor, CT 06095 203-683-2222
Medbar	71-08 51st Ave. Woodside, NY 11377 800-621-6203
Minolta Corp.	101 Williams Dr. Ramsey, NJ 07446 201-825-4000

Murata Business Systems	5560 Tennyson Parkway Plano, TX 75024 214-403-3300
NEC America	110 Rio Robles San Jose, CA 95134 800-222-4632
Okidata	532 Fellowship Rd. Mount Laurel, NJ 08054 800-OKI-DATA
Olivetti USA	765 U.S. Highway 202 Somerville, NJ 08876-1289 800-447-4700
Ricoh Corp.	5 Dedrick Place West Caldwell, NJ 07006 201-882-2000
Sanyo Business Systems Corp.	51 Joseph St. Moonachie, NJ 07074 201-440-9300
Sharp Electronics Corp.	Sharp Plaza Mahway, NJ 07430-2135 800-BE-SHARP
Toshiba America, Inc.	13131 West Little York Rd. Houston, TX 77041 713-466-0277

Modems

ADT (American Data Tech)	44 W. Bellevue Dr. Pasadena, CA 91105 818-578-1339
Advanced Transducer Devices	1150 Morse Ave. Sunnyvale, CA 94088 800-624-4920
Amstrad	1915 Westridge Dr. Irving, TX 75038 800-777-0395
Anchor Automation, Inc.	20675 Bahama St. Chatsworth, CA 91311 818-998-6100
Aprotek	1071-A Avenida Acaso Camarillo, CA 93010 800-962-5800
AT&T Paradyne (Ark)	8445 126th Ave. North Largo, FL 34649-2826 800-482-3333

ATI Technologies Inc.	3761 Victoria Park Ave. Scarborough, Ontario CN M1W 3S2 416-756-0718
Best Data Products, Inc.	5907 Noble Ave. Van Nuys, CA 91411 800-632-2378
Cardinal Technologies, Inc.	1827 Freedom Rd. Lancaster, PA 17601 800-722-0094
CLEO Communications	3796 Plaza Dr. Ann Arbor, MI 48108 800-233-2536
Codex Corp.	20 Cabot Blvd. Mansfield, MA 02048 800-426-1212
Datafox Computer Products	2215 East University Phoenix, AZ 85034 800-228-0641
Data Race	12758 Cimarron Path San Antonio, TX 78249 512-692-3909
Datatrek	4505 Wyland Dr. Elkhart, IN 46516 219-522-8000
E-Tech Research	2700 Augustine Dr. Santa Clara, CA 95054 408-982-0270
Emucom	225 Stedman St. Lowell, MA 01851 800-521-1030
Epson America	2780 Lomita Blvd. Torrance, CA 90505 800-922-8911
Everex Systems	48431 Milmont Dr. Fremont, CA 94538 800-821-0806
First Class Peripherals	3579 Highway 50 East Carson City, NV 89706 800-982-3232
Fujitsu Bus. Communications	3190 Miraloma Ave. Anaheim, CA 92806 800-654-0715

Goldstar Technology	3003 N. First St. San Jose, CA 95134-2004 408-432-1331
GVC Chenel Corp.	99 Demarest Rd. Sparta, NJ 07871 800-CHENEL-2
Hayes Microcomputer Products	705 Westech Dr. Norcross, GA 30092 404-449-8791
Hyundai Electronics America	166 Bay Point Parkway San Jose, CA 95134 800-727-6972
Incomm Data Systems, Inc.	652 South Wheeling Rd. Wheeling, IL 60090 800-346-2660
Link Computer, Inc.	560 South Melrose St. Placentia, CA 92670 714-993-6976
Longshine Technology, Inc.	2013 North Capitol Ave. San Jose, CA 95132 408-942-1746
Lotus Development Corp.	55 Cambridge Pkwy. Cambridge, MA 02142 617-577-8500
Mark Computer Products Corp.	25 Birch St. Milford, MA 01757 800-762-MARK
Memotec Datacom Inc.	40 High St. North Andover, MA 01845 800-CDS-BITS
Microsoft Corp.	10700 Northup Way, Box 97200 Bellevue, WA 98009 800-426-9400
Microtek Inc.	5555-H Magnatron Blvd., Suite H San Diego, CA 92111 619-569-0900
Mitsuba Technology	557 Covina Blvd. San Dimas, CA 91773 714-592-6003
MultiTech Systems, Inc.	2205 Woodale Dr. Mounds View, MN 55112 800-328-9717

NEC America, Inc.	110 Rio Robles San Jose, CA 95134 800-222-4632
NSA (Network Software Assn.)	22982 Mill Creek Laguna Hills, CA 92653 714-768-4013
Novation, Inc.	32 South Wendy Dr. Newbury Park, CA 91320 800-848-6636
Osicom Technologies	198 Green Pond Rd. Rockaway, NJ 07866 800-922-0881
PC House	841 East Artesia Blvd. Carson, CA 90746 213-324-8621
Packard Bell	9425 Canoga Ave. Chatsworth, CA 91311 800-733-4411
Practical Peripherals	31245 La Baya Dr. Westlake Village, CA 91362 800-641-0814
Product R & D Corp.	1194 Pacific St. San Luis Obispo, CA 93401 800-234-5584
Shiva Corp.	155 Second St. Cambridge, MA 02141 800-458-3550
Supra Corp.	1133 Commercial Way Albany, OR 97321 503-967-9075
Telcor Systems Corp.	12 Michigan Dr. Natick, MA 01760 800-826-2938
Telebit Corp.	1345 Shorebird Way Mountain View, CA 94043-1329 800-TELE-BIT
Telenetics Corp.	5109 East La Palma Ave. Anaheim, CA 92807 800-826-6336
Tri-Data Systems, Inc.	1450 Kifer Rd. Sunnyvale, CA 94086-5306 800-TRI-DATA

U.S. Robotics, Inc.	8100 McCormick Blvd. Skokie, IL 60076 800-342-5877
Ven-Tel, Inc.	2121 Zanker Rd. San Jose, CA 95131-2177 800-538-5121
Western Datacom	P.O. Box 45113 Cleveland, OH 44145 800-262-3311

Chapter 10: Upgrading Your System with Software

3COM Corp.	1390 Shorebird Way P.O. Box 7390 Mountain View, CA 94039 415-961-9602
Access Technology Inc.	6 Pleasant St. South Natick, MA 01760 617-655-9191
Act Marketing Corp.	104 Lakefront Dr. Hunt Valley, MD 21031 800-922-9232
Adobe Systems	1585 Charleston Rd. Mountain View, CA 94039 415-962-2000
Aedex Corp.	181 West Orangethorpe Placentia, CA 92670 714-528-4700
Alpha Software Corp.	30 B St. Burlington, MA 01803 800-451-1018
Ami Pro	5600 Glenridge Dr. Atlanta, GA 30342 800-831-9679
Articulate Publications	402 N. Larchmont Blvd. Los Angeles, CA 90004 213-871-1350
Artificial Intelligence Inc.	P.O. Box 81045 Seattle, WA 98018 206-271-8633
Ashton-Tate	10150 West Jefferson Blvd. Culver City, CA 90230 213-204-5570

AT&T Information Systems	P.O. Box 1955 Morristown, NJ 07960 201-898-8000
ATASI	2075 Zanker Rd. San Jose, CA 95131 408-995-0335
Attache Software	4251 Plymouth Rd. Ann Arbor, MI 48105 313-663-1166
Autodesk Inc.	150 Shoreline Highway, Bldg. B Mill Valley, CA 94941 415-332-2344
Borland International	4113 Scotts Valley Dr. Scotts Valley, CA 95066 408-438-8400
Digital Research	60 Garden Ct. Monterey, CA 93942 800-382-1800
Hewlett-Packard Corp.	3000 Hanover St. Palo Alto, CA 94304 800-531-5205
IBM	1133 Westchester Ave. White Plains, NY 10604 914-642-4618
Lotus Development Corp.	P.O. Box 1165 Cambridge, MA 02142 800-532-7672
MicroSoft Corp.	10700 Northup Way Bellevue, WA 98009 800-426-9400
Novell	1170 N. Industrial Park Dr. Orem, UT 84057 801-226-8202
Software Publishing Corp.	1901 Landings Dr. Mountain View, CA 94043 415-962-8910
WordPerfect Corp.	1555 N. Technology Way Orem, UT 84057 801-225-5000
WordStar International	33 San Pablo Ave. San Rafael, CA 94903 408-499-7676

INDEX

Absolute joystick, 169
Absolute/rate joystick, 169
Acoustic couplers, 292
Acousto-mechanical, 172
Amplitude modulation (AM), 288
Analog mice, 172, 174
Antiglare coating, 115
Application-specific integrated circuit (ASIC), 36
Artificial intelligence, 207
Auto Key, 164
Average access time, 138

Background operation, 281
Barium-ferrite, 130
Basic I/O system (BIOS), 9, 38, 43, 111, 138
Bit map, 95
Blackouts, 252, 255
Blind ink, 182
Broadcasting, 281
Brownouts 250–251, 255, 259

Caddy, 210–213
Call scheduling, 281
Camera-based scanners, 188
Camera-type flatbed scanner, 198
Cathode ray tube (CRT), 95-97
CCD, 181, 184–87, 198
CCITT V.22, 293
CCITT V.32, 293
CD-audio disks, 209
CD-ROM, 4, 39, 151, 207–11, 273, 277
Cell matrix, 73
Charge-coupled device (CCD), 180, 184
Color filter array (CFA), 184
Color hand-held scanners, 193
Comite Consultatif International Telephonique et Telegraphique (International Telephone Consultative or CCITT), 293
Compact disk, 19
Compact disk read-only memory, 207
CPU, 1, 2, 20, 89, 142, 155
CRT, 95–97
Cyclic-redundancy-checking (CRC), 131

DAT, 270
Data-compression, 148
Data-over-voice (DOV), 289, 291–92
DC 600, 260
DC 2000, 260–61
DDD modems, 290–91
DDD network, 292
Defragment, 144
Defragmenting, 144
Digitizing tablets, 176
DIP, 87
Direct-memory-access (DMA), 54
Disk utilities, 143

DMA, 55, 132
Dot pitch, 113
Dots per inch (dpi), 113, 226
Draft-mode speed, 226
DRAM, 69, 99
Drum printers, 223
Dvorak, 163
Dynamic Data Exchange (DDE) 301, 303, 305, 309, 324, 336
Dynamic RAM, 69

8086, 16, 76, 78–79
8086 CPU, 13
8087 MCP, 13, 15
8088, 62, 76, 78, 79, 86, 111
8088 CPU, 13, 15
8088 microprocessor, 17
8088-2 CPU, 15
80286, 26, 62, 76, 85
80286 CPU, 13–14, 16
80287 math processor, 13–14, 16
80287 MCP, 26
80386, 27, 65
80387SX, 31
EISA, 35, 37, 41, 89
Electrostatic tablet, 177
Electrosensitive-matrix printers, 223
E-mail interface, 334–35
EMS, 79–81, 84, 88, 315
Enhanced-small device interfaces (ESDI), 27, 37, 152
Expanded memory manager (EMM), 80
Expanded memory specification (EMS), 77
Expanded memory specification (XMS), 79
Extended Industry Standard Architecture, (EISA), 33
Extended graphics array (XGA), 37
Extremely low frequency (ELF), 118

Fat bits, 195
Feeder scanners, 188
Ferric-oxide, 129–30
File access table (FAT), 143–44
Flatbed scanners, 188
Floating-point unit (FPU), 59
Force-actuated joystick, 166
Formatted capacity, 139
Frequency modulation (FM), 288–89

GANTT charts, 331
GEM, 315–16
Glare, 115
Grains, 188
Graphics boards, 7
Gray scale, 187, 193, 199
Gray-scale monitor, 117
GUI, 322

Halftone scanning, 194
High-definition television (HDTV), 185
High memory are (HMA), 311, 312
High Sierra format, 209
Home, 234
Horizontal scan frequency, 113
Hysteresis, 135

IBM AT, 8
IBM PC, 1
IBM XT, 8
IDA, 40–41
IDE, 35–36, 152

Inboard, 63, 386
Institute of Electrical and Electronics Engineers (IEEE), 56
Integrated Drive Electronics (IDE), 33
Integrated Services Digital Networks (ISDN), 281
Intel above board, 5
Intel 8028, 6, 55
Intel 8086, 25–26
Intel 8088, 3, 8, 54
Intel 80286, 8, 26
Intelligent drive array (IDA), 39
Interleave, 24
ISA, 42, 89
Isometric joysticks, 168
ISO 9660, 209

Jewel cases, 210
Joyswitch, 169

Landscape, 242
Laser image digitizing, 184
Linearity, 114
Line drivers, 292
Line-following system, 187
Local-area data transports (LADTs), 291

Magneto-optic media, 276
Magnetostrictive tablet, 177
Malton, 163
Math coprocessor, 12
MCA, 23, 88
MCGA, 117
MCP, 12
Media, 136
Memory cache, 148
Message Handling Service (MHS), 334
Metal-oxide-semiconductor (MOS), 71

MFM, 140, 152, 154
Micro channel, 23, 38, 56, 58, 119, 148
Micro Networking Protocol (MNP), 294
M-Motion multimedia board, 38
Modem eliminators, 292
Modified frequency modulation (MFM), 127
Modified Huffman, 280
Modified MFM (M2FM), 127
Monochrome hand-held scanners, 193
MSCDEX, 210, 212, 213
Multicolor graphics array (MCGA), 25
Multifunction cards, 50
Multihead matrix printers, 223

NetWare 29, 34, 39, 154, 386
Near-letter-quality (NLQ), 215, 232–33
Noise, 226, 252
Nonreturn-to-zero (NRZ), 127

OCR-A, 181
Optical character recognition (OCR), 179–182, 193–194, 197, 285
Optical disk drive, 24
Opto-mechanical, 171–72
OS/2 320, 322–23, 27
Outage, 250, 252
Overhead scanners, 188
Oxide media, 136

Page-mode interleaving, 43
Parity checking, 75
Park, 234
Pattern-recognition, 203
PCL, 243–44
PERT, 331
Phase-change media, 276
Phase modulation (PM), 288–89
Phase shift keying (PSK), 289
Pitch, 113
Pixel, 91, 95, 103, 113–14, 117, 188
Platen, 231
Platters, 135
Plotter add-on scanner, 193
Polling, 281
Portrait, 242
Printer add-on scanner, 193
Printer control language (PCL), 234
Printer emulations, 227
Program information files (PIF), 320
Programmable Option Select (POS), 57–58
PS/2, 21–22, 56, 63, 88, 117, 119

Quarter Inch Cartridge (QIC), 261, 272
QWERTY, 162

RAM, 3, 64, 68–69, 75–78, 80–89, 95–97, 145–46, 148, 150, 182, 226, 237, 244, 246, 287, 326
RAM disk, 4, 5
Range-of-brightness setting, 114
Raster display, 91
Rate joystick, 169
Read-only memory (ROM), 3, 49, 68–69, 95–97, 99, 217
Real bits, 195
Red-green-blue interface (RGBI), 15
Refreshing, 69
Refresh rate, 114
Resolution, 91, 113, 188
RGB, 93, 102, 104, 109
RISC, 29
RLL, 140–54

Sags, 250–51, 255
Scanner settings, 195
SCRAM, 95
Screen flicker, 114
Sectors, 124–26, 139, 142, 144–45
Short cards, 51
SIMM, 30, 43-44, 85–88
Single Inline Memory Module (SIMMs), 32, 86
Single Inline Packaging (SIP), 24
SIPP, 85
Slide scanners, 188
Small computer system interfaces (SCSI), 37–39, 62, 88, 150–53, 155–59, 211–12, 261
Software caching, 149
Speaker-dependent recognition, 202
Speaker-dependent systems, 203
Speaker-independent systems, 203
Special function keys, 19
Speech-recognition chips, 205
Speech recognizers, 200
Spikes, 250–51
Spot size, 114
Start-a-Program list, 321
Static electricity, 53, 75
Static RAM (SCRAM), 64
ST-506, 140
Streaming tape drive, 24
Stripe pitch, 113
Structured Query Language (SQL), 324
Sun Microsystems, 7
Super VGA (SVGA), 33, 101, 105, 107, 118–19
Surges, 250–51, 253
Systems Network Architecture (SNA), 323

Teasing, 174

Terminate-and-stay-resident (TSR), 310, 312, 314
Text editing, 178
Thin-film media, 136
TIFF, 196
Track-to-track speed, 138
Transaction log, 281
Transistor-transistor-logic (TTL), 71
TT-compatible, 109

Undelete, 143
Unerase, 143
Unformat, 145
Unformatted capacity, 139
UNIX, 7, 30, 39, 79, 82
User-addressable base memory, 81

VA, 259
VAX, 6
Video graphics adapter (VGA), 26–27, 30, 32, 37, 41–42, 80, 89, 100–1, 104–6, 110–11, 117–20, 287
Video graphic array, 25
Vines, 29, 386
Virtual 8086 mode, 28
Virtual memory, 4
Volt-amps, 259

Watts, 259
Weitek 4167 numeric coprocessor, 41, 43
Word recognizers, 200
Write-once-read-many (WORM), 273, 275, 277
WYSIWYG, 332

X.400, 334
XGA, 38, 41
XMODEM, 302, 306

YMODEM, 302, 306

ZMODEM, 302, 306–8
Zoom, 319